The Logic of the Gift

THE
Logic
OF THE
Gift

Toward an Ethic of Generosity

▣

Edited by
Alan D. Schrift

Routledge   New York   London   1997

Published in 1997 by
Routledge
29 West 35th Street
New York, NY 10001

Published in Great Britain by
Routledge
11 New Fetter Lane
London EC4P 4EE

Copyright © 1997 by Routledge

Printed in the United States of America on acid-free paper.

Émile Benveniste, "Gift and Exchange in the Indo-European Vocabulary," in *Problems in General Linguistics*. Translated by Mary Elizabeth Meek. © 1971 by the University of Miami Press. Pierre Bourdieu, Selections from *The Logic of Practice*. Translated by Richard Nice, with the permission of the publishers, Stanford University Press. © 1990 by Polity Press, Cambridge in association with Blackwell Publishers, Oxford. Hélène Cixous, Selections from "Sorties: Out and Out: Attacks/Ways Out/Forays," in *The Newly Born Woman,* by Hélène Cixous and Catherine Clément. Originally published in France as *La Jeune Née* © 1975 by Union Générale d'Éditions, Paris. English translation and introduction © 1986 by the University of Minnesota. Published by the University of Minnesota Press. Jacques Derrida, "The Time of the King," in *Given Time: 1. Counterfeit Money*. Translated by Peggy Kamuf. © 1992 by the University of Chicago Press. Marcel Mauss, "Gift, Gift," in *Oeuvres* vol. 3. © 1969 by Éditions de Minuit. Rodolphe Gasché, "L'échange héliocentrique," in *L'Arc* 48. © 1972. Luce Irigaray, "Women on the Market," in *This Sex Which Is Not One*. Translated by Catherine Porter. © 1985 by Cornell University Press. Claude Lévi-Strauss, Selections from *Introduction to the Work of Marcel Mauss*. Translated by Felicity Baker. © 1987 by London, Routledge & Kegan Paul. Marilyn Strathern, "Partners and Consumers: Making Relations Visible," in *New Literary History*. © 1991 by the Johns Hopkins University Press. Marshall Sahlins, "The Spirit of the Gift," in *Stone Age Economics* (New York: Aldine de Gruyter). Copyright © 1972 by Marshall Sahlins. Gary Shapiro, "On Presents and Presence," in *Alcyone: Nietzsche on Gifts, Noise, and Women*. © 1991 by State University of New York Press.

Library of Congress Cataloging-in-Publication Data

The logic of the gift : toward an ethic of generosity / edited by Alan D. Schrift.
p. cm.
Includes bibliographical references and index.
ISBN 0-415-91098-6. — ISBN 0-415-91099-4 (pb)
1. Generosity. 2. Gifts. I. Title.
BJ1533.G4S37 1997
179'.9—dc20
96-41607
CIP

. . . a gift-giving virtue is the highest virtue.

For Gail, who has given so much,
and for Benjamin, who gives without knowing,
and of course for Jill, who has taught me the joy of giving

Table of Contents

PART FOUR: ANGLO-AMERICAN INTERVENTIONS

Acknowledgments

This volume has benefited from many conversations with and suggestions by scholars too numerous to mention who work in the fields of anthropology, economics, sociology, literature, and philosophy. That said, I would like to acknowledge several individuals whose help has been essential to this volume: Koen Decoster, Richard Nice, and Morris Parslow for their excellent translations; Robert Bernasconi, Pierre Bourdieu, and Allan Stoekl for the generous gift of their time in writing pieces especially for this volume; Sharon Olds for the gift of her marvelous poem, which appears here for the first time; Felicity Baker for her kind permission to use her translation of Lévi-Strauss's *Introduction to the Work of Marcel Mauss*; Aletta Biersack, whose conversations and suggestions to me while I was a fellow at the Oregon Humanities Center had a much greater role in the development of this project than she probably realizes; the students in my 1995 philosophy seminar on "Gifts and Exchange" at Grinnell College, who served as a sounding board for many of my ideas and who worked through what proved to be an early version of the contents of this collection; and the friends and colleagues at Grinnell and elsewhere with whom I have discussed issues related to what I have called the logic of the gift: Johanna Meehan, Jeffrey Nealon, Kelly Oliver, Gary Shapiro, Paula Smith, Maura Strassberg, and Janelle Taylor.

I would also like to thank my editor at Routledge, Maureen MacGrogan, who has been an enthusiastic advocate for this project; her support throughout its duration is greatly appreciated.

The manuscript was prepared by several skilled typists who dealt with a variety of technical problems in the transcription of the essays, and I would like to thank Lisa Mulholland, Deniece Walker, and especially Helyn Wohlwend and Jeanette Copeman for their careful attention to details and their patience.

I have benefited from the able assistance of several students at Grinnell —Ann Murphy, Rodney Ast, Sarah Wohlford, Tanya Hedges, Kelley Wagers, Sarah Piltch, and Maggie McKee—who worked in various capacities as proofreaders, typists, and research assistants. I have also benefited from the technical support of Diana Clay at Computer Services, the Burling Library staff at Grinnell, and the financial support of the Trustees of Grinnell College and the Grinnell College Grant Board which, under the direction of Dean Charles Duke, I gratefully acknowledge.

The debt one owes to one's friends and family is as easy to acknowledge as it is difficult to repay. To Joan, Leonard, and Jill, your limitless generosity is appreciated without reserve.

More Blessèd

When the flight attendant offers me coffee
I offer him Extra Strength Bufferin, which I'm tapping
into my palm. No, he smiles,
—You wouldn't have any Sudafed?
Of *course* I have Sudafed,
I exclaim loudly. What I mean is I have
what he needs, I am a mother. We discuss his dose;
I think if he's used to two he should stay
with two. Can I give you a complimentary
Bailey's in that coffee? Oh no, I say, Thanks—
as if I would shift this new balance
of payments in the universe—it is
Love-Nothing. And the pills were in a packet,
the silver bubbles Sudafed come in, so he
didn't have to worry about my germs. Suddenly
I realize my mother taught me the bliss
of giving, she trained me in it,
the way one might become wise, with a lover,
in the bliss of loving. She so loved
to receive, she was so grateful for it.
Her father must have given her things before his
early death, because she claps her little
hands and yodels and twinkles—every
gift is erotic. The pleasure of giving
is a sexual pleasure. It is a power. I have it.

Sharon Olds

Introduction: Why Gift?

Alan D. Schrift

Since Marcel Mauss's well-known and influential *Essai sur le don* first appeared in 1924, gifts and gift exchange have been frequent topics of inquiry within the field of anthropology. But for the other disciplines in the social sciences and humanities, gifts and gift giving were not a theme able to sustain much attention. Until quite recently, that is. In fact, over the past two decades, the theme of gifts and gift giving has emerged as a central issue within a range of divergent fields. Whether inscribed within a tradition that traces itself to Marcel Mauss's *Essai sur le don,* to Georges Bataille's articulation of a general economy of expenditure, or to Martin Heidegger's reflections on the *"es gibt"* of Being, philosophers, literary critics, and literary theorists have with increasing frequency joined anthropologists and sociologists in reflecting upon various economic phenomena in the context of their attempts to theorize gift exchange.

This tendency in contemporary discourse to focus on questions of gifts, gift giving, reciprocity, and exchange can be traced to two important recent developments. The first is the appearance in 1991 of Jacques Derrida's *Donner le temps. 1. La fausse monnaie,* translated into English the following year as *Given Time: 1. Counterfeit Money.* The date of publication for this text is misleading, however, for Derrida acknowledges that his text follows closely the trajectory of "a seminar given under the same title in 1977–78 at the Ecole Normale Supériere in Paris and the next year at Yale University."[1] His thinking on the aporia of the gift, therefore, has been known to many of his "students" for almost twenty years. And as Derrida himself notes in the foreword to *Given Time,* the problematic of the gift, whether or not named as such, had been at work in his texts "wherever it is a question of the *proper* (appropriation, expropriation, exappropriation), economy, the trace, the name, and especially the *rest,* of course, which is to say more or less constantly."[2] More specifically, although the gift was for the most part overlooked by his early commentators, I would suggest it was a central and recurrent Derridean theme in his texts of the 1970s, ranging from *Spurs: Nietzsche's Styles,*[3] in which the giving of woman is joined to Heidegger's question of the proper, property, and the gift of Being, through *The Post Card: From Socrates to Freud and Beyond,*[4] in which

1

Derrida addresses issues surrounding giving and the gift in terms of *envois* and their failure to arrive at their destinations, the giving and return of the *fort/da* in Freud, the giving/theft of the purloined letter in Poe, and the *es gibt* of *Sein* and *Ereignis* in Heidegger. In fact, in the foreword to *Given Time*, Derrida draws attention to pages from virtually all his important texts in which the vocabulary of the gift is inscribed. While this problematic of the gift is curiously absent in most of the early discussions of Derrida's work, it is worth noting that one place it was not ignored was in feminist readings of Derrida's works and deconstruction in general. In this regard, one might go so far as to argue that a "sexual difference" among Derrida's "commentators" emerged concerning whether or not they regard the thematics of the gift in Derrida as a topic worthy of comment.[5] With the publication of *Given Time*, however, this has all changed. And the economic question already is and promises to remain a major focus of future Derridean scholarship.

The question of gender points to the second development within contemporary critical theory that has brought the problematic of the gift to the center of critical attention. Within the discipline of anthropology, as Gayle Rubin put it two decades ago, an inquiry into the relation between gender and the gift has been ongoing since Claude Lévi-Strauss, in *The Elementary Structures of Kinship*, added "to the theory of primitive reciprocity the idea that marriages are a most basic form of gift exchange, in which it is women who are the most precious of gifts."[6] Since 1980, a number of monographs have appeared that challenge some of the anthropological and economic assumptions that have become almost canonical since Mauss's *Essai*. For example, anthropologist C. A. Gregory, in *Gifts and Commodities*, makes a distinction that allows us to connect the economic reflections of anthropology with the more philosophical/ethical concerns of deconstruction. Gregory distinguishes between commodity and gift exchange in the following way: "Commodity exchange establishes objective quantitative relationships between the objects transacted, while gift exchange establishes personal qualitative relationships between the subjects transacting."[7] Where commodity exchange is focused on a transfer in which objects of equivalent exchange value are reciprocally transacted, gift exchange seeks to establish a relationship between subjects in which the actual objects transferred are incidental to the value of the relationship established. Commodity exchange thus exhibits the values that, for example, Carol Gilligan associates with an ethic of rights based on abstract principles of reciprocity, while gift exchange exhibits the forming of and focus on relationships that she associates with an ethic of care based on interpersonal needs and responsibilities, an ethic that speaks in a voice different from the one that has heretofore dominated the moral tradition.[8]

The theme of the gift, then, can be located at the center of current discussions of deconstruction, gender, ethics, philosophy, anthropology, and economics. It is, I would argue, one of the primary focal points at which contemporary disciplinary and interdisciplinary discourses intersect. And, as the essays collected in this volume demonstrate, while the problematic of the gift may not always have been at the center of critical attention, its appearance is not and has not been limited to the discourses of anthropologists. In fact, as Ralph Waldo Emerson's essay "Gifts," written in 1844, makes clear, the paradoxical and problematic character of the gift has been apparent for quite a while. This essay, which Mauss recalled at the opening of the conclusion to his *Essai* as "curious,"[9] already noted that the unreciprocated gift left the receiver feeling inferior and vengeful at the intrusion on one's independence and the incursion of this debt to repay. And in so doing, Emerson's short essay already raised a fundamental question that all analyses of the gift must address, namely, should the analysis focus on the object given, on the relationship established between the giver and the receiver, or on the inextricable interconnections between these object(s) and relationship(s)?

A few decades after Emerson, Friedrich Nietzsche echoed these sentiments when he opened *Thus Spoke Zarathustra* with a reflection on gifts and the necessity of giving. When Zarathustra first goes down from his cave to rejoin humanity, like the bee that has gathered too much honey or the cup that wants to overflow, he is overfull and needs to locate those to whom he can bring the gift of his teaching. Zarathustra soon comes to stand in relation to his followers as a giver of gifts, and his followers are only too eager to receive his teachings as gifts from on high. But unlike his followers, Zarathustra knows the dangers involved in gift giving; he knows that the gift is a *pharmakon*,[10] for those who benefit from receiving the gifts often feel beholden to the one who gave to them. Zarathustra thus cautions those who have nothing to give to be reserved in accepting, because "Great indebtedness does not make men grateful, but vengeful; and if a little charity is not forgotten, it turns into a gnawing worm."[11]

To be able to give gifts rightly, Zarathustra claims, is an "*art* [*Kunst*],"[12] and great care and skill is required in order to prevent feelings of indebtedness in the recipients of one's generosity. One repays one's teacher badly if one remains only a student, Zarathustra tells his followers at the end of part one, in a chapter entitled "On the Gift-Giving Virtue," as he urges them to lose him and find themselves. To remain a student is to return the teacher's gifts in kind, either by simple obedience to the teacher's lessons or by presenting the teacher with a comparable countergift in return. Neither response takes the gift freely and with forgetfulness of its origin. For Zarathustra, overfull with wisdom, giving is a "necessity,"[13] and while his followers may return eternally to the words of their teacher, the return on Zarathustra's gifts will not return to him, as he confesses not to know the happiness of those who receive. This, Zarathustra realizes, is his ultimate poverty: his hand never rests from giving. Yet by remaining committed to the affirmation of giving even beyond what he possesses, Zarathustra is never impoverished by this need to give, nor does he ever reconsider his judgment that the gift-giving virtue is the highest virtue.

While Emerson's and Nietzsche's reflections on the gift hover in the background of many of the discussions that follow, three early twentieth-century thinkers who have reflected on the logic of the gift occupy a much more central position in the current discussions: Marcel Mauss, Georges Bataille, and Martin Heidegger. Although this is not the place for an extensive discussion of their thought and its influence, a brief comment on their general views will help situate many of the following essays. As suggested earlier, Mauss's _The Gift_ is without doubt the text that initiates the modern reflections on gifts and gift giving. Insofar as a reading of this text will be the focus of the essays in section two, here we need only mention some of the most basic features of Mauss's essay. First and foremost is Mauss's thesis that although the gift might appear free and disinterested, it is in fact both constrained and quite interested. That is to say, in the archaic societies he examines, Mauss finds that the gift is given in a context in which both its reception and its reciprocal return are obligated in terms of well-articulated social rules. Thus, much of Mauss's text involves analyzing gift-giving practices in an effort to disclose the underlying rules that govern the ongoing circulation of gifts. His purpose in this analysis is twofold. On the one hand, he wants to show that contrary to what has been believed, the phenomenon of the market did not first arise with the invention of money. Rather, as a human phenomenon, the market "is not foreign to any known society," and he argues that even in apparently non-market archaic societies, their exchanges are governed by rules and contracts that, insofar as they are different from our own, show the possibility of systems of exchange other than those based upon modern notions of money and commodity transactions.[14]

On the other hand, there is a clear political agenda guiding Mauss's analysis, for he is explicit in claiming that the analysis of the social rules at work in these archaic societies allows us to draw some moral conclusions concerning the organizational principles that ground our own society. He closes his essay with a self-named lesson in "civics" that offers a response both to the recent violence of the First World War and the continuing unequal distribution of wealth. His analysis of the agonistic expenditure of the potlatch shows it to be in no way disinterested, for through such gifts a social and economic hierarchy is established. If our society is to avoid such hierarchies, and the social instability that results from them, it can do so, Mauss argues, only by more equitably distributing access to the "common store of wealth." Mauss closes his essay by noting that what one finds, at the conclusion of the research he has provided, is that "societies have progressed in so far as they themselves, their subgroups, and lastly, the individuals in them, have succeeded in stabilizing relationships, giving, receiving, and finally, giving in return. . . . Goodness and happiness [will then be found] in the peace that has been imposed, in well-organized work, alternately in common and separately, in wealth amassed and then redistributed, in the mutual respect and reciprocating generosity that is taught by education."[15]

Georges Bataille puts forward his economic reflections from within a paradigm framed very much by Mauss's *Essai*. But he does so in order to accomplish a "Copernican transformation" of economic and ethical thinking.[16] That is to say, Bataille's goal, articulated first in his influential 1933 essay "The Notion of Expenditure"[17] and revised over the next sixteen years until its final formulation in volume one of *The Accursed Share*, is to overturn the economic principles of utilitarian calculation that define the rationality of what he calls "restrictive economy." This overturning will make possible a different economic logic, one based on the unproductive expenditure of excess that defines the workings of a "general economy." According to Bataille, this unproductive expenditure animates the potlatch analyzed by Mauss, and Bataille goes on to argue that it is a necessary, albeit heretofore unacknowledged, requirement for continued economic growth. Basing his argument in part on a naturalism that sees the paradigm of general economy in the unreciprocated expenditure of solar energy (one of the many points at which Bataille is rightfully situated as an heir to the Nietzschean discourse on squandering),[18] Bataille claims that modern economic forces of commodity accumulation obscure "the basic movement that tends to restore wealth to its function, to gift-giving, to squandering without reciprocation."[19] Like Mauss, Bataille's reflections are motivated by political concerns: convinced that a part of wealth "is doomed to destruction or at least unproductive use without any possible profit, it is logical, even *inescapable*, to surrender commodities without return."[20] In the past, potlatch, religious sacrifice, and, most destructively, warfare have been the means for expending that excessive wealth/energy that could no longer be accumulated. The events of the Second World War only confirm Bataille's thesis that there are limits to what can be accumulated, and *The Accursed Share* ends on the hopeful note that perhaps the Marshall Plan will emerge as a new kind of unproductive expenditure of excess that can avoid the catastrophes of war.

Martin Heidegger takes a decidedly different approach to the gift, locating it not within a cycle or circle of exchange but within the context of a fundamental ontology quite different from the one sketched in *Being and Time*. That is to say, Heidegger's reflections on the gift come in the context of a reflection on *Ereignis* as the gift-event of Being. While there are many ways to develop the implications of Heidegger's turn away from Being/*Sein* and toward *Ereignis* (which has been translated as "the event of appropriation"), the point I want to emphasize here is that this turn makes the non-substantive and event-ual nature of Being more explicit than was the case when Heidegger earlier tried to express his thinking through the language of ontological difference (Being vs. being, *Sein* vs. *Seiende*). Oversimplifying to the extreme, to say that *Ereignis* appears in the context of Heidegger's reflection on the "*es gibt*" of *Sein*, the "there is/it gives" of Being, is to say that Being *is*, not as a thing, but as an event, a happening. To say that "there is/it gives Being" means that Being happens, that Being *is* as event. When Heidegger comes to speak of *Ereignis*, he is reformulating the fundamental ontological insight of *Being and Time* that temporality (*Zeitlichkeit*) is the meaning of the Being of Dasein. Heidegger's earlier account of the forgetting of the ontological difference, of the difference between Being and beings, now gets refigured as the forgetting of the gift-event of Being. And the call to recollect this event (*Ereignis*) of the gift (of Being) that has been forgotten is thus a call, if not an imperative, to receive this gift appropriately. The overcoming of this forgetfulness is, for Heidegger, the task of thinking that is at present called upon to think of Being not as "what is" but as "what happens," "what unfolds in time." Whether or not Heidegger's own reflections take us very far toward understanding the gift may be debated, but what is beyond debate is that by posing the question of the gift in terms of time and forgetting, his thought continues to inform many of the positions articulated in the following pages.

The selections that follow fall loosely into four groups. The first section includes three "documents": Ralph Waldo Emerson's "curious" essay, "Gifts" (1844), Marcel Mauss's early note on the etymology of 'gift' "Gift, Gift" (1924), and Émile Benveniste's important philological-linguistic account of the peculiarities of 'gift' and 'exchange' in Indo-European languages, "Gift and Exchange in the Indo-European Vocabulary" (1948–49).

Together, these selections point out several of the conceptual and linguistic peculiarities that must frame all reflection on the gift. Emerson, for example, notes that the only true gift is a gift of one's self, for a "real gift" must be something painful to give. That gift must also be unnecessary to the receiver; it must be excessive, for if it is needed, it loses its status *as* gift. While gifts challenge the autonomy of the receiver, the true gift nevertheless unites the giver and receiver, and Emerson concludes that the gift finds perhaps its most perfect expression in the gifts of love.

Mauss focuses in his "technical" account on the peculiar and ambivalent etymology of '*gift*' in Germanic languages. Noting that the single word '*gift*' has given rise to meaning both 'present' and 'poison', Mauss traces this back to the "typical prestation" for the ancient Germans and Scandinavians: the gift of drink. Anticipating quite specifically the undecidability of the Derridean *pharmakon*, Mauss notes that the recipient would always be uncertain whether the gift about to be drunk was a drink-present or a drink-poison. This uncertainty, he suggests, anticipates the conjoined pleasure and displeasure "we still feel when receiving presents" (31), and this, he concludes, sets the stage for his future study on "the obligation to return presents." That study turned out to be, of course, his essay on *The Gift*, a work that Marshall Sahlins described as Mauss's "own gift to the ages" in his essay republished in this volume.

Benveniste, in his widely cited essay, delves further into the ambiguous and ambivalent etymology of both gift and exchange. Where Mauss stops with the undecidability of the gift as present/poison, Benveniste locates a more foundational undecidability in the notion of giving itself, which he argues can be shown in Indo-European languages to have evolved from the root *$d\bar{o}$-, which can mean 'give' or 'take' depending on the construction. Benveniste then draws the startling conclusion that "'to give' and 'to take' thus proclaim themselves here, in a very ancient phase of Indo-European, as notions that were organically linked by their polarity and which were susceptible of the same expression." (34) He goes on to trace a link philologically between certain early forms of expenditure and the institution of potlatch, noting that the distance between the ostentatious expenditure of food and wealth associated with "archaic" potlatch and the great festive banquets of today may not be as great as is often assumed, as evidenced by such contemporary expressions as the "giving of a reception."

The second section reprints selections from three important readings of Mauss's *Essai sur le don*. Claude Lévi-Strauss was one of the first readers of the *Essai* to develop Mauss's suggestion that the implications of his research extended far beyond the field of Melanesian anthropology. For Lévi-Strauss, the importance of Mauss's essay lay in the fact that it attempted to explain empirically observed behavior and communication in terms of a society's unconscious rules of exchange. And insofar as it sought to formalize these unconscious rules, Lévi-Strauss reads Mauss's essay as the first attempt at a structural anthropology. In introducing the notion of a "total social fact," Mauss named those social phenomena that involve "the totality of society and its institutions" that "are at the same time juridical, economic, religious, and even aesthetic and morphological, etc." and that must be analyzed in terms of the totality of their connections.[21] In these phenomena, "all kinds of institutions are given expression at one and the same time—religious, juridical, and moral, which relate to both politics and the family; likewise economic ones, which suppose special forms of production and consumption, or rather, of performing total services and of distribution."[22] Yet Mauss's analysis fails in the end and, according to Lévi-Strauss, his failure—a failure ultimately to become a structuralist—rests on his resorting to a mystical quality, the *Hau*, to explain the circulation of gifts that he observed. What Mauss should have done, Lévi-Strauss claims, was to account for this circulation in terms of a single *structural* relation of exchange involving three parts: giving, receiving, and reciprocating. Lévi-Strauss argues that Mauss missed this point because he forgot his own central discovery of the total social fact; that is to say, he mistook as three distinct operations what were in reality simply *parts* of the complex social *whole* of exchange. Because he mistook parts for wholes, he found it necessary to posit the *Hau* as a principle to explain the interconnection among giving, receiving, and reciprocating. Had he seen these three operations simply as parts of the primary structural process of exchange as a whole, Lévi-Strauss concludes, there would have been no need to posit the *Hau*. (55)

For Lévi-Strauss, the *Hau* is a conscious attribution by the indigenous group of a name to the underlying unconscious rules that govern social practices. (55–56) These rules cannot be recognized *as* rules, however, for if they were, the gift would become simply a barter or a loan. The appeal to *Hau*, Lévi-Strauss argues, takes Mauss away from his fundamental assumption regarding the understanding of social life as a system of conscious and unconscious relations. Thus, Lévi-Strauss concludes that the *Hau* is a "floating signifier," a "magical name" that gets attached to a variety of signifieds and thereby allows the indigenous peoples, or any linguistic community for that matter, to make sense of their social world.

Marshall Sahlins, in "The Spirit of the Gift," offers an extended commentary on the Maori *Hau* and its relation to the general theme of social contract. He argues that rather than a first attempt at a *structural* anthropology, Mauss's essay shows the way to a future *economic* anthropology.

Responding to three critical commentaries on Mauss's essay—those of Lévi-Strauss, Raymond Firth, and J. Prytz Johansen—Sahlins reads Mauss in the context of Hobbes's political philosophy and claims that "for the war of every man against every man, Mauss substitutes the exchange of everything between everybody" (83). The parallels Sahlins brings out between Mauss's essay and Hobbes's *Leviathan* are striking. Both Hobbes and Mauss show society choosing reason over war: for Hobbes, the rational motivation is the fear of violence; for Mauss, it is the choice of economic over military competition, a choice that also opts for a mode of opposition other than violence. And both Hobbes's and Mauss's theories are shown to rest upon a paradox. When Hobbes argues that the power of the sovereign is necessary to ensure reciprocity, he faces the paradox of realizing the natural condition of a reasoned peace only by means of something artificial: the State. Similarly, when Mauss resorts to the *Hau* in order to ensure reciprocity, he faces the paradoxical situation of grounding reason (social stability) in the form of the irrational: the *Hau* as a spiritual-magical force. Sahlins concludes by suggesting that while close to Hobbes, Mauss also remains close to Marx insofar as he seeks, with the concept of the *Hau*, to understand the force within things as something akin to their fetishized "exchange-value" that makes equivalences possible. Mauss's importance thus resides in his moving the alternatives of war and trade from the periphery to the center of social life as he demonstrates that exchange, as a material transaction, is always already a social relation.

Rodolphe Gasché, in his "Heliocentric Exchange," offers yet another reading, this time deconstructive, of Mauss's *The Gift*, arguing that the logic of Mauss's argument depends on his falling victim to the same ambiguity that he seeks to clarify in his analysis of primitive exchange. In Mauss's effort to distinguish the obligations to give, to receive, and to reciprocate, Gasché shows him resting his supposedly clear distinctions on the very ambiguities (reciprocity as rivalry, generosity as interested, the free return as obligatory) that he sought to clarify. More to the point, Gasché argues that Mauss's appeal to the *Hau* as the force in the gift that obligates the receiver to reciprocate establishes the circulation of the gift by virtue of avoiding a central feature of the practices analyzed, namely, asking what obligates the donor's giving of the gift in the first place. Insofar as Mauss sees the movement of the gift as circular—from giver to receiver and back again to the giver—he never explains why the donor gives at all. In other words, why is there gift? As Gasché argues, were Mauss to have asked this question, he would have recognized that there is no originary gift, no first prestation. Rather, the donor is already implicated in the cycle—not the circle—of exchange: any prestation is always already a counterprestation,

(112) "the donor is always already a *donee*" (115). This implication is Mauss's "unthought" as he fails to recognize that whenever a gift is given, relations of exchange (obligations to give/receive/reciprocate) have always already been established. Gasché concludes that because he fails to decenter the circle of reciprocal exchange, Mauss is unable to think beyond a restricted economy to the sort of generalized expenditure that Bataille had sought to make room for in his own articulation of the logic of the gift.

The third section presents selections from four of the leading voices in contemporary French theory that intervene in the space opened by Mauss's reflections on gift and exchange. Two of these, Jacques Derrida's and Pierre Bourdieu's, respond directly to the problematic of the gift as framed by Mauss. The others, essays by Hélène Cixous and Luce Irigaray, respond less directly to Mauss's discourse as they address broader social issues concerning the economics of gift and exchange.

As mentioned earlier, the problematic of the gift and questions of (textual, libidinal) economy have been at work throughout Derrida's writings. In the selection reprinted here, chapter one of *Given Time*, Derrida outlines several dimensions of what he regards as the fundamental aporia of the gift. Moving from Mauss's gift to the gift of Being in Heidegger, Derrida seizes upon the impossibility of the gift, an impossibility comparable to the impossibility of *différance*,[23] namely, the conditions of the possibility of the gift are precisely the conditions of its impossibility. That is to say, once the gift is recognized *as* gift, it is no longer a gift; it becomes an obligation that demands reciprocity and once reciprocated, Derrida argues, it has been annulled (128). Because he framed the gift in terms of the circle of reciprocal obligation, Derrida suggests somewhat playfully that "Mauss's *The Gift* speaks of everything but the gift: it deals with economy, exchange, contract (*do et des*), it speaks of raising the stakes, sacrifice, gift *and* counter-gift—in short, of everything that in the thing itself impels the gift *and* the annulment of the gift" (138). For Derrida, on the other hand, the gift defies the metaphysics of presence—it appears but can never present itself as a gift, it can never be (a) present. The gift, therefore, is intimately connected with forgetting; it is, in fact, coextensive with a radical forgetting that demands that the gift be forgotten by both the donor (who will resent the gift until it has been returned) and the donee (who will feel it as a duty to repay until such restitution is discharged). Derrida concludes that the structure of the gift, like the structure of Being and of time, is not a thing, is nothing (140); it has, instead, the structure of an event, an event of forgetting and deferral, an event of *différance*.[24] In fact, what the gift gives, in the end, is time, nothing but time—time to forget, time to return, time for a delayed reciprocation that is no longer simply a return. Insofar as the gift reciprocates an obligation that is always already forgotten, he suggests that it escapes the economic logic that governs relations of simple exchange. Derrida closes by offering (as a gift?) Baudelaire's "Counterfeit Money," to which the remaining three chapters of *Given Time* make constant reference. But already in this selection, the pertinence of Baudelaire's story for Derrida's account is clear: like the gift, counterfeit money retains its value only so long as it is not recognized; and like the narrator's friend, who Derrida suggests is reproached for not knowing how to give, we might ask whether we must fault Mauss for his own attempt to calculate the circulation of the gift under a law of return somewhere between the economic and the noneconomic.

In the excerpt published in this volume from her contribution to *The Newly Born Woman*, Hélène Cixous rephrases Mauss's and Derrida's insights that the gift is inscribed under the law of return in terms of a gendered unconscious. She notes the lack of ease with which a masculine economy confronts generosity: "Giving: there you have a basic problem, which is that masculinity is always associated—in the unconscious, which is after all what makes the whole economy function—with debt."[25] The phallocentric desire that animates the Hegelian dialectic of self and other is a desire for appropriation: one confronts the other as different and unequal and one seeks to make the other one's own. The desire to possess, to receive a return on one's investments, animates an economy that Cixous suggests we call "masculine," in part because it "is erected from a fear that, in fact, is typically masculine: the fear of expropriation, of separation, of losing the attribute" (151). Founded on a system of returns, economies of the *propre* —proper economies, economies based on the possession of private property—are driven not so much by the desire to appropriate; they are structured instead around the fear of loss, the fear of losing what is already possessed: a fear of being expropriated that Cixous qualifies as "masculine." Where masculine economies can make only quid pro quo exchanges to recoup a direct profit, Cixous claims that feminine economies transact their business differently. They are not constrained to giving as a means of deferred exchange in order to obligate a countergift in return; instead, they encourage giving as an affirmation of generosity. No longer understandable in classical "exchangist" economic terms, a feminine economy allows for the possibility of giving without expectation of return, for giving that is truly generous. It is not that women's gifts escape the law of return; rather "all the difference lies in the why and how of the gift, in the values that the gesture of giving affirms, causes to circulate" (158) Which is to say, playing on the polysemy of the French "*rapport*," for a masculine economy the only return (*rapport*) worth securing is conceived in terms of revenues and profit, while a feminine economy seeks not to secure profit but to establish *rapport*/relations. A feminine economy, she writes, "is an economy which has a more supple relation to property, which can stand separation and detachment, which signifies that it can also stand freedom—for instance, the other's freedom."[26] It is an economy, in other words, in which direct profit can be deferred, perhaps infinitely, in exchange for the continued circulation of giving.

Cixous emphasizes the difference between feminine and masculine economies in terms of the former promoting the establishing of relationships through the giving of gifts. In particular, she draws our attention to maternal gifts as ones that escape the logic of appropriation that structures the commodity economy she labels "masculine." Mother and child do not stand in a relationship of self vs. other, opposing parties with competing interests, and the gift to the child of a mother's love or a mother's breast is not comprehensible in terms of quantifiable exchange values or the law of return that governs an economy based on the exchange of commodities. Nor are these maternal gifts understandable in terms of the fear of expropriation, for the mother, she suggests, is willing to expend these gifts without reserve or expectation of return. In fact, like Bataille, Cixous emphasizes and affirms the positive value of plenitude, but unlike Bataille, she wants to gender this positive value feminine as she articulates a set of economic principles that refuse to accept the assumption of conditions of scarcity as given. By escaping the proprietary constraints on subjectivity, women are able to exist in a "relationship to the other in which the gift doesn't calculate its influence" (163). And she argues that this escape is what makes possible *écriture féminine* as a writing that puts the isolated, autonomous self at risk, questioning and being questioned in the between of same and of other. Such radical questioning goes to the roots of our historical-cultural gender constructions, and she hopes it will make possible radical transformations of gender relations and intersubjective identities.

Luce Irigaray, in "Women on the Market," also focuses on gender as essential to our thinking the economic because our society, so we are told, "is based upon the exchange of women" (174). But whereas Lévi-Strauss framed this economic order in terms of gift exchange, Irigaray argues instead that women are exchanged not as gifts but as commodities. As such, she appeals to Marx's analysis to help disclose the social status of women as objects of exchange whose value is split between its natural form (as a [re]productive body) and its social form (as a body possessing value insofar as it can be exchanged). She thus brings to bear Marx's analysis of use vs. exchange value, suggesting that the stereotypical male fantasies of woman as mother, virgin, or prostitute exemplify woman respectively as use value, exchange value, and usage that is exchanged. Moreover, Marx's analysis of the fetishism of commodities helps explain how women have been framed as fetish objects: while Marx's commodity fetishism substitutes relations among things for relations between men, as fetish objects, women's role in exchanges manifests and circulates the power of the Phallus as it establishes relationships of men with each other. Like Cixous, Irigaray suggests that it is an exclusively masculine form of desire that has "presided over the evolution of a certain social order, from its primitive form, private property, to its developed form, capital" (183–84). And like Cixous, she concludes that were women freed from their objectification within an exchange system that prohibits their occupying the position of subject, the current social order could not be maintained. Instead of an economic and social order committed to rules of commodity exchange under conditions of scarcity, a new social order would be possible, an order characterized by a different "relation to nature, matter, the body, language, and desire"(189).

In his first selection in this volume, reprinted from *The Logic of Practice,* Pierre Bourdieu develops an analysis of gifts that seeks to avoid the pitfalls of both phenomenological and structuralist theories of the gift. Grounded on a theory of practice, Bourdieu accounts for gift exchange in terms of a specific logic that, by focusing on an economy of symbolic goods, offers two advantages: it can account for the ambiguity of the gift as it passes through time, and it permits an understanding of the agent of gift exchange neither as a phenomenologically construed intending subject nor as a structurally constructed and self-deluded follower of social rules. Like Derrida, Bourdieu focuses his account of gifts on the theme of time, specifically the time lag between gift and countergift. It is, he argues, precisely this time lag that stands as the condition for the possibility of the gift. Bourdieu is critical of an objectivist account like Lévi-Strauss's for focusing almost entirely on the relation of reciprocal equivalence between gift and countergift. This focus on reciprocity renders the objectivist account unable to distinguish gift exchange from either "swapping," which "telescopes gift and countergift into the same instant," or "lending, in which the return of the loan, explicitly guaranteed by a legal act, is in a sense already performed at the very moment when a contract is drawn up ensuring the predictability and calculability of the acts it prescribes" (197–98). But the alternative to the objectivist account is not a subjectivist account that distinguishes gift from swap or loan exclusively in terms of the differing intentions of the giver and receiver. Rather, Bourdieu's account of the gift is grounded on the necessity of a deferred and different countergift that is made possible by the individual and collective misrecognition of the social rules that govern the act of reciprocation. This misrecognition, moreover, does not facilitate a violation of the social rules; instead, it is itself part of the social rules, part of the *habitus,* by which Bourdieu names the "systems of durable, transposable dispositions, structured structures predisposed to function as structuring structures, that is, as principles which generate and organize practices and representations that can be objectively adapted to their outcomes without presupposing a conscious aiming at ends or an express mastery of the operations necessary in order to obtain them."[27]

Gift exchange is, for Bourdieu, "the paradigm of all the operations through which symbolic alchemy produces the reality-denying reality that the collective consciousness aims at as a collectively produced, sustained and maintained misrecognition of the 'objective' truth" (203). It is precisely this "symbolic alchemy" that objectivist theories overlook. By overdetermining "value" and "interest" exclusively as "*economic* value" and "*economic* interest," Bourdieu claims that objectivist accounts are guilty of ethnocentrism in that their economistic assumptions render them incapable of recognizing any form of value or interest other than that produced by capitalism (205). Archaic economies, Bourdieu reminds us, operate in terms of the double-sided conceptual vocabulary analyzed by Benveniste, in which giving is taking, gifts are debts, and the line between the economic and the noneconomic is constantly blurred. In his attempt to understand the logic of practice that blurs this line, Bourdieu develops the notion of "symbolic capital" as capital whose social value is recognized by virtue of its material value having been *mis*recognized. Taking account of "the acts of cognition that are implied in misrecognition and recognition," he puts forward the theory of agency that underlies his theory of practice, a theory of agency that acknowledges these acts of cognition as part of the social reality produced by a "socially constituted subjectivity" that itself "belongs to objective reality" (215).

In Bourdieu's second selection, written especially for this volume, he returns to his earlier analysis of gifts to highlight the ambiguity of the gift that must play between the "individual and collective self-deception" that, reminiscent of a Sartrean collective "bad faith," refuses to attend to egoistic and interested calculations of exchange while at the same time remaining aware of that very logic of exchange. The appropriate response to this ambiguity, however, is not to reduce the gift, as perhaps Derrida does, to an antinomy whose conditions of possibility are precisely its conditions of impossibility (e.g., the gift that is recognized as a gift ceases thereby to be a gift). Rather, in a move that brings him close to Cixous, Bourdieu argues that we must challenge the very ethnocentric economistic assumptions that have led gift economy "to shrink to an island in the ocean of equivalent-exchange economy" (235). For these assumptions, Bourdieu suggests, frame giving and generosity in a context in which the demand for return is so foundational to social practice that economic capital is transfigured into social capital and "economic domination (of the rich over the poor, master over servant, man over woman, adults over children, etc.) [is transformed] into personal dependence (paternalism, etc.), even devotion, filial piety or love" (238).

The question of the gift, Bourdieu concludes, is ultimately a *political* question. He writes, "The purely speculative and typically scholastic question of whether generosity and disinterestedness are possible should give way to the political question of the means that have to be implemented in order to create universes in which, as in gift economies, people have an interest in disinterestedness and generosity" (240). When established in conditions of "lasting asymmetry" that exclude the possibility of equivalent return or "active reciprocity, which is the condition of possibility of genuine autonomy," the apparently "most gratuitous and least costly relations of exchange"—e.g., expressions of concern, kindness, consideration or advice, acts of generosity or charity—"are likely to create lasting relations of dependence" (238). An analysis of gift and exchange thus is doomed to fail if it does not begin with a logic of practice but begins instead with the assumption that agents act as isolated atoms; for by doing so, it ignores "the economic and social conditions in which historical agents are produced and reproduced, endowed (through their upbringing) with durable dispositions that make them able and inclined to enter into exchanges, equal or unequal, that give rise to durable relations of dependence" (239).

The fourth and final section presents recent discussions by four thinkers who represent the diversity of ways the logic of the gift—framed in part by the selections of the first three sections—can be seen at work in the critical discourses of the humanities and social sciences in the United States and Great Britain. Allan Stoekl, in "Bataille, Gift-Giving, and the Cold War," examines the closing chapters of volume one of Bataille's *The Accursed Share* (1949) and argues that Bataille's comments on the Marshall Plan, written at the start of the cold war, may suggest the continuing importance of a "general economy" in the contemporary, post–cold war context. Where the notion of a general economy as a gift giving without return has been appropriated in a wide range of literary and philosophical contexts, Stoekl suggests that Bataille introduced this concept not so much for its literary implications as for its social and cultural effects. The "logic" of *The Accursed Share*, which begins with a theoretical account of the meaning and laws of general economy, thus works toward a conclusion that reads the Marshall Plan as "an immense, State-sponsored potlatch" (248). Stoekl recalls that for Bataille, where the Soviet system was based upon "conservation and recuperation, the American is one of expenditure without return"

(249). Bataille argued, in fact, that the American expenditure of the Marshall Plan arose as a (calculated?) response to precisely this Soviet conservation, and Stoekl suggests that in this way, Bataille's work may already be a post–cold war document in that it predicts that, with the fall of the Soviet conservation, another force of conservation will need to arise to rival the opposing tendency toward excessive consumption. In this way, the opposition between the US and Japan in fact may be reproducing the early cold war relations between the US and the USSR as functions of "the same profound posthistorical opposition, that between conservation and expenditure, sense and show" (253). And, by implication, Stoekl leads us to consider whether this same opposition between conservation and expenditure is not being played out in the contemporary cultural battles over the conservative agenda of cutting back on foreign aid and care (read "gifts") for the poor, closing the borders to those who will consume without returning, and, in general, the call for eliminating the state-sponsored gift giving that has rested at the heart of the social welfare state.

Robert Bernasconi, in "What Goes Around Comes Around: Derrida and Levinas on the Economy of the Gift and the Gift of Genealogy," juxtaposes Derrida's account of the logic of the gift with that of Emmanuel Levinas, and he argues that while these accounts appear to differ on many points, they both in fact share the same assumption of the gift's fundamentally aporetic nature. Their proximity on this point is obscured somewhat in that Levinas presents the problem not in terms of the gift but in terms of work, a work that must be "radically generous" and a "departure without return" (258). Here, like the gift, work must be undertaken outside the context of any return or reciprocity. Therefore, Bernasconi suggests that neither work nor gift can be thought of in terms of the model of exchange. In this sense, he wants to read Derrida's discussion of the gift as a challenge to the very heart of Levinas's ethics, which must be construed not in terms of reciprocal duties but as an absolute, asymmetrical duty to the Other. Like the gift, ethics must be without calculation—goodness, if it is to be, must be absolute, that is, it must be undertaken with no thought of reward or of benefit returning to the self. Bernasconi suggests, however, that Derrida and Levinas might be able to avoid the aporia to which they are both led were their accounts less ahistorical and more *genealogical*. To show this, he examines almsgiving, a topic discussed by Derrida in *Given Time* and a topic central to Levinasian ethics. While Derrida is critical of Levinas for focusing on the ahistorical (and paradoxical) notion of "duty without debt," Bernasconi argues that Derrida is guilty of the same lack of genealogy that Derrida himself recognizes (in "Force of Law"[28] and elsewhere) as central to the deconstructive project. That is to say, both Derrida and Levinas are guilty of the same totalizing gesture that too quickly combines the Hebraic with the Greek traditions and takes the Greek/Western concept of rationality to be universal. Were they to attend more explicitly to the genealogy of the concept of intention, Bernasconi suggests, they would "avoid some of the mystifications that a lack of historical awareness produces" (270). And in the case of the gift, they would recognize that the specific account of the aporia to which they both assent is grounded on a Kantian/Judeo-Christian version of intention (and goodness) that is not only not universal but is challenged directly by the Aristotelian notion of *proairesis*. By indissolubly linking the "intention in giving" to the "inherent value of what is given" (267), Bernasconi concludes that *proairesis* allows us to think "intention" other than as it is conceived within the "ethics of intention"; that is to say, it gives us a way to address the value of the gift without necessarily disconnecting it from the intentions or motivations that led to the gift being given, the very disconnection that leads Derrida and Levinas to their aporetic conclusions.

Gary Shapiro, in "The Metaphysics of Presents: Nietzsche's Gift, the Debt to Emerson, Heidegger's Values," offers a provocative reading of the gift in response to Nietzsche's Zarathustra's naming "the gift-giving virtue" as the "unnameable." Along the way, he puts Nietzsche's discourse on gifts and gift giving in contact with Mauss's *The Gift*, which claimed that the gift practices of the Melanesians could not be named or understood from within the perspective of the market, and he brings to light Nietzsche's debt to Emerson, with whose essays Nietzsche was familiar, and whose affinities with Nietzsche on the logic of the gift Shapiro makes explicit. Like Emerson, Nietzsche sees the gift as both valuable and dangerous. And like Emerson, Nietzsche sees genuine giving as a difficult virtue to master. In the end, Shapiro argues that Nietzsche/Zarathustra's account of the gift more closely resembles Bataille's wasteful and transgressive expenditure than Mauss's account of the gift as a force of social stability. In so doing, he positions Nietzsche to respond to Heidegger's critical account of Nietzsche as the culmination of the Western metaphysical tradition. For, among other things, Heidegger places Nietzsche at this culminating point precisely because Nietzsche, while escaping many of the prejudices of the nineteenth century, was in his view not able to escape the perspective of values and value thinking. Shapiro, on the other hand, shows that Heidegger's own account of value in Nietzsche fails to place any value on Nietzsche's affirmation of squandering, an affirmation that, rather than reckoning on returns of equal value, puts forward as a sign of power the disengaged and disinterested destruction of what is valued. Where Heidegger sees Nietzsche offering his "transvaluation of values" as a reversal of the traditional hierarchy of values, Shapiro suggests that we view Nietzsche's transvaluation, as exemplified in his account of the logic of the gift, as a transformation of valuative thinking. The gift-giving virtue names the unnameable, therefore, precisely because as the highest virtue, it is the destroyer of the value of presence/presents par excellence.

Marilyn Strathern, in "Partners and Consumers: Making Relations Visible," extends her analysis of gift economy in Melanesia (put forward in *The Gender of the Gift: Problems with Women and Problems with Society in Melanesia* [1988][29]) toward analyzing certain practices within Euro-American consumer culture and, in particular, toward practices pertaining to the new reproductive technologies. The propriety of this extension would seem, on the surface, to be obvious. We speak, do we not, of organ or sperm *donation*, of *donor* eggs and *donor* sperm, of the *gift* of life. The procedure itself of gamete intra-fallopian transfer, she notes, is not by mere coincidence referred to by its felicitous acronym GIFT. She cautions, however, that the surface similarities may obscure more profound differences, differences that derive from the contrasting conceptions of persons that animate each culture. In late-twentieth-century Euro-American consumer culture, the person is understood as a free-standing individual and "gift-giving seems a highly personalized form of transaction" (295). Gifts in this context are conceived "as extensions of the self insofar as they carry the expression of sentiments" (302) and gift giving "presupposes two kinds of relationships: an individual person's relations with others and an individual person's relations with society" (307). For the Melanesians, on the other hand, persons are understood relationally and the gift is understood in the context not of an initial establishment but of the *re*-establishment of these relations. Rather than presupposing two kinds of relationships, "Melanesian gifts on the other hand presuppose two kinds of persons, partners divided by their transaction: paternal from maternal kin, fetus from placenta, clansmen from the ground they cultivate, descendants from ancestors" (307). The coercive nature of gift giving in Melanesia, Strathern notes, makes the partnering relationship established between donor and recipient both finite and enduring. Furthermore, gifting, as it takes place in the altruistic and voluntaristic context of the new reproductive technologies, is anything but enduring, and Strathern concludes by asking whether it is, for all that, any less coercive.

The trajectory of the essays reprinted in this collection should make one thing quite clear: the question of the gift is a political question, a question of the *polis*, which addresses fundamental issues of intersubjective interaction. From Emerson and Mauss to Bourdieu and Strathern, the discussions of the gift never stray too far from basic ethical and political questions concerning how human beings do and should treat one another. This should not be surprising inasmuch as giving gifts is a social act that unavoidably takes one outside oneself and puts one in contact with an other or others. That the logic of the gift, then, is infused with assumptions of reciprocity should also not be surprising given that our fundamental notion of justice, embodied in the image of the balanced scales, is a notion of equitable exchange. Justice as equity demonstrates the depth to which contractarian notions of equal exchange inform our most fundamental model of human interaction, a depth reflected in many of the essays that follow whose discourse on the gift remains to some extent infected by a contractarian thematics of quid pro quo exchange between individuals.

The widespread appearance and urgency of the contemporary discourses of the humanities and social sciences on gifts and gift giving may, therefore, itself be viewed as a response to the current political climate. That is to say, the appeal of the gift as a topic for consideration and research may reflect a renewed concern for the establishment of more politically acceptable relations between citizens in response to the recent neoconservative attacks on many of the fundamental principles underlying a notion of social welfare and the accompanying neoconservative championing of a return to a fundamentally contractarian notion of human relations. This attack has allowed a narrowly self-interested notion of reciprocal return to emerge and dominate the current political discourse on giving. Focusing only on those "gifts" that can, should, and must be returned leads, among other things, to viewing foreign-aid decisions exclusively in terms of national self-interest; viewing welfare as a "free ride" that must be replaced by a more contractarian relation in which repayment can be assured ("workfare"); viewing taxes as the unjust extortion of "gifts" that "givers" are forced against their will to give to those who need and benefit from the social programs supported by those taxes; viewing charity not as a generous donation to society's less fortunate members but as a prudent tax-avoidance strategy; etc. One must wonder what sorts of assumptions regarding gift giving and generosity are operating in a society that views public assistance to its least advantaged members as an illegitimate gift that results in an unjustifiable social burden that can no longer be tolerated while at the same time viewing corporate bailouts and tax breaks for its wealthiest citizens as legitimate investments in a nation's future. To combat such views requires challenging some of the assumptions basic to the modern liberal democratic state, including perhaps the very notion of a property-possessing individual empowered to demand full and unimpeded authority to control all that he or she owns.

If we depart from the more traditional accounts of gift exchange that presuppose a misrecognition or forgetting of the debt that its reception entails, would this allow us to avoid describing gift-giving practices as a mis-recognition of what is in reality reciprocal exchange? Might we then retrieve gift giving from the economic necessities imposed upon it within an exchangist economy and reframe the practices of giving in an account that does not restrict transactions to private proprietary relationships in which loans and loans paid back masquerade as the bestowal of gifts? Could we escape the limits of the Hegelian ideal of autonomy—the *nomos* of the *autos*—as a law of the self, which might make it possible to exceed the limits of ourselves and enter into the between of self and other without losing ourselves in the process? To free ourselves from the oppositional logic of "self vs. all others" might allow for our self-construction as something other than isolated and atomistic subjectivities. Freed from the constraints of an atomistic and autonomous individualism, might possibilities be opened for establishing nonproprietary relations of cooperative ownership in which a fully intersubjective self could be at home in the between of self and other? And might such nonproprietary relations facilitate the formulation of an alternative logic of the gift, one liberated from the presuppositions of more classical exchangist logics that imprison gift giving within the constraints of the economic assumptions of commodity trading? Mauss looked to "archaic society and to the elements in it" to find "the joy of public giving; the pleasure in generous expenditure on the arts, in hospitality, and in the private and public festival; social security, the solicitude arising from reciprocity and co-operation," and the like.[30] It is toward facilitating such possibilities that the essays in this collection have been compiled, in the hope that we might move closer, at last, to an ethic of generosity.

Notes

1. Jacques Derrida, *Given Time*, trans. Peggy Kamuf (Chicago: University of Chicago Press, 1992), p. ix.

2. Ibid., p. ix.

3. Jacques Derrida, *Spurs: Nietzsche's Styles*, trans. Barbara Harlow (Chicago: University of Chicago Press, 1979).

4. Jacques Derrida, *The Post Card: From Socrates to Freud and Beyond*, trans. Alan Bass (Chicago: University of Chicago Press, 1987).

5. I am thinking here of the work of Peggy Kamuf, Christie V. McDonald, and Alice Jardine, among others. One might also cite Hélène Cixous's discussion in her chapter "Sorties" in Hélène Cixous and Catherine Clément, *The Newly Born Woman*, trans. Betsy Wing (Minneapolis: University of Minnesota Press, 1986). While by no means a "commentary" on the work of Derrida, here Cixous nevertheless seems to be responding in part to Derrida's economic discourse on Nietzsche/woman. For a discussion of Cixous in this context see my "On the Gynecology of Morals: Nietzsche and Cixous on the Logic of the Gift," in *Nietzsche and the Feminine*, ed. Peter J. Burgard (Charlottesville: University of Virginia Press, 1994),

pp. 210–229, reprinted with minor revisions in my *Nietzsche's French Legacy: A Genealogy of Poststructuralism* (New York: Routledge, 1995), pp. 82–101.

6. Gayle Rubin, "The Traffic in Women," in *Toward an Anthropology of Women*, ed. Rayna Reiter (New York and London: Monthly Review Press, 1975), p. 173.

7. C. A. Gregory, *Gifts and Commodities* (London: Academic Press, 1982), p. 41. Gregory's sharp distinction between gifts and commodities has been challenged, however. See, for example, Arjun Appadurai, "Introduction: Commodities and the Politics of Value," in *The Social Life of Things*, ed. Arjun Appadurai (Cambridge: Cambridge University Press, 1986), pp. 3–63; and Alan Smart, "Gifts, Bribes, and *Guanxi*: A Reconsideration of Bourdieu's Social Capital,"*Cultural Anthropology* 8, 3 (1993): 388–408, esp. 396.

8. See Carol Gilligan, *In a Different Voice* (Cambridge: Harvard University Press, 1982).

9. Marcel Mauss, *The Gift: The Form and Reason for Exchange in Archaic Societies*, trans. W. D. Halls (New York: Norton, 1990), p. 65.

10. Derrida frequently draws attention to the gift as *pharmakon*, often in the context of a comment on Mauss. For example, in "Plato's Pharmacy," he cites Mauss's call to examine the etymology of "gift," which comes from the Latin *dosis*, Greek δοσιξ, a dose of poison (*Dissemination*, trans. Barbara Johnson [Chicago: University of Chicago Press, 1981], pp. 131–132). More recently, he makes several references to the gift as *pharmakon* in *Given Time*.

11. Friedrich Nietzsche, *Thus Spoke Zarathustra*, in *The Viking Portable Nietzsche*, trans. and ed. Walter Kaufmann (New York: The Viking Press, 1967), "On the Pitying."

12. Ibid., "The Voluntary Beggar."

13. See Ibid., "On the Great Longing."

14. Mauss, *The Gift*, p. 4.

15. Ibid., pp. 82–83.

16. Georges Bataille, *The Accursed Share: An Essay on General Economy, Vol I: Consumption*, trans. Robert Hurley (New York: Zone Books, 1988), p. 25.

17. Georges Bataille, "The Notion of Expenditure," in *Visions of Excess: Selected Writings, 1927–39*, ed. Allan Stoekl, trans. Allan Stoekl with Carl R. Lovitt and Donald M. Leslie Jr. (Minneapolis: University of Minnesota Press, 1985), pp. 116–29.

18. We should here recall that Zarathustra's very first words are directed toward the sun's overflowing expenditure.

19. Bataille, *The Accursed Share*, p. 38.

20. Ibid., p. 25.

21. Mauss, *The Gift*, pp. 78–79.

22. Ibid., p. 3.

23. Derrida recalls in a later footnote that the question of the gift was inscribed in the essay "*Différance*": "In recalling the Heideggerian remark ('the gift of presence is a property of Appropriating [*Die Gabe von Anwesen ist Eigentum des Ereignens*],' *Zeit und Sein*, p. 22), I was interested then in underscoring that 'there is no essence of différance,' that 'it (is) that which not only could never be appropriated in the *as such* of its name or its appearing, but also that which threatens the authority of the *as such* in general. . . .' Which is, in effect, what is being said here about the gift, and thus one must hesitate to say: about the gift *itself*"(*Given Time*, pp. 127–28, note 12).

24. Ibid., p. 40.

25. Hélène Cixous, "Castration or Decapitation?" trans. Annette Kuhn, *Signs: Journal of Women in Culture and Society* 7, 1(1981): 48.

26. Hélène Cixous, "An exchange with Hélène Cixous," trans. Verena Andermatt Conley, in *Hélène Cixous: Writing the Feminine* (Lincoln: University of Nebraska Press, 1984), p. 137.

27. Pierre Bourdieu, *The Logic of Practice*, trans. Richard Nice (Cambridge: Polity Press, 1990), p. 53.

28. Jacques Derrida, "Force of Law: The 'Mystical Foundation of Authority,'" trans. by Mary Quaintance, *Cardozo Law Review*, 11, 5–6 (July/August 1990): 920–1045.

29. Marilyn Strathern, *The Gender of the Gift: Problems with Women and Problems with Society in Melanesia* (Berkeley: University of California Press, 1988).

30. Mauss, *The Gift*, p. 69.

Part One

□

DOCUMENTS

Gifts

Ralph Waldo Emerson

It is said that the world is in a state of bankruptcy, that the world owes the world more than the world can pay, and ought to go into chancery, and be sold. I do not think this general insolvency, which involves in some sort all the population, to be the reason of the difficulty experienced at Christmas and New Year, and other times, in bestowing gifts; since it is always so pleasant to be generous, though very vexatious to pay debts. But the impediment lies in the choosing. If at any time, it comes into my head, that a present is due from me to somebody, I am puzzled what to give, until the opportunity is gone. Flowers and fruits are always fit presents; flowers, because they are a proud assertion that a ray of beauty outvalues all the utilities of the world. These gay natures contrast with the somewhat stern countenance of ordinary nature: they are like music heard out of a work-house. Nature does not cocker us: we are children, not pets: she is not fond: everything is dealt to us without fear or favor, after severe universal laws. Yet these delicate flowers look like the frolic and interference of love and beauty. Men use to tell us that we love flattery, even though we are not deceived by it, because it shows that we are of importance enough to be courted. Something like that pleasure, the flowers give us: what am I to whom these sweet hints are addressed? Fruits are acceptable gifts, because they are the flower of commodities, and admit of fantastic values being attached to them. If a man should send to me to come a hundred miles to visit him, and should set before me a basket of fine summer-fruit, I should think there was some proportion between the labor and the reward.

For common gifts, necessity makes pertinences and beauty every day, and one is glad when an imperative leaves him no option, since if the man at the door have no shoes, you have not to consider whether you could procure him a paint-box. And as it is always pleasing to see a man eat bread, or drink water, in the house or out of doors, so it is always a great satisfaction to supply these first wants. Necessity does everything well. In our condition of universal dependence, it seems heroic to let the petitioner be the judge of his necessity, and to give all that is asked, though at great inconvenience. If it be a fantastic desire, it is better to leave to others the office of punishing him. I can think of many parts I should prefer playing to that of the Furies. Next to things of necessity, the rule for a gift, which one of my friends prescribed, is, that we might convey to some person that which properly belonged to his character, and was easily associated with him in thought. But our tokens of compliment and love are for the most part barbarous. Rings and other jewels are not gifts, but apologies for gifts. The only gift is a portion of thyself. Thou must bleed for me. Therefore the poet brings his poem; the shepherd, his lamb; the farmer, corn; the miner, a gem; the sailor, coral and shells; the painter, his picture; the girl, a handkerchief of her own sewing. This is right and pleasing, for it restores society in so far to its primary basis, when a man's biography is conveyed in his gift, and every man's wealth is an index of his merit. But it is a cold, life-less business when you go to the shops to buy me something, which does not represent your life and talent, but a goldsmith's. This is fit for kings, and rich men who represent kings, and a false state of property, to make presents of gold and silver stuffs, as a kind of symbolical sin-offering, or payment of black-mail.

The law of benefits is a difficult channel, which requires careful sailing, or rude boats. It is not the office of a man to receive gifts. How dare you give them? We wish to be self-sustained. We do not quite forgive a giver. The hand that feeds us is in some danger of being bitten. We can receive anything from love, for that is a way of receiving it from ourselves; but not from any one who assumes to bestow. We sometimes hate the meat which we eat, because there seems something of degrading dependence in living by it.

"Brother, if Jove to thee a present make,
Take heed that from his hands thou nothing take."

We ask the whole. Nothing less will content us. We arraign society, if it do not give us besides earth, and fire, and water, opportunity, love, reverence, and objects of veneration.

He is a good man, who can receive a gift well. We are either glad or sorry at a gift, and both emotions are unbecoming. Some violence, I think, is done, some degradation borne, when I rejoice or grieve at a gift. I am sorry when my independence is invaded, or when a gift comes from such as do not know my spirit, and so the act is not supported; and if the gift pleases me overmuch, then I should be ashamed that the donor should read my heart, and see that I love his commodity, and not him. The gift, to be true, must be the flowing of the giver unto me, correspondent to my flowing unto him. When the waters are at level, then my goods pass to him, and his to me. All his are mine, all mine his. I say to him, How can you give me this pot of oil, or this flagon of wine, when all your oil and wine is mine, which belief of mine this gift seems to deny? Hence the fitness of beautiful, not useful things for gifts. This giving is flat usurpation, and therefore when the beneficiary is ungrateful, as all beneficiaries hate all Timons, not at all considering the value of the gift, but looking back to the greater store it was taken from, I rather sympathize with the beneficiary, than with the anger of my lord Timon. For, the expectation of gratitude is mean, and is continually punished by the total insensibility of the obliged person. It is a great happiness to get off without injury and heart-burning, from one who has had the ill luck to be served by you. It is a very onerous business, this of being served, and the debtor naturally wishes to give you a slap. A golden text for these gentlemen is that which I so admire in the Buddhist, who never thanks, and who says, "Do not flatter your benefactors."

The reason of these discords I conceive to be, that there is no commensurability between a man and any gift. You cannot give anything to a magnanimous person. After you have served him, he at once puts you in debt by his magnanimity. The service a man renders his friend is trivial and selfish, compared with the service he knows his friend stood in readiness to yield him, alike before he had begun to serve his friend, and now also. Compared with that good-will I bear my friend, the benefit it is in my power to render him seems small. Besides, our action on each other, good as well as evil, is so incidental and at random, that we can seldom hear the acknowledgments of any person who would thank us for a benefit, without some shame and humiliation. We can rarely strike a direct stroke, but must be content with an oblique one; we seldom have the satisfaction of yielding a direct benefit, which is directly received. But rectitude scatters favors on every side without knowing it, and receives with wonder the thanks of all people.

I fear to breathe any treason against the majesty of love, which is the genius and god of gifts, and to whom we must not affect to prescribe. Let him give kingdoms or flower-leaves indifferently. There are persons, from whom we always expect fairy tokens; let us not cease to expect them. This is prerogative, and not to be limited by our municipal rules. For the rest, I like to see that we cannot be bought and sold. The best of hospitality and of generosity is also not in the will, but in fate. I find that I am not much to you; you do not need me; you do not feel me; then am I thrust out of doors, though you proffer me house and lands. No services are of any value, but only likeness. When I have attempted to join myself to others by services, it proved an intellectual trick,—no more. They eat your service like apples, and leave you out. But love them, and they feel you, and delight in you all the time.

From *Essays*, Second Series, 1844.

Gift, Gift

Marcel Mauss

The two meanings of "present" and "poison," into which this single word has diverged in the different Germanic languages, seem so far removed from each other that etymologists find it difficult to explain the passage from one to the other and their common origin. The very destiny of the word differs according to the languages, the meaning of poison being almost the only one to be kept in modern German, the sense of present and endowment being the only one to be maintained in English, Dutch having two words, one being neuter, the other feminine for indicating the poison and the present or dowry respectively. Here, one sense has eroded, there another, and nowhere is the semantic derivation clear. As far as I see it in the great etymological dictionaries of German and English, the Murray and the Kluge,[1] no satisfactory explanation has been provided for it. The important remarks made by Hirt concerning the German *gift*, however, have to be taken into account.[2] It is indeed clear that *gift* "poison" is a euphemism resulting from a taboo concerning a word one was reluctant to use: just like in Latin *venenum* corresponds to **venesnom* "Liebestrank." But why is it precisely the word *gift* and the idea of bestowal it evokes that have been chosen as symbols of poison? That is what still remains to be explained.

Now, for the sociologist and for the historian of Germanic law, the filiation of these meanings offers no difficulty.

For the benefit of clarity, we ask the reader to allow us to touch on a few principles that have not yet become well-known enough to make it unnecessary for us to explain them again.

◻

In the Germanic world, the social system that I have proposed to call a "system of total prestations" ["*système des prestations totales*"] has particularly flourished. In this system, which is not only juridical and political but economical and religious as well, clans, families, and individuals create bonds through perpetual services and counter-services of all kinds, usually in the form of free gifts and services of a religious nature or otherwise.[3]

After having believed for a long time that this system has been widespread only in backward societies, we now see that it exists in a large part of the ancient legal systems of European societies.[4] In particular the groups forming the ancient Germanic societies create bonds through marriages, through daughters-in-law and sons-in-law, through the children born from both lineages, nephews, cousins, grandfather and grandson, raised with one another, some fed by others, some served by others,[5] etc.—by military services and initiations, enthronings and the festivities they give rise to;— by deaths, funerary meals and successions, usufructs, the reciprocation of gifts they entail;—by gratuitous gifts, usurious loans returned or to be returned. An unceasing circling of both goods and persons, of permanent and temporary services, of honors and feasts given, returned and to be returned; this is how one has to imagine a good part of the social life of the ancient peoples of Germany and Scandinavia.

Other ancient European societies, for instance the Celts, have further developed other elements of those rites and those ancient legal systems. The theme of rivalry, that of single combat, that of emulating extravagant spending, of challenges and tournaments has been exacerbated in the Gallic, Welsh, and Irish countries.[6] These societies clearly practice the form of total prestations of an agonistic type we have proposed to name "pot-latch," after the Chinook and the jargon of the traders and the American Indians, and to the juridical aspects of which Mr. Davy has drawn attention.[7] We know that these particular forms have been well developed in the American Northwest and in Melanesia. Potlatch in the strict sense of the word is not foreign to the customs of the ancient Germans and Scandinavians either.

But it is the gift, the pawn that is most interesting to study with these societies. Indeed, the *Gabe*, the *gift* [*la ou le* gift], the present appears there with more pronounced features; it is more clearly visible there than in many other types of societies and certainly more than in other Indo-European societies. The German language in particular has quite an extremely rich range of words and of words invented for expressing its different kinds of nuances, from *Gabe* and *Mitgift* to *Morgengabe, Liebesgabe, Abgabe,* and the curious *Trotzgabe*.[†]

◻

Now, in all these numerous societies, on many different levels of civilization, in the Maori legal system in particular, these exchanges and gifts of objects that link the people involved, function on the basis of a common fund of ideas: the object received as a gift, the received object in general, engages, links magically, religiously, morally, juridically, the giver and the receiver. Coming from one person, made or appropriated by him, being from him, it gives him power over the other who accepts it. In the case where the prestation provided is not rendered in the prescribed juridical, economical, or ritual form, the giver obtains power over the person who has participated in the feast and has taken in its substances, the one who has married the girl or has bound himself by blood relations, the beneficiary who uses an object enchanted with the whole authority of the giver.

The chain of these ideas is particularly evident in the Germanic legal system and languages, and one can easily see how the two senses of the word *gift* are integrated in it. Indeed, the typical prestation for the ancient Germans and Scandinavians is the gift of drink,[8] of beer; in German, the present par excellence[9] is what one pours (*Geschenk, Gegengeschenk*). It would be unnecessary to refer here to a very substantial number of topics of Germanic law and mythology. But one can see that the uncertainty about the good or bad nature of the presents could have been nowhere greater than in the case of the customs of the kind where the gifts consisted essentially in drinks taken in common, in libations offered or to be rendered. The drink-present can be a poison; in principle, with the exception of a dark drama, it isn't; but it can always become one. It is always a charm anyway (the word *"gift"* has kept this meaning in English) which permanently links those who partake and is always liable to turn against one of them if he would fail to honor the law. The kinship of meaning linking gift-present to gift-poison is therefore easy to explain and natural.

There are, moreover, other words belonging to this legal system that also possess, in the Germanic lands, this ambiguity. The pawn corresponded as well, in ancient law, to this mutual charm. Mr. Huvelin has, in a classical paper,[10] suspected the origin of the legal tie comparable to the Latin *nexum*, to reside in this magical exchange. Let's make this more clear. The *gage, wage, -wadium, vadi*, that creates a bond between master and servant, creditor and debtor, buyer and seller is a magical and ambiguous thing. It is at the same time good and dangerous; it is thrown at the feet of the contracting party in a gesture that is at the same time one of confidence and of prudence, of distrust and of defiance. Oddly enough, this is still the most solemn way of exchanging amongst the bold navigators and tradesmen of the Melanesian Trobriand Islands.[11] And it is the reason why one still speaks in English of "throwing the gage" for throwing down the gauntlet.

Besides, all these ideas have two faces. In other Indo-European languages it is the notion of poison that is uncertain. Kluge and the etymologists rightly compare the series *potio* "poison" and *gift, gift*. It is still worthwhile to read the agreeable discussion of Aulus Gellius[12] on the ambiguity of the Greek φάρμακον and the Latin *venenum*. For the *Lex Cornelia de Sicariis et Veneficis*, of which Cicero fortunately has preserved the very "recitation," still specifies *venenum malum*.[13] The magic potion, the delicious charm,[14] can be either good or bad. Neither is the Greek φίλτρον necessarily a sinister term, and the drink of friendship, of love, is only dangerous if the enchanter wants it to be so.

◙

These conclusions are only a technical and philological elaboration concerning a single fact that will be mentioned only later. For it is part of an ensemble of observations taken from all sorts of law systems, of magics, of religions and economies of all kinds of societies, from the Melanesian and Polynesian and North American to our own morality. On this matter and without leaving the field of the Germanists, one could call to mind one of Emerson's essays: *On Gifts and Presents* [*sic*][15] points out very well the pleasure and the displeasure we still feel when receiving presents. One will find an account of all these facts in a work on "the obligation to return presents," to be published in the first issue of the new series of *l'Année sociologique*.††

First published in *Mélanges offerts à M. Charles Andler
par ses amis et ses élèves* [1924].
Reprinted in *Oeuvres*, Vol. 3 [1969].
Translated by Koen Decoster for this volume.

Notes

1. Kluge feels that the same thing must have happened to these words as has happened to *vergeben, vergiften*. *Etymol. Wörterb*, 1915 [TN: *Etymologisches Wörterbuch der deutschen Sprache* (Strassburg: Trubner, 8. verbesserte und verm. Aufl.)], p. 171.

2. *Etymol. d. neuhochd. Sprache*, 1909 [TN: *Etymologie der neuhochdeutschen Sprache: Darstellung des deutschen Wortschatzes in seiner geschichtlichen Entwicklung* (Handbuch des deutschen Unterrichts an hoheren Schulen 4, 2) (München: Beck)], p. 297. The connection Hirt makes with the series: Gotic lubja, Old High German *luppi* "Liebe-Zaubertrank" [TN: "love-potion"] is also interesting and well-founded.

3. For a short survey of these questions, see Davy, *Eléments de sociologie*, I [TN: Georges Davy, *Sociologie politique* (*Eléments de sociologie* 1) (Paris: Vrin, deuxième éd., 1950)], p. 156f.

4. Mauss, "Une forme archaïque de contrat chez les Thraces," *Rev. des études grecques*, 1921.

5. I'm alluding here to "fosterage" and similar customs.

6. In a forthcoming issue of the *Revue celtique*, one will find notes by Mr. Hubert and Mr. Mauss on this topic [EN: *Revue celtique* 42 (1925)].

7. *La foi jurée*. (*Travaux de l'Année sociologique*.) [TN: Georges Davy, *La foi jurée: étude sociologique du problème du contrat. La formation du lien contractuel*

(Bibliothèque de philosophie contemporaine. Travaux de l'Année sociologique) (Paris: Alcan, 1922).]

† TN: *Mitgift* has, apart from the general meaning of a gift the receiver takes with (*"mit"*) him, the specific sense of the gift a bride is given by her relatives to take with her when she marries. *Morgengabe* belongs to the same register: it can be the gift a husband gives his wife the morning after the wedding, it can also be the dowry paid by the husband to the relatives of his bride, or it can designate the *"Mitgift"* just mentioned. The old German dictionary of the Grimm brothers discusses both terms in great detail: *Deutsches Wörterbuch* von Jacob Grimm und Wilhelm Grimm (Leipzig: Hirzel, 1854-1922). *Liebesgabe* is a gift out of charity or pity. *Abgabe* is the giving away (*"ab"*) of something. *Trotzgabe* is a "curious" word indeed: it is not mentioned in the Duden, Brockhaus-Wahrig, or Grimm dictionaries, but it should designate a gift in spite of, notwithstanding (*"trotz"*) something.

8. Von Amira, *Nordgermanisches Obligationenrecht*, II [TN: Karl Von Amira, *Nordgermanisches Obligationenrecht. 2: Westnordgermanisches Obligationenrecht* (Leipzig: Veit, 1895)], pp. 362, 363, and above all Maurice Cahen, *La libation, Et. s. le vocabul. religieux,* etc. [TN: *Etudes sur le vocabulaire religieux du vieux-scandinave: la libation* (Paris: Alcan, 1922)], p. 58, etc.

9. To be complete, one should also mention the "paraphernalia" given by the husband to the wife of which Tacitus describes the circuit between families in chapter 18 of the Germania (in a usually misunderstood though perfectly clear sentence).

10. "Magie et droit individuel," *Année sociologique* 10, p. 30ff.

11. See B. Malinowski, *Argonauts of the Western Pacific,* London, 1922, p. 473; see especially the beautiful photographs, plates XXI, LXII, and the cover illustration.

12. [TN: *Noctes Atticae*] 19, 9 with a pertinent quotation from Homer.

13. *Pro Cluentio,* 148. The *Digest* [TN: Emperor Justinian's Digest of Roman Law] still requires to specify with which kind of *"venenum," "bonum, sive malum,"* one is dealing.

14. If the etymology linking *venenum* (see Walde, *Lat. Etymol. Wört.* [TN: Alois Walde, *Lateinisches Etymologisches Wörterbuch* (Indogermanische Bibliothek), 2. umgearb. Aufl. (Heidelberg: Winter, 1910)], ad. verb.) of *Venus* and the Sanskrit *van, vanati* is exact, as seems likely.

15. *Essays,* see the second series. [EN: Reprinted above, pp. 25–27.]

†† TN: A reference to Mauss's *Essai sur le don. Forme et raison de l'échange dans les sociétés archaïques,* reedited several times since and recently retranslated by W. D. Halls as *The Gift. The Form and Reason for Exchange in Archaic Societies,* foreword by Mary Douglas (London: Routledge, 1990).

Gift and Exchange
in the Indo-European Vocabulary

Émile Benveniste

It was the very great contribution of Marcel Mauss, in his now classic *Essai sur le don*,[1] to have revealed the functional relationship between gift and exchange and to have defined thereby a whole group of religious, economic, and judicial phenomena belonging to archaic societies. He showed that the gift is only one element in a system of reciprocal prestations which are at once free and constraining, the freedom of the gift obliging the recipient to a countergift, which engenders a continuous flow of gifts offered and gifts given in return. Here is the principle of an *exchange* which, generalized not only between individuals but also between groups and classes, stimulates the circulation of wealth throughout the entire society. The game is determined by rules that become fixed in institutions of all sorts. A vast network of rites, celebrations, contracts, and rivalries organizes the mechanics of these transactions.

The demonstration made by Mauss was based primarily upon archaic societies, which furnished him with a mass of conclusive evidence. If one seeks to verify this mechanism in ancient societies, particularly in the Indo-European world, convincing examples become much more rare. It is true that Mauss himself described "an archaic form of contract among the Thracians," and he also discovered in ancient India and Germany traces of analogous institutions. In addition, one must allow for chance discoveries, always possible in this vast domain in which the investigation has not been systematically pursued. The fact remains that these societies are much more difficult to explore and that, as far as usable documents are concerned, one cannot count on a large amount of sure and specific evidence, if one wishes it to be explicit.

We do have nevertheless some less apparent facts, which are all the more valuable for not having run the risk of being distorted by conscious interpretations. These are the facts presented by the vocabulary of the Indo-European languages. One cannot use them without an elaboration based on the comparison of attested forms. But that comparison will result in conclusions which will supply to a rather large degree the absence of evi-

dence for the most ancient periods of our societies. Several examples will
be brought forth and analyzed in order to obtain whatever information
they can offer about the prehistoric notions of gift and exchange.

In most Indo-European languages, "to give" is expressed by a verb from
the root *$d\bar{o}$*- which also has a large number of nominal derivatives. There
seemed to be no possible doubt about the constancy of this signification until
it was established that the Hittite verb *$d\bar{a}$*- meant not "give" but "take." This
caused considerable confusion, which still lasts. Should Hittite *$d\bar{a}$*- be considered a different verb? We cannot assume this without misgivings. Must we,
on the other hand, admit that the original sense of *$d\bar{o}$*- was "take," faithfully
preserved in Hittite *$d\bar{a}$*- as well as in Indo-Iranian *$\bar{a}$-$d\bar{a}$*- "receive"? This
would reverse the problem without making it any easier; it would remain to
be explained how "give" could have come from "take." In reality the problem seems insoluble if we seek to derive "take" from "give" or "give" from
"take." But the problem is wrongly put. We shall consider that *$d\bar{o}$*- properly
means neither "take" nor "give" but either the one or the other, depending
on the construction. It must have been employed like English "take," which
permits two opposed meanings: "to take something from someone" but also
"to take something to someone, to deliver something to someone." Cf. also,
"to betake oneself, to go"; besides, in Middle English, *taken* meant "to
deliver" as well as "to take." Similarly, *$d\bar{o}$*- indicated only the fact of taking
hold of something; only the syntax of the utterance differentiated it as "to
take hold of in order to keep" (= take) and "to take hold of in order to offer"
(= give). Each language made one of these acceptations prevail at the expense
of the other in order to construct the antithetical and distinct expressions for
"taking" and "giving." Accordingly, in Hittite *$d\bar{a}$*- means "take" and is
opposed to *pai*- "give," while in most of the other languages it is *$d\bar{o}$*- which
means "give," and a different verb which assumes the meaning of "take."
Some traces of the double possibility survive; even though the distribution
was fixed in Indo-Iranian, the verb *$d\bar{a}$*- "to give," with the preverb *$\bar{a}$*- indicating movement toward the subject, means "to receive."

It seems, then, that the most characteristic verb for "to give" was
marked by a curious semantic ambivalence, the same sort of ambivalence
affecting more technical expressions like "buy" and "sell" in Germanic
(Germ. *kaufen: verkaufen*) or "borrow" and "lend" in Greek (δανείζω :
δανείζομαι). "To give" and "to take" thus proclaim themselves here, in a
very ancient phase of Indo-European, as notions that were organically
linked by their polarity and which were susceptible of the same expression.

Now *$d\bar{o}$*- is not the only example of this. For a long time there has been
a question about the etymology of the verb for "take" in Germanic: Goth.
niman, Germ. *nehmen*, which assumes a root *nem*-. One would naturally

think of relating it to Gr. νέμω. Comparatists have always refused to do this, claiming that there was a difference in meaning.[2] But the meaning must be defined with some precision before it can be decided if it is really an obstacle to the relationship. The Greek verb νέμω has the two values of "to give legally as an allotment" (Ζεὺς νέμειὄλβον ἀνθρώποισι [Od. 16. 188] and "to have legally as an allotment" (πόλιν νέμειν) [Hdt. 1. 59]).[3] In Gothic, niman does indeed mean "to take" in various acceptations. But a compound of this verb is of special interest: it is arbi-numja "heir," lit. "the one who takes (= receives) the inheritance." Now the Greek term that arbi-numja translates is κληρονόμος "heir." Is it chance that (κληρο)νόμος and (arbi) numja are formed from νέμω in Greek and from niman in Gothic? Here we have hold of the missing link which allows us to join the meanings which history has separated. Goth. niman means "to take," not in the sense of "to take hold of" (which is greipan, Germ. greifen) but in the sense of "to receive" and more exactly, of "to receive as an allotment, into possession," which is precisely the same as one of the two acceptations of Gr. νέμω. The connection between νέμω and niman is now restored, and is confirmed by the ambivalence of *nem-, which indicates legal attribution as given or as received.[4]

Let us now turn to the very notion of "gift" in the form which is the most constant throughout most of the Indo-European languages. We observe that, in general, nominal forms derived from *dō- were used. Now, it happens—and this fact has been barely noticed—that within a single language, several of these derivatives will be employed simultaneously, being differentiated by their suffixes. The coexistence of these "synonyms" should arouse attention and call for a strict verification, first because they are not synonyms and, more especially, because the simplicity of a notion such as "gift" would not seem to require multiple expressions.

Ancient Greek had no fewer than five distinct and parallel words for "gift," *dō-, and our dictionaries and translations render them identically as "gift, present": δώς, δόσις, δῶρον, δωρεά, δωτίνη.[5] We must try to define each one of them specifically by virtue of its formation. The first, δώς, has only one example, in Hesiod: δώς, ἀγαθή, ἄρπαξ, δὲ κακή "to give is good, to ravish is evil" (Works 354); a root word which, like ἄρπαξ must have been an invention of the poet for an expression as simple and as little differentiated as possible for "gift." In δόσις the notion is presented as an effective accomplishment; it is the act of giving susceptible of being realized in a gift:[6] καί οἱ δόσις ἔσσεται ἐσθλή "(the one who will devote himself), we shall give him a precious gift" (Il. 10. 213). This time, the gift is promised in advance, designated in detail, and is to recompense a bold deed. The next two, δῶρον and δωρεά must be taken together: the first, δῶρον, is indeed the gift of generosity, of gratitude, or of homage, which is incorporated into the object offered; and δωρεά properly designates, as an abstraction, "the providing of presents" (cf. Hdt. 3. 97) or the "totality of presents" (ibid. 3. 84), whence the adverbial use δωρεάν "in the manner of a present, gratuitously." Aristotle defines δωρεά precisely as a δόσις ἀναπόδοτος (*Top.* 125a. 18), a δόσις that does not impose the obligation of a gift in return. Finally there remains the most significant term, δωτίνη, which is also a gift but of a completely different sort. The δωτίνη, in Homer, is the obligatory gift offered to a chief whom one wishes to honor (*Il.* 9. 155. 297) or the gift that is due one as a guest; Ulysses, received by Polyphemus, feels he has a right to count on the δωτίνη, which is a part of the duties of hospitality: εἴ τι πόροις ξεινήιον ἠὲ καὶ ἄλλως | δοίης δωτίνην ἥτε | ξείνων θέμις ἐστίν (*Od.* 9. 267).[†] Alcinous, welcoming Ulysses at his home, does not wish to let him leave without having brought together the whole δωτίν that is meant for him: εἰς ὅ κε πᾶσαν | δωτίνην τελέσω (*Od.* 11. 351). The uses of the word in Herodotus confirm this technical sense. A man, wishing to befriend the husband of a woman whom he desires, offers him as a δωτίνη any of his possessions that the husband might desire, but on condition of reciprocity (Hdt. 6. 62). One cannot emphasize more clearly the functional value of the δωτίνη, of this gift that obliges a gift in return. This is the invariable sense of the word in Herodotus; whether the δωτίνη is intended to call forth a gift in return or whether it serves to compensate for a previous gift, it always includes the idea of reciprocity: it is the gift that a city is compelled to give the person who has done it a service (1. 61); the gift sent to a people in order to engage their friendship (1. 69).[7] Whence δωτινάξω (2. 180) "to collect the δωτῖναι' in the form of voluntary contributions from the cities towards a common work. In an inscription from Calauria, δωτίνη relates to the "rent" due in kind from one who has obtained a concession of land (*I.G.* 4. 841. 11; third century B.C.). We have in δωτίνη the notion of a gift in return or a gift which calls for a return. The mechanism of the reciprocity of the gift is revealed by its very meaning and is related to a system of offerings of homage or hospitality.

Up to this point we have considered words whose sense brought them to our attention immediately. But a valid inquiry must and can go well beyond the terms that have an explicit reference to the gift. There are some which are less apparent, not immediately obvious, and which sometimes can be recognized only by certain particular qualities in the meaning. Others preserve their proper value in only one part of the Indo-European domain. We must make use of both in order to reconstruct this complex prehistory.

An obvious connection joins the notion of the gift to that of hospitality. But one must distinguish among the terms relating to hospitality. The etymology of some of them, like Greek ξένος, is not certain. The study of the word is thus involved with that of the institution and should be left to the historian of Hellenic society. More interesting are the terms whose evolution we can follow, even, and perhaps especially, if this evolution has produced divergences in the meaning. One of these is the Latin word *hostis*. The term *hostis* will here be considered in its relation with other Latin words of the same family, which includes more than Latin (Goth. *gasts*, O.Slav. *gosti* "guest/host"), but we shall put aside *hospes*, which cannot be analyzed with any certitude although it is certainly related.

Well-known Latin evidence assists in the reconstruction of the history of *hostis* in Rome. The word still means "foreigner" in the Law of the XII Tables, and this sense was familiar to Roman scholars. Varro (*L.L.* 5. 3) states: "hostis . . . tum eo verbo dicebant peregrinum qui suis legibus uteretur, nunc dicunt eum quem dicebant perduellem." And Festus (414. 37) gives us this important definition in addition: ". . . ab antiquis hostes appellabantur quod erant pari iure cum populo Romano atque *hostire* ponebatur pro *aequare*."

There is actually a series of proofs that *hostire* did indeed signify *aequare*. Several derivatives confirm it, some of which are related to material operations, others to judicial or religious institutions. In Festus himself, we find *red-hostire* "referre gratiam," and in Plautus: promitto . . . *hostire* contra ut merueris "I promise to pay you back as you deserve" (*Asin.* 377). In addition, *hostimentum* is defined as "beneficii pensatio" and "aequamentum" (Nonius 3. 26) and, according to a gloss, more precisely, "*hostimentum* dicitur lapis quo pondus exaequatur" (*C.G.L.* 5. 209. 3). This meaning appears in Plautus, where it indicates the "compensation" for work and wages: "par pari datum hostimentumst, opera pro pecunia" (*Asin.* 172). The same notion is present in *hostus*, which Varro specifies as a rural term: "*hostum* vocant quod ex uno facto olei reficitur: factum dicunt quod uno tempore conficiunt" (*R.R.* 1. 24. 3); the sense is properly "compensation, that oil which is obtained as a compensation for one pressing." *Hostorium* was the name for the stick used to *level* the bushel (lignum quo modius aequatur, Prisc. 2. 215. 17; *C.G.L.* 5. 503. 36). Augustine (*Civ. Dei.* 4. 8) mentions a *dea Hostilina* who was in charge of equalizing the ears of grain (or perhaps of equalizing the harvest with the work realized). These clear and concordant indications are not diminished by certain glosses in the abridgement of Festus and Nonius, according to which *hostire* would mean "ferire, comprimere, caedere"; this sense was deduced from archaic citations that were not exactly understood and which moreover refute it: in *hostio ferociam* (Pacuvius) and *hostit voluntatem tuam* (Naevius), the verb does not mean "destroy" but "compensate, counterbalance."

An important term for this family is gained by annexing to it the word *hostia*. *Hostia* does not designate any offered victim at all but only the one which was intended to "compensate for" the anger of the gods. Just as important in another domain is the term *hostis*, whose relation to all the others which surround it can be seen. The primary meaning of *hostis* is indeed the one Festus gives it: not just any "foreigner" but the foreigner who is *pari iure cum populo Romano*. *Hostis* thereby takes on the meaning of both "foreigner" and "guest." The equal rights that he enjoyed with respect to the Roman citizen were connected with his status as a guest. *Hostis* is properly one who compensates and enjoys compensation, one who obtains from Rome the counterpart of the advantages which he has in his own country and the equivalent of which he owes in his turn to the person whom he pays reciprocally. This old relationship was weakened, then abolished, as the status of *civis* came to be more rigorously defined and the *civitas* became the sole and ever stricter norm of judicial participation in the Roman community. The relationships regulated by personal or family agreements were wiped out in the face of rules and duties imposed by the state; *hostis* then became the "foreigner" and then the "public enemy" by a change in meaning that is connected with the political and judicial history of the Roman state.

Through *hostis* and the related terms in early Latin we can discern a certain type of *compensatory offering* that is the basis of the notion of "hospitality" in the Latin, Germanic, and Slavic societies; equality of status transposes into law the parity between persons confirmed by reciprocal gifts.

In order to approach a different aspect of the same notions, we shall resort to another Latin word whose meaning has been more stable but also more complex. An entire Indo-European phenomenology of "exchange," of which fragments survive in the numerous forms derived from the root **mei-*, might be traced through and around *munus*. We should study in particular the Indo-Iranian notion of *mitra*, the contract and the god of the contract, a term whose authentic meaning largely overlaps that of the "contract." It is the equivalent in the human world of what the *ṛta* is in the cosmic world, that is, the principle of total reciprocity that bases human society on rights and obligations to the point that the same expression (Sans. *druh*, Av. *drug-*) indicates the one who violates the *mitra* and the one who transgresses the *ṛta*. This profound and rich expression takes on a particular acceptation in Lat. *munus*. In literary use, *munus* means "function, office," or "obligation" or "task" or "favor" or, finally, "public spectacle, gladiatorial contest," all acceptations relating to the social sphere. The formation of *munus* is characteristic in this regard; it contains the suffix **nes-* which, as Meillet correctly observed, is attached to designations of a social or judicial nature (cf. *pignus, fenus, funus, facinus*). The unity of meanings in *munus* is found in the notion of respects paid or service accomplished, and this itself goes back to what Festus defined as a *donum quod officii causa datur*. In accepting a *munus*, one contracts an obligation to repay it publicly by a distribution of favors or privileges, or by holding games, etc. The word contains the double value of a charge conferred as a distinction and of donations imposed in return. Here is the basis of "community," since *communis* signifies literally "one who shares in the *munia* or *munera*"; each member of the group is compelled to give in the same proportion as he receives. Charges and privileges are the two faces of the same thing, and this alternation constitutes the community.

An "exchange" which is constituted of "gifts" accepted and returned is something quite different from utilitarian commerce. It must be generous in order to be judged profitable. When one gives, he must give the most precious thing he has. This is what can be learned from certain terms that are etymologically of the same family as *munus*: O.Irish *māin*, *mōin*, which means "present" and "precious thing," and especially Goth. *maiþms* "δῶρον," O.Ice. *meidmar* pl. "jewels," O.E. *madum* "treasure, jewel." It is worth noticing that Goth. *maiþms* is not a gift in the sense that English "gift" would express. This word appears in the translation of Mark 7: II, to render δῶρον, but as the equivalent of the Hebrew word κορβᾶν "offering to the Treasure of the Temple." The choice of *maiþms* shows that in Gothic as in the other Germanic languages, the present of exchange must be of signal value.

A comparison of vocabulary will reveal to us an institution analogous to the ones we have just discussed, but not so obvious. It is a type of donation almost abolished in historical societies and which we can only rediscover by interpreting the rather dissimilar significations of a group of words derived from **dap-*: Lat. *daps* "sacred banquet," O.Ice. *tafn* "sacrificial animal," Arm. *tawn* "feast," Gr. δαπάνη "expense" (cf. δάπτω "break to pieces, consume, destroy"), and also Lat. *damnum* "damage" (**dap-nom*). The religious sense of some of these terms is clear. But in each of them the meaning has been narrowed down to only one particular aspect of a representation which goes beyond the sphere of the sacred and is realized in the domains of law and economy as well.

As the nucleus of the meaning we shall set up the notion of "expense" as a manifestation both religious and social: a festive and sumptuous expense, an offering that consists of a large consumption of food, made for prestige and as a "pure loss." This definition seems to account for all the special acceptations arising from the fragmentation of an archaic conception. The Roman *daps* was a banquet offered to the gods, a real banquet with roast meat and wine which the participants ceremoniously consumed after having desacralized it. The antiquity of this rite can be seen in the formulae that consecrated it; according to Cato, these prayers were addressed to Jupiter: *Jupiter dapalis, quod tibi fieri oportet, in domo familia mea culignam vini dapi, eius rei ergo macte hac illace dape pollucenda esto . . . Jupiter dapalis, macte istace dape pollucenda esto* (Cato *Agr.* 132). The use of *pol-*

lucere with *daps* emphasizes the magnificence of it: the verb always accompanies splendid consecrations in the ancient religious vocabulary. This can actually be seen in Ovid (*Fasti* 5. 515ff) when the poor peasant Hyrieus offers Jupiter, who is visiting him, a whole ox, his only possession, as a *daps*. Moreover, ancient derivatives of *daps* confirm the fact that this word implied largesse and associate it with festive banquets of hospitality: "*dapatice* se acceptos dicebant antiqui, significantes magnifice, et *dapaticum negotium* amplum ac magnificum" (Festus). The verb *dapinare*, whether it is connected with *daps* or whether it is an adaptation of Gr. δαπανᾶν, signifies, in the only example of it that survives, "to treat royally at the table": *aeternum tibi dapinabo victum, si vera autumas* (Pl. *Capt.* 897).

In Greek, δαπάνη, of which, in general, only the commonplace acceptation of "expense" is retained, also implies largesse, an expense for display and prestige, although the term is no longer restricted to religious use. In Herodotus (2. 169), δαπάνη signifies "sumptuous ornamentation" in the decoration of a building. Pindar (*Isthm.* 4. 29) provides a significant use of it: Πανελλάνεσσι δ᾽ ἐριζόμενοι δαπάνα χαῖρον ἵππων "(the competitors in the games) in rivalry with the peoples of all Hellas took pleasure in expenditures on horses." It really is, in effect, an expense of rivalry and prestige. If a new proof is necessary, it will be found in the sense of the adjective δαψιλής "abundant, splendid," which passed into Latin, in which *dapsilis* "magnificent, sumptuous," is associated secondarily with *daps* and renews an ancient etymological connection. The verb δαπανᾶν means "to spend," but it must be understood in a stronger sense: "to spend" here means "to consume, to destroy"; cf. δαπανηρός "prodigal, extravagant." Hence, with the strict notion of a "sacrifice with food" (Lat. *daps*, O.Ice. *tafn*) and of "feast" (Arm. *tawn*) must be associated the idea of an ostentatious prodigality which is at the same time the consumption of food and the destruction of wealth. This clarifies the word *damnum*, so curiously separated from this semantic group. In *damnum*, there remains only the sense of "damage suffered," of material and especially pecuniary loss: it is the "expense" imposed upon someone and no longer consented to freely, the "loss" which is prejudicial and no longer a voluntary sacrifice; in short, a detriment or a penalty instead of a magnificent squandering. Jurists, who were also peasants, thus narrowed and reduced to a penalty what had been the sign of largesse and generosity. Whence *damnare* "damno afficere, to impose a fine," and in general, "to condemn."

All these features help us perceive, in an Indo-European prehistory which is not so ancient, a socioreligious phenomenon of which we still retain many traces in our vocabulary today. In English we say "*to give* a reception" and in French "*offrir* un banquet"; there are "expenses" of food and "sacrifices" of possessions made as social obligations and as fulfillments of the duty of hospitality. This analysis leads us finally to recognize, in the Indo-European world, the institution known as potlatch. It does not seem that the ancient classical societies knew that aggravated form of potlatch that several writers, Mauss in particular, have described among the Kwakiutl or the Haïda, or those extravagant challenges in which chiefs who were jealous of their prestige provoked one another to enormous destructions of wealth. But the fact still remains that the terms analyzed here refer to a custom of the same type as the potlatch. Although the theme of rivalry no longer appears, the essential features are really the same: the feast with an abundance of food, the expense which is purely ostentatious and intended to maintain rank, the festive banquet—all this would have no sense if those who had the profit of this largesse were not committed to requite it by the same means. Moreover, is it chance that the term *potlatch* is related in essence to offerings of food and means literally, "to nourish, to consume"?[8] Among all the varieties of potlatch, this must have been the most usual in societies in which the authority and the prestige of the chiefs were maintained by the largesse they distributed and from which they benefited in turn.

It would be easy to extend these considerations further, either by pursuing the etymological relations of the terms examined, or, on the other hand, by studying the different Indo-European expressions for notions that are apparently identical. One example will show in what unpredictable form the notion of "exchange" may be revealed.

As one might guess, "exchange" gives rise to a large vocabulary for specifying economic relations. But terms of this type have almost always been renewed, so that we must consider each language for itself. There is, however, one term which is at least fairly widespread in Indo-European and which is unvarying in meaning: it is the one that properly designates "value." It is represented by Gr. ἀλφάνω, Sans. arh- "to have worth, to be worthy" (cf. *arhat* "deserving") also Av. *arz-*, Lth. *algà* "price, wages." In Indo-Iranian and in Lithuanian, the sense appears to be rather general and abstract, not lending itself to a more precise determination. But in Greek, ἀλφάνω allows for a more exact interpretation than the dictionaries indicate in rendering it by "to earn, to yield."

In Homer, ἀλφάνω means indeed "to get a profit," but this sense is connected to a well-defined situation: the profit in question is the one that a captive brings to the man who sells him. It suffices to enumerate the Homeric examples. In order to move Achilles to pity, when he is ready to kill him, Lycaon implores him: "You once took me and led me to be sold at the market at Lemnos, where I brought you the price of a hundred oxen" ἑκατόμβοιον δέ τοι ἦλφον (*Il.* 21. 79). About a little slave who is offered for sale: "he will bring you a thousand times his price" ὁ δ᾽ ὑμῖν μυρίον ὦνον ἄλφοι (*Od.* 15. 453). Melantheus threatens to sell Eumaeus far from

Ithaca "so that he will bring me a good living" ἵνα μοι βίοτον πολύν ἄλφοι (*Od.* 17. 250), and the suitors invite Telemachus to sell his guests at the market in Sicily "where they will bring you a good price" ὅθεν κέ τοι ἄξιον ἄλφοι (*Od.* 20. 383). There is no variation in the meaning of the verb and the full force of it is found in the epithet that describes maidens: παρθένοι ἀλφεσίβοιαι they "bring in oxen" for their father who gives them in marriage.

"Value" is characterized, in its ancient expression, as a "value of exchange" in the most material sense. It is the value of exchange that a human body possesses which is delivered up for a certain price. This "value" assumes its meaning for whoever disposes of a human body, whether it is a daughter to marry or a prisoner to sell. There we catch a glimpse, in at least one part of the Indo-European domain, of the very concrete origin of a notion connected to certain institutions in a society based on slavery.[††]

From *Problems in General Linguistics* [1948–49] translation 1971.

Translated by Mary Elisabeth Meek.

Notes

1. *L'Année sociologique,* new series, 1 (1923–1924): 30–186.

2. As a recent instance, cf. Sigmund Feist, *Etymologisches Wörterbuch der Gotischen Sprache,* 3rd ed. (Leyden: E. J. Brill, 1939), p. 376.

3. Just as Fr. *partager* means "to give as a share" and "to have as a share."

4. There are other proofs of this: O. Irish *gaibim* "take, have," corresponds to Germ. *geben* "give"; while O. Slav. *berǫ* means "I take," the same form in Irish, *do-biur,* means "I give," etc. These terms are affected by an apparent instability which in reality reflects the double value inherent in verbs with this sense. Etymologists often refuse to admit these opposed meanings or try to retain only one, thus rejecting obvious parallels and spoiling the interpretation.

5. There is even a sixth, δόμα, but it is late and need not detain us.

6. Cf. Benveniste, *Noms d'agent et noms d'action en indo-europeén* (Paris: Adrien-Maisonneuve, 1948), p. 76.

†. EN: Benveniste's citation appears incorrectly in the English translation as *Od.* II. 267.

7. This meaning of δωτίνη, once fixed, helps to settle a philological problem. We read in Herodotus 6. 89 that the Corinthians, by way of friendship, ceded to the Athenians some ships with the "symbolic" price of five drachmas, "because their law forbade a completely free gift" δωτίνην (var. δωρέην) γὰρ ἐν τῷ νόμῳ οὐκ ἐξῆν δοῦναι. The sense of a "free gift," which is that of δωρέη, not of δωτίνη, should cause the adoption of the reading δωρεὴν of ABCP, in opposition to the editors (Kallenberg, Hude, Legrand) who admit δωτίνην, following DRSV.

8. Cf. Mauss, *L'Année sociologique,* new series, 1 (1923–1924): 38, n. 1.

††. EN: I would like here to acknowledge the assistance of Rodney L. Ast in checking all the Greek citations (several of which were transcribed erroneously in the English translation) against Benveniste's French text, and Joseph Cummins for checking Benveniste's citations against the original Greek and Latin sources

Part Two

READINGS OF MAUSS

Selections from *Introduction to the Work of Marcel Mauss*

Claude Lévi-Strauss

Chapter II

The three other essays which make up this book (and even form the larger part of it) are the *Théorie de la magie* (1902–3), the *Essai sur le don* (1923–4), and *La Notion de personne* (1938).[1] These three essays bring to the fore another, even more decisive, aspect of Mauss's thinking, namely, the notion of the total social fact; this aspect would have emerged more clearly if we could have punctuated the twenty years between *La Magie* and *Le Don* with a few landmarks: *L'Art et le mythe* (1909); *Anna-Virâj* (1911); *Les Origines de la notion de monnaie* (1914a); *Dieux Ewhe de la monnaie et du change* (1914b); *Une Forme archaïque de contrat chez les Thraces* (1921b); *Commentaires sur un texte de Posidonius* (1925). The notion of total social fact would be further clarified if the major *Essai sur le don* had been accompanied by texts that move in the same direction: *De Quelques formes primitives de classification* (1903, in collaboration with Durkheim); *Essai sur les variations saisonnières des sociétés Eskimo* (1904–5); *Gift, Gift* (1924b); *Parentés à plaisanteries* (1926b); *Wette, wedding* (1928); *Biens masculins et féminins en droit celtique* (1929a); *Les Civilisations* (1929b); *Fragment d'un plan de sociologie générale descriptive* (1934).[2]

It really would be a great mistake to isolate the *Essai sur le don* from the rest of the work, even though it is quite undeniably the masterwork of Marcel Mauss, his most justly famous writing, and the work whose influence has been the deepest. It is the *Essai sur le don* which introduced and imposed the notion of *total social fact*; but it is not hard to see how that notion is linked to considerations, only apparently different, which I mentioned in the preceding pages. It could even be said to command those considerations, since it is like them but is more inclusive and systematic in the way that it arises from the concern to define social reality, or, better, to define the social *as* reality. Now the social is only real when integrated in a system, and that is a first aspect of the notion of total fact: "After sociologists have, as they must, analyzed and abstracted rather too much, they must then force themselves to recompose the whole."[3] One might be tempted to apprehend the total fact through any one aspect of society exclusively: the familial aspect, the technical, economic, juridical, or religious aspect; that would be an error; but the total fact does not emerge as total simply by reintegrating the discontinuous aspects. It must also be embodied in an individual experience, and that, from two different viewpoints: first, in an individual history which would make it possible to "observe the comportment of total beings, not divided up into their faculties";[4] and after that, in what I would like to call (retrieving the archaic meaning of a term whose applicability to the present instance is obvious) an *anthropology*, that is, a system of interpretation accounting for the aspects of all modes of behavior simultaneously, physical, physiological, psychical, and sociological, "Only to study that fragment of our life which is our life in society is not enough."

The total social fact therefore proves to be three-dimensional. It must make the properly sociological dimension coincide with its multiple synchronic aspects; with the historical or diachronic dimension; and finally, with the physio-psychological dimension. Only in individuals can these three dimensions be brought together. If you commit yourself to this "study of the concrete which is a study of the whole,"[5] you cannot fail to note that "what is true is not prayer or law, but the Melanesian of this or that island, Rome, Athens."[6]

Consequently, the notion of total fact is in direct relation to the twofold concern (which until now we had encountered on its own), to link the social and the individual on the one hand, and the physical (or physiological) and the psychical on the other. But we are better able to understand the reason for it, which is also twofold. On the one hand, it is at the end of a whole series of reductive procedures that we can grasp the total fact, which includes: (1) different modes of the social (juridical, economic, aesthetic, religious, and so on); (2) different moments of an individual history (birth, childhood, education, adolescence, marriage, and so on); (3) different forms of expression, from physiological phenomena such as reflexes, secretions, decreased and increased rates of movement, to unconscious categories and conscious representations, both individual and collective. All of that is definitely social, in one sense, since it is only in the form of a social fact that these elements, so diverse in kind, can acquire a global signification and become a whole. But the converse is no less true, for the only guarantee we can have that a total fact corresponds to reality, rather than being an arbitrary accumulation of more or less true details, is that it can be grasped in a concrete experience: first, in that of a society localized in space or time, "Rome, Athens"; but also, in that of any individual at all in any one at all of the societies thus localized, "the Melanesian of this or that island." So it really is true that, in one sense, any psychological phenomenon is a sociological phenomenon; that the mental is identified with the social. But on the other hand, in a different sense, it is all quite the reverse: the proof of the social cannot be other than mental; to put it another way, we can never be sure of having reached the meaning and the function of an institution, if we are not in a position to relive its impact on an individual consciousness. As that impact is an integral part of the institution, any valid interpretation must bring together the objectivity of historical or comparative analysis and the subjectivity of lived experience. When I followed, earlier, what seemed to me to be one of the directions of Mauss's thinking, I arrived at the hypothesis that the psychical and the social are complementary. That complementarity is not static, as would be that of two halves of a puzzle; it is dynamic and it arises from the fact that the psychical is both at once a simple *element of signification* for a symbolic system which transcends it, and the only *means of verification* of a reality whose manifold aspects can only be grasped as a synthesis inside it.

There is much more to the notion of total social fact, therefore, than a recommendation that investigators remember to link agricultural techniques and ritual, or boat-building, the form of the family agglomeration and the rules of distribution of fishing hauls. To call the social fact *total* is not merely to signify that *everything observed is part of the observation*, but also, and above all, that in a science in which the observer is of the same nature as his object of study, *the observer himself is a part of his observation*. I am not alluding, here, to the modifications which ethnological observation inevitably produces in the functioning of the society where it occurs, for that difficulty is not peculiar to the social sciences; it is encountered wherever anyone sets out to make fine measures, that is, wherever the observer (either he himself, or else his means of observation) is of the same order of magnitude as the observed object. In any case, it was physicists who brought that difficulty to light, and not sociologists; it merely imposes itself on sociologists in the same way. The situation particular to the social sciences is different in nature; the difference is to do with the intrinsic character of the object of study, which is that it is object and subject both at once; or both 'thing' and 'representation', to speak the language of Durkheim and Mauss. It could doubtless be said that the physical and natural sciences are in the same circumstance, since any element of the real is an object, and yet it triggers representations; and that a full explanation of the object should account simultaneously for its own structure and for the representations through which our grasp of its properties is mediated. In theory, that is true; a total chemistry should explain not just the form and the distribution of a strawberry's molecules, but how there results from the arrangement a unique flavor. However, history can prove that a satisfactory science does not need to go so far, and that for centuries on end, and even millennia perhaps (since we do not know when it will complete its work), it can progress in the knowledge of its object by virtue of an eminently unstable distinction between qualities pertaining to the object which are the only ones that the science seeks to explain, and other qualities which are a function of the subject, and which need not be taken into consideration.

When Mauss speaks of total social facts, he implies, on the contrary, (if I am interpreting him correctly) that that easy and effective dichotomy is denied to the sociologist, or at least, that it could only correspond to a temporary and transient state of the development of the science. An appropriate understanding of a social fact requires that it be grasped *totally*, that is, from outside, like a thing; but like a thing which comprises within itself the subjective understanding (conscious or unconscious) that we would have of it, if, being inexorably human, we were living the fact as indigenous people instead of observing it as ethnographers. The problematic thing is to know how it is possible to fulfil that ambition, which does not consist only of grasping an object from outside and inside simultaneously, but also requires much more; for the insider's grasp (that of the indigenous person, or at least that of the observer reliving the indigenous person's experience) needs to be transposed into the language of the outsider's grasp, providing certain elements of a whole which, to be valid, has to be presented in a systematic and coordinated way.

The task would not be feasible if the distinction between the objective and the subjective, rejected by the social sciences, were as rigorous as it has to be when the physical sciences provisionally allow it. But that is precisely the difference: the physical sciences bow (temporarily) to a distinction that they intend shall be rigorous, whereas the social sciences reject (permanently) a distinction which could only be a hazy one. I should like to explain further what I mean by that. I mean that, in so far as the distinction is, as a theoretical distinction, an impossible one, it can in practice be pushed much further, to the point where one of its terms becomes negligible, at least relative to the order of magnitude of the observation. The subject itself—once the object-subject distinction is posited—can then be split and duplicated in the same way, and so on without end, without ever being reduced to nothing. Sociological observation, seemingly sentenced by the insurmountable antinomy that we isolated in the last paragraph, *extricates itself* by dint of the subject's capacity for indefinite self-objectification, that is to say (without ever quite abolishing itself as subject) for projecting outside itself ever-diminishing fractions of itself. Theoretically, at least, this fragmentation is limitless, except for the persistent implication of the existence of the two extremes as the condition of its possibility.

The prominent place of ethnography in the sciences of man, which explains the role it already plays in some countries, under the name of social and cultural anthropology, as inspirer of a new humanism, derives from the fact that it offers this unlimited process of objectification of the subject, which is so difficult for the individual to effect; and offers it in a concrete, experimental form. The thousands of societies which exist or have existed on the earth's surface are human, and on that basis we share in them in a subjective way; we could have been born into them, and so we can seek to understand them as if we were. But at the same time, all of them taken together (as compared to any one of them on its own) attest the subject's capacity to objectify himself in practically unlimited propor- tions, since the society which is the reference group, which constitutes only a tiny fraction of the given, is itself always exposed to being subdivided into two different societies, one of which promptly joins the enormous mass of that which, for the other one, has and always will have the status of object; and so it goes on indefinitely. Any society different from our own has the status of object; any group of our own society, other than the group we come from ourselves, is object; and even every custom of our own group to which we do not adhere. That limitless series of objects constitutes, in ethnography, the Object, and is something that the individual subject would have to pull painfully away from himself, if the diversity of mores and customs did not present him with a prior fragmenting. But never could the historical and geographical closing of gaps induce him to forget (at the risk of annihilating the results of his efforts) that all those objects proceed from him, and that the most objectively conducted analysis of them could not fail to reintegrate them inside the analyst's subjectivity.

▣

The ethnographer, having embarked on that work of identification, is always threatened by the tragic risk of falling victim to a *misunderstanding*; that is, the subjective grasp he reaches has nothing in common with that of the indigenous individual, beyond the bald fact of being subjective. That difficulty would be insoluble, subjectivities being, in hypothetical terms, incomparable and incommunicable, if the opposition of self and other could not be surmounted on a terrain which is also the meeting place of the objective and the subjective; I mean the unconscious. Indeed, on the one hand, the laws of unconscious activity are always outside the subjective grasp (we can reach conscious awareness of them, but only as an object); and yet, on the other hand, it is those laws that determine the modes of their intelligibility.

So it is not surprising that Mauss, imbued with a sense of the necessity for a close collaboration between sociology and psychology, referred con- stantly to the unconscious as providing the common and specific character of social facts: "In magic, as in religion, it is the unconscious ideas which are the active ones."[7] In the essay on magic from which that quotation is taken, we can see an effort, doubtless still hesitant, to formulate ethnological problems by other means than through "rigid, abstract categories of our language and our thinking"; to do so in terms of a "non-intellectualist psychology" foreign to our "adult European understanding." It would be quite mistaken to perceive that as concordant (before the fact) with Lévy-Bruhl's idea of a prelogical mentality, an idea that Mauss was never to accept. We must rather seek its meaning in the attempt he himself made, in connection with the notion of *mana*, to reach a sort of "fourth dimension" of the mind, a level where the notions of "unconscious category" and "category of collective thinking" would be synonymous.

Mauss's perception was accurate, therefore, when from 1902 he affirmed that "in sum, as soon as we come to the representation of magical properties, we are in the presence of phenomena similar to those of language."[8] For it is linguistics, and most particularly structural linguistics, which has since familiarized us with the idea that the fundamental phenomena of mental life, the phenomena that condition it and determine its most general forms, are located on the plane of unconscious thinking. The unconscious would thus be the mediating term between self and others. Going down into the givens of the unconscious, the extension of our understanding, if I may put it thus, is not a movement toward ourselves; we reach a level which seems strange to us, not because it harbors our most secret self, but (much more normally) because, without requiring us to move outside ourselves, it enables us to coincide with forms of activity which are both at once *ours* and *other*: which are the condition of all the forms of mental life of all men at all times. Thus, the grasp (which can only be objective) of the unconscious forms of mental activity leads, nevertheless, to subjectivisation; since, in a word, it is the same type of operation which in psychoanalysis allows us to win back our most estranged self, and in ethnological inquiry gives us access to the most foreign other as to another self. In both cases, the same problem is posed; that of a communication sought after, in the one instance between a subjective and an objective self, and in the other instance between an objective self and a subjective other. And, in both cases also, the condition of success is the most rigorously positive search for the unconscious itineraries of that encounter; itineraries traced once and for all in the innate structure of the human mind and in the particular and irreversible history of individuals or groups.

In the last analysis, therefore, the ethnological problem is a problem of communication; and that realization must be all that is required to show the radical separation of the path Mauss follows when he identifies *unconscious* with *collective*, from the path of Jung, which one might be tempted to define the same way. For it is not the same thing, to define the unconscious as a category of collective thinking, and to divide it up into sectors according to the individual or collective character of the content attributed to it. In both cases, the unconscious is conceived as a symbolic system; but for Jung, the unconscious is not reduced to the system; it is filled full of symbols, and even filled with symbolized things which form a kind of substratum to it. But that substratum is either innate or acquired. If it is innate, one must object that, without a theological hypothesis, it is inconceivable that the content coming from experience should precede it; if it is acquired, the problem of the hereditary character of an acquired unconscious would be no less awesome than that of acquired biological features. In fact, it is not a matter of translating an extrinsic given into symbols, but of reducing to their nature as a symbolic system things which never fall outside that system except to fall straight into incommunicability. Like language, the social *is* an autonomous reality (the same one, moreover); symbols are more real than what they symbolize, the signifier precedes and determines the signified. We will encounter this problem again in connection with *mana*.

The revolutionary character of the *Essai sur le don* (1923–4) is that it sets us on that path. The facts it puts forward are not new discoveries. Two years before, G. Davy had analyzed and discussed potlatch on the basis of the enquiries of Boas and Swanton, whose importance Mauss himself had taken care to emphasize in his teaching even before 1914,[9] and the whole of the *Essai sur le don* emerges, in the most direct way, out of Malinowski's *Argonauts of the Western Pacific*, also published in 1922, which was to lead Malinowski himself, independently, to conclusions very close to those of Mauss.[10] That is a parallel which might induce us to see the indigenous Melanesians themselves as the real authors of the modern theory of reciprocity. So what is the source of the extraordinary power of those disorganized pages of the *Essai*, which look a little as if they are still in the draft stage, with their very odd juxtaposition of impressionistic notations and (usually compressed into a critical apparatus that dwarfs the text) inspired erudition, which gathers American, Indian, Celtic, Greek, or Oceanian references seemingly haphazardly, and yet always equally penetratingly? Few have managed to read the *Essai sur le don* without feeling the whole gamut of the emotions that Malebranche described so well when recalling his first reading of Descartes: the pounding heart, the throbbing head, the mind flooded with the imperious, though not yet definable, certainty of being present at a decisive event in the evolution of science.

What happened in that essay, for the first time in the history of ethnological thinking, was that an effort was made to transcend empirical observation and to reach deeper realities. For the first time, the social ceases to

belong to the domain of pure quality—anecdote, curiosity, material for
moralizing description or for scholarly comparison—and becomes a system,
among whose parts connections, equivalences, and interdependent aspects
can be discovered. First, it is the products of social activity, whether technical, economic, ritual, aesthetic, or religious (tools, manufactured products,
foodstuffs, magical formulae, ornaments, chants, dances, and myths), which
are made comparable to one another through that common character they
all have of being transferable; the modes of their transferability can be analyzed and classified, and even when they seem inseparable from certain types
of values, they are reducible to more fundamental forms, which are of a
general nature. Furthermore, these social products are not only comparable,
but often substitutable, in so far as different values can replace one another
in the same operation. And, above all, it is the operations themselves which
admit reduction to a small number. However diverse the operations may
seem when seen through the events of social life—birth, initiation, marriage, contract, death, or succession, and however arbitrary they may seem
in the number and distribution of the individuals that they involve as mem-
bers-elect, intermediaries, or donors—it is these operations, above all else,
which always authorize a reduction to a smaller number of operations,
groups, or persons, in which there finally remain only the fundamental terms
of an equilibrium, diversely conceived and differently realized according to
the type of society under scrutiny. So the types become definable by these
intrinsic characteristics; and they become comparable to one another, since
those characteristics are no longer located in a qualitative order, but in the
number and the arrangement of elements which are themselves constant in
all the types. To take an example from a scholar who, perhaps better than
anyone else, has managed to understand and exploit the possibilities opened
up by this method:[11] the interminable series of celebrations and gifts which
accompany marriage in Polynesia, which involve tens or even hundreds of
persons and seem to defy empirical description, can be broken down into
thirty or thirty-five prestations effected among five lineages which are in a
constant relation to one another, and are decomposable into four cycles of
reciprocity between the lineages A and B, A and C, A and D, and A and E.
The total operation expresses a certain type of social structure such that, for
example, there are no cycles allowed between B and C, or between E and B
or D, or, finally, between E and C, whereas a different form of society
would give these cycles pride of place. The method is so strictly applicable
that, if an error appeared in the solution to the equations obtained from it,
it would be more likely to be imputable to a gap in knowledge about the
indigenous institutions than to a miscalculation. Thus, in the example just
cited, we can ascertain that the cycle between A and B is opened by a prestation having no counterpart; that would at once lead us to seek, if we were

not already aware of it, the presence of a unilateral action, prior to the matrimonial ceremonies, although directly related to them. Such, precisely, is the role played in that society by the abduction of the fiancée, whose first prestation represents—according to the indigenous terminology itself—the 'compensation'. So the abduction could have been inferred, had it not been a matter of observation.

It will be noted that that operator technique is very close to that which Trubeckoj and Jakobson were perfecting, at the same time as Mauss was writing the *Essai*, and which was to enable them to found structural linguistics; for them too, it was a matter of distinguishing a purely phenomenological given, on which scientific analysis has no hold, from an infrastructure simpler than that given, to which the given owes its whole reality.[12] Thanks to the notions of 'optional variants', 'combinatory variants', 'terms in a system or set,' and 'neutralization', phonological analysis was precisely to create the possibility of defining a language by a small number of constant relations; the diversity and apparent complexity of its phonetic system merely illustrate the possible range of authorized combinations.

The *Essai sur le don* therefore inaugurates a new era for the social sciences, just as phonology did for linguistics. The importance of that double event (in which Mauss's part unfortunately remained in the outline stage) can best be compared to the discovery of combinatorial analysis for modern mathematical thinking. It is one of the great misfortunes of contemporary ethnology that Mauss never undertook to exploit his discovery, and that he thus unconsciously incited Malinowski (of whom we may, without prejudice to his memory, acknowledge that he was a better observer than theorist) to launch out alone upon the elaboration of the corresponding system, on the basis of the same facts and analogous conclusions, which the two men had reached independently.

It is difficult to know in what direction Mauss would have developed his doctrine, if he had been willing. The principal interest of one of his last works, *La Notion de personne* (1938), also published in *Sociologie et anthropologie*, is not so much in the argumentation, which we can find cursory and at times careless, as in the tendency which emerges in it to extend to the diachronic order a technique of permutations which the *Essai sur le don* had rather conceived as a function of synchronic phenomena. In any event, Mauss would probably have encountered some difficulties if he had tried to take the system to a further level of elaboration; we will shortly see why. But he certainly would not have given it the regressive form that Malinowski was to give it; for while Mauss construed the notion of *function* following the example of algebra, implying, that is, that social values are knowable *as functions of* one another, Malinowski transforms the meaning along the lines of what could seem to be a naïve empiricism, in that it no longer designates anything more than the practical usefulness for society of its customs and institutions. Whereas Mauss had in mind a *constant relation* between phenomena, which would be the site of their explanation, Malinowski merely wonders *what they are useful for*, to seek a justification for them. Such a posing of the problem annihilates all the previous advances, since it reintroduces an apparatus of assumptions having no scientific value.

The most recent developments in the social sciences, on the other hand, attest that Mauss's was the only way of posing the problem that was well founded; these new developments give us cause to hope for the progressive mathematization of the field. In certain essential domains, such as that of kinship, the analogy with language, so strongly asserted by Mauss, could enable us to discover the precise rules by which, in any type of society, cycles of reciprocity are formed whose automatic laws are henceforth known, enabling the use of deductive reasoning in a domain which seemed subject to the most total arbitrariness. On the other hand, by associating more and more closely with linguistics, eventually to make a vast science of communications, social anthropology can hope to benefit from the immense prospects opened up to linguistics itself, through the application of mathematical reasoning to the study of phenomena of communication.[13] Already, we know that a large number of ethnological and sociological problems, some on the level of morphology, some even on the level of art or religion, are only waiting upon the goodwill of mathematicians who could enable ethnologists collaborating with them to take decisive steps forward, if not yet to a solution of those problems, at least to a preliminary unification of them, which is the condition of their solution.

Chapter III

Why did Mauss halt at the edge of those immense possibilities, like Moses conducting his people all the way to a promised land whose splendor he would never behold? I am impelled to seek the reason, not from any wish to criticize, but out of a duty not to let the most fruitful aspect of his thinking be lost or vitiated. Mauss might have been expected to produce the twentieth-century social sciences' *Novum Organum*;[1] he held all the guidelines for it, but it has only come to be revealed in fragmented form. An omission must no doubt explain this. There must be some crucial move, somewhere, that Mauss missed out.

A curious aspect of the argumentation of the *Essai sur le don* will put us on the track of this difficulty. In this essay, Mauss seems—rightly—to be controlled by a logical certainty, namely, that *exchange* is the common denominator of a large number of apparently heterogeneous social activities. But exchange is not something he can perceive on the level of the facts. Empirical observation finds not exchange, but only, as Mauss himself says, "three obligations: giving, receiving, returning."[2] So the whole theory calls for the existence of a structure, only fragments of which are delivered by experience—just its scattered members, or rather its elements. If exchange is necessary, but not given, then it must be constructed. How? By applying to the isolated parts, which are the only present elements, a source of energy which can synthesize them. "One can . . . prove that in the exchanged objects . . . there is a property which forces the gifts to circulate, to be given and returned."[3] But this is where the difficulty comes in. Does this property exist objectively, like a physical property of the exchanged goods? Obviously not. That would in any case be impossible, since the goods in question are not only physical objects, but also dignities, responsibilities, privileges—whose sociological role is nonetheless the same as that of material goods. So this property must be conceived in subjective terms. But then we find ourselves faced with an alternative: either the property is nothing other than the act of exchange itself as represented in indigenous thinking, in which case we are going round in a circle, or else it is a power of a different nature, in which case the act of exchange becomes, in relation to this power, a secondary phenomenon.

The only way to avoid the dilemma would have been to perceive that the primary, fundamental phenomenon is exchange itself, which gets split up into discrete operations in social life; the mistake was to take the discrete operations for the basic phenomenon. Here as elsewhere—but here above all—it was necessary to apply a precept Mauss himself had already formulated in the *Essai sur la magie*: "The unity of the whole is even more real than each of the parts."[4] But instead, in the *Essai sur le don*, Mauss strives to reconstruct a whole out of parts; and as that is manifestly not possible, he has to add to the mixture an additional quantity which gives him the illusion of squaring his account. This quantity is *hau*.

Are we not dealing with a mystification, an effect quite often produced in the minds of ethnographers by indigenous people? Not, of course, by "indigenous people" in general since no such beings exist, but by a given indigenous group, about whom specialists have already pondered problems, asked questions, and attempted answers. In the case in point, instead of applying his principles consistently from start to finish, Mauss discards them in favor of a New Zealand theory—one which is immensely valuable as an ethnological document; yet it is nothing other than a theory. The fact that Maori sages were the first people to pose certain problems and to resolve them in an infinitely interesting but strikingly unsatisfactory manner does not oblige us to bow to their interpretation. *Hau* is not the ultimate explanation for exchange; it is the conscious form whereby men of a

given society, in which the problem had particular importance, apprehended an unconscious necessity whose explanation lies elsewhere.

We may infer that Mauss is seized by hesitation and scruples at the most
crucial moment. He is no longer quite sure whether he must draw a picture
of indigenous theory, or construct a theory of indigenous reality. He is very
largely right to be unsure, for indigenous theory is much more directly
related to indigenous reality than a theory developed from our own categories or problems would be. So it was a very great progress, at the time
when Mauss was writing, to approach an ethnographic problem from the
starting-point of his New Zealand or Melanesian theory, rather than to call
upon Western notions such as animism, myth or participation. But indigenous or Western, theory is only ever a theory. At best, it offers us a path of
access; for, whether they be Fuegians or Australian Aboriginals, the interested parties' beliefs are always far removed from what they actually think
or do. Once the indigenous conception has been isolated, it must be
reduced by an objective critique so as to reach the underlying reality. We
have very little chance of finding that reality in conscious formulations; a
better chance, in unconscious mental structures to which institutions give
us access, but a better chance yet, in language. *Hau* is a product of indigenous reflection; but reality is more conspicuous in certain linguistic features which Mauss does not fail to note, although he does not make as
much of them as he should. "Papuan and Melanesian," he notes, "have
only one word to designate buying and selling, lending and borrowing.
Antithetical operations are expressed by the same word."[5] That is ample
proof that the operations in question are far from "antithetical"; that they
are just two modes of a selfsame reality. We do not need *hau* to make the
synthesis, because the antithesis does not exist. The antithesis is a subjective illusion of ethnographers, and sometimes also of indigenous people
who, when reasoning about themselves—as they quite often do—behave
like ethnographers, or more precisely, like sociologists; that is, as colleagues
with whom one may freely confer.

When I endeavor to reconstruct Mauss's thinking in this way, without
recourse to magical or affective notions (whose use by Mauss seems to me
to be merely residual), some may reproach me for drawing him too far in a
rationalist direction. My reply to such a reproach is that Mauss took upon
himself, from the very start of his career, in the *Esquisse d'une théorie
générale de la magie*, this same effort to understand social life as a system of
relations, which is the life-blood of the *Essai sur le don*. It is not I, it is he
who asserts the necessity for understanding the magical act as a mode of
thinking. He is the one who introduces into ethnographic criticism a fundamental distinction between analytic thinking and synthetic thinking, a
distinction whose philosophical origin is in the theory of mathematical

notions. Mauss was only able to conceive the problem of thinking in the terms of classical logic. Certain notions take the place of the copula in his argumentation; he says it in so many words: "*Mana* . . . plays the role of the copula in a proposition."[6] If he had been able to formulate the problem of thinking, instead, in terms of relational logic, am I not justified in saying that the very function of the copula would have been undone, and with it, the notions to which he attributes this function—namely, *mana* in his theory of magic, and *hau* in his theory of the gift?

◙

After a gap of twenty years, the argument of the *Essai sur le don* reproduces that of the *Théorie de la magie*: or at least, the opening part of it does. That alone would justify including in this volume a work whose early date (1902) must be borne in mind in order not to judge it unfairly. Comparative ethnology was eventually to renounce, largely at Mauss's own instigation, what he in *Le Don* called "that constant comparison which mixes everything up together and makes institutions lose all their local color and documents their savor."[7] But that had not yet been given up, at the time of *La Magie*. Only later was Mauss to apply himself to focussing our attention on societies "which really represent maxima, excesses, which can better show the facts than in societies where, although no less essential, they are still tiny and involuted." But the *Esquisse* is exceptionally valuable for understanding the history of his thinking and isolating some of its constants. And that is true, not only for the grasp of Mauss's thinking, but for an appreciation of the French sociological school, and of the exact relationship between Mauss's thought and the thought of Durkheim. Analyzing the notions of *mana*, *wakan*, and *orenda*, building on that foundation an overall interpretation of magic, and so making contact with what he regards as fundamental categories of the human mind, Mauss anticipates by ten years the organization and some of the conclusions of *Les Formes élémentaires de la vie religieuse* (1912).[8] The *Esquisse* thus shows the importance of Mauss's contribution to Durkheim's thinking; it enables us to reconstitute something of that close collaboration between uncle and nephew, which was not limited to the ethnographic field; for we know, in a different context, the essential role that Mauss played in the preparation of *Le Suicide* (1897).[9]

But what interests us most, here, is the logical structure of the work. It is entirely grounded in the notion of *mana*, and we know that a lot of water has flowed under that bridge since then. To keep up with the current, it would be necessary to add to the *Esquisse* the most recent results obtained in the field as well as those derived from linguistic analysis.[10] It would also be necessary to complete the different types of *mana* by introducing into that already vast, and not very harmonious, family the notion very common among the indigenous South Americans of a sort of substantial and usually negative *mana*: a fluid that the shaman controls, which can cover objects in an observable form, which provokes displacements and levitations, and which is generally considered harmful in its effects. Instances are the *tsaruma* of the Jivaro; *nandé*, a Nambikwara representation which I have myself studied;[11] and all the analogous forms reported among the Amniapâ, the Apapocuva, the Apinayé, the Galibi, the Chiquito, the Lamisto, the Chamicuro, the Xebero, the Yameo, the Iquito, and others.[12] What would be left of the notion of *mana* after such a reformulation? It is hard to say; in any event, it would emerge *profaned*. Not that Mauss and Durkheim were wrong, as is sometimes claimed, to bring notions together from far-flung parts of the world, and to constitute them as a category. Even if history confirms the findings of linguistic analysis, and the Polynesian *term* 'mana' is a distant derivative of an Indonesian term defining the efficacy of personal gods, it would by no means follow that the *notion* connoted by that term in Melanesia and Polynesia was a residue or a vestige of a more highly elaborated form of religious thinking. Despite all the local differences, it seems quite certain that *mana, wakan, orenda* do represent explanations of the same type; so it is legitimate to construct the type, seek to classify it, and analyze it.

The trouble with the traditional position regarding *mana* seems to me to be of a different kind. Contrary to what was believed in 1902, conceptions of the *mana* type are so frequent and so widespread that it is appropriate to wonder whether we are not dealing with a universal and permanent form of thought, which, far from characterizing certain civilizations, or archaic or semi-archaic so-called "stages" in the evolution of the human mind, might be a function of a certain way that the mind situates itself in the presence of things, which must therefore make an appearance whenever that mental situation is given. In the *Esquisse*, Mauss cites a most profound remark of Father Thavenet about the Algonquian notion of *manitou*:

> It more particularly designates any being which does not yet have a
> common name, which is unfamiliar; of a salamander, a woman said she
> was afraid: it was a *manitou*; people laughed at her, telling her the name
> salamander. Trade beads are *manitou*'s scales, and cloth, that wonderful
> thing, is the skin of a *manitou*.[13]

Likewise, the first group of semi-civilized Tupi-Kawahib Indians, with whose help we were to reach an unknown village of the tribe in 1938, admired the lengths of red flannel we presented to them and exclaimed: "O que é este bicho vermelho?" ("What is this red animal?"), which was neither evidence of primitive animism, nor the translation of an indigenous notion, but merely an idiomatic expression of the *falar cabóclo*, the rustic Portuguese of the interior of Brazil. But, inversely, the Nambikwara, who had never seen oxen before 1915, designate them as they have always designated stars, by the name of *atásu*, whose connotation is very close to the Algonquian *manitou*.[14]

These assimilations are not so extraordinary; we do the same type of assimilating, doubtless more guardedly, when we qualify an unknown object, or one whose function is unclear, or whose effectiveness amazes us, by the French terms *truc* or *machin*. Behind *machin* is machine, and, further back, the idea of force or power. As for *truc*, the etymologists derive it from a medieval term which signifies the lucky move in games of skill or games of chance, that is, one of the precise meanings given to the Indonesian term in which some see the origin of the word *mana*.[15] Of course, we do not say of an object that it *has* these qualities of *truc* or *machin*; but we do say of a person that he or she "has something"; and when American slang says that a woman has got "oomph," it is not certain, if we call to mind the sacred and taboo-laden atmosphere which permeates sexual life, in America even more than elsewhere, that we are very far removed from the meaning of *mana*. The difference comes not so much from the notions themselves, such as the human mind everywhere unconsciously works these out, as from the fact that, in our society, these notions have a fluid, spontaneous character, whereas elsewhere they serve as the ground of considered, official interpretative systems; a role, that is to say, which we ourselves reserve for science. But always and everywhere, those types of notions, somewhat like algebraic symbols, occur to represent an indeterminate value of signification, in itself devoid of meaning and thus susceptible of receiving any meaning at all; their sole function is to fill a gap between the signifier and the signified, or, more exactly, to signal the fact that in such a circumstance, on such an occasion, or in such a one of their manifestations, a relationship of non-equivalence[16] becomes established between signifier and signified, to the detriment of the prior complementary relationship.

So we set ourselves on a path closely parallel to that of Mauss when he invoked the notion of *mana* as grounding certain *a priori* synthetic judgments. But we shall not go along with him when he proceeds to seek the origin of the notion of *mana* in an order of realities different from the relationships that it helps to construct: in the order of feelings, of volitions and of beliefs, which, from the viewpoint of sociological explanation, are epiphenomena, or else mysteries; in any case, they are objects extrinsic to the field of investigation. That is, to my mind, the reason why such a rich, penetrating, illuminating inquiry veers off and ends with a disappointing conclusion. *Mana* finally comes down to "the expression of social sentiments which are formed—sometimes inexorably and universally, sometimes fortuitously—with regard to certain things, chosen for the most part in an arbitrary fashion. . . ."[17] But the notions of sentiment, fated inexorability, the fortuitous and the arbitrary are not scientific notions. They do not shed light on the phenomena we set out to explain; they are a party to those phenomena. So we can see that in one case, at least, the notion of *mana* does present those characteristics of a secret power, a mysterious force, which Durkheim and Mauss attributed to it: for such is the role it plays in their own system. *Mana* really is *mana* there. But at the same time, one wonders whether their theory of *mana* is anything other than a device for imputing properties to indigenous thought which are implied by the very peculiar place that the idea of *mana* is called on to occupy in their own thinking.

Consequently, the strongest warning should be sounded to those sincere admirers of Mauss who would be tempted to halt at that first stage of his thinking; their gratitude would be not for his lucid analyses so much as for his exceptional talent for rehabilitating certain indigenous theories in their strangeness and their authenticity: for he would never have looked to that contemplation for the idle refuge of a vacillating mind. If we confined ourselves to what is merely a preliminary procedure in the history of Mauss's thinking, we would risk committing sociology to a dangerous path: even a path of destruction, if we then went one step further and reduced social reality to the conception that man—savage man, even—has of it. That conception would furthermore become empty of meaning if its reflexive character were forgotten. Then ethnography would dissolve into a verbose phenomenology, a falsely naïve mixture in which the apparent obscurities of indigenous thinking would only be brought to the forefront to cover the confusions of the ethnographer, which would otherwise be too obvious.

There is nothing to prevent us from continuing Mauss's thinking in the other direction: the direction which the *Essai sur le don* was to define, after overcoming the equivocation that we noted earlier in reference to *hau*. For, luckily, whereas *mana* comes at the end of the *Esquisse*, *hau* only appears at the beginning of the *Essai sur le don*, and it is treated throughout as a point of departure, and not a goal. If we were to project the conception of exchange, which Mauss there invites us to formulate, back on to the notion of *mana*, where would it take us? It has to be admitted that, like *hau*, *mana* is no more than the subjective reflection of the need to supply an unperceived totality. Exchange is not a complex edifice built on the obligations of giving, receiving, and returning, with the help of some emotional-mystical cement. It is a synthesis immediately given to, and given by, symbolic thought, which, in exchange as in any other form of communication, surmounts the contradiction inherent in it; that is the contradiction of perceiving things as elements of dialogue, in respect of self and others simultaneously, and destined by nature to pass from the one to the other. The fact that those things may be *the one's* or *the other's* represents a situation which is derivative from the initial relational aspect. But does not the same apply in the case of magic? Magical reasoning, implied in the action of producing smoke to elicit clouds and rain, is not grounded in a primordial distinction between smoke and cloud, with an appeal to *mana* to weld the one to the other, but in the fact that a deeper level of thinking identifies smoke with cloud; that the one is, at least in a certain respect, the same thing as the other: that identification is what justifies the subsequent association, and not the other way round. All magical operations rest on the restoring of a unity; not a lost unity (for nothing is ever lost) but an unconscious one, or one which is less completely conscious than those operations themselves. The notion of *mana* does not belong to the order of the real, but to the order of thinking, which, even when it thinks itself, only ever thinks an object.

It is in that relational aspect of symbolic thinking that we can look for the answer to our problem. Whatever may have been the moment and the circumstances of its appearance in the ascent of animal life, language can only have arisen all at once. Things cannot have begun to signify gradually. In the wake of a transformation which is not a subject of study for the social sciences, but for biology and psychology, a shift occurred from a stage when nothing had a meaning to another stage when everything had meaning. Actually, that apparently banal remark is important, because that radical change has no counterpart in the field of knowledge, which develops slowly and progressively. In other words, at the moment when the entire universe all at once became *significant*, it was none the better *known* for being so, even if it is true that the emergence of language must have hastened the rhythm of the development of knowledge. So there is a fundamental opposition, in the history of the human mind, between symbolism, which is characteristically discontinuous, and knowledge, characterized by continuity. Let us consider what follows from that. It follows that the two categories of the signifier and the signified came to be constituted simultaneously and interdependently, as complementary units; whereas knowledge, that is, the intellectual process which enables us to identify certain aspects of the signifier and certain aspects of the signified, one by reference to the other—we could even say the process which enables us to choose, from the entirety of the signifier and from the entirety of the signified, those parts which present the most satisfying relations of mutual agreement—only got started very slowly. It is as if humankind had suddenly acquired an immense domain and the detailed plan of that domain, along with a notion of the reciprocal relationship of domain and plan; but had spent millennia learning which specific symbols of the plan represented the different aspects of the domain.

The universe signified long before people began to know what it signified; no doubt that goes without saying. But, from the foregoing analysis, it also emerges that from the beginning, the universe signified the totality of what humankind can expect to know about it. What people call the progress of the human mind and, in any case, the progress of scientific knowledge, could only have been and can only ever be constituted out of processes of correcting and recutting of patterns, regrouping, defining relationships of belonging, and discovering new resources, inside a totality which is closed and complementary to itself.

We appear to be far removed from *mana*, but in reality we are extremely close to it. For, although the human race has always possessed an enormous mass of positive knowledge, and although the different societies have devoted more or less effort to maintaining and developing it, it is nonetheless in very recent times that scientific thinking became established as authority and that forms of societies emerged in which the intellectual and moral ideal, at the same time as the practical ends pursued by the social body, became organized around scientific knowledge, elected as the center of reference in an official and deliberate way. The difference is one of degree, not of nature, but it does exist. We can therefore expect the relationship between symbolism and knowledge to conserve common features in the non-industrial societies and in our own, although those features would not be equally pronounced in the two types of society. It does not mean that we are creating a gulf between them, if we acknowledge that the work of equalizing of the signifier to fit the signified has been pursued more methodically and rigorously from the time when modern science was born, and within the boundaries of the spread of science. But everywhere else, and still constantly in our own societies (and no doubt for a long time to come), a fundamental situation perseveres which arises out of the human condition: namely, that man has from the start had at his disposition a signifier-totality which he is at a loss to know how to allocate to a signified, given as such, but no less unknown for being given. There is always a non-equivalence or "inadequation" between the two, a non-fit and overspill which divine understanding alone can soak up; this generates a signifier-surfeit relative to the signifieds to which it can be fitted. So, in man's effort to understand the world, he always disposes of a surplus of signification (which he shares out among things in accordance with the laws of the symbolic thinking which it is the task of ethnologists and linguists to study). That distribution of a supplementary ration—if I can express myself thus— is absolutely necessary to ensure that, in total, the available signifier and the mapped-out signified may remain in the relationship of complementarity which is the very condition of the exercise of symbolic thinking.

I believe that notions of the *mana* type, however diverse they may be, and viewed in terms of their most general function (which, as we have seen, has not vanished from our mentality and our form of society) represent nothing more or less than that *floating signifier* which is the disability of all finite thought (but also the surety of all art, all poetry, every mythic and aesthetic invention), even though scientific knowledge is capable, if not of staunching it, at least of controlling it partially. Moreover, magical thinking offers other, different methods of channeling and containment, with different results, and all these methods can very well coexist. In other words, accepting the inspiration of Mauss's precept that all social phenomena can be assimilated to language, I see in *mana*, *wakan*, *orenda*, and other notions of the same type, the conscious expression of a *semantic function*, whose role is to enable symbolic thinking to operate despite the contradiction inherent in it. That explains the apparently insoluble antinomies attaching to the notion of *mana*, which struck ethnographers so forcibly, and on which Mauss shed light: force and action; quality and state; substantive, adjective, and verb all at once; abstract and concrete; omnipresent and localized. And, indeed, *mana* is all those things together; but is that not precisely because it is none of those things, but a simple form, or to be more accurate, a symbol in its pure state, therefore liable to take on any symbolic content whatever? In the system of symbols which makes up any cosmology, it would just be a *zero symbolic value*, that is, a sign marking the necessity of a supplementary symbolic content over and above that which the signified already contains, which can be any value at all, provided it is still part of the available reserve, and is not already, as the phonologists say, a term in a set.[18]

That conception seems to me to be rigorously faithful to Mauss's thinking. In fact, it is nothing other than Mauss's conception, translated from its original expression in terms of class logic into the terms of a symbolic logic which summarizes the most general laws of language. The translation is not of my making, nor is it the result of my taking liberties with the initial conception. It merely reflects an objective evolution which has occurred in the psychological and social sciences in the course of the last thirty years; the value of Mauss's teaching lay in its being a first manifestation of that evolution, and in having contributed greatly to it. Mauss was, indeed, one of the very first to expose the insufficiency of traditional psychology and logic, and to break open their rigid frameworks, revealing different forms of thought, seemingly "alien to our adult European minds."[19] At the time when he was writing (remember that the essay on magic dates from a time when Freud's ideas were completely unknown in France) that discovery could scarcely have been expressed otherwise than negatively, through a call for a "nonintellectualist psychology." But no one would have had more cause than

Mauss to rejoice in the fact that that psychology eventually became formulatable as a *differently* intellectualist psychology, the generalized expression of the laws of human thought, of which the individual manifestations, in different sociological contexts, are simply the various modes. He would have been glad, first, because it was the *Essai sur le don* which was to define the method for that task, and, above all, because Mauss himself had assigned to ethnology the essential goal of contributing to the enlargement of the scope of human reason. So, for the cause of reason, he claimed in advance all the discoveries that could yet be made, in those obscure zones where mental forms, not easily accessible because buried both at once at the farthest limits of the universe and in the most secret recesses of our minds, are often perceived only as refracted in a cloudy halo of emotion. It is evident that Mauss was obsessed throughout his life by Comte's precept, which appears and reappears constantly in the essays collected in [*Sociologie et anthropologie*]; that is the precept that psychological life can only acquire a meaning on two levels: that of the social, which is language; or that of the physiological, which is, for living things, the other form, the mute form of necessity.[20] Never was he truer to his underlying thinking, never did he map the ethnologist's mission as astronomer of the human constellations better than in that formulation which draws together the method, the means, and the ultimate goal of our sciences; a formulation which any institute of ethnology could inscribe over its portal:

> We must, before all else, compile as large as possible a catalogue of categories; we must begin with all those which we can know that mankind has used. Then it will be seen that in the firmament of reason there have been, and there still are, many moons that are dead, or pale, or obscure.[21]

From *Introduction to the Work of Marcel Mauss* [1950] translation 1987.

Translated by Felicity Baker.

Notes

Chapter II

1. *La Notion de personne* should be read in conjunction with *L'âme, le nom et la personne* (1929b), which completes it. [EN: In Chapter I, Lévi-Strauss had discussed the three essays *Psychologie et sociologie* (1924), *L'Idée de mort* (1926), and *Les Techniques du corps* (1936).]

2. See bibliography for the aforementioned articles by Mauss.

3. Mauss, *Essai sur le don*, in *Sociologie et anthropologie*, p. 276 (*The Gift*, 1954, p. 78).

4. Ibid.

5. Ibid.

6. Ibid.

7. Mauss, *La Magie*, p. 109 (*Magic*, 1972, p. 116).

8. Ibid., pp. 71–2 (p. 79).

9. G. Davy, *La Foi jurée* (1922).

10. B. Malinowski, *Argonauts of the Western Pacific*, 1922. On this point, see Malinowski's note in *Crime and Custom in Savage Society*, 1926, p. 41, note 57.

11. R. Firth, *We, the Tikopia*, 1936, ch. 15; *Primitive Polynesian Economy*, 1939, p. 323.

12. N. S. Trubeckoj (also spelled Trubetskoi, Troubetzkoy, etc.), *Grundzüge der Phonologie*, 1939; and articles by R. Jakobson included in the Appendix of the French translation, *Principes de phonologie*, 1949. For reference to the English translations of these writings, see bibliographical entries under R. Jakobson, 1930, 1936, 1939; and N. S. Trubeckoj, 1939.

13. N. Wiener, *Cybernetics*, 1948; C. E. Shannon and W. Weaver, *The Mathematical Theory of Communication*, 1949.

Chapter III

1. TN: Francis Bacon's *Novum Organum* (1620) describes aphoristically the method of universalization of knowledge; its principles of investigation gave impetus to experimental science.

2. Mauss, *Essai sur le don*, p. 205 (*The Gift*, p. 37).

3. Ibid., p. 214 (p. 41).

4. Mauss, *La Magie*, p. 81 (*Magic*, p. 88).

5. *Le Don*, p. 193 (*The Gift*, pp. 30–1). Mauss is here quoting J. H. Holmes, *In Primitive New Guinea*, 1924.

6. *La Magie*, p. 116 (*Magic*, p. 122).

7. *Le Don*, p. 149 (*The Gift*, p. 3).

8. E. Durkheim, *Les Formes élémentaires de la vie religieuse*, 1912.

9. E. Durkheim, *Le Suicide*, 1897.

10. A. M. Hocart, "Mana," 1914; "Mana again," 1922; "Natural and supernatural," 1932. H. I. Hogbin, "Mana," 1935–6. A. Capell, "The word 'mana': a linguistic study," 1938. R. Firth, "The analysis of mana: an empirical approach," 1940; "An analysis of mana," 1941. G. Blake-Palmer, "Mana, some Christian and Moslem parallels," 1946. G. J. Schneep, "El concepto de mana," 1947. B. Malinowski, *Magic, Science and Religion*, 1948.

11. C. Lévi-Strauss, "La Vie familiale et sociale des Indiens Nambikwara" (1948b).

12. A. Métraux, "La causa y el tratamiento mágico de las enfermedades entre los indios de la Región Tropical Sud-Americana" (1944a); "Le Shamanisme chez les Indiens de l'Amérique du Sud tropicale" (1944b).

13. Mauss, *La Magie*, p. 108 (*Magic*, p. 114). [TN: Mauss is here quoting Father Thavenet out of E. Teza, *Intorno agli studi del Thavenet sulla lingua algonchina: osservazioni*, 1880. The reference is given inaccurately by Mauss as "Tesa, *Studi del Thavenet*, 1881," and reproduced in the same form in the 1972 English translation.]

14. C. Lévi-Strauss, "La Vie familiale . . ." (1948b), pp. 98–9; "The Tupi-Kawahib" (1948a), pp. 299–305.

To be compared with the Dakota, who say of the first horse, brought, according to myth, by lightning: "He smelled differently from a human being. They thought it might be a dog, only he was bigger than a pack-dog, so they named him *šúnka wakhán*, 'Mysterious Dog'" (M. W. Beckwith, "Mythology of the Oglala Dakota," 1930, p. 379).

15. On the derivation of the word *mana*, cf. A. Capell (1938).

16. TN: For clarity, I have used *non-equivalence* instead of *inadequation* (the French term being *inadéquation*), which is obsolete. Seventeenth-century examples cited in *O.E.D.* refer to the "inadequation to the truth" of man's knowledge of his inner states, and to "difference arising . . . from the inadequation of languages"; both of these are clearly precursors of the *inadequation of signifier and signified* proposed in this passage.

17. Mauss, *La Magie*, p. 115 (*Magic*, p. 121). Decisive though Mauss's procedure was, when he assimilated social phenomena to language, it was to give sociological thinking some trouble in one respect. Ideas like the ones expressed in the passage quoted could, in fact, get support from what was for a long time to be considered the impregnable rampart of Saussurean linguistics: that is, the theory of the arbitrary nature of the linguistic sign, but today, there is no position that we more urgently need to put behind us.

18. Linguists have already been led to formulate hypotheses of this type. For instance:

> A zero-phoneme . . . is opposed to all other French phonemes by the absence both of distinctive features and of a constant sound characteristic. On the other hand, the zero-phoneme . . . is opposed to the absence of any phoneme whatsoever. (R. Jakobson and J. Lotz, "Notes on the French phonemic pattern," 1949, p. 155)

19. Mauss, *La Magie*, p. 100 (*Magic*, p. 107).

20. TN: Auguste Comte (1798–1857), founder of Positivist philosophy, a system confined to recognition of facts, observable phenomena, and their objective relations. His *Cours de philosophie* (1830–42) is famous for its classification of the sciences and its history of social evolution.

21. Mauss, *Rapports réels et pratiques de la psychologie et de la sociologie*, in *Sociologie et anthropologie*, 1950, p. 309 ("Real and practical relations . . . ," *Sociology and Psychology*, 1979a, p. 32).

† EN

Works Cited

Beckwith, Martha W. 1930. "Mythology of the Oglala Dakota." *Journal of American Folklore* 43: 339–442.

Blake-Palmer, G. 1946. "Mana, some Christian and Moslem parallels." *Journal of the Polynesian Society* 55: 263–75.

Capell, Arthur. 1938. "The word 'mana': a linguistic study." *Oceania* 9: 89–96.

Davy, Georges. 1922. *La Foi jurée. Étude sociologique du problème du contrat. La formation du lien contractuel*. Paris: Alcan.

Durkheim, Émile. 1897. *Le Suicide. Étude de sociologie*. Paris: Alcan. (English translation by J. A. Spaulding and G. Simpson, *Suicide. A Study in Sociology*. Edited with an introduction by G. Simpson. London: Routledge & Kegan Paul, 1952.)

————. 1912. *Les Formes élémentaires de la vie religieuse. Le système totémique en Australie.* Paris: Alcan. (English translation by J. W. Swain, *The Elementary Forms of the Religious Life.* London: George Allen & Unwin, 1915.)

Durkheim, Émile, and Marcel Mauss. 1903. "De Quelques formes primitives de classification. Contribution à l'étude des représentations collectives." *Année sociologique.* 1901–2, 6: 1–72. Republished in Mauss, 1969–75, *Oeuvres*, Vol. 2. Pp. 13–89. (English translation and introduction by R. Needham, *Primitive Classification.* London: Cohen & West, 1963; second ed. 1967.)

Firth, Raymond. 1936. *We, the Tikopia. A Sociological Study of Kinship in Primitive Polynesia.* London: George Allen & Unwin.

————. 1939. *Primitive Polynesian Economy.* London: G. Routledge & Sons.

————. [1940. "The analysis of mana: an empirical approach." *Journal of the Polynesian Society* 49: 483–510. Republished in *Tikopia Ritual and Belief.* London: Allen & Unwin, 1967.

————. [1941. "An analysis of mana." *Polynesian Anthropological Studies:* 198–218.

Hocart, Arthur M. 1914. "Mana." *Man* 46: 97–101.

————. 1922. "Mana again." *Man* 79: 139–41.

————. 1932. "Natural and supernatural." *Man* 78: 59–61.

Hogbin, Herbert Ian. 1935–6. "Mana." *Oceania* 6: 241–74.

Holmes, John H. 1924. *In Primitive New Guinea.* London: Seeley, Service & Co.

Jakobson, Roman. 1930. "Principes de phonologie historique": présenté à la Réunion phonologique internationale à Prague, 20 décembre 1930. Published in German in the *Travaux du cercle linguistique de Prague* 4, 1931; revised for French edition in appendix of N. S. Trubeckoj, *Principes de phonologie*; republished in R. Jakobson, *Selected Writings*, Vol. 1, *Phonological Studies.* The Hague: Mouton, 1962. Pp. 202–20.

————. 1936. "Sur la théorie des affinités phonologiques entre les langues": rapport au Quatrième Congrès international de linguistes, Copenhague, août 1936, publié dans les Actes du Congrès, 1938. Revised for publication in appendix of N. S. Trubeckoj, *Principes de phonologie*; republished in R. Jakobson, *Selected Writings*, Vol. 1, *Phonological Studies.* The Hague: Mouton & Co., 1962. Pp. 234–46.

————. 1939. "Les Lois phoniques du langage enfantin": communication préparée pour le Cinquième Congrès international de linguistes convoqué à Bruxelles, septembre 1939. Published in appendix of N. S. Trubeckoj, *Principes de phonologie*; republished in R. Jakobson, *Selected Writings*, Vol. 1, *Phonological Studies.* The Hague: Mouton, 1962. Pp. 317–27.

Jakobson, Roman, and J. Lotz. 1949. "Notes on the French phonemic pattern." *Word* 5, 2. Republished in R. Jakobson, *Selected Writings*, Vol. 1, *Phonological Studies.* The Hague: Mouton, 1962. Pp. 426–34.

Lévi-Strauss, Claude. 1948a. "The Tupi-Kawahib." *Handbook of South American Indians*, 3: 299–305.

————. 1948b. "La Vie familiale et sociale des Indiens Nambikwara." *Journal de la Société des Américanistes*, n.s., 37: 1–131.

Malinowski, Bronislaw. 1922. *Argonauts of the Western Pacific. An Account of Native Enterprise and Adventure in the Archipelagos of Melanesian New Guinea.* London: Routledge, 1922; republished London: Routledge & Kegan Paul, 1978.

————. 1926. *Crime and Custom in Savage Society.* London: Kegan Paul & Co.

————. 1948. *Magic, Science and Religion, and Other Essays.* New York: Free Press; republished New York: Doubleday Anchor Books, 1954; London: Souvenir Press, 1974.

Mauss, Marcel. 1902–3. "Esquisse d'une théorie générale de la magie." En collaboration avec H. Hubert, *Année sociologique.* Paris: Presses Universitaires de France; republished in Mauss, *Sociologie et anthropologie.* Pp. 1–141. (English translation by R. Brain, *A General Theory of Magic.* London: Routledge & Kegan Paul, 1972.)

————. 1904–5. "Essai sur les variations saisonnières des sociétés Eskimo. Etude de morphologie sociale," avec la collaboration partielle de H. Beuchat. *Année sociologique* 9: 39–132. Republished in second and third editions of Mauss, *Sociologie et anthropologie,* 1966 and 1973. Pp. 389–475. (English translation by J. J. Fox, *Seasonal Variations of the Eskimo. A Study in Social Morphology.* London: Routledge & Kegan Paul, 1979.)

————. 1909. "L'Art et le mythe d'après M. Wundt." *Revue philosophique de la France et de l'étranger* 66 (July–December): 48–78.

————. 1911. "Anna-Virâj," in *Mélanges d'indianisme offerts par ses élèves à M. Sylvain Lévy.* Paris: Ernest Leroux. Pp. 333–41. Republished in Mauss, *Oeuvres,* Vol. 2. Pp. 593–600.

————. 1914a. "Les Origines de la notion de monnaie." Communication faite à l'Institut Français d'Anthropologie; publiée dans les comptes rendus des séances, 2, tome 1, Supplément à l'*Anthropologie* 25. Republished in Mauss, *Oeuvres,* Vol. 2, in the section Valeur magique et valeur d'échange, pp. 106–20, which includes further discussions from *Anthropologie* 25, with reference to the religion and magic of the Ewhe.

————. 1914b. "Dieux Ewhe de la monnaie et du change." See preceding entry.

————. 1921b. "Une Forme archaïque de contrat chez les Thraces." *Revue des études grecques* 34: 388–97. Republished in Mauss, *Oeuvres,* Vol. 3. Pp. 35–43.

————. 1923–4. "Essai sur le don. Forme et raison de l'échange dans les sociétés archaïques." *Année sociologique* 2e série, 1: 30–186. Republished in Mauss, *Sociologie et anthropologie.* Pp. 143–279.

————. 1924a. "Rapports réels et pratiques de la psychologie et de la sociologie": communication présentée le 10 janvier 1924 à la Société de Psychologie. *Journal de psychologie normale et pathologique* 21: 892–922. Republished in Mauss, *Sociologie et anthropologie.* Pp. 281–310. (English translation by Ben Brewster, "Real and practical relations between psychology and sociology." In Mauss, *Sociology and Psychology.* Pp. 1–33.)

————. 1924b. "Gift, Gift." In *Mélanges offerts à Charles Andler par ses amis et ses élèves.* Strasbourg: Istra. Pp. 243–7. Republished in Mauss, *Oeuvres,* Vol. 3. Pp. 46–51.

————. 1925. "Commentaires sur un texte de Posidonius. Le suicide, contre-prestation suprême." *Revue celtique* 42: 324–9. Republished in Mauss, *Oeuvres,* Vol. 3. Pp. 52–7.

————. 1926b. "Parentés à plaisanteries": communication présentée à l'Institut Français d'Anthropologie, 1926; *Annuaire de l'Ecole pratique des hautes études,* section des sciences religieuses, 1928. Republished in Mauss, *Oeuvres,* Vol. 3. Pp. 109–24.

————. 1928. "Wette, wedding." In *Procès-verbaux de la Société d'Histoire du droit.*

————. 1929a. "Biens masculins et féminins en droit celtique." In *Procès-verbaux des Journées d'Histoire du droit.*

————. 1929b. "Les Civilisations: éléments et formes." *Civilisation. Le mot et l'idée.* Paris: Le Renaissance du livre, 1930, pp. 81–108. Republished in Mauss, *Oeuvres,* Vol. 2. Pp. 456–87.

————. 1929c. "L'âme, le nom et la personne." Intervention à la suite d'une communication de L. Lévy-Bruhl, "L'âme primitive." *Bulletin de la Société française de philosophie* 29: 124–7. Republished in Mauss, *Oeuvres,* Vol. 2. Pp. 131–5.

————. 1934. "Fragment d'un plan de sociologie générale descriptive. Classification et méthode d'observation des phénomènes généraux de la vie sociale dans les sociétés de type archaïque (phénomènes spécifiques de la vie intérieure de la société)." *Annales sociologiques,* série A, fascicule 1: 1–56. Republished in Mauss, *Oeuvres,* Vol. 3. Pp. 303–54.

————. 1938. "Une Catégorie de l'esprit humain: la notion de personne, celle de 'moi'." *Journal of the Royal Anthropological Institute* 263–362. (English translation by Ben Brewster, "A category of the human mind: the notion of person, the notion of 'self'." In Mauss, *Sociology and Psychology.* Pp. 57–94.)

————. 1950. *Sociologie et anthropologie.* Précédé d'une *Introduction à l'oeuvre de Marcel Mauss* par Claude Lévi-Strauss. Paris: Presses Universitaires de France.

————. 1954. *The Gift. Forms and Functions of Exchange in Archaic Societies.* Trans. Ian Cunnison. Introduction by E. E. Evans-Pritchard. London: Cohen & West.

————. 1969–75. *Oeuvres.* 3 Vols. Ed. Victor Karady. Paris: Editions de Minuit.

————. 1972. *A General Theory of Magic.* Trans. R. Brain. Foreword by D. F. Pocock. London: Routledge & Kegan Paul.

————. 1979a. *Sociology and Psychology.* Trans. Ben Brewster. London: Routledge & Kegan Paul.

————. 1979b. *Seasonal Variations of the Eskimo. A Study in Social Morphology.* Trans. J. J. Fox. London: Routledge & Kegan Paul.

Métraux, Alfred. 1944a. "La causa y el tratamiento mágico de las enfermedades entre los indios de la Región Tropical Sud-Americana." *America Indígena* 4, 2 (April): 157–64.

————. 1944b. "Le Shamanisme chez les Indiens de l'Amérique du Sud tropicale." *Acta Americana* 2, 3 (July–September): 197–219; 4 (October–December): 320–41.

Schneep, G. J. 1947. "El concepto de mana." *Acta Anthropologica* 11, 3.

Shannon, Claude E., and Warren Weaver. 1949. *The Mathematical Theory of Communication.* Urbana: University of Illinois Press.

Teza, Emilio. 1880. *Intorno agli studi del Thavenet sulla lingua algonchina: osservazioni.* Pisa: Nistri.

Trubeckoj, N. S. 1939. *Grundzüge der Phonologie.* Prague. French translation by J. Cantineau, *Principes de phonologie.* Paris: Klincksieck, 1949. English translation by C. A. M. Baltaxe, *Principles of Phonology.* Berkeley and Los Angeles: University of California Press, 1969.

Wiener, Norbert. 1948. *Cybernetics or Control and Communication in the Animal and the Machine.* New York: John Wiley & Sons.

The Spirit of the Gift

Marshall Sahlins

Marcel Mauss's famous *Essay on the Gift* becomes his own gift to the ages. Apparently completely lucid, with no secrets even for the novice, it remains a source of an unending ponderation for the anthropologist *du métier*, compelled as if by the *hau* of the thing to come back to it again and again, perhaps to discover some new and unsuspected value, perhaps to enter into a dialogue which seems to impute some meaning of the reader's but in fact only renders the due of the original. This chapter is an idiosyncratic venture of the latter kind, unjustified moreover by any special study of the Maori or of the philosophers (Hobbes and Rousseau especially) invoked along the way. Yet in thinking the particular thesis of the Maori *hau* and the general theme of social contract reiterated throughout the *Essay*, one appreciates in another light certain fundamental qualities of primitive economy and polity, mention of which may forgive the following overextended commentary.

"Explication de Texte"

The master concept of the *Essai sur le don* is the indigenous Maori idea *hau*, introduced by Mauss as "the spirit of things and in particular of the forest and the game it contains . . ." (1950, p. 158).[1] The Maori before any other archaic society, and the idea of *hau* above all similar notions, responded to the central question of the *Essay*, the only one Mauss proposed to examine "à fond": "*What is the principle of right and interest which, in societies of primitive or archaic type, requires that the gift received must be repaid? What force is there in the thing given which compels the recipient to make a return?*" (p. 148).

The *hau* is that force. Not only is it the spirit of the *foyer*, but of the donor of the gift; so that even as it seeks to return to its origin unless replaced, it gives the donor a mystic and dangerous hold over the recipient.

Logically, the *hau* explains only why gifts are repaid. It does not of itself address the other imperatives into which Mauss decomposed the process of reciprocity: the obligation to give in the first place, and the obligation to receive. Yet by comparison with the obligation to reciprocate, these aspects Mauss treated only summarily, and even then in ways not always detached from the *hau*: "This rigorous combination of symmetrical and opposed rights and duties ceases to appear contradictory if one realizes that it consists above all of a melange of spiritual bonds between things which are in some degree souls, and individuals and groups which interact in some degree as things" (p. 163).

Meanwhile, the Maori *hau* is raised to the status of a general explanation: the prototypical principle of reciprocity in Melanesia, Polynesia, and the American northwest coast, the binding quality of the Roman *traditio*, the key to gifts of cattle in Hindu India—"What you are, I am; become on this day of your essence, in giving you I give myself" (p. 248).

Everything depends then on the "texte capitale" collected by Elsdon Best (1909) from the Maori sage, Tamati Ranapiri of the Ngati-Raukawa tribe. The great role played by the *hau* in the *Essay on the Gift*—and the repute it has enjoyed since in anthropological economics—stems almost entirely from this passage. Here Ranapiri explained the *hau* of *taonga*, that is, goods of the higher spheres of exchange, valuables. I append Best's translation of the Maori text (which he also published in the original), as well as Mauss's rendering in French.
Best, 1909, p. 439:

> I will now speak of the *hau*, and the ceremony of *whangai hau*. That *hau* is not the *hau* (wind) that blows—not at all. I will carefully explain to you. Suppose that you possess a certain article, and you give that article to me, without price. We make no bargain over it. Now, I give that article to a third person, who, after some time has elapsed, decides to make some return for it, and so he makes me a present of some article. Now, that article that he gives me is the *hau* of the article I first received from you then gave to him. The goods that I received for that item I must hand over to you. It would not be right for me to keep such goods for myself, whether they be desirable items or otherwise. I must hand them over to you, because they are a *hau* of the article you gave me. Were I to keep such an equivalent for myself, then some serious evil would befall me, even death. Such is the *hau*, the *hau* of personal property, or the forest *hau*. Enough on these points.

Mauss, 1950, pp. 158–159:

> Je vais vous parler du *hau*. . . . Le *hau* n'est pas le vent qui souffle. Pas du tout. Supposez que vous possédez un article déterminé (*taonga*) et que vous me donnez cet article; vous me le donnez sans prix fixé. Nous ne faisons pas de marché à ce propos. Or, je donne cet article à une

troisième personne qui, après qu'un certain temps s'est écoulé, décide de
rendre quelque chose en paiement (*utu*), il me fait présent de quelque
chose (*taonga*). Or, ce *taonga* qu'il me donne est l'esprit (*hau*) du *taonga*
que j'ai reçu de vous et que je lui ai donné à lui. Les *taonga* que j'ai reçus
pour ces *taonga* (venus de vous) il faut que je vous les rende. Il ne serait
pas juste (*tika*) de ma part de garder ces *taonga* pour moi, qu'ils soient
désirables (*rawe*), ou désagréables (*kino*). Je dois vous les donner car ils
sont un *hau* du *taonga* que vous m'avez donné. Si je conservais ce deuxième *taonga* pour moi, il pourrait m'en venir du mal, sérieusement,
même la mort. Tel est le *hau*, le *hau* de la propriété personnelle, le *hau*
des *taonga*, le *hau* de la forêt. *Kati ena*. (Assez sur ce sujet.)

Mauss complained about Best's abbreviation of a certain portion of the
original Maori. To make sure that we would miss nothing of this critical
document, and in the hope further meanings might be gleaned from it, I
asked Professor Bruce Biggs, distinguished student of the Maori, to prepare a new interlinear translation, leaving the term "*hau*," however, in the
original. To this request he responded most kindly and promptly with the
following version, undertaken without consulting Best's translation:[2]

> *Na, mo te hau o te ngaaherehere. Taua mea te hau, ehara i te mea*
> Now, concerning the *hau* of the forest. This *hau* is not the *hau*
>
> *ko te hau e pupuhi nei. Kaaore. Maaku e aata whaka maarama ki a koe.*
> that blows (the wind). No. I will explain it carefully to you.
>
> *Na, he taonga toou ka hoomai e koe mooku. Kaaore aa taaua*
> *whakaritengo*
> Now, you have something valuable which you give to me. We have no
>
> *uto mo too taonga. Na, ka hoatu hoki e ahau mo teetehi atu tangata, aa,*
> agreement about payment. Now, I give it to someone else, and,
>
> *ka roa peaa te waa, aa, ka mahara taua tangata kei a ia raa taug taonga*
> a long time passes, and that man thinks he has the valuable,
>
> *kia hoomai he utu ki a au, aa, ka hoomai e ia. Na, ko taua taonga*
> he should give some repayment to me, and so he does so. Now, that
>
> *i hoomai nei ki a au, ko te hau teenaa o te taonga i hoomai ra ki a au*
> valuable which was given to me, that is the *hau* of the valuable which was
>
> *i mua. Ko taua taonga me hoatu e ahau ki a koe. E kore*
> given to me before. I must give it to you. It would not

rawa e tika kia kaiponutia e ahau mooku; ahakoa taonga pai rawa,
taonga
be correct for me to keep it for myself, whether it be something very
good,

kino raanei me tae rawa taua taonga i a au ki a koe. No te mea he hau
or bad, that valuable must be given to you from me. Because that valuable

no te taonga teenaa taonga na. Ki te mea kai kaiponutia e ahau taua
taonga
is a *hau* of the other valuable. If I should hang onto that valuable

mooku, ka mate ahau. Koina te hau, hau taonga
for myself, I will become *mate.* So that is the *hau—hau* of valuables,

hau ngaaherehere. Kaata eenaa.
hau of the forest. So much for that.

Concerning the text as Best recorded it, Mauss commented that—despite
marks of that "esprit théologique et juridique encore imprécis" characteristic of Maori—"it offers but one obscurity: the intervention of a third person." But even this difficulty he forthwith clarified with a light gloss:

> But in order to rightly understand this Maori jurist, it suffices to say:
> "*Taonga* and all strictly personal property have a *hau*, a spiritual power.
> You give me a *taonga*, I give it to a third party, the latter gives me
> another in return, because he is forced to do so by the *hau* of my present;
> and I am obliged to give you this thing, for I must give back to you what
> is in reality the product of the *hau* of your *taonga.*" (1950, p. 159)

Embodying the person of its giver and the *hau* of its forest, the gift
itself, on Mauss's reading, obliges repayment. The receiver is beholden by
the spirit of the donor; the *hau* of a *taonga* seeks always to return to its
homeland, inexorably, even after being transferred hand to hand through a
series of transactions. Upon repaying, the original recipient assumes power
in turn over the first donor; hence, "la circulation obligatoire des richesses,
tributs et dons" in Samoa and New Zealand. In sum:

> . . . it is clear that in Maori custom, the bond of law, bond by way of
> things, is a bond of souls, because the thing itself has a soul, is soul. From
> this it follows that to present something to someone is to present some-
> thing of oneself. . . . It is clear that in this system of ideas it is necessary

to return unto another what is in reality part of his nature and substance; for, to accept something from someone is to accept something of his spiritual essence, of his soul; the retention of this thing would be dangerous and mortal, not simply because it would be illicit, but also because this thing which comes from a person, not only morally but physically and spiritually—this essence, this food, these goods, movable or immovable, these women or these offspring, these rites or these communions—give a magical and religious hold over you. Finally, this thing given is not inert. Animate, often personified, it seeks to return to what Hertz called its "*foyer d'origine*" or to produce for the clan and the earth from which it came some equivalent to take its place. (*op. cit.*, p. 161)

The Commentaries of Lévi-Strauss, Firth, and Johansen

Mauss's interpretation of the *hau* has been attacked by three scholars of authority, two of them experts on the Maori and one an expert on Mauss. Their critiques are surely learned, but none I think arrives at the true meaning of the Ranapiri text or of the *hau*.

Lévi-Strauss debates principles. He does not presume to criticize Mauss on Maori ethnography. He does, however, question the reliance on an indigenous rationalization: "Are we not faced here with one of those instances (not altogether rare) in which the ethnologist allows himself to be mystified by the native?" (Lévi-Strauss, 1950, p. 38.) The *hau* is not the reason for exchange, only what one people happen to believe is the reason, the way they represent to themselves an unconscious necessity whose reason lies elsewhere. And behind Mauss's fixation on the *hau*, Lévi-Strauss perceived a general conceptual error that regrettably arrested his illustrious predecessor short of the full structuralist comprehension of exchange that the *Essay on the Gift* had itself so brilliantly prefigured: "like Moses leading his people to a promised land of which he would never contemplate the splendor" (p. 37). For Mauss had been the first in the history of ethnology to go beyond the empirical to a deeper reality, to abandon the sensible and discrete for the system of relations; in a unique manner he had perceived the operation of reciprocity across its diverse and multiple modalities. But, alas, Mauss could not completely escape from positivism. He continued to understand exchange in the way it is presented to experience—fragmented, that is to say, into the separate acts of giving, receiving, and repaying. Considering it thus in pieces, instead of as a unified and integral principle, he could do nothing better than to try to glue it back again with this "mystic cement," the *hau*.

Firth likewise has his own views on reciprocity, and in making them he scores Mauss repeatedly on points of Maori ethnography (1959, pp. 418–21). Mauss, according to Firth, simply misunderstood the *hau*, which is a difficult and amorphous concept, but in any event a more passive spiritual principle than Mauss believed. The Ranapiri text in fact gives no evidence that the *hau* passionately strives to return to its source. Nor did the Maori generally rely on the *hau* acting by itself to punish economic delinquency. Normally in the event of a failure to reciprocate, and invariably for theft, the established procedure of retribution or restitution was witchcraft (*makutu*): witchcraft initiated by the person who had been bilked, usually involving the services of a "priest" (*tohunga*), if operating through the vehicle of the goods detained.[3] Furthermore, adds Firth, Mauss confused types of *hau* that in the Maori view are quite distinct—the *hau* of persons, that of lands and forests, and that of *taonga*—and on the strength of this confusion he formulated a serious error. Mauss simply had no warrant to gloss the *hau* of the *taonga* as the *hau* of the person who gives it. The whole idea that the exchange of gifts is an exchange of persons is *sequitur* to a basic misinterpretation. Ranapiri had merely said that the good given by the third person to the second was the *hau* of the thing received by the second from the first.[4] The *hau* of persons was not at issue. In supposing it was, Mauss put his own intellectual refinements on Maori mysticism.[5] In other words, and Lévi-Strauss notwithstanding, it was not a native rationalization after all; it was a kind of French one. But as the Maori proverb says, "the troubles of other lands are their own" (Best, 1922, p. 30).

Firth for his part prefers secular to spiritual explanations of reciprocity. He would emphasize certain other sanctions of repayment, sanctions noted by Mauss in the course of the *Essay*:

> The fear of punishment sent through the *hau* of goods is indeed a supernatural sanction, and a valuable one, for enforcing repayment of a gift. But to attribute the scrupulousness in settling one's obligations to a belief in an active, detached fragment of personality of the donor, charged with nostalgia and vengeful impulses, is an entirely different matter. It is an abstraction which receives no support from native evidence. The main emphasis of the fulfillment of obligation lies, as the work of Mauss himself has suggested, in the social sanctions—the desire to continue useful economic relations, the maintenance of prestige and power—which do not require any hypothesis of recondite beliefs to explain. (1959, p. 421)[6]

The latest to apply for entrance to the Maori "house of learning," J. Prytz Johansen (1954), makes certain clear advances over his predecessors in the reading of the Ranapiri text. He at least is the first to doubt that the old Maori had anything particularly spiritual in mind when he spoke of the *hau* of a gift. Unfortunately, Johansen's discussion is even more labyrinthal than Tamati Ranapiri's, and once having reached the point he seems to let go, searches a mythical rather than a logical explanation of the famous exchange *à trois* and ends finally on a note of scholarly despair.

After rendering due tribute and support to Firth's critique of Mauss, Johansen observes that the word *hau* has a very wide semantic field. Probably several homonyms are involved. For the series of meanings usually understood as "life principle" or something of the sort, Johansen prefers as a general definition, "a part of life (for example, an object) which is used ritually in order to influence the whole," the thing serving as *hau* varying according to the ritual context. He then makes a point that hitherto had escaped everyone's notice—including, I think, Best's. Tamati Ranapiri's discourse on gifts was by way of introduction to and explanation of a certain ceremony, a sacrificial repayment to the forest for the game birds taken by Maori fowlers.[7] Thus the informant's purpose in this expositing passage was merely to establish the principle of reciprocity, and "*hau*" there merely signified "countergift"—"the Maori in question undoubtedly thought that *hau* means countergift, simply what is otherwise called *utu*" (Johansen, 1954, p.118).

We shall see momentarily that the notion of "equivalent return" (*utu*) is inadequate for the *hau* in question; moreover, the issues posed by Ranapiri transcend reciprocity as such. In any event, Johansen, upon taking up again the three-party transaction, dissipated the advance he had made. Unaccountably, he credited the received understanding that the original donor performs magic on the second party through the goods the latter received from the third, goods that become *hau* in this context. But since the explication is "not obvious," Johansen found himself compelled to invoke a special unknown tradition, "to the effect that when three persons exchanged gifts and the intermediary party failed, the counter-gift which had stopped with him might be *hau*, i.e., might be used to bewitch him." He then finished gloomily: "However a certain uncertainty is involved in all these considerations and it seems doubtful whether we shall ever attain to actual certainty as regards the meaning of the *hau*" (ibid., p. 118).

The True Meaning of the Hau of Valuables

I am not a linguist, a student of primitive religions, an expert on the Maori, or even a Talmudic scholar. The "certainty" I see in the disputed text of Tamati Ranapiri is therefore suggested with due reservations. Still, to adopt the current structuralist incantation, "everything happens as if" the

Maori was trying to explain a religious concept by an economic principle, which Mauss promptly understood the other way around and thereupon proceeded to develop the economic principle by the religious concept. The *hau* in question really means something on the order of "return on" or "product of," and the principle expressed in the text on *taonga* is that any such yield on a gift ought to be handed over to the original donor.

The disputed text absolutely should be restored to its position as an explanatory gloss to the description of a sacrificial rite.[8] Tamata Ranapiri was trying to make Best understand by this example of gift exchange—an example so ordinary that anybody (or any Maori) ought to be able to grasp it immediately—why certain game birds are ceremoniously returned to the *hau* of the forest, to the source of their abundance. In other words, he adduced a transaction among men parallel to the ritual transaction he was about to relate, such that the former would serve as paradigm for the latter. As a matter of fact, the secular transaction does not prove directly comprehensible to us, and the best way to understand it is to work backwards from the exchange logic of the ceremony.

This logic, as presented by Tamati Ranapiri, is perfectly straightforward. It is necessary only to observe the sage's use of "*mauri*" as the physical embodiment of the forest *hau,* the power of increase—a mode of conceiving the *mauri* that is not at all idiosyncratic, to judge from other writings of Best. The *mauri*, housing the *hau*, is placed in the forest by the priests (*tohunga*) to make game birds abound. Here then is the passage that followed that on the gift exchange—in the intention of the informant, as night follows day.[9]

> I will explain something to you about the forest *hau*. The *mauri* was placed or implanted in the forest by the *tohunga* [priests]. It is the *mauri* that causes birds to be abundant in the forest, that they may be slain and taken by man. These birds are the property of, or belong to, the *mauri*, the *tohunga*, and the forest: that is to say, they are an equivalent for that important item, the *mauri*. Hence it is said that offerings should be made to the *hau* of the forest. The *tohunga* (priests, adepts) eat the offering because the *mauri* is theirs: it was they who located it in the forest, who caused it to be. That is why some of the birds cooked at the sacred fire are set apart to be eaten by the priests only, in order that the *hau* of the forest-products, and the *mauri*, may return again to the forest—that is, to the *mauri*. Enough of these matters. (Best, 1909, p. 439)

In other words, and essentially: the *mauri* that holds the increase-power (*hau*) is placed in the forest by the priests (*tohunga*); the *mauri* causes game birds to abound; accordingly, some of the captured birds should be ceremoniously returned to the priests who placed the *mauri*; the consumption of these birds by the priests in effect restores the fertility (*hau*) of the forest (hence the name of the ceremony, *whangai hau*, "nourishing *hau*").[10] Immediately then, the ceremonial transaction presents a familiar appearance: a three-party game, with the priests in the position of an initiating donor to whom should be rendered the returns on an original gift. The cycle of exchange is shown in Figure 4.1.

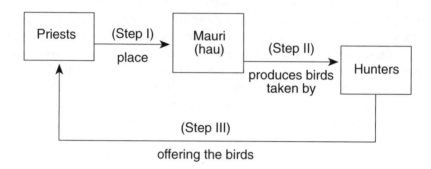

Figure 4.1

Now, in the light of this transaction, reconsider the text, just preceding, on gifts among men. Everything becomes transparent. The secular exchange of *taonga* is only slightly different in form from the ceremonial offering of birds, while in principle it is exactly the same—thus the didactic value of its position in Ranapiri's discourse. *A* gives a gift to *B* who transforms it into something else in an exchange with *C*, but since the *taonga* given by *C* to *B* is the product (*hau*) of *A*'s original gift, this benefit ought to be surrendered to *A*. The cycle is shown in Figure 4.2.

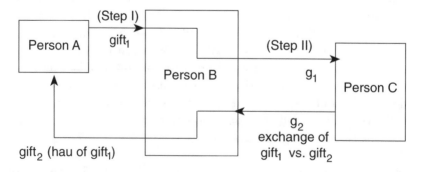

Figure 4.2

The meaning of *hau* one disengages from the exchange of *taonga* is as secular as the exchange itself. If the second gift is the *hau* of the first, then the *hau* of a good is its yield, just as the *hau* of a forest is its productiveness. Actually, to suppose Tamati Ranapiri meant to say the gift has a spirit which forces repayment seems to slight the old gentleman's obvious intelligence. To illustrate such a spirit needs only a game of two persons: you give something to me; your spirit (*hau*) in that thing obliges me to reciprocate. Simple enough. The introduction of a third party could only unduly complicate and obscure the point. But if the point is neither spiritual nor reciprocity as such, if it is rather that one man's gift should not be another man's capital, and therefore the fruits of a gift ought to be passed back to the original holder, then the introduction of a third party is necessary. It is necessary precisely to show a *turnover*: the gift has had issue; the recipient has used it to advantage. Ranapiri was careful to prepare this notion of advantage beforehand by stipulating[11] the absence of equivalence in the first instance, as if *A* had given *B* a free gift. He implies the same, moreover, in stressing the delay between the reception of the gift by the third person and the repayment—"a long time passes, and that man thinks that he has the valuable, he should give some repayment to me." As Firth observes, delayed repayments among Maori are customarily larger than the initial gift (1959, p. 422); indeed, it is a general rule of Maori gift exchange that, "the payment must if possible be somewhat in excess of what the principle of equivalence demanded" (ibid., p. 423). Finally, observe just where the term *hau* enters into the discussion. Not with the initial transfer from the first to the second party, as well it could if it were the spirit in the gift, but upon the exchange between the second and third parties, as logically it would if it were the yield on the gift.[12] The term "profit" is economically and historically inappropriate to the Maori, but it would have been a better translation than "spirit" for the *hau* in question.

Best provides one other example of exchange in which *hau* figures. Significantly, the little scene is again a transaction *à trois*:

> I was having a flax shoulder-cape made by a native woman at Ruatahuna. One of the troopers wished to buy it from the weaver, but she firmly refused, lest the horrors of *hau whitia* descend upon her. The term *hau whitia* means "averted *hau*." (1900–01, p. 198)

Only slightly different from the model elaborated by Tamati Ranapiri, this anecdote offers no particular difficulty. Having commissioned the cape, Best had the prior claim on it. Had the weaver accepted the trooper's offer, she would have turned this thing to her own advantage, leaving Best with nothing. She appropriates the product of Best's cape; she becomes subject to the evils of a gain unrightfully turned aside, "the horrors of *hau whitia*."[13] Otherwise said, she is guilty of eating *hau*—*kai hau*—for in the introduction to this incident Best had explained,

> Should I dispose of some article belonging to another person and not hand over to him any return or payment I may have received for that article, that is a *hau whitia* and my act is a *kai hau*, and death awaits, for the dread terrors of *makutu* [witchcraft] will be turned upon me (1900–01, pp. 197–98).[14]

So as Firth observed, the *hau* (even if it were a spirit) does not cause harm on its own initiative; the distinct procedure of witchcraft (*makutu*) has to be set in motion. It is not even implied by this incident that such witchcraft would work through the passive medium of *hau*, since Best, who was potentially the deceived party, had apparently put nothing tangible into circulation. Taken together, the different texts on the *hau* of gifts suggest something else entirely: not that the goods withheld are dangerous, but that withholding goods is *immoral*—and therefore dangerous in the sense the deceiver is open to justifiable attack. "'It would not be *correct* to keep it for myself,' said Ranapiri, 'I will become *mate* (ill, or die).'"

We have to deal with a society in which freedom to gain at others' expense is not envisioned by the relations and forms of exchange. Therein lies the moral of the old Maori's economic fable. The issue he posed went beyond reciprocity: not merely that gifts must be suitably returned, but that returns rightfully should be given back. This interpretation it is possible to sustain by a judicious selection among the many meanings of *hau* entered in H. Williams's (1921) Maori dictionary. *Hau* is a verb meaning to "exceed, be in excess," as exemplified in the phrase *kei te hau te wharika nei* ("this mat is longer than necessary"); likewise, *hau* is the substantive, "excess, parts, fraction over any complete measurement." *Hau* is also "property, spoils." Then there is *haumi*, a derivative meaning to "join," to "lengthen by addition," to "receive or lay aside"; it is also, as a noun, "the piece of wood by which the body of a canoe is lengthened."

The following is the true meaning of Tamati Ranapiri's famous and enigmatic discourse on the *hau* of *taonga*:

> I will explain it carefully to you. Now, you have something valuable which you give to me. We have no agreement about payment. Now, I give it to someone else, and, a long time passes, and that man thinks he has the valuable, he should give some repayment to me, and so he does

so. Now, that valuable which was given to me, that is the product of
[*hau*] the valuable which was given to me [by you] before. I must give it
to you. It would not be right for me to keep it for myself, whether it be
something good, or bad, that valuable must be given to you from me.
Because that valuable is a return on [*hau*] the other valuable. If I should
hang onto that valuable for myself, I will become ill [or die].

. . .

The Larger Significance of Hau

Returning now to the *hau*, it is clear we cannot leave the term merely with
secular connotations. If the *hau* of valuables in circulation means the yield
thereby accrued, a concrete product of a concrete good, still there is a *hau*
of the forest, and of man, and these do have spiritual quality. What kind of
spiritual quality? Many of Best's remarks on the subject suggest that the
hau-as-spirit is not unrelated to the *hau*-as-material-returns. Taking the two
together, one is able to reach a larger understanding of that mysterious *hau*.

Immediately it is clear that *hau* is not a spirit in the common animistic
sense. Best is explicit about this. The *hau* of a man is a quite different thing
from his *wairua*, or sentient spirit—the "soul" of ordinary anthropological
usage. I cite from one of Best's most comprehensive discussions of *wairua*:

> In the term *wairua* (soul) we have the Maori term for what anthropolo-
> gists style the soul, that is the spirit that quits the body at death, and
> proceeds to the spirit world, or hovers about its former home here on
> earth. The word *wairua* denotes a shadow, any unsubstantial image;
> occasionally it is applied to a reflection, thus it was adopted as a name
> for the animating spirit of man. . . . The *wairua* can leave the sheltering
> body during life; it does so when a person dreams of seeing distant
> places or people. . . . The *wairua* is held to be a sentient spirit; it leaves
> the body during sleep, and warns its physical basis of impending dan-
> gers, of ominous signs, by means of the visions we term dreams. It was
> taught by high-grade native priests that all things possess a *wairua*, even
> what we term inanimate objects, as trees and stones. (Best, 1924, vol. 1,
> pp. 299–301)[15]

Hau, on the other hand, belongs more to the realm of animatism than
animism. As such it is bound up with *mauri*, in fact, in the writings of the
ethnographic experts, it is virtually impossible to distinguish one from the
other. Firth despairs of definitively separating the two on the basis of Best's

overlapping and often corresponding definitions—"the blurred outline of the distinction drawn between *hau* and *mauri* by our most eminent ethnographic authority allows one to conclude that these concepts in their immaterial sense are almost synonymous" (Firth, 1959, p. 281). As Firth notices, certain contrasts sometimes appear. In reference to man, the *mauri* is the more active principle, "the activity that moves within us." In relation to land or the forest, "*mauri*" is frequently used for the tangible representation of an incorporeal *hau*. Yet it is clear that "*mauri*" too may refer to a purely spiritual quality of land, and, on the other hand, the *hau* of a person may have concrete form—for example, hair, nail clippings, and the like used in witchcraft. It is not for me to unscramble these linguistic and religious mysteries, so characteristic of that Maori "esprit théologique et juridique encore imprécis." Rather, I would emphasize a more apparent and gross contrast between *hau* and *mauri*, on one side, and *wairua* on the other, a contrast that also seems to clarify the learned words of Tamati Ranapiri.

Hau and *mauri* as spiritual qualities are uniquely associated with fecundity. Best often spoke of both as the "vital principle." It is evident from many of his observations that fertility and productivity were the essential attributes of this "vitality." For example (the italics in the following statements are mine):

> The *hau* of land is its vitality, *fertility* and so forth, and also a quality which we can only, I think, express by the word prestige. (Best, 1900–01, p. 193)

> The *ahi taitai* is a sacred fire at which rites are performed that have for their purpose the protection of the life principle and *fruitfulness* of man, the land, forests, birds, etc. It is said to be the *mauri* or *hau* of the home. (p. 194)

> . . . when Hape went off on his expedition to the south, he took with him the *hau* of the *kumara* [sweet potato], or, as some say, he took the *mauri* of the same. The visible form of this *mauri* was the stalk of a *kumara* plant, it represented the *hau*, that is to say, the vitality and *fertility* of the *kumara*. (p. 196; cf. Best, 1925, pp. 106–107)

> The forest *mauri* has already received our attention. We have shown that its function was to protect the *productiveness* of the forest. (p. 6)

> Material *mauri* were utilized in connection with agriculture; they were placed in the field where crops were planted, and it was a firm belief that they had a highly beneficial effect on the growing crops. (1922, p. 38)

Now, the *hau* and *mauri* pertain not only to man, but also to animals, land, forests and even to a village home. Thus the *hau* or vitality, or *productiveness*, of a forest has to be very carefully protected by means of certain very peculiar rites. . . . For *fecundity* cannot exist without the essential *hau*. (1909, p. 436)

Everything animate and inanimate possesses this life principle (*mauri*): without it naught could *flourish*. (1924 vol. 1, p. 306)

So, as we had in fact already suspected, the *hau* of the forest is its fecundity, as the *hau* of a gift is its material yield. Just as in the mundane context of exchange *hau* is the return on a good, so as a spiritual quality *hau* is the principle of fertility. In the one equally as in the other, the benefits taken by man ought to be returned to their source, that it may be maintained as a source. Such was the total wisdom of Tamati Ranapiri.

"Everything happens as if" the Maori people knew a broad concept, a general principle of productiveness, *hau*. It was a category that made no distinctions, of itself belonging neither to the domain we call "spiritual" nor that of the "material," yet applicable to either. Speaking of valuables, the Maori could conceive *hau* as the concrete product of exchange. Speaking of the forest, *hau* was what made the game birds abound, a force unseen but clearly appreciated by the Maori. But would the Maori in any case need to so distinguish the "spiritual" and the "material"? Does not the apparent "imprecision" of the term *hau* perfectly accord with a society in which "economic," "social," "political," and "religious" are indiscriminately organized by the same relations and intermixed in the same activities? And if so, are we not obliged once more to reverse ourselves on Mauss's interpretation? Concerning the spiritual specifics of the *hau*, he was very likely mistaken. But in another sense, more profound, he was right. "Everything happens as if" *hau* were a total concept. *Kaati eenaa.*

Political Philosophy of the *Essay on the Gift.*

For the war of every man against every man, Mauss substitutes the exchange of everything between everybody. The *hau*, spirit of the donor in the gift, was not the ultimate explanation of reciprocity, only a special proposition set in the context of a historic conception. Here was a new version of the dialogue between chaos and covenant, transposed from the explication of political society to the reconciliation of segmentary society. The *Essai sur le don* is a kind of social contract for the primitives.

Like famous philosophical predecessors, Mauss debates from an original condition of disorder, in some sense given and pristine, but then overcome dialectically. As against war, exchange. The transfer of things that are in some degree persons and of persons in some degree treated as things, such is the consent at the base of organized society. The gift is alliance, solidarity, communion—in brief, peace, the great virtue that earlier philosophers, Hobbes notably, had discovered in the State. But the originality and the verity of Mauss was exactly that he refused the discourse in political terms. The first consent is not to authority, or even to unity. It would be too literal an interpretation of the older contract theory to discover its verification in nascent institutions of chieftainship. The primitive analogue of social contract is not the State, but the gift.

The gift is the primitive way of achieving the peace that in civil society is secured by the State. Where in the traditional view the contract was a form of political exchange, Mauss saw exchange as a form of political contract. The famous "total prestation" is a "total contract," described to just this effect in the *Manuel d'ethnographie*:

> We shall differentiate contracts into those of total *prestation* and contracts in which the *prestation* is only partial. The former already appear in Australia; they are found in a large part of the Polynesian world . . . and in North America. For two clans, total *prestation* is manifest by the fact that to be in a condition of perpetual contract, everyone owes everything to all the others of his clan and to all those of the opposed clan. The permanent and collective character of such a contract makes it a veritable *traité*, with the necessary display of wealth *vis-à-vis* the other party. The *prestation* is extended to everything, to everyone, at all times. . . . (1967, p. 188)

But as gift exchange, the contract would have a completely new political realization, unforeseen and unimagined in the received philosophy and constituting neither society nor State. For Rousseau, Locke, Spinoza, Hobbes, the social contract had been first of all a pact of society. It was an agreement of incorporation: to form a community out of previously separate and antagonistic parts, a superperson of the individual persons, that would exercise the power subtracted from each in the benefit of all. But then, a certain political formation had to be stipulated. The purpose of the unification was to put end to the strife born of private justice. Consequently, even if the covenant was not as such a contract of government, between ruler and ruled, as in medieval and earlier versions, and whatever the differences between the sages over the locus of sovereignty, all had to imply by the contract of society the institution of State. That is to say, all had to insist on the alienation by agreement of one right in particular: private force. This was the essential clause, despite that the philosophers went on to debate its comprehensiveness: the surrender of private force in favor of a Public Power.

The gift, however, would not organize society in a corporate sense, only in a segmentary sense. Reciprocity is a "between" relation. It does not dissolve the separate parties within a higher unity, but on the contrary, in correlating their opposition, perpetuates it. Neither does the gift specify a third party standing over and above the separate interests of those who contract. Most important, it does not withdraw their force, for the gift affects only will and not right. Thus the condition of peace as understood by Mauss—and as in fact it exists in the primitive societies—has to differ politically from that envisioned by the classic contract, which is always a structure of submission, and sometimes of terror. Except for the honor accorded to generosity, the gift is no sacrifice of equality and never of liberty. The groups allied by exchange each retain their strength, if not the inclination to use it.

Although I opened with Hobbes (and it is especially in comparison with *Leviathan*[16] that I would discuss *The Gift*), it is clear that in sentiment Mauss is much closer to Rousseau. By its segmentary morphology, Mauss's primitive society rather returns to the third stage of the *Discourse on Inequality* than to the radical individualism of a Hobbesian state of nature (cf. Cazaneuve, 1968). And as Mauss and Rousseau had similarly seen the oppositions as social, so equally their resolutions would be sociable. That is, for Mauss, an exchange that "extends to everything, to everyone, to all time." What is more, if in giving one gives himself (*hau*), then everyone spiritually becomes a member of everyone else. In other words, the gift approaches even in its enigmas that celebrated contract in which, "Chacun de nous met en commun sa personne et toute sa puissance sous la suprême direction de la volonté générale; et nous recevons en corps chaque membre comme partie indivisible du tout."

But if Mauss is a spiritual descendant of Rousseau, as a political philosopher he is akin to Hobbes. Not to claim a close historic relation with the Englishman, of course, but only to detect a strong convergence in the analysis: a basic agreement on the natural political state as a generalized distribution of force, on the possibility of escaping from this condition by the aid of reason, and on the advantages realized thereby in cultural progress. The comparison with Hobbes seems to best bring out the almost concealed scheme of *The Gift*. Still, the exercise would have little interest were it not that this "*problématique*" precisely at the point it makes juncture with Hobbes arrives at a fundamental discovery of the primitive polity, and where it differs from Hobbes it makes a fundamental advance in understanding social evolution.

Political Aspects of The Gift and Leviathan

In the perspective of Mauss, as it was for Hobbes, the understructure of society is war. This in a special sense, which is sociological.

The "war of every man against every man," spectacular phrase, conceals an ambiguity; or at least in its insistence on the nature of man it ignores an equally striking structure of society. The state of nature described by Hobbes was also a political order. True that Hobbes was preoccupied with the human thirst for power and disposition to violence, but he wrote too of an allocation of force among men and of their liberty to employ it. The transition in *Leviathan* from the psychology of man to the pristine condition seems therefore at the same time continuous and disjunctive. The state of nature was *sequitur* to human nature, but it also announced a new level of reality that as polity was not even describable in the terms of psychology. This war of each against all is not just the disposition to use force but the *right* to do so, not merely certain inclinations but certain *relations* of power, not simply a passion for supremacy but a sociology of dominance, not only the instinct of competition but the legitimacy of the confrontation. The state of nature is already a kind of society.[17]

What kind? According to Hobbes, it is a society without a sovereign, without "a common Power to keep them all in awe." Said positively, a society in which the right to give battle is retained by the people in severalty. But this must be underlined: it is the right that endures, not the battle. The emphasis is Hobbes's own, in a very important passage that carried the war of nature beyond human violence to the level of structure, where rather than fighting it appears as a *period of time* during which there is no assurance to contrary, and the will to contend is sufficiently known:

> For WARRE, consisteth not in Battell onely, or the act of fighting; but in a tract of time, wherein the Will to contend by Battell is sufficiently known: and therefore the notion of *Time*, is to be considered in the nature of Warre; as it is in the nature of Weather. For as the nature of Foule weather, lyeth not in a shower or two of rain; but in an inclination thereto of many dayes together; So the nature of Warre, consisteth not in actual fighting; but in the known disposition thereto, during all the time there is no assurance to the contrary. All other time is PEACE.
> (Part I, Chapter 13)

Happily, Hobbes frequently used the archaic spelling, "Warre," which gives us the opportunity of taking it to mean something else, a determinate political form. To repeat, the critical characteristic of Warre is free recourse to force: everyone reserves that option in pursuit of his greater gain or glory, and in defense of his person and possessions. Unless and until this partite strength was rendered to a collective authority, Hobbes argued, there would never be assurance of peace; and though Mauss discovered that assurance in the gift, both agreed that the primitive order is an absence of law; which is the same as saying that everyone can take the law into his own hands, so that man and society stand in continuous danger of a violent end.

Of course, Hobbes did not seriously consider the state of nature as ever a general empirical fact, an authentic historic stage—although there are some people who "live to this day in that brutish manner," as the savages of many places in America, ignorant of all government beyond the lustful concord of the small family. But if not historical, in what sense was the state of nature intended?

In the sense of Galilean logic, it is sometimes said: a thinking away of the distorting factors in a complex appearance to the ideal course of a body moving without resistance. The analogy is close, but insofar as it slights the tension and the stratification of the complex appearance, it perhaps does not do justice, neither to Hobbes nor to the parallel in Mauss. This "Warre" does exist, if it is only that people "lock their doors behind" and princes are in "constant jealousy." Yet though it exists, it has to be imagined because all appearance is *designed* to repress it, to overlay and deny it as an insupportable menace. So it is imagined in a way that seems more like psychoanalysis than physics: by probing for a hidden substructure that in outward behavior is disguised and transfigured into its opposite. In that event, the deduction of the pristine state is not a direct extension of experimental approximations, still consistent with the empirical even as it is projected beyond the observable. The real is here counterposed to the empirical, and we are forced to understand the appearance of things as the negation rather than the expression of their truer character.

In just this manner, it seems to me, Mauss posited his general theory of the gift on a certain nature of primitive society, nature not always evident—but that exactly because it is contradicted by the gift. It was, moreover, a society of the same nature: Warre. The primitive order is a contrived agreement to deny its inherent fragility, its division at base into groups of distinct interest and matched strength, clanic groups "like the savage people in many places of America," that can join only in conflict or else must withdraw to avoid it. Of course, Mauss did not begin from Hobbesian principles of psychology. His view of human nature is certainly more nuanced than that "perpetual and restless desire of Power after power, that ceaseth only in Death."[18] But his view of social nature was an anarchy of group poised against group with a will to contend by battle that is sufficiently

known, and a disposition thereto during all that time there is no assurance
to the contrary. In the context of this argument, the *hau* is only a dependent proposition. That supposed adoption by the ethnologist of a native
rationalization is itself, by the scheme of *The Gift*, the rationalization of a
deeper necessity to reciprocate whose reason lies elsewhere: in threat of
war. The compulsion to reciprocate built into the *hau* responds to the
repulsion of groups built into the society. The force of attraction in things
thus dominates the attractions of force among men.

Less spectacular and sustained than the argument from *hau*, that from
Warre nevertheless reappears persistently in *The Gift*. For Warre is contained in the premises, constructed by Mauss in the very definition of
"total prestation": those exchanges, "undertaken in seemingly voluntary
guise . . . but in essence strictly obligatory, *on pain of private or open warfare*" (1950, p. 151; emphasis mine). Similarly: "To refuse to give or to fail
to invite is, like refusing to accept, equivalent to a declaration of war; it is
to refuse alliance and communion" (pp. 162–63).

Perhaps it strains the point to insist on Mauss's appreciation of the
potlatch as a sort of sublimated warfare. Let us pass on to the concluding
paragraphs of the essay, where the opposition between Warre and exchange
is developed with progressive amplitude and clarity, first in the metaphor
of the Pine Mountain Corroboree, finally in a general statement that
begins . . .

> All the societies we have described above, except our own European, are
> segmentary societies. Even the Indo-Europeans, the Romans before the
> *Twelve Tables*, the Germanic societies until very late—up to the Edda—
> Irish society until the time of its principal literature, all were still based
> on clans, or at the least great families, more or less undivided internally
> and isolated from one another externally. All these societies are or were
> far removed from our own degree of unification, as well as from that
> unity with which they are endowed by inadequate historical study.
> (1950, p. 277)

From this organization, a time of exaggerated fear and hostility, appears
an equally exaggerated generosity:

> When, during tribal feasts and ceremonies of rival clans and of families
> that intermarry or initiate reciprocally, groups visit each other; even
> when, among more advanced societies—with a developed law of "hospi-
> tality"—the law of friendship and contracts with the gods have come to
> assure the "peace" of the "market" and the towns; for a very long period

of time and in a considerable number of societies, men confront each
other in a curious frame of mind, of exaggerated fear and hostility and of
generosity equally exaggerated, which is however mad in no one's eyes
but our own. (p. 277)

So the people "come to terms" (*traiter*), happy phrase whose double
meaning of peace and exchange perfectly epitomizes the primitive contract:

In all the societies that have immediately preceded ours and that still
surround us, and even in numerous usages of our own popular morality,
there is no middle way: either complete trust or complete mistrust. One
lays down one's arms, renounces magics and gives everything away from
casual hospitality to one's daughters and goods. It is in conditions of
this kind that men put aside their self-concern and learnt to engage in
giving and returning. But then they had no choice. Two groups of men
that meet can only withdraw—or in case of mistrust or defiance, battle—
or else come to terms. (p. 277)

By the end of the essay, Mauss had left far behind the mystic forests of
Polynesia. The obscure forces of *hau* were forgotten for a different explanation of reciprocity, consequent on the more general theory, and the
opposite of all mystery and particularity: *Reason*. The gift is Reason. It is
the triumph of human rationality over the folly of war—

It is by opposing reason to emotion, by setting up the will for peace
against rash follies of this kind, that peoples succeed in substituting
alliance, gift and commerce for war, isolation and stagnation. (p. 278)

I stress not only this "reason," but the "isolation" and "stagnation."
Composing society, the gift was the liberation of culture. Oscillating permanently between confrontation and dispersion, the segmentary society is
otherwise brutish and static. But the gift is progress. That is its supreme
advantage—and Mauss's final appeal:

Societies have progressed in the measure that they themselves, their subgroups and finally their individuals have been able to stabilize their relations, to give, receive, and to repay. In order to trade it was necessary
first to lay down the spear. It is then that one succeeded in exchanging
goods and persons, not only between clan and clan, but between tribe
and tribe, nation and nation, and, above all, between individuals. It is
only consequently that people became capable of mutually creating and

satisfying their interests, and finally of defending them without recourse to arms. It is thus that clans, tribes, peoples have learned—and it is thus that tomorrow in our world called civilized the classes, nations, and also individuals must learn—how to oppose without massacring one another, and how to give without sacrificing one to another. (pp. 278–79)

The "incommodities" of the Hobbesian state of nature had been likewise a lack of progress. And society was similarly condemned to stagnation. Here Hobbes brilliantly anticipated a later ethnology. Without the State (commonwealth) he is saying, lacking special institutions of integration and control, culture must remain primitive and uncomplicated—just as, in the biological realm, the organism had to remain relatively undifferentiated until the appearance of a central nervous system. In some degree, Hobbes even went beyond modern ethnology, which still only in an unconscious way, and without serious attempt to justify its decision, is content to see in the formation of the state the great evolutionary divide between "primitive" and "civilized," while in the meantime subjecting that famous passage of Hobbes's where it is explained just why the criterion is good, to nasty, brutish, and short burlesques. Hobbes at least gave a functional justification of the evolutionary distinction, and an indication that qualitative change would alter the quantity:

> *The incommodities of such a Warre.* Whatsoever therefore is consequent to a time of Warre, where every man is Enemy to every man; the same is consequent to the time, wherein men live without other security, than what their own strength, and their own invention shall furnish them withall. In such condition, there is no place for industry; because the fruit thereof is uncertain: and consequently no Culture of the Earth, no Navigation, nor use of the commodities that may be imported by Sea; no commodious Building; no Instruments of moving, and removing such things as require much force; no Knowledge of the face of the Earth; no account of Time, no Arts; no Letters; no Society; and which is worst of all, continuall feare, and danger of violent death; And the life of man, solitary, poore, nasty, brutish and short. (Part 1, Chapter 13)

But to pursue the resemblance to Mauss, from this insecurity and poverty man seeks to escape: for reasons largely of emotion, according to Hobbes, but by means strictly of *reason*. Menaced by material deprivation and haunted by fear of violent death, men would incline to reason, which "suggesteth certain convenient Articles of Peace, upon which men may be drawn to agreement." Thus Hobbes's well-known Laws of Nature, which are counsels of reason in the interest of preservation, and of which the first and fundamental is *"to seek Peace, and follow it."*

> And because the condition of Man, (as hath been declared in the precedent Chapter) is a condition of Warre of every one against everyone; in which case every one is governed by his own Reason; and there is nothing he can make use of, that may not be a help unto him, in preserving his life against his enemyes; It followeth, that in such a condition, every man has a Right to every thing; even to one another's body. And therefore, as long as this naturall Right of every man to every thing endureth, there can be no security to any man, how strong or wise soever he be, of living out the time, which Nature ordinarily alloweth men to live. And consequently it is a precept, or generall rule of Reason, *That every man, ought to endeavour Peace, as farre as he has hope of obtaining it; and when he cannot obtain it, that he may seek, and use, all helps, and advantages of Warre.* The first branch of which Rule, containeth the first, and Fundamentall Law of Nature; which is, to seek Peace, and follow it. (Part 1, Chapter 14)

That Hobbes had even foreseen the peace of the gift is too strong a claim. But this first law of nature was followed by eighteen others, all in effect designed to realize the injunction that men seek peace, and the second through fifth in particular founded on the same principle of reconciliation of which the gift is merely the most tangible expression—founded also, that is to say, on reciprocity. So in structure the argument unites with Mauss's. To this point, at least, Hobbes understands the suppression of Warre neither through the victory of one nor by the submission of all, but in a *mutual surrender.* (The ethical importance is obvious, and Mauss would duly emphasize it, but theoretically too the point is in opposition to the cult of power and organization that was to mark a later evolutionism—and to which Hobbes went on to contribute.)

On the deeper analogy of reciprocity, one may thus juxtapose to gift exchange Hobbes's second law of nature, *"That a man be willing, when others are so too, as farre-forth, as for Peace, and defence of himselfe he shall think it necessary, to lay down this right to all things; and be contented with as much liberty against other men, as he would allow other men against himselfe"*; and the third law, *"That men performe their Covenants made"*; and again, the fifth, *"That every man strive to accomodate himselfe to the rest."* But of all these apposite precepts, the fourth law of nature touches nearest the gift:

The fourth law of nature, gratitude. As Justice dependeth on Antecedent
Covenant; so does GRATITUDE depend on Antecedent Grace that is
to say, Antecedent Free-gift: and is the fourth Law of Nature; which may
be conceived in this Forme, *That a man which receiveth Benefit from
another of meer Grace, Endeavour that he which giveth it, have no reasonable cause to repent him of his good will.* For no man giveth, but with
intention of Good to himselfe; because Gift is Voluntary; and of all
Voluntary Acts, the Object is to every man his own Good; of which if
men see they shall be frustrated, there will be no beginning of benevo-
lence, or trust; nor consequently of mutuall help; nor of reconciliation
of one man to another; and therefore they are to remain still in the condition of *War*; which is contrary to the first and Fundamentall Law of
Nature, which commandeth men to *Seek Peace.* (Part I, Chapter 15)

Thus the close correspondence between the two philosophers: including, if not exactly the gift, at least a similar appreciation of reciprocity as
the primitive mode of peace; and also, if this more marked in Hobbes than
in Mauss, a common respect for the rationality of the undertaking.
Furthermore, the convergence continues with a negative parallel. Neither
Mauss nor Hobbes could trust in the efficacy of reason alone. Both con-
cede, Hobbes the more explicitly, that reason against the force of an
imprinted rivalry is insufficient to guarantee the contract. Because, says
Hobbes, the laws of nature, even if they be reason itself, are contrary to our
natural passions, and men cannot be expected unfailingly to obey unless
they are generally coerced to do so. On the other hand, to honor the laws
of nature without the assurance that others do likewise is unreasonable; for
then the good become prey, and the strong arrogant. Men, says Hobbes,
are not bees. Men are driven constantly to compete for honor and dignity,
out of which arises hate, envy, and finally, war. And "covenants without the
sword, are but words, and of no strength to secure a man at all." Hobbes
consequently is led to this paradox: that the laws of nature cannot succeed
outside the frame of a contrived organization, outside the commonwealth.
Natural law is established only by artificial Power, and Reason enfranchised
only by Authority.

I stress again the political character of Hobbes's argument. The commonwealth put an end to the state of nature but not to the nature of man.
Men agreed to surrender their right to force (except in self-defense), and
to put all their strength at the disposal of a sovereign, who would bear their
person and save their lives. In this conception of state formation, Hobbes
once more rings very modern. What more fundamental sense has since
been made of the state than that it is a differentiation of the generalized

primitive order: structurally, the separation of a public authority out of the society at large; functionally; the special reservation to that authority of coercive force (monopoly control of force)?

> The only way to erect such a Common Power, as may be able to defend them from the invasion of Forraigners, and the injuries of one another, and thereby to secure them in such sort, as that by their owne industry, and by the fruites of the Earth, they may nourish themselves and live contentedly; is, to conferre all their power and strength upon one Man, or upon one Assembly of men, that may reduce all their Wills, by plurality of voices, unto one Will: which is as much as to say, to appoint one Man, or Assembly of men, to beare their Person; and every one to owne, and acknowledge himselfe to be the Author of whatsoever that he that so beareth their Person, shall Act, or cause to be Acted, in those things which concern the Common Peace and safetie; and therein to submit their Wills, every one to his Will, and their Judgements, to his Judgement. (Part 2, Chapter 17)

But Mauss's resolution of Warre also had historic merit: it corrected just this simplified progression from chaos to commonwealth, savagery to civilization, that had been the work of classical contract theory.[19] Here in the primitive world Mauss displayed a whole array of intermediate forms, not only of a certain stability, but that did not make coercion the price of order. Still, Mauss too was not confident that reason alone had been responsible. Or perhaps it was just an afterthought, upon looking back over the peace of the gift, that he saw in it the signs of an original wisdom. For the rationality of the gift contradicted everything he had said before on the subject of *hau*. Hobbes's paradox was to realize the natural (reason) in the artificial; for Mauss, reason took the form of the irrational. Exchange is the triumph of reason, but lacking the embodied spirit of the donor (*hau*), the gift is not requited.

A few last words about the fate of *The Gift*. Since Mauss, and in part by way of rapprochement with modern economics, anthropology has become more consistently rational in its treatment of exchange. Reciprocity is contract pure and mainly secular, sanctioned perhaps by a mixture of considerations of which a carefully calculated self-interest is not the least (cf. Firth, 1967). Mauss seems in this regard much more like Marx in the first chapter of *Capital*: if it can be said without disrespect, more animistic. One quarter of corn is exchangeable for X hundredweight iron. What is it in these things, so obviously different, that yet is equal? Precisely, the question was, for Marx, what *in these things* brings them into agreement?—and not what is it about these parties to the exchange? Similarly, for Mauss; "What force is there in the thing given that makes the beneficiary reciprocate?" And the same kind of answer, from "intrinsic" properties: here the *hau*, if there the socially necessary labor time. Yet "animistic" is manifestly an improper characterization of the thought involved. If Mauss, like Marx, concentrated singularly on the anthropomorphic qualities of the things exchanged, rather than the (thinglike?) qualities of the people, it was because each saw in the transactions respectively at issue a determinate form and epoch of alienation: mystic alienation of the donor in primitive reciprocity, alienation of human social labor in commodity production (cf. Godelier, 1966, p. 143). They thus share the supreme merit, unknown to most "Economic Anthropology," of taking exchange as it is historically presented, not as a natural category explicable by a certain eternal disposition of humanity.

In the total prestations between clan and clan, said Mauss, things are related in some degree as persons and persons in some degree as things. More than irrational, it exaggerates only slightly to say that the process approaches clinical definitions of neurosis: persons are treated as objects; people confuse themselves with the external world. But even beyond the desire to affirm the rationality of exchange, a large section of Anglo-American anthropology has seemed instinctively repelled by the commercialization of persons apparently implied in the Maussian formula.

Nothing could be farther apart than the initial Anglo-Saxon and French responses to this generalized idea of prestation. Here was Mauss decrying the *inhumanity* of modern abstract distinctions between real and personal law, calling for a return to the archaic relation between men and things, while the Anglo-Saxons could only congratulate the ancestors for having finally liberated men from a debasing confusion with material objects. And especially for thus liberating women. For when Lévi-Strauss parlayed the "total prestation" into a grand system of marital exchanges, an interesting number of British and American ethnologists recoiled at once from the idea, refusing for their part to "treat women as commodities."

Without wanting to decide the issue, not at least in these terms, I do wonder whether the Anglo-American reaction of distrust was ethnocentric. It seems to presume an external separation of the economic, having to do with getting and spending, and besides always a little off-color, from the social sphere of moral relationships. For if it is decided in advance that the world in general is differentiated as is ours in particular, economic relations being one thing and social (kinship) another, than to speak of groups exchanging women does appear an immoral extension of business to marriage and a slander of all those engaged in the traffic. Still, the conclusion forgets the great lesson of "total prestation," both for the study of primitive economics and of marriage.

The primitive order is generalized. A clear differentiation of spheres into social and economic does not there appear. As for marriage, it is not that commercial operations are applied to social relations, but the two were never completely separated in the first place. We must think here in the same way we do now about classificatory kinship: not that the term for "father" is "extended" to father's brother, phrasing that smuggles in the priority of the nuclear family, but rather that we are in the presence of a broad kinship category that knows no such genealogical distinctions. And as for economics, we are similarly in the presence of a generalized organization for which the supposition that kinship is "exogenous" betrays any hope of understanding.

I mention a final positive contribution of *The Gift*, related to this point but more specific. At the end of the essay, Mauss in effect recapitulated his thesis by two Melanesian examples of tenuous relations between villages and peoples: of how, menaced always by deterioration into war, primitive groups are nevertheless reconciled by festival and exchange. This theme too was later amplified by Lévi-Strauss. "There is a link," he wrote, "a continuity, between hostile relations and the provision of reciprocal prestations. Exchanges are peacefully resolved wars and wars are the result of unsuccessful transactions" (1969, p. 67; cf. 1943, p. 136). But this implication of *The Gift* is, I think, even broader than external relations and transactions. In posing the internal fragility of the segmentary societies, their constituted decomposition, *The Gift* transposes the classic alternatives of war and trade from the periphery to the very center of social life, and from the occasional episode to the continuous presence. This is the supreme importance of Mauss's return to nature, from which it follows that primitive society is at war with Warre, and that all their dealings are treaties of peace. All the exchanges, that is to say, must bear in their material design some political burden of reconciliation. Or, as the Bushman said, "'The worse thing is not giving presents. If people do not like each other but one gives a gift and the other must accept, this brings a peace between them. We give what we have. That is the way we live together'" (Marshall, 1961, p. 245).

And from this comes in turn all the basic principles of an economics properly anthropological, including the one in particular at the heart of [the final two chapters of *Stone Age Economics*]: that every exchange, as it embodies some coefficient of sociability, cannot be understood in its material terms apart from its social terms.

From *Stone Age Economics*, 1972.

Notes

1. An English translation of *L'Essai sur le don* has been prepared by Ian Cunnison, and published as *The Gift* (London: Cohen and West, 1954).

2. Hereinafter, I will use the Biggs version except where the argument about Mauss's interpretation requires that one cite only the documents available to him. I take this opportunity to thank Professor Biggs for his generous help.

3. It seems from Firth's account that the same procedure was used both against thieves and ingrates. I appeal here to Maori authorities for clarification. From my own very limited and entirely textual experience, it seems that the goods of a victimized party were used particularly in sorcery against thieves. Here, where the culprit usually is not known, some portion of the goods remaining—or something from the place they were kept—is the vehicle for identifying or punishing the thief (for example, Best, 1924, vol. 1, p. 311). But sorcery against a known person is typically practiced by means of something associated with *him*; thus, in a case of failure to repay, the goods of the deceiver would be more likely to serve as vehicle than the gift of the owner. For further interest and confusion, such a vehicle associated with the victim of witchcraft is known to the Maori as *hau*. One of the entries under "*hau*" in W. Williams's dictionary is: "something connected with a person on whom it is intended to practice enchantment; such as a portion of his hair, a drop of his spittle, or anything which has touched his person, etc., which when taken to the *tohunga* [ritual expert] might serve as a connecting link between his incantations and their object" (Williams, 1892).

4. The intervention of a third party thus offers no obscurity to Firth. The exchange between second and third parties was necessary to introduce a second good that could stand for the first, or for the *hau* of the first (cf. Firth, 1959, p. 420 n.).

5. "When Mauss sees in the gift exchange an interchange of personalities, 'a bond of souls,' he is following, not native belief, but his own intellectualized interpretation of it" (Firth, 1959, p. 420).

6. In his latest word on the subject, Firth continues to deny the ethnographic validity of Mauss's views on the Maori *hau*, adding also that no such spiritual belief is involved in Tikopian gift exchange (1967). Too, he now has certain critical reservations on Mauss's discussion of the obligations to give, receive, and reciprocate. Yet at one level he would agree with Mauss. Not in the sense of an actual spiritual entity, but in the more generalized social and psychological sense of an extension of the self, the gift does partake of its donor (ibid., pp. 10–11, 15–16).

7. In the original Maori as published by Best, the passage on gifts was actually intercalculated as an explanatory aside between two descriptions of the ceremony. The continuous English translation, however, deletes the main part of the first description, this Best having cited a page earlier (1909, p. 438). Besides, both English and Maori texts begin with a discussion of witchcraft spells, not apparently related to the ceremonial or the gift exchange, but about which more later.

8. There is a very curious difference between the several versions of Best, Mauss, and Tamati Ranapiri. Mauss appears to deliberately delete Best's reference to the ceremony in the opening phrase. Best had cited "'I will now speak of the *hau*, and the ceremony of *whangai hau*'"; whereas Mauss has it merely, "'Je vais vous [*sic*] parler du *hau* . . .'" (ellipsis is Mauss's). The interesting point is raised by Bigg's undoubtedly authentic translation, much closer to that of Mauss, as it like-

wise does not mention *whangai hau* at this point: "'Now, concerning the *hau* of the forest.'" However, even in this form the original text linked the message on *taonga* with the ceremony of *whangai hau*, "fostering" or "nourishing *hau*," since the *hau* of the forest was not the subject of the immediately succeeding passage on gifts but of the consequent and ultimate description of the ceremony.

9. I use Best's translation, the one available to Mauss. I also have in hand Bigg's interlinear version; it does not differ significantly from Best's.

10. The earlier discussion of this ritual, preceding the passage on *taonga* in the full Maori text, in fact comments on two related ceremonies: the one just described and another, performed before, by those sent into the forest in advance of the fowling season to observe the state of the game. I cite the main part of this earlier description in Bigg's version: "The *hau* of the forest has two 'likenesses.' 1. When the forest is inspected by the observers, and if birds are observed to be there, and if birds are killed by them that day, the first bird killed by them is offered to the *mauri*. It is simply thrown away into the bush, and is said, 'that's for the *mauri*.' The reason, lest they get nothing in the future. 2. When the hunting is finished (they) go out of the bush and begin to cook the birds for preserving in fat. Some are set aside first to feed the *hau* of the forest; this is the forest *hau*. Those birds which were set aside are cooked on the second fire. Only the priests eat the birds of the second fire. Other birds are set aside for the *tapairu* from which only the women eat. Most of the birds are set aside and cooked on the *puuraakau* fire. The birds of the *puuraakau* fire are for all to eat. . . ." (cf. Best, 1909, pp. 438, 440–41, 449f; and for other details of the ceremonies, 1942, pp. 13, 184f, 316–17).

11. And in Best's translation, even reiterating: "'Suppose that you possess a certain article, and you give that article to me, without price. We make no bargain over it.'"

12. Firth cites the following discussion to this point from Gudgeon: "'If a man received a present and passed it on to some third person then there is no impropriety in such an act; but if a return present is made by the third party then it must be passed on to the original grantor or it is a *hau ngaro* (consumed *hau*)'" (Firth, 1959, p. 418). The lack of consequence in the first of these conditions is again evidence against Mauss's nostalgic *hau*, ever striving to return to its *foyer*.

13. *Whitia* is the past participle of *whiti*. *Whiti*, according to H. Williams's dictionary, means: (1) *v.i.*, cross over, reach the opposite side; (2) change, turn, to be inverted, to be contrary; (3) *v.t.*, pass through; (4) turn over, prise (as with a lever); (5) change (Williams, 1921, p. 584).

14. Best's further interpretation lent itself to Mauss's views: "For it seems that that article of yours is impregnated with a certain amount of your *hau*, which presumably passes into the article received in exchange therefore, because if I pass that second article on to other hands it is a *hau whitia*" (1900–01, p. 198). Thus "it seems." One has a feeling of participating in a game of ethnographic folk-etymology, which we now find, from Best's explanation, is a quite probable game *à quatre*.

15. Thus Mauss's simple translation of *hau* as spirit and his view of exchange as a *lien d'âmes* is at least imprecise. Beyond that, Best repeatedly would like to distinguish *hau* (and *mauri*) from *wairua* on the grounds that the former, which ceases to exist with death, cannot leave a person's body on pain of death, unlike *wairua*. But here Best finds himself in difficulty with the material manifestation of a person's *hau* used in witchcraft, so that he is alternatively tempted to say that some part of the *hau* can be detached from the body or that the *hau* as witchcraft is not the "true" *hau*.

16. I use the Everyman's edition for all citations from *Leviathan* (New York: Dutton, 1950), as it retains the archaic spelling, rather than the more commonly cited *English Works* edited by Molesworth (1839).

17. Why this should seem particularly so in *Leviathan* in comparison with the earlier *Elements of Law* and *De Cive* becomes intelligible from McNeilly's recent analysis to the effect that *Leviathan* completes the transformation of Hobbes's argument into a formal rationality of interpersonal relations (in the absence of a sovereign power), which involves abandonment, as concerns the logic of argument, of the prior stress on the content of human passions. Hence if in the early works, "Hobbes attempts to derive political conclusions from certain (very doubtful) propositions about the specific nature of individual human beings . . . in *Leviathan* the argument depends on an analysis of the *formal* structure of the *relations* between individuals" (McNeilly, 1968, p. 5).

18. Mauss did note in certain transactions of the present day some "fundamental motives of human activity: emulation between individuals of the same sex, that 'deep-seated imperialism' of men, at base part social, part animal and psychological. . . ." (1950, pp. 258–59). On the other hand, if as Macpherson (1965) argues, Hobbes's conception of human nature is just the bourgeois eternalized, then Mauss is squarely opposed to it (1950, pp. 271–72).

19. Hobbes's particular inability to conceive primitive society as such is manifest by his assimilation of it, that is of the patriarchal chiefdom, to the commonwealth. This is clear enough in the passages of *Leviathan* on commonwealths by acquisition, but even more definitive in the parallel sections of *Elements of Law* and *De Cive*. Thus, in the latter: "A *father* with his *sons* and *servants*, grown into a civil person by virtue of his paternal jurisdiction, is called a *family*. This *family*, if through multiplying of *children* and acquisition of *servants* it becomes numerous, insomuch as without casting the uncertain die of war it cannot be subdued, will be termed an *hereditary kingdom*. Which though it differ from an *institutive monarchy*, being acquired by force, in the original and manner of its constitution; yet being constituted, it hath all the same properties, and the right of authority is everywhere the same; insomuch as it is not needful to speak anything of them apart" (*English Works* [Molesworth, ed.], 1839, vol. 2, pp. 121–22).

Works Cited

Best, Elsdon.
   1900–01. "Spiritual Concepts of the Maori." *Journal of the Polynesian Society* 9: 173–99; 10: 1–20.
   1909. "Maori Forest Lore . . . Part III." *Transactions of the New Zealand Institute* 42: 433–81.
   1922. *Spiritual and Mental Concepts of the Maori*. Dominion Museum Monographs No. 2.
   1924. *The Maori*. 2 vols. Memoirs of the Polynesian Society No. 5.
   1925. *Maori Agriculture*. Dominion Museum Bulletin No. 9.
   1942. *Forest Lore of the Maori*. Dominion Museum Bulletin No. 14.
Cazaneuve, Jean.
   1968. *Sociologie de Marcel Mauss*. Paris: Presses Universitaires de France.
Firth, Raymond.
   1959. *Economics of the New Zealand Maori*. 2d ed. Wellington: R. E. Owen, Government Printer.

1967. "Themes in Economic Anthropology: A General Comment." In *Themes in Economic Anthropology,* ed. Raymond Firth. London: Tavistock, ASA Monograph 6.

Godelier, Maurice.
1966. *Rationalité et irrationalité en économie.* Paris: Maspero.

Hobbes, Thomas.
1950. *Leviathan.* New York: Dutton.

Johansen, J. Prytz.
1954. *The Maori and His Religion.* Copenhagen: Musksgaard.

Lévi-Strauss, Claude.
1943. "Guerre et commerce chez les Indiens de l'Amerique du Sud." *Renaissance* 1: 122–39.
1950. "Introduction à l'oeuvre de Marcel Mauss." In *Sociologie et anthropologie,* by Marcel Mauss. Paris: Presses Universitaires de France.
1969. *The Elementary Structures of Kinship.* London: Eyre and Spottiswoode.

Marshall, Lorna.
1961. "Sharing, Talking, and Giving: Relief of Social Tensions Among !Kung Bushmen." *Africa* 31: 231–49.

Macpherson, C. B.
1965. "Hobbes's Bourgeois Man." In *Hobbes Studies.* Ed. K. C. Brown. Oxford: Blackwell.

Mauss, Marcel.
1950. "Essai sur le don: Forme et raison de l'échange dans les sociétés archaïques." In *Sociologie et anthropologie.* (First published 1923–24 in *L'Année Sociologique.*) Paris: Presses Universitaires de France.
1967. *Manuel d'ethnographie.* (First published 1947.) Paris: Payot.

McNeilly, F. S.
1968. *The Anatomy of Leviathan.* London: Macmillan.

Molesworth, Sir William, ed.
1839. *English Works of Thomas Hobbes.* London: J. Bohn.

Williams, Herbert.
1921. *A Dictionary of the Maori Language.* Auckland, N.Z.: Williams and Northgate.

Williams, William.
1892. *A Dictionary of the New Zealand Language.* Auckland, N.Z.: Williams and Northgate.

Heliocentric Exchange

Rodolphe Gasché

I. Hybrid Blooming

The archeology[1] proposed by Marcel Mauss in *Essai sur le don*[2] is not without its difficulties: like any science it digs down through empirical data and the various historical and ethnic layers to find an identical, transparent, and ultimate object. Now, that mostly ethnographic[3] material is anything but homogeneous. But it is not its multiple, disparate origin, which is dependent upon ethnographic research as well as secondary sources, in every sense of the word, that will concern us here. It is rather a matter of the very nature of exchange in archaic societies that Mauss is trying to encircle in order to set it up as an object. At the first approach the object eludes any attempt at a univocal denomination. From the beginning, with his "program," Mauss runs into this difficulty: striving to isolate within the set of "very complex themes" and the "multiplicity of social things in motion" one peculiar feature of prestations, a theme whose priority in the structural approach to the material is not fortuitous, as we will see further on, he is immediately confronted with its contrary. The "voluntary character" of the prestations is only voluntary, in effect, "so to speak, apparently free and gratuitous, and yet constrained and interested." Although the prestations in question have "almost always assumed the form of the present or gift generously offered," "underneath there is obligation and economic interest" (p. 147). In that first attempt at circumscribing the object "exchange" by isolating one of its features, Mauss is led into a twofold paradox: first, the object does not let itself be defined by one characteristic, turning up as essentially ambiguous and always evoking the contrary of each definition; second, by proceeding in this way, Mauss himself is led into the confusion of terms that he is going to disclose in primitive thought, especially in its language. So on this level of the text he is obliged to repeat, without being able to master it, the very ambiguity he intended to reduce.

But first let's see the whole extent of the ambiguity in primitive prestations. The first classification he effects between total or simple prestations and agonistic prestations is already problematic. Whereas in total prestations "everything is complementary" (p. 151) and, as he notes in his

Manuel d'ethnographie[4] (p. 129), reciprocity is "total," total prestations of the agonistic type are "unequal" and "competitive" (ibid. p. 131). The rules that classify the two types, however, are the same: an obligation to receive, to give, and to take; so the latter type seems to differ from the former only by its "essentially interest-bearing and sumptuary" character; it shows up as struggle and war (*ED*, p. 152–53). But like the type of simple, total prestations, it too corresponds "to a system of rivalries between people bound to reciprocity" (*ME*, idem). It too leads to "complete circuits" (idem). And if we admit that the gift in its aspect as a present is, as Mauss himself says, only "fiction, formalism, and social lying" (*ED*, p. 147), we can infer that the characteristic of disinterestedness is itself a sumptuary effect insofar as the present is really not disinterested and obliges the other to give it back with interest. So all the criteria are united in simple prestation with total reciprocity and equality to make it possible to disclose in it the rivalry that defines agonistic prestations. The difference is at most one of mere degree. So we can conclude that the classification resting on the opposition between reciprocity and rivalry is, let us say, artificial and that the phenomenon, if there is one, proceeds just as well from the one as from the other.

All the other categories that Mauss sets forth run into the same difficulty. As we had already seen, the gift is at once generous and interested, free and obligatory. And likewise, trying to describe the sentiments prevalent in exchanges in primitive societies, Mauss feels obliged to say that "they fraternize, and yet they remain strangers: they communicate and they oppose one another in a gigantic commerce and an ongoing tournament" (p. 205). The parties engaged are, he says further on, in "an odd state of mind, of exaggerated fear and hostility and equally exaggerated generosity" (p. 277). There is an "instability between festivity and war" (p. 278).

All the denominations and all the conceptualization brought to bear do not succeed in defining the "object" which, instead, turns out to be unnameable. It always shows up as an other, as a non-object; and as it is always more and always less than the oppositions that are manifest in its ambiguity, there is no exhaustive series of oppositions that could empty it out. At most, all that can be reported is the ambiguity, which in and of itself eludes any attempt at enunciation and conceptualization.

Now, as we have seen, at an early stage of his reflection Mauss is led, in spite of himself, to feel that difficulty: in an essay, *Gift-Gift*, which appeared at about the same time as his memoir on the gift (1924), the problem is posed in perhaps its most fully worked-out form; and it may not be by chance that the passage in question is mentioned in *Essai sur le don* only in passing, in a footnote (p. 225). In *Gift-Gift*, Mauss had shown that the germanic word *Gift*, which means *Gabe*, that is, gift, signifies at the same time poison, thus indicating the obligation inherent in the gift to be given back upon penalty of enchantment or death. And he goes on:

> Besides, all these ideas have two faces. In other Indo-European languages it is the notion of poison that is uncertain. Kluge and the etymologists rightly compare the series *potio* "poison" and *gift, gift*. (M. Mauss, *Oeuvres*, III, p. 50)[†]

So the ideas and the facts in question would be branded with an irreducible ambiguity and derive from a system whose fundamental structure is twofold.

At that point, a point which, in the text of the *Essai*, is not *within* the logic of its development, and we will come back to that, but which is rather apart from it, Mauss glimpses the possibility of thinking the complete alterity of his object and of the societies to which it seems to pertain. Thus, and again in a footnote, Mauss criticizes Boas, whom he has just cited in terms of praise (p. 198), for having used modern economic categories in the analysis of prestation societies. He thereby implies that such notions are not pertinent in the description of the total alterity of these total formations. And criticizing his own procedure, he writes:

> One can dissolve, stir up, color, and define differently the principal notions we have used. The terms we have employed: present, offering, gift, are themselves not altogether exact. It is simply that we have not found any others. The concepts of law and economics that we like to put in opposition—freedom and obligation; on the one hand liberality, generosity, luxury and on the other thrift, interest, utility; we would do well to put them back in the *creuset* [melting pot]. (p. 267)

Thus it is clearly made manifest that those pairs of oppositions pertain, properly speaking, to our (restricted) economy and that only a displacement of such notions, a recasting or pulverizing of them, would perhaps make it possible to describe the fundamental otherness of those societies, their practices and ideas. That process would likewise be the condition required for the neutralization of the leveling off that such notions bring about and which leads to an effacement of all differences, wrenching the so-called primitive societies into the perspective of Western culture. The success of such a recasting of the notions and categories hitherto employed would lead, however, to an effect whose consequences would be uncontrollable: the otherness, the difference between the societies, would be insurmountable and Western thought would be thrown back, for once at least, onto itself and would remain alone with its wretchedness; for henceforth the radical otherness of archaic societies could no longer be considered as the hidden essence of Western culture, its possible supplement, a remedy for its difficulties, and, in a word, its *arché*. And at the same time the project of an archeology would be reduced to pure vanity. That apprehension, the fear of such consequences, may be precisely the reason why Mauss will abandon that approach.

But let's come back to the metaphor of the *creuset* [melting pot]. The question we would like to pose is that of the possibility of thinking the otherness, starting from a recasting of the usual terms. Without relying too much on the etymological definition, it might be of some interest to recall that the word *creuset* has its origin in the word *croix* [cross], *crux*. So recasting the oppositional pairs would be, in a way, to put them on a cross, or, again, to uncover the criss-cross figure which is also a crossing out [*rature*] of the pairs of oppositions. This cross at the bottom of the *creuset* on which the respective terms are laid out would uncover not so much a synthesis, a new concept apt for naming the unnameable, as the other of those same concepts: their arrangement, their articulation, in a word, their "logic." Then, from the recasting, would surge up the unthought system of classification by oppositions, a "repressed" system which frees the oppositions from their inscription so as to allow them to begin to designate and name unequivocally. And, following Mauss's suggestion, we will get to a reflection of ethnology upon itself, to its deconstruction; for what surges up from the bottom of the *creuset* is, in a way, an other, which, in its otherness, is no less strange than the other that archaic society represented. Not a new concept, which would only reduce once again the ambiguity and otherness disclosed in the social formations in question and which would thereby prolong the project of assimilation by an ethnology which in its essence can only be ethnocentric, but a certain "logic" which would show that ethnological discourse only grasps its object always already emasculated, as Bataille would say. The other which a society would be whose practices would not permit themselves to be subordinated to a concept, that other does not permit itself to be introduced into the ethnological project except in the form of a restricted metaphor. So what shows up clearly at the bottom of the melting pot would be the economy whose occultation produces this necessity, whose occultation is precisely what makes possible a science like ethnology and the idea of its object. But as we have already said, that is not the path Mauss will choose.

On the contrary, the *Essai sur le don* will be built entirely around a project for the reduction and appropriation of the savage originary ambiguity. We will attempt to trace this logic of reappropriation, of submission to form and reason, along the chain of Mauss's arguments, but without any ambition of accounting for it exhaustively. The first step Mauss takes in this direction attributes the ambiguity of indigenous practices and institutions to an incapacity of the primitive mind to apprehend its own practice. That ineptitude would be manifest at the level of the mind itself as well as in its language, its vocabulary. Mauss thinks he can discern in the vocabulary of Melanesian societies, for example, an "odd ineptitude for dividing and defining" coupled with "odd refinements in nomenclature." From that he deduces pejoratively that the language of the Trobrianders is "a bit immature" (p. 191). It would imply their "incapacity to abstract and distinguish their economic and juridical concepts" even though, moreover, they have no need to do so, as, moreover, he says himself. And if they have no need to do so, ought we not think that their practice is of an order that makes it unnecessary? Yet that does not occur to Mauss and he goes on (p. 193):

> "antithetical" operations are expressed by the same word . . .
> These men have neither the idea of selling nor the idea of lending, and
> yet they carry out juridical and economic operations corresponding to
> those words.

From which fact it would follow that the social practice of archaic societies is in flagrant contradiction with the forms of indigenous reflection. Although they have only one word for naming actions as different as selling and buying, Mauss, who had objected to Boas by denouncing his use of modern notions in the analysis of primitive societies, presupposes here that indigenous practices would have the same function as those of the so-called cultural societies. So Mauss has to conclude that primitive thought, like its language, is characterized by an odd "confusion" which makes everything, principally things and souls, *blend together*. And Mauss writes, summing up in a figure what he has just denounced: "A sort of hybrid has bloomed over yonder" (p. 267).

So hybrid blooming, a producer of many-headed flowers, over-grown monstrosities, is opposed to the concept, whose signification is clear and distinct and which seems to bear its one head on an upright body. Mauss is bent on finding the concept in order to be able to master the overgrowth and the undecidable ambiguity. The hybrid figure oddly resembles the headless figure resulting from the cutting off of a single head which was trying to rise above the body. And it is this function of deconstruction, of destruction of univocity, that is carried out in the decapitated or many-headed figure that, along with Bataille, we will oppose to the Maussian project for recuperating or setting up an unequivocal meaning.[5]

II. An Air of Pure Expenditure

[Then we show[6] how Mauss reduces expenditure to "an air of pure expenditure," that is, to an *effect*. Prestations which are in no wise disinterested are merely "dressed up," as Mauss puts it (p. 147), in a wrapping of generosity. The wrapping is only a social lie, travesty, and external form. It *is added* to the commonplace transmission of goods, to simple barter. The sumptuary moment is not, however, gratuitous. It is a constitutive moment in a model of exchange which seemed, at first view, to be dominated by "real wastage" (*Oeuvres*, III, p. 36), but later turns out to be the model of reciprocity par excellence.]

The society Mauss is describing is a social formation of total prestation in which is inscribed the archaic form of exchange as "the exchange of gifts presented and given back" (p. 227). This system of total prestation in which *everything* is exchanged at every instant—as Mauss sees it we are dealing, in effect, with simple, not agonistic, prestation—is a system of perfect harmony. It knows no accumulation of wealth and power, for we have here a system of "prestations and immediate counter-prestations" where "everything is given back, eventually or even right away, to be immediately redistributed" (p. 213). The rediscovery of systems of total prestation leads to a displacement: if we had the impression that pure expenditure was the archaic moment, which Mauss contrasts with the avarice of present-day societies, henceforth it will be the aspects of total immediacy and reciprocity which appear as the essence of those societies whose practice results from a "primitive contract," "that brings whole groups face to face in communal feasts . . ." (*Oeuvres*, III, p. 34). In this context the idea of pure expenditure now finds its "rightful" place: denounced as a pure effect, in its role as supplement it becomes the integrating factor, the decisive moment for the mechanism of reciprocity. And wherever it might try to go beyond that restricted constitutive function, it will be exposed as a late product of a degeneration of the archaic form of exchange. Such is the case for total prestations of the agonistic type, which are derivative practices, "monstrous products," as Mauss puts it somewhere. For in the case of the potlatch or the kula, specific forms of competitive exchanges, the production of antagonisms seems to endanger the very idea of reciprocity; sumptuary expenditure of considerable wealth seems able to bring about a fall into the original chaos that preceded the primitive contract establishing reciprocity with total prestations.

III. Warm Hoarding

[Here we show most notably how the idea of reciprocity itself is reduced to an effect. By a kind of redefinition of the interest at stake in exchange in archaic societies, "one is interested, but in a way different from that of our times. . . . Interest there is, but that interest is only analogous to the interest which, so it is said, guides us" (p. 271). Interest remains the same as in our societies, but it is pursued by other means which enable everyone to participate in the wealth. The whole difference resides in the fact that in the warm societies which are ours, cool reason is determined by an interest of an accumulative nature, whereas in cool societies a warm reason prescribes a prestative interest and a warm hoarding. Warm reason has for its end the effect of a greater participation of all individuals in the process of the communication and exchange of goods. But since the interests of the donors do not differ fundamentally from what they are in our societies, reciprocity in that economy becomes merely a means of realizing them more perfectly: of acquiring power over one's contemporaries. . . . Reciprocity, which is an effect because it is a means and exterior, is added, like expenditure, to the common practice of the exchange of wealth. The result is the conciliation of antagonisms, which thus remain in a relationship of complementarity.

So the difference between the two types of societies is seen to be reduced to the functioning of these two types of effects (expenditure and reciprocity) which control the primitive economy and lend it an air of homogeneity lacking in ours. Such operations are necessary for Mauss in order to conceptualize the practice initially so foreign to any concept, the ambiguous practice we were talking about at the beginning.]

IV. A Firmly Fixed Figure

Now we will turn our attention to a figure that will reinforce both the similarity and the dissimilarity of archaic societies in comparison with ours. This figure, which in "the incessant circulus" (*Oeuvres*, III, p. 61) of prestations is superimposed like a rule and a purpose on the supplementation accomplished by the effects (expenditure, generosity, and reciprocity), this figure, which is extracted from that incessant motion and which has been successfully fixed, is none other than the circle. Mauss introduces it into his text as a metaphor whose purpose is precisely to arrest the incessant motion, to fix it and make it signify. Thus the figure will be not only the consequence of the motion of supplementation but already, in a much more fundamental manner, what will condition the supplementation itself. Having translated as a circle the specific form of Trobriander exchange, the kula, he says (p. 176):

> And indeed it is *as if* [my emphasis, R.G.] the tribes, the sea journeys,
> the precious things and useful objects, the foods and feastings, the ser-

vices of all sorts, ritual and sexual, the men and women, all were caught in a circle and around that circle kept up a regular movement in both space and time.

All the phenomena in those societies which, in a simple enumeration, appear to be only an accumulation of more or less odd and disparate incidents are controlled by that figure, through which they take on meaning. The metaphor of the circle will give a regularity to the social economy of those peoples, a regularity which, as an incessant circulus, relates everything to everything and turns out to be the very figure of reciprocity.

Let's not forget, however, that modern economy too is described according to the circulus of circulation. Yet the circulation seems to be somehow deficient because a certain privilege of accumulation tends to produce absolute impoverishment. The privilege of accumulation makes closure of the circle of circulation as well as its compensatory action simply impossible. So the interest that an ethnocentric ethnology takes in primitive societies resides in the wish to find in them a still valid model of the compensatory circular movement which has almost completely disappeared from our agonistic societies and vestiges of which, at most, are to be found in the unconsciousness of the masses and obscure practices of our civilization.

By the simple fact that it confers on the circle a peculiarity that will raise the efficacy of the metaphor to its highest pitch, a supplementary determination of the circle appears further to reinforce what we have said thus far. Mauss reports (pp. 165–66) the following fact:

> Indeed, the Eskimos of Asia have invented a sort of mechanism, a wheel decorated with all sorts of provisions, mounted on a kind of Maypole, and topped off with a walrus head. The mast protrudes above the tent of which it forms the center pole. It is maneuvered from inside the tent by means of another wheel and made to turn in the direction of the sun's movement.

Much could be said about that mechanism, but here we want only to single out the fact which Mauss himself observes, namely, the articulation of exchange with nature. Wheel, circle, sun, and exchange appear as superimposed and interchangeable figures: it is evident that the definition of primitive exchange as an incessant circulus is patterned on the motion of the sun. As the metaphor of the sun has always represented the idea of truth in mythology and Western philosophy, it appears then that primitive exchange, which is grafted onto the sun's motion, participates in the truth. Although Mauss never says so explicitly (but that is stereotypical of all his other propositions, such as the immanent implication of the representation of exchange as a circulus), we can say that the exchange whose circulation reproduces the perfect circularity of the solar star must be true exchange, participating in, being none other than, the truth itself; nothing is more logical than to conclude that this figure is the form buried and forgotten by our deficient contemporary economy.

Since, according to their definition as given here, the metaphors of circle, wheel, and sun belong to the set of fundamental metaphors of Western thought, one can presume that their transposition, their effect of metaphorization on ethnographic material which seemed at the outset to be ambiguous by nature, an incessant, elusive movement, on the one hand imposes this rotary motion of the circle/exchange on the ethnographic material and, on the other hand, manages to shape it into a "firmly fixed figure" (p. 194). The immobilization brought about in constant, indeterminant motion by the figure of the circle as an ideal form of that motion, a shaped and reasonable motion, seems therefore to be another figure controlling the attempt to master the originary ambiguity, a moment of the logic of recuperation that will provide Western societies with the means to be able to revolve once again in the light and around the axis centered on the truth that the sun is.

The limitation of exchange to the figure of the circle is, moreover, a means of reducing expenditure. We have already shown how Mauss had rendered expenditure subservient by its incorporation into the movement of supplementation. As a pure effect, being added to ordinary exchanges, it is completing them; as pure expenditure, on the contrary, it rendered the circulus, the return to the initial point, and the compensatory movement impossible. So the figure of the circle is also the means for mastering an expenditure without a return, of reducing it to the function of an effect, and of giving it its "rightful" place in an economy that we will have to call restricted.

All these gestures have for their purpose to dominate exchange itself, otherwise the difference would become too great in relation to ethnological interests, thus rendering any filiation impossible. Still we may well wonder whether the logic of re-appropriation of the ambiguous by the circumscription of transposed metaphors is inevitable.

Relating exchange to the sun need not automatically signify a relation with truth. Bataille's thinking, it so happens, could show us another path to follow, a path which, however, presupposes the radical abolition of the project of recuperation and of the attribution of a reasonable meaning to those indigenous practices. If indeed we conceive the possibility of an irremediable expenditure, with no return, in whose emptiness death would loom, the sun, as a figure of permanent dissolution and waste—it is the sun, according to Bataille, that is the figure of limitless waste, represented, and for good reason, as an acephalic figure—then the relationship between the sun and the practice of exchange takes on a different character. As a figure of the dilapidation of meaning it is grafted onto a practice which, it too, leads to dissolution by its constant rejection of any appropriable wealth, of any determinable meaning. Such metaphorization no longer pursues meaning; like instability itself it only denotes what can have no meaning.

V. The Force in Things

Having specified the circle as the master figure dominating exchange in primitive societies, let's enlarge our catalog of Mauss's figures by another element, by the nature of the thing exchanged. What circulates between donor and *donee* is conceived in such a way as to guarantee the limiting figure of its circular course as well as its infinite repetition. The principal question which from the very first pages inaugurates the whole development of *Essai sur le don* already implies the answer by the nature of its terms. Here is the question: "What force is there in the thing given that causes the *donee* to give it back?" (p. 148). In the unfolding of exchange something enters, then, that maintains a force that not only obliges the *donee* to give back what he has received but to give it back with interest. To put it differently, there participates in the exchange and is an element in the exchange only that which, like the *hau*, wants to come back "to its birthplace" (p. 160). Finally, that alone is an element of exchange which, by its nature, may remain clear and distinct during the whole trajectory of the transaction, that is to say, what can preserve the ineffaceable character of its proprietor. The thing exchanged is brought back to its proprietor at the end of a brief course that can be taken in at a glance; it is used without being used up; to the contrary, it pays off. That force in the thing remains visible throughout its course and is not effaced like the metaphor in a concept or the image on a coin.

"The power that forces gifts to circulate, to be given and given back" (p. 214), the attribute whose effect is that "the thing given is not inert" (p. 161), consists in the fact that the thing is *inhabited* by the power, contains it like a recipient. That is suggested by the many metaphors Mauss uses as well as by the ethnographic material he cites. We refer to pages 218ff. for examples of boxes, houses, baskets, and embellished boxes. Likewise, Mauss determines the *donee* as a *"receptacle"* (in italics in the text); the *donee* becomes a receptacle of the *mana* of the donor upon accepting the gift.[7]

Now let's do a reading of the practice of the gift and exchange in those terms: the donor, who is initially the receptacle of the *mana* proper to him, gives the *donee* an object laden with his *mana*. He separates himself from what is proper to him, his property [*propriété*] or propriety [*propreté*], to transfer it into the receptacle that the *donee* is. There follows the working up and wearing away of the *mana* in that other, who gives it back to the donor in one form or another, whereby the donor regains possession of what is properly his, laden with the fruit of another's labor. So we would have before us here a simple model of an alienation which is not only reconciled after a short, transparent circuit but which in addition has brought back to the initiator some "surplus" value. Isn't that an almost paradisiacal version of the relationship between master and slave, a relationship where the fruit of the labor of the other cannot be appropriated without the loss of the master's substance? Doesn't the insistence on the force inhabiting the things thrust into the circuit of exchange, the force which seems to be the essential of the thing exchanged and of exchange, help to create the illusion that this is not a matter of exploitation or sordid, despicable dealings but of a practice as noble as the reappropriation of one's alienated own [*propre*]? If such is the case, the fascination that this "commerce . . . noble, replete with etiquette and generosity" (p. 202) has for Mauss is easily explained.

The "surplus" value acquired by the donor now confers on him the opposite role of *donee* and he will be obliged to give back the present laden with the *mana* of the other: thus the latter, who at first had the role of slave, becomes, like the donor, a master. Since the participants in the exchange are many, the donor may be reflected in any member of the society whomsoever; he communicates virtually with the entire community, with everything. In the network of the exchange each one is a possible equivalent for every one, with no subordination to anyone whomsoever, who re-appropriates for himself what had been lost. So everything takes place as if the individual donors remained out of the circuit, making it serve only for the constitution of their identity; later, of course, they can let themselves be caught up in it, mimicking the slave's role to guarantee the identification, the self-constitution of the other, who thus manages, he too, to exclude himself from the circle so as to put into it only what cannot be lost.

So the society, the community, appears as the element of the mediation by which individuals, always already outside of that element, put into play their propriety to reappropriate it after a little detour, thus consolidating all the more successfully their exteriority with respect to the community. Consequently, the community appears as merely a pretense, a means of stabilizing their initial position, and not an end in itself. And since this whole memoir on the gift is also intended for the rich and those who hold power in our society, a statement like the following, which concludes the chapter on "Moral Conclusions," takes on a rather cynical meaning:

> Let us adopt as a principle of our lives what has always been and always will be a principle: to come out of ourselves, to give freely and as an obligation: we run no risk of making a mistake. (p. 265)

Are we in the presence here of a shareholders' prospectus which gets around the necessity for the prior universal alienation that Rousseau talked about? Let's remember what Althusser said concerning the social contract:

> for the possibility of exchange to make any sense, initially there must take place that total gift which cannot be the object of any exchange. So Rousseau posits as the a priori condition of any possible exchange that total alienation which cannot be payed for in any exchange. (L. Althusser, "Sur le 'Contrat Social,'" *Cahiers pour l'Analyse*, no. 8, p. 23)

That calls for a comparison with Mauss's statement that the ideal potlatch is the one that would never be given back. Now, for Mauss it is a matter uniquely of an ideal which is added to the common practice of barter. The unconditional gift that cannot be recovered never happens because the donor gives only what he can be absolutely sure of finding again at the end of its course through the circuit of exchange. The originary gift, the founder of absolute reciprocity, is rendered impossible by the fact that the donor remains outside the circulation: he is not a point on the wheel he would be a part of but an immobile point that the wheel merely touches. Thus the gift which, for Mauss, inaugurates each and every exchange circuit never explains why there is a gift: the force in things makes clear only why the gift is given back. The obligation to give, for which Mauss offers no theory, remains in the shadow of an individual decision which could just as well not have been made. For to explain the reasons why the donor gives, to account for that act of which Mauss says that it too is obligatory, would be to show that the donor is already in the game at the start of the game. That is, his prestation is always already a counter-prestation. And since the latter implication is the unthought for Mauss, always present as a necessity for thinking and always occulted anew, we are led once again to the realization that exchange, as Mauss thinks of it, is only a particular, restricted form of a generalized exchange in which there would be neither inside nor outside. This exchange would be anterior *de facto* and *de jure* to the logic of the gift, of the thing received (gift + force) and the thing given back (gift + force + surplus). The terms thus designated would constitute only a restricted circuit, circular par excellence, one of whose terms is posited as originary, a parody of the universal alienation of which Rousseau was speaking, because it effaces its obligatory character, its inscription in the game that has always already begun and which makes of it simply the trace of an anterior exchange. Always already a counter-prestation.

And if exchange is a process of supplementation for an initial lack, for something which has been lost, as has already been noted several times (notably by Goux), it seems to us that such an exchange constitutes the restricted form we have just described. Indeed, any exchange becomes possible for Mauss only through the project of a recuperation of an alienated self by an ego who conceives himself, however, as out of the circle and, by that very conceit, as an irreducible plenitude, as much an imposture as the object thrust into the circuit, which is merely the substitute for his self [*propre*]. This primary exchange of what would have been lost opens and limits the exchange. The alienation of self is fictive, since the ego that enters into the exchange believes himself to be outside with respect to the exchange, believes himself to be an irreducible plenitude by virtue of the occultation of the originary alienation, which causes him to be always already caught up in the exchange and which is added to the alienation as a repetition of the originary loss, a repetition that procures the illusion of a recuperable, conditional loss. And as we have seen that the restricted exchange is practiced only for prestige and the acquisition of "surplus," we can deduce that the exchange, and the fictive alienation that starts it, is essentially the logic of the production of property. The fantasm of the self would be the condition for it.

The fiction of the self would be, at this level, the general standard that makes equivalents possible, a standard, however, that would still not have the abstract character of the value form of money but which is still rich in its effigy, in the imprint of the ego. Thus the objects thrust into the exchange, loaded with the force of the donor's *mana,* will come back to him obligatorily: no loss will be possible. We might well compare the process with the oral phase of incorporation as Freud described it: certain metaphors that Mauss uses make the comparison possible, such as the translation of potlatch as food, the expression that in the potlatch one group eats another. . . .

> "Just as no commodity can make the form of its own value out of its natural form" but must "necessarily take for its equivalent another commodity whose use value thus serves as its value form" [Marx], likewise any form and any formation of the ego can only pass through "an erotic relationship in which the (human) individual affixes himself to an image which alienates him."[8]

Thus each individual wanting to form an ego, his difference with respect to another, must abandon himself to the other in the gesture of giving, so that what he gave up may, in the final reckoning, be given back to him. The gift seems to be an expression of that endeavor, or rather of the preservation of the plenitude of an original, fictive, disengaged ego, which, through the cleavage of society into antagonistic classes, has been made impossible and whose return Mauss is dreaming of in what he thinks to be reciprocity.

VI. The Transfer of the Boxes

Trying to sketch out the way one might treat "the complete theory of these three obligations (to give back, to receive, to give), of these three themes of the same complexus" (p. 161), Mauss tells us that "this tight blending . . . ceases to appear contradictory if we realize that it is first and foremost a blending of spiritual bonds between things which pertain to some degree to the soul and the individuals and groups which, to some degree, treat one another as things" (p. 163). And he goes on to say: "Everything comes and goes as if there were a constant exchange of a spiritual matter . . ." (p. 164).

Mauss saw clearly, and therein consists the originality of his analysis, that this exchange cannot be understood on the empirical level, for example, as a simple bartering, as a common practice of accumulation. Not only do three forms of practices which in our society are clearly distinguished—to give back, to give, and to receive—"lose even any meaning" (Mallarmé), but also what is exchanged and the exchangers themselves have no univocal status: they are sometimes a thing, sometimes a soul. Since what the ethnologist observes has no meaning on the empirical, immanent level, he draws the conclusion—thus practicing the opposition between soul and thing, terms pertaining to Western culture and whose nonpertinence he had, however, realized—that because it is not a matter of a material exchange for material purposes, there must be a spiritual purpose. The *since* of the sentence betrays the transposition of a metaphor, a moment of the process of "Sinn-gebung," applied to a material that turns up as equivocal.

That conclusion of the ethnologist is also at the basis of his theory of ensoulment, which underlies the idea of the force in things. From the fact that indigenous thought goes about naming everything around it and that all things seem to be actors on the vast stage of a theater, Mauss deduces that they are quickened by supernatural powers. "Everything speaks, the roof, the fire, carvings, paintings" (p. 120); he draws the conclusion that "things are confounded with the spirits who made them . . ." etc. (p. 221).

His conclusion, consistent with the ideas of his time, seems to us, however, to manifest a lack of comprehension of the nature of savage thought [*pensée sauvage*]. Since Lévi-Strauss, at least, we know that for savage thought naming means fitting into a relationship, into a system, defining by opposition to. . . . The names that savage thought applies that way to the things designated are merely simple distinctive features, means to distinguish among them, and they are in nowise names that would bespeak the essence of the things, their inherent force, for example, as Western thought has always conceived names. So now a different reading of the ethnographic material gathered by Mauss becomes possible, a reading for which we will provide some guideposts for what has concerned us up to this point.

If the name or the attributes of a thing are merely differential markers, then the self-proclaimed individual character, the soil from which the object thrust into the circuit is torn, is also just a distinctive feature of that object and in no way an essence of the thing, a hidden force. And if that distinctive marker is nothing more and nothing less than a differential feature of the thing, the thing can no longer serve as a means of explanation for exchange. And the guarantee that the object will come back to its point of origin is also effaced. The nature of the sign, "a sign of wealth," said Mauss, is thereby profoundly altered, since henceforth the relationship between signifier and signified, or as Mauss said, the object/force of the thing, is no longer a relationship of representation. The object thrust into the course no longer carries with it any signifying content, (the essence of the master), the thing is nothing other than the sum of its features or, says Mauss, a "bond": "The thing itself, given and engaged in the pledge, is, by its own power, a bond" (p. 253). A bond, not between a force and a thing or between a plenary donor outside the cycle of exchange and his partner; for, as we have noted, that plenitude is only an appearance, the donor being always already caught up in the network of the exchange, so that he himself is only a bundle of traces, a bond, comparable to the signs exchanged.

Now, taking into account those presuppositions, let's reconsider exchange itself, the circulation of goods, as well as the production of propriety and property. According to Mauss, exchange is the transfer of goods in a broad sense of the word. The word *tonga* connotes "everything that is property properly so-called," and which, then, can be exchanged. Conversely, everything that is exchanged must, by its nature, be property. In order to be able to enter into the circuit of the circulation, that property must be torn from its native ground (a person, a clan, etc.). Because of that founding act the object is rich with the soul of its proprietor, which it carries with it and which inaugurates the circulation; with that object there takes place the first substitution and consequently the production of equivalents. The thing that comes back to its proprietor at the end of the circuit is no longer the same; it is laden with the interest it collected. So much for the logic of the propriety and property such as Mauss has used it. But we have seen that the inaugural act by an outside ego was only an imposture: the donor is always already a *donee*. Thus, the fixed point of departure to which one could return does not exist, and with it collapses the possibility of thinking something such as originary propriety or property.

If there is no absolute beginning, what then are the objects exchanged and what goes on during exchange? If there is valorization, what does the surplus that the signs take on signify? To answer that, let's look at Mauss's revealing statement about the value of what he believes to be one of the first forms of money:

> It is still true that those values are unstable and lack the characteristic necessary for a standard, a measure: for example, their price increases and decreases with the number and magnitude of the transactions in which they have been used. Mr. Malinowski compares very nicely the *vaygu'a* of the Trobrianders acquiring prestige in the course of their sea journeys with the crown jewels. Similarly, the emblazoned coppers of the northwestern American and the mats of Samoa increase in value with each potlatch, each exchange. (p. 178)

If the thing exchanged, at first bearing only the feature of its origin, gets richer in the course of its journey, it will only be by enlarging its wrapper, which hides nothing, with auxiliary features, signifiers it acquires in the course of its passage, like the traces left on the wrapper by the hands through which the thing has passed. This sign represents and conveys only itself; it tells only the redoubling of its bonds, the acquisition or loss of its features. What it signifies, if that word still has a meaning here, is only itself, its nature as a signifier, its own transferability.

Let's remember that among the objects exchanged there also figure those which, as we know from Lévi-Strauss, serve explicitly for distinguishing among groups and persons, that is, blazons and, especially, totems. "In the course of the life of individuals and clans there is a commerce in blazons that finds expression in the *potlatch*. . . . One loses his blazon in the *potlatch*; one loses it in war too," writes Mauss in a text of 1910; and a little further on he speaks of the circulation of totems "from clan to clan" as an object of exchange or a gift (*Oeuvres*, III, pp. 80–82). For Mauss, who thinks those names must be of religious nature because they would represent ancestors, such exchange could only have become possible by the effacement of their religious character. But if we consider primitive thought, as well as its practices, as a differential activity that confers identity through distinctive features, an identity thus essentially unstable by the very nature of the signifier, nothing is more "natural" than that such an identity may be exchanged, then, for another in the constant process of coming and going. For if the distinctive feature bespeaks only its transfer, it is only by the incessant production of traces, by a continual dismemberment of the differential network, by an ever-new transposition, that it becomes manifest. This activity, boundless but always going beyond the bounds, having neither a center nor an exterior, I will henceforth call exchange, or again, generalized exchange.

It is clear that this practice cannot be grasped by any of the traditional notions: it is an empty practice. And terms like property and propriety cannot account for this activity unless, as Mauss does, one attempts to fix the incessant motion in a figure which is itself firmly fixed, a master and mastering figure, the closed circuit, the circle. Only then does the activity make sense, no longer going around and around unloaded; and what circulates is ensouled.

We have seen, however, that what the signs in exchange, the products of a transfer, carry is only their own transferential power: metaphoric in the broadest sense of the word, they say nothing except their metaphoricity; they redouble, ad infinitum. That permits us to say that savage thought too is an empire of signs if "it is understood that these signs are empty and that the ritual is without a god," as Roland Barthes puts it (*L'Empire des signes*, p. 145).†† And what he says about Japanese packages we can also apply to those miraculous boxes, the objects of transfer par excellence, of which Mauss had said that there "can be boxes within boxes, a great number of them nested within one another (Haida)" (p. 218).[9]

First published in *L'Arc* 48, 1972.
Translated by Morris Parslow for this volume.

Notes

1. The theory of exchange sketched out by Mauss discovers a buried floor, the "human rocks on which our societies are built": it reaches "conclusions that are in a sense archeological about the nature of human transactions in the societies that surround us or have immediately preceded us" (*Essai sur le don*, p. 148). The gesture of this archeological research which consists of discovering under different layers a forgotten identity, the meaning and very reason of any ulterior development and of any departure from the norm that it represents, Mauss is already putting it to work in the subtitle of *Essai sur le don*. It is a question here of the form and reason of exchange in archaic societies: all of which makes us think that the structure of exchange that Mauss will propose to us as an unyielding block will be an exchange ship-shape and boarded for inspection: which will already be obedient to a certain number of formal rules, especially to a reason: it will be an exchange which will pur-

sue a goal and will have a precise meaning. Thus the archeology will be the accomplice of a certain eschatology.

2. In M. Mauss, *Sociologie et anthropologie*, Paris: Presses Universitaires de France, 1950.

3. For the most part shifted to the bottom of the page as an apparatus of notes so as not to burden the text and perhaps too so as not to pile up obstacles to the progress of thought ("The notes and everything not in big print are indispensable only to specialists," p. 149, note 2), a gesture that gives us pause.

4. Paris, 1967.

* *ED* = *Essai sur le don. ME* = *Manuel d'ethnographie*.

† EN: Paris: Les Éditions de Minuit, 1969. Mauss's essay is translated above, pp. 28–32.

5. See my article on Georges Bataille in number 44 of *L'Arc*.

6. I have bracketed in the next two [sections] passages that I have condensed.

7. In a similar vein, we would need to think about the feminine connotation of the goods exchanged in Samoa, a connotation which may not be explained just by the fact that women are the objects of exchange par excellence but also by the fact that they are inhabited by a new being during their pregnancy. The translation of *hau* as a force impregnating things exchanged, as a spirit, a breath, etc., would deserve reconsideration from this point of view.

8. Jean-Joseph Goux, "Numismatiques I," *Tel Quel*, 35, p. 68. [EN: Cf. Jean-Joseph Goux, *Symbolic Economies: After Marx and Freud*, trans. Jennifer Curtiss Gage (Ithaca: Cornell University Press, 1990), p. 14. The first quotes attributed to Karl Marx come from "The equivalent form of value," chap. I, sec. 3.A3 of *Capital*, vol. 1. The final quote, unattributed by Goux, appears to come from Lacan.]

†† EN: Geneva: Editions d'Art Albert Skira, S.A., 1970. (*L'Arc* incorrectly lists p. 148.) English translation: *The Empire of Signs*, trans. Richard Howard (New York: Hill and Wang, 1982), p. 108.

9. This text was part of a presentation given in 1969–70 at L'Ecole Normale Supérieure in the seminar conducted by J. Derrida, whom I would like to thank here.

Part Three

◨

FRENCH RE-APPRAISALS

The Time of the King

Jacques Derrida

Epigraph
  The King takes all my time; I give the rest to Saint-Cyr, to whom I would like to give all.

It is a woman who signs.

For this is a letter, and from a woman to a woman. Madame de Maintenon is writing to Madame Brinon. This woman says, in effect, that to the King she gives all. For in giving all one's time, one gives all or the all, if all one gives is in time and one gives all one's time.

It is true that she who is known to have been the influential mistress and even the morganatic wife of the Sun King[1] (the Sun and the King, the Sun-King will be the subjects of these lectures), Madame de Maintenon, then, did not say, in her letter, literally, that she was *giving* all her time but rather that the King *was taking* it from her ("the King takes all my time"). Even if, in her mind, that means the same thing, one word does not equal the other. What she *gives*, for her part, is not time but the *rest*, the rest of the time: "I give the rest to Saint-Cyr, to whom I would like to give all." But as the King *takes* it all from her, then the rest, by all good logic and good economics, is nothing. She can no longer *take* her time. She has none left, and yet she gives it. Lacan says of love: It gives what it does not have, a formula whose variations are ordered by the *Ecrits* according to the final and transcendental modality of the woman inasmuch as she is, supposedly, deprived of the phallus.[2]

Here Madame de Maintenon is *writing*, and she says *in writing*, that she gives the rest. What is the rest? *Is* it, the rest? She gives the rest which is nothing, since it is the rest of a time concerning which she has just informed her correspondent she has nothing of it left since the King takes it all from her. And yet, we must underscore this paradox, even though the King takes all *her* time, she seems to have some left, as if she could return the change. "The King takes all *my* time," she says, a time that belongs to her therefore. But how can a time belong? What is it *to have time*? If a time belongs, it is because the word *time* designates metonymically less time itself than the things with which one fills it, with which one fills the form of time, time *as form*. It is a matter, then, of the things one does *in the meantime* [cependant] or the things one has at one's disposal *during* [pendant] this time. Therefore, as time does not belong to anyone as such, one can no more *take* it, itself, than *give* it. Time already begins to appear as that which undoes this distinction between taking and giving, therefore also between receiving and giving, perhaps between receptivity and activity, or even between being-affected and the affecting of any affection. Apparently and according to common logic or economics, one can only exchange, one can only take or give, by way of metonymy, what is *in* time. That is indeed what Madame de Maintenon seems to *want to say* on a certain surface of her letter. And yet, even though the King takes it all from her, altogether, this time or whatever fills up the time, she has some left, a remainder that is not nothing since it is

121

beyond everything, a remainder that is nothing but that *there is* since she *gives it*. And it is even essentially what she gives, *that very thing*. The King takes all, she gives the rest. The rest is not, there is the rest that is given or that gives itself. It does not give itself to someone, because, as everyone knows, Saint-Cyr is not her lover, and it is above all not masculine. Saint-Cyr is a—very feminine—place, a charity, an institution, more exactly a *foundation* of Madame de Maintenon's. Saint-Cyr is the name of a charitable institution for the education of impoverished young ladies of good families. Its founder retired there and no doubt was able to devote all her time to it, in accordance with her declared wish, after *the death of the King* in 1715. Would we say, then, that the question of the rest, and of the rest of given time, is secretly linked to a death of the king?

Thus the rest, which *is* nothing but which *there is* nevertheless, does not give itself to someone but to a foundation of young virgins. *And it never gives itself enough, the rest:* "I give the rest to Saint-Cyr, to whom I would like to give all." She never gets enough of giving this rest that she does not have. And when she writes, Madame de Maintenon, that she would like to give all, one must pay attention to the *literal* writing of her *letter, to the letter of her letter*. This letter is almost untranslatable; it defies exchange from language to language. Let us underscore the fact that we are dealing with a letter since things would not be said in the same way in a different context. So when she writes that she would like to give *all* [*elle voudrait* le tout *donner*], she allows two equivocations to be installed: *le* can be a personal pronoun (in an inverted position: *je voudrais tout le donner*, I would like to give it all, that is, all of it) or it can be an *article* (before the word *tout*, which is thus nominalized: I would like to give *all*, that is, everything). That would be the first equivocation. The second equivocation: *tout* or *le tout* can be understood to refer to *time* (all of which the King takes from her) as well as to the *rest* of time: of the time and of what presents itself there, occupying it thus, or of the rest and of what presents itself there, likewise occupying it. This phrase lets one hear the infinite sigh of unsatisfied desire. Madame de Maintenon says to her correspondent that everything leaves her something to be desired. Her wish is not fulfilled or attained either by what she allows herself to take from the King nor even by the rest that she gives—in order to *make a present* of it, if you will, to her young virgins.

Her desire would be there where she *would like*, in the conditional, to give what she cannot give, the all, that rest of the rest of which she cannot make a present. Nobody takes it all from her, neither the King nor Saint-Cyr. This rest of the rest of time of which she cannot make a present, that is what Madame de Maintenant (as one might call her) desires, that is in truth what she would desire, not for herself but so as to be able to give it [*pour le pouvoir donner*]—for the power of giving [*pour le pouvoir de donner*], perhaps, so as to give herself this power of giving. She lacks not lacking time, she lacks not giving enough. She lacks this leftover time that is left to her and that she cannot give—that she doesn't know what to do with. But this rest of the rest of time, of a time that moreover is nothing and that belongs properly to no one, this rest of the rest of time, that is the whole of her desire. Desire and the desire to give would be the same thing, a sort of tautology. But maybe as well the tautological designation of the impossible. Maybe the impossible. The impossible may be—if giving and taking are also the same—the same, the same thing, which would certainly not be a thing.

One could accuse me here of making a big deal and a whole *history* out of words and gestures that remain very clear. When Madame de Maintenon says that the

King takes her time, it is because she is glad to give it to him and takes pleasure from it: the King takes nothing from her and gives as much as he takes. And when she says "I give the rest to Saint-Cyr, to whom I would like to give all," she opens herself up to her correspondent about a *daily* economy concerning the leisures and charities, the works and days of a "grande dame" somewhat overwhelmed by her obligations. None of the words she writes has the sense of the unthinkable and the impossible toward which my reading would have pulled them, in the direction of giving-taking, of time and the rest. She did not mean to say that, you will say.

What if . . . yes she did [*Et si*].

And if [*Et si*] what she wrote meant to say that, then what would that have to suppose? How, where, on the basis of what and when can we read this letter fragment as I have done? How could we even divert it as I have done, while still respecting its literality and its language?

Let us begin by the impossible.

To join together, in a title, time and the gift may seem to be a laborious artifice. What can time have to do with the gift? We mean: what would there be to see in that? What would they have to do with each other, or more literally, to see together, *qu'est-ce qu'ils auraient à voir ensemble*, one would say in French. Of course, they have nothing to *see* together and first of all because both of them have a singular relation to the visible. Time, in any case, gives nothing to see. It is at the very least the element of invisibility itself. It withdraws whatever could give itself to be seen. It itself withdraws itself from visibility. One can only be blind to time, to the essential *disappearance* of time even as, nevertheless, in a certain manner nothing *appears* that does not require and take time. Nothing sees the light of day, no phenomenon, that is not on the measure of day, in other words, of the *revolution* that is the rhythm of a sun's course. And that orients this course from its endpoint: from the rising in the east to the setting in the west. The works and days, as we said a moment ago.

We will let ourselves be carried away by this word *revolution*. At stake is a certain *circle* whose figure precipitates both time and the gift toward the possibility of their impossibility.

To join together, in a title, at once time and the gift may seem to be a laborious artifice, as if, for the sake of economy, one sought to treat two subjects at once. And that is in fact the case, for reasons of economy. But economy is here the subject. What is economy? Among its irreducible predicates or semantic values, economy no doubt includes the values of law (*nomos*) and of home (*oikos*, home, property, family, the hearth, the fire indoors). *Nomos* does not only signify the law in general, but also the law of distribution (*nemein*), the law of sharing or partition [*partage*], the law as partition (*moira*), the given or assigned part, participation. Another sort of tautology already implies the economic within the nomic as such. As soon as there is law, there is partition: as soon as there is *nomy*, there is economy. Besides the values of law and home, of distribution and partition, economy implies the idea of exchange, of circulation, of return. The figure of the circle is obviously *at the center*, if that can still be said of a circle. It stands at the center of any problematic of *oikonomia*, as it does of any economic field: circular exchange, circulation of goods, products, monetary signs or merchandise, amortization of expenditures, revenues, substitution of use values and exchange values. This motif of circulation can lead one to think that the law of economy is the—circular—return to the point of departure, to the origin, also to the home. So one would have to follow the *odyssean* structure of the economic narrative. *Oikonomia* would always follow the path of Ulysses. The latter returns to the side of his loved ones or to himself, he goes away in view of *repatriating* himself, in order to return to the home from which [*à partir duquel*] the signal for departure is given and the part assigned, the side chosen [*le parti pris*], the lot divided, destiny commanded (*moira*). The being-next-to-self of the Idea in Absolute Knowledge would be odyssean in this sense, that of an *economy* and a *nostalgia*, a "homesickness," a provisional exile longing for reappropriation.

Now the gift, *if there is any*, would no doubt be related to economy. One cannot treat the gift, this goes without saying, without treating this relation to economy, even to the money economy. But is not the gift, if there is any, also that which interrupts economy? That which, in suspending economic calculation, no longer gives rise to exchange? That which opens the circle so as to defy reciprocity or symmetry, the common measure, and so as to turn aside the return in view of the no-return? If there is gift, the *given* of the gift (*that which* one gives, *that which* is given, the gift as given thing or as act of donation) must not come back to the giving (let us not already say to the subject, to the donor). It must not circulate, it must not be exchanged, it must not in any case be exhausted, as a gift, by the process of exchange, by the movement of circulation of the circle in the form of return to the point of departure. If the figure of the circle is essential to economics, the gift must remain *aneconomic*. Not that it remains foreign to the circle, but it must *keep* a relation of foreignness to the circle, a relation without relation of familiar foreignness. It is perhaps in this sense that the gift is the impossible.

Not impossible but *the* impossible. The very figure of the impossible. It announces itself, gives itself to be thought as the impossible. It is proposed that we begin by this.

And we will do so. We will begin later. By the impossible.

The motif of the circle will obsess us throughout this cycle of lectures. Let us provisionally set aside the question of whether we are talking about a geometric figure, a metaphorical representation, or a great symbol, the symbol of the symbolic itself. We have learned from Hegel to treat this problem. Saying that the circle will obsess us is another manner of saying that it will encircle us. It will besiege us all the while that we will be regularly attempting to exit [la sortie]. But why exactly would one desire, along with the gift, if there is any, the exit? Why desire the gift and why desire to interrupt the circulation of the circle? Why wish to get out of it [en sortir]? Why wish to get through it [s'en sortir]?

The circle has already put us onto the trail of time and of that which, by way of the circle, circulates between the gift and time. One of the most powerful and ineluctable representations, at least in the history of metaphysics, is the representation of time as a circle. Time would always be a process or a movement in the form of the circle or the sphere. Of this privilege of circular movement in the representation of time, let us take only one index for the moment. It is a note by Heidegger, the last and the longest one in *Sein und Zeit*. Some time ago I attempted a reading of it in "*Ousia* and *Grammē*: Note on a Note from *Being and Time*."[3] Since this Note and this Note on a note will be part of our premises, it will help to recall at least the part concerning the absolute insistence of this figure of the circle in the metaphysical interpretation of time. Heidegger writes:

> The priority which Hegel has given to the "now" which has been leveled off, makes it plain that in defining the concept of time he is under the sway of the manner in which time is *ordinarily* understood; and this means that he is likewise under the sway of the traditional conception of it. It can even be shown that his conception of time has been drawn *directly* from the "physics" of Aristotle. [. . .] Aristotle sees the essence of time in the *nun*, Hegel in the "now" [*jetzt*]. Aristotle takes the *nun* as *oros*; Hegel takes the "now" as "boundary" [*Grenze*]. Aristotle understands the *nun* as *stigmē*; Hegel interprets the "now" as a point. Aristotle describes the *nun* as *tode ti*; Hegel calls the "now" the "absolute this" [*das "absolute Dieses"*]. Aristotle follows tradition in connecting *khronos* with *sphaira*, Hegel stresses the "circular course" [*Kreislauf*] of time. [. . .] In suggesting a direct connection between Hegel's conception of time and Aristotle's analysis, we are not accusing Hegel of any "dependence" on Aristotle, but are calling attention to the *ontological import which this filiation has in principle* for the *Hegelian logic*.[4]

There would be more to say on the figure of the circle in Heidegger. His treatment is not simple. It also implies a certain affirmation of the circle, which is assumed. One should not necessarily flee or condemn circularity as one would a bad repetition, a vicious circle, a regressive or sterile process. One must, in a *certain way* of course, inhabit the circle, turn around in it, live there a feast of thinking, and the gift, the gift of thinking, would be no stranger there. That is what *Der Ursprung des Kunstwerks* (*The Origin of the Work of Art*) suggests. But this motif, which is not a stranger to the motif of the hermeneutic circle either, coexists with what we might call a delimitation of the circle: the latter is but a particular figure, the "particular case" of a structure of *nodal* coiling up or interlacing that Heidegger names the *Geflecht* in *Unterwegs zur Sprache* (*On the Way to Language*).

If one were to stop here with this first somewhat simplifying representation or with these hastily formulated premises, what could one already say? That wherever there is time, wherever time predominates or conditions experience in general, wherever *time as circle* (a "vulgar" concept, Heidegger would therefore say) is predominant, the gift is impossible. A gift could be possible, there could be a gift only at the instant an effraction in the circle will have taken place, at the instant all circulation will have been interrupted and *on the condition* of this instant. What is more, this instant of effraction (of the temporal circle) must no longer be part of time. That is why we said "on the condition of this instant." This condition concerns time but does not *belong* to it, does not pertain to it without being, for all that, more logical than chronological. There would be a gift only at the instant when the *paradoxical* instant (in the sense in which Kierkegaard says of the paradoxical instant of decision that it is madness) tears time apart. In this sense one would never have the time of a gift. In any case, time, the "present" of the gift, is no longer thinkable as a now, that is, as a present bound up in the temporal synthesis.

The relation of the gift to the "present," in all the senses of this term, also to the presence of the present, will form one of the essential knots in the interlace of this discourse, in its *Geflecht*, in the knot of that *Geflecht* of which Heidegger says precisely that the circle is perhaps only one figure or a particular case, an inscribed possibility. That a gift is called a present, that "to give" may also be said "to make a present," "to give a present" (in French as well as in English, for example), this will not be for us just a verbal clue, a linguistic chance or *aléa*.

We said a moment ago: "Let us begin by the impossible." By the impossible, what ought one to have understood?

If we are going to speak of it, we will have to name something. Not to present the thing, here the impossible, but to try with its name, or with some name, to give an understanding of or to think this impossible thing, this impossible itself. To say we are going to "name" is perhaps already or still to say too much. For it is perhaps the name of name that is going to find itself put in question. If, for example, the gift were impossible, the name or noun "gift," what the linguist or the grammarian believes he recognizes to be a name, would not be a name. At least, it would not name what one thinks it names, to wit, the unity of a meaning that would be that of the gift. Unless the gift were the impossible but not the unnameable or the unthinkable, and unless in this gap between the impossible and the thinkable a dimension opens up where *there is* gift—and even where *there is* period, for example time, where *it gives* being and time (*es gibt das Sein* or *es gibt die Zeit*, to say it in a way that anticipates excessively what would be precisely a certain essential excess of the gift, indeed an excess of the gift over the essence itself).

Why and how *can I think that the gift is the impossible?* And why is it here a matter precisely of *thinking*, as if thinking, the word *thinking*, found its fit only in this disproportion of the impossible, even announcing itself—as thought irreducible to intuition, irreducible also to perception, judgment, experience, science, faith—only on the basis of *this* figure of the impossible, on the basis of the impossible *in the figure of the gift?*

Let us suppose that someone wants or desires to give to someone. In our logic and our language we say it thus: someone wants or desires, someone *intends-to-give* something to someone. Already the complexity of the formula appears formidable. It supposes a subject and a verb, a constituted subject, which can also be collective—for example, a group, a community, a nation, a clan, a tribe—in any case, a subject identical to itself and conscious of its identity, indeed seeking through the gesture of the gift to constitute its own unity and, precisely, to get its own identity recognized so that that identity comes back to it, so that it can reappropriate its identity: as its property.

Let us suppose, then, an intention-to-give: Some "one" wants or desires to give. Our common language or logic will cause us to hear the interlace of this already complex formula as incomplete. We would tend to complete it by saying "some 'one'" (A) intends-to-give B to C, some "one" intends to give or gives "something" to "someone other." This "something" may not be a thing in the common sense of the word but rather a symbolic object; and like the donor, the donee may be a collective subject; but in any case A gives B to C. These three elements, identical to themselves or on the way to an identification with themselves, look like what is presupposed by every gift event. For the gift to be possible, for there to be gift event, according to our common language and logic, it seems that this compound structure is indispensable. Notice that in order to say this, I must already suppose a certain precomprehension of what *gift* means. I suppose that I know and that you know what "to give," "gift," "donor," "donee" mean in our common language. As well as "to want," "to desire," "to intend." This is an unsigned but effective contract between us, indispensable to what is happening here, namely, that you accord, lend, or give some attention and some meaning to what I myself am doing by giving, for example, a lecture. This whole presupposition will remain indispensable at least for the *credit* that we accord each other, the faith or good faith that we lend each other, even if in a little while we were to argue and disagree about everything. It is by making this precomprehension (credit or faith) explicit that one can authorize oneself to state the following axiom: In order for there to be gift, gift event, some "one" has to give some "thing" to someone other, without which "giving" would be meaningless. In other words, if giving indeed means what, in speaking of it among ourselves, we think it means, then it is necessary, in a certain situation, that some "one" give some "thing" to some "one other," and so forth. This appears tautological, it goes without saying, and seems to imply the defined term in the definition, which is to say it defines nothing at all. Unless the discreet introduction of "one" and of "thing" and especially of "other" ("someone other") does not portend some disturbance in the tautology of a gift that cannot be satisfied with giving or with giving (to) *itself* [se *donner*] without giving something (other) to someone (other).

For this is the impossible that seems to give itself to be thought here: these conditions of possibility of the gift (that some "one" gives some "thing" to some "one other") designate simultaneously the conditions of the impossibility of the gift. And already we could translate this in other terms: these conditions of possibility define or produce the annulment, the annihilation, the destruction of the gift.

Once again, let us set out in fact from what is the simplest level and let us still entrust ourselves to this semantic precomprehension of the word "gift" in our language or in a few familiar languages. For there to be a gift, there must be no reciprocity, return, exchange, countergift, or debt. If the other *gives* me *back* or *owes* me or has to give me back what I give him or her, there will not have been a gift, whether this restitution is immediate or whether it is programmed by a complex calculation of a long-term deferral or differance. This is all too obvious if the other, the donee, gives me back *immediately* the same thing. It may, moreover, be a matter of a good thing or a bad thing. Here we are anticipating another dimension of the problem, namely, that if giving is spontaneously evaluated as *good* (it is *well* and *good* to give and what one gives, the present, the *cadeau*, the gift, is a good), it remains the case that this "good" can easily be reversed. We know that as good, it can also be bad, poisonous (*Gift, gift*), and this from the moment the gift puts the other in debt, with the result that giving comes down to hurting, to doing harm; here one need hardly mention the fact that in certain languages, for example in French, one may say as readily "to give a gift" as "to give a blow" [*donner un coup*], "to give life" [*donner la vie*] as "to give death" [*donner la mort*], thereby either dissociating and opposing them or identifying them. So we were saying that, quite obviously, if the donee gives back the same thing, for example an invitation to lunch (and the example of food or of what are called consumer goods will never be just one example among others), the gift is annulled. It is annulled each time there is restitution or countergift. Each time, according to the same circular ring that leads to "giving back" [*"rendre"*], there is payment and discharge of a debt. In this logic of the debt, the circulation of a good or of goods is not only the circulation of the "things" that we will have offered to each other, but even of the values or the symbols that are involved there [*qui s'y engagent*][5] and the intentions to give, whether they are conscious or unconscious. Even though all the anthropologies, indeed the metaphysics of the gift have, *quite rightly and justifiably*, treated *together*, as a system, the gift and the debt, the gift and the cycle of restitution, the gift and the loan, the gift and credit, the gift and the countergift, we are here *departing*, in a peremptory and distinct fashion, from this tradition. That is to say, from tradition itself. We will take our point of departure in the dissociation, in the overwhelming evidence of this other axiom: There is gift, if there is any, only in what interrupts the system as well as the symbol, in a partition without return and without division [*répartition*], without being-with-self of the gift-counter-gift.

For there to be a gift, *it is necessary* [*il faut*] that the donee not give back, amortize, reimburse, acquit himself, enter into a contract, and that he never have contracted a debt. (This "it is necessary" is already the mark of a duty, of a debt owed, of the duty-not-to [*le devoir de-ne-pas*]: The donee owes it *to himself* even not to give back; he *ought* not *owe* [*il a le devoir de ne pas* devoir], and the donor ought not count on restitution.) It is thus necessary, at the limit, that he not *recognize* the gift as gift. If he recognizes it *as* gift, if the gift *appears to him as such*, if the present is present to him *as present*, this simple recognition suffices to annul the gift. Why? Because it gives back, in the place, let us say, of the thing itself, a symbolic equivalent. Here one cannot even say that the symbolic *re*-constitutes the exchange and annuls the gift in the debt. It does not re-constitute an exchange, which, because it no longer takes place as exchange of things or goods, would be transfigured into a symbolic exchange. The symbolic opens and constitutes the order of exchange and of debt, the law or the order of circulation in which the gift gets annulled. It suffices therefore for the other to *perceive the gift*—not only to perceive it in the sense in which, as one says in French, "on *perçoit*," one receives, for example, merchandise, payment, or compensation—but to perceive its nature of gift, the meaning or intention, the *intentional meaning* of the gift, in order for this simple *recognition* of the gift *as* gift, *as such*, to annul the gift as gift even before *recognition* becomes *gratitude*. The simple identification of the gift seems to destroy it. The simple identification of the passage of a gift as such, that is, of an identifiable thing among some identifiable "ones," would be nothing other than the process of the destruction of the gift. It is as if, between the event or the institution of the gift *as such* and its destruction, the difference were destined to be constantly annulled. *At the limit, the gift as gift* ought *not appear as gift: either to the donee or to the donor.* It cannot be gift as gift except by not being present as gift. Neither to the "one" nor to the "other." If the other perceives or receives it, if he or she keeps it as gift, the gift is annulled. But the one who gives it must not see it or know it either; otherwise he begins, at the threshold, as soon as he intends to give, to pay himself with a symbolic recognition, to praise himself, to approve of himself, to gratify himself, to congratulate himself, to give back to himself symbolically the value of what he thinks he has given or of what he is preparing to give. The temporalization of time (memory, present, anticipation; retention, protention, imminence of the future; "ecstases," and so forth) always sets in motion the process of a destruction of the gift: through keeping, restitution, reproduction, the anticipatory expectation or apprehension that grasps or comprehends in advance.

In all these cases, the gift can certainly keep its phenomenality or, if one prefers, its appearance as gift. But its very appearance, the simple phenomenon of the gift annuls it as gift, transforming the apparition into a phantom and the operation into a simulacrum. It suffices that the other perceive and *keep*, not even the object of the gift, the object given, the thing, but the meaning or the quality, the gift property of the gift, its intentional meaning, for the gift to be annulled. We expressly say: It suffices that the gift *keep* its phenomenality. But *keeping* begins by *taking*. As soon as the other accepts, as soon as he or she takes, there is no more gift. For this destruction to occur, it suffices that the movement of acceptance (of prehension, of reception) last a little, however little that may be, more than an instant, an instant already caught up in the temporalizing synthesis, in the *syn* or the *cum* or the being-with-self of time. There is no more gift as soon as the other *receives*—and even if she refuses the gift that she has perceived or recognized as gift. As soon as she keeps for the gift the signification of gift, she loses it, there is no more *gift*. Consequently, if there is no gift, there is no gift, but if there is gift held or beheld *as* gift by the other, once again there is no gift; in any case the gift does not *exist* and does not *present* itself. If it presents itself, it no longer presents itself.

We can imagine a first objection. It concerns the at least implicit re-course that we have just had to the values of subject, self, consciousness, even intentional meaning and phenomenon, a little as if we were limiting ourselves to a phenomenology of the gift even as we declared the gift to be irreducible to its phenomenon or to its meaning and said precisely that it was destroyed by its own meaning and its own phenomenality. The objec-tion would concern the way in which we are describing the intentionality of intention, reception, perception, keeping, recognition—in sum, every-thing by means of which one or the other, donee and donor, *take part* in the symbolic and thus annul the gift in the debt. One could object that this description is still given in terms of the self, of the subject that says I, *ego*, of intentional or intuitive perception-consciousness, or even of the con-scious or unconscious ego (for Freud the ego or a part of the ego can be unconscious). One may be tempted to oppose this description to another that would substitute for the economy of perception-consciousness an economy of the unconscious: Across the forgetting, the non-keeping, and the non-consciousness called up by the gift, the debt and the symbolic would reconstitute themselves for the subject of the Unconscious or the unconscious subject. As donee or donor, the Other would keep, bind him-self, obligate himself, indebt himself according to the law and the order of the symbolic, according to the figure of circulation,[6] even as the conditions of the gift—forgetfulness, non-appearance, non-phenomenality, non-per-ception, non-keeping—would have been fulfilled. We are indicating here only the principle of a problematic displacement that we would have to go into more carefully.

The necessity of such a displacement is of the greatest interest. It offers us new resources of analysis, it alerts us to the traps of the would-be *gift* without debt, it activates our critical or ethical vigilance. It permits us always to say: "Careful, you think there is gift, dissymmetry, generosity, expenditure, or loss, but the circle of the debt, of exchange, or of symbolic equilibrium reconstitutes itself according to the laws of the unconscious; the 'generous' or 'grateful' consciousness is only the phenomenon of a cal-culation and the ruse of an economy. Calculation and ruse, economy in truth would be the truth of these phenomena."

But such a displacement does not affect the paradox with which we are struggling, namely, the impossibility or the double bind of the gift: For there to be gift, it is necessary that the gift not even appear, that it not be perceived or received as gift. For if we added "not even *taken* or *kept*," it was precisely so that the generality of these notions (of *taking* and espe-cially of *keeping*) could cover a wider reception, sense, and acceptation than that of consciousness or of the perception-consciousness system. We had in mind also the keeping in the Unconscious, memory, the putting into reserve or temporalization as effect of repression. For there to be gift, not only must the donor or donee not perceive or receive the gift as such, have no consciousness of it, no memory, no recognition; he or she must also forget it right away [*à l'instant*] and moreover this forgetting must be so radical that it exceeds even the psychoanalytic categoriality of forgetting. This forgetting of the gift must even no longer be forgetting in the sense of repression. It must not give rise to any of the repressions (originary or secondary) that reconstitute the debt and exchange by putting in reserve, by keeping or saving up what is forgotten, repressed, or censured. Repression does not destroy or annul anything; it keeps by displacing. Its operation is systemic or topological; it always consists of keeping by exchanging places. And, by keeping the meaning of the gift, repression annuls it in symbolic recognition. However unconscious this recognition may be, it is effective and can be verified in no better fashion than by its effects or by the symptoms it yields up [*qu'elle donne*] for decoding.

So we are speaking here of an absolute forgetting—a forgetting that also absolves, that unbinds absolutely and infinitely more, therefore, than excuse, forgiveness, or acquittal. As condition of a gift event, condition for the advent of a gift, absolute forgetting should no longer have any relation with either the psycho-philosophical category of forgetting or even with the psychoanalytic category that links forgetting to meaning or to the logic of the signifier, to the economy of repression, and to the symbolic order. The thought of this radical forgetting as thought of the gift should accord with a certain experience of the *trace* as *cinder* or *ashes* in the sense in which we have tried to approach it elsewhere.[7]

And yet we say "forgetting" and not nothing. Even though it must leave nothing behind it, even though it must efface everything, including the traces of repression, this forgetting, this *forgetting of the gift* cannot be a simple non-experience, a simple non-appearance, a self-effacement that is carried off with what it effaces. For there to be gift event (we say event and not act), something must come about or happen, in an instant, in an instant that no doubt does not belong to the economy of time, in a time without time, in such a way that the forgetting forgets, that it forgets *itself,* but also in such a way that this forgetting, without being something present, presentable, determinable, sensible, or meaningful, is not nothing. What this forgetting and this forgetting of forgetting would therefore give us to think is something other than a philosophical, psychological, or psychoanalytic category. Far from giving us to think the possibility of the gift, on the contrary, it is on the basis of what takes shape in the name *gift* that one could *hope* thus to think forgetting. For there to be forgetting in this sense, there must be gift. The gift would also be the *condition* of forgetting. By condition, let us not understand merely "condition of possibility," system of premises or even of causes, but a set of traits defining a given situation in which something, or "that" ["ça"], is established (as in the expressions "the human condition," "the social condition," and so forth). We are not talking therefore about conditions in the sense of conditions posed (since forgetting and gift, if there is any, are in this sense unconditional),[8] but in the sense in which forgetting would be in the *condition of the gift* and the gift in the *condition of forgetting*; one might say on the mode of being of forgetting, if "mode" and "mode of being" did not belong to an ontological grammar that is exceeded by what we are trying to talk about here, that is, gift and forgetting. But such is the condition of all the words that we will be using here, of all the words given in our language—and this linguistic problem, let us say rather this problem of language before linguistics, will naturally be our obsession here.

Forgetting and gift would therefore be each in the condition of the other. This already puts us on the path to be followed. Not a particular path leading here or there, but on *the* path, on the *Weg* or *Bewegen* (path, to move along a path, to cut a path), which, leading nowhere, marks the step that Heidegger does not distinguish from thought. The thought on whose path we are, the thought as path or as movement along a path is precisely what is related to that *forgetting* that Heidegger does not name as a psychological or psychoanalytic category but as the condition of Being and of the truth of Being. This truth of Being or of the meaning of Being was foreshadowed, for Heidegger, on the basis of a question of Being posed, beginning with the first part of *Sein und Zeit*, in the transcendental horizon of the question of time. The explicitation of time thus forms the horizon of the question of Being as question of presence. The first line of *Sein und Zeit* says of this question that it "has today fallen into oblivion [*in Vergessenheit*]. Even though in our time [*unsere Zeit*] we deem it progressive to give our approval to 'metaphysics' again. . . . "

Here we must be content with the most preliminary and minimal selection within the Heideggerian trajectory; we will limit ourselves to situating that which links the question of time to the question of the gift, and then both of them to a singular thinking of forgetting. In fact, forgetting plays an essential role that aligns it with the very movement of history and of the truth of Being (*Sein*) which is nothing since it is not, since it is not being (*Seiendes*), that is, being-present or present-being. Metaphysics would have interpreted Being (*Sein*) as being-present/present-being only on the basis of, precisely, a pre-interpretation of time, which pre-interpretation grants an absolute privilege to the now-present, to the temporal ecstasis named present. That is why the transcendental question of time (and within it a

new existential analysis of the temporality of *Dasein*) was the privileged
horizon for a reelaboration of the question of Being. Now, as we know, this
movement that consisted in interrogating the question of Being within the
transcendental horizon of time was not interrupted (even though *Sein und
Zeit* was halted after the first half and even though Heidegger attributed
this interruption to certain difficulties linked to the language and the
grammar of metaphysics), but rather led off toward another turn or turning (*Kehre*). After this turning, it will not be a matter of subordinating the
question of Being to the question of the *Ereignis*, a difficult word to translate (event or propriation that is inseparable from a movement of dis-pro-
priation, *Enteignen*). This word *Ereignis*, which commonly signifies event,
signals toward a thinking of appropriation or of de- propriation that cannot
be unrelated to that of the gift. So from now on it will not be a matter of
subordinating, through a purely logical inversion, the question of Being to
that of *Ereignis*, but of conditioning them otherwise one by the other, one
with the other. Heidegger sometimes says that Being (*das Seyn*, an archaic
spelling that attempts to recall the word to a more thinking— *denkerisch*—
mode) is *Ereignis*.[9] And it is in the course of this movement that Being
(*Sein*)—which is not, which does not exist as being-present/present-
being—is signaled on the basis of the gift.

This is played out around the German expression *es gibt*, which, moreover, in *Sein und Zeit* (1928) had made a first, discreet appearance that was
already obeying the same necessity.[10] We translate the idiomatic locution *es
gibt Sein* and *es gibt Zeit* by "il y a l'être" in French and in English "there is
Being" (Being is not but there is Being), "il y a le temps," "there is time"
(time is not but there is time). Heidegger tries to get us to hear in this
[*nous donner à y entendre*] the "it gives," or as one might say in French, in
a neutral but not negative fashion, "ça donne," an "it gives" that would
not form an utterance in the propositional structure of Greco-Latin grammar, that is, bearing on present-being/being-present and in the subject-
predicate relation (S/P). The enigma is concentrated both in the "it" or
rather the "*es*," the "ça" of "ça donne," which is not a thing, and in this
giving that gives but without giving anything and without anyone giving
anything—nothing but Being and time (which are nothing). In *Zeit und
Sein* (1952), Heidegger's attention bears down on the giving (*Geben*) or
the gift (*Gabe*) implicated by the *es gibt*. From the beginning of the meditation, Heidegger recalls, if one can put it this way, that in itself time is nothing temporal, since it is nothing, since it is not a thing (*kein Ding*). The
temporality of time is not temporal, no more than proximity is proximate
or treeness is woody. He also recalls that Being is not being (being-pre-
sent/present-being), since it is not something (*kein Ding*), and that there-

fore one cannot say either "time is" or "Being is," but "*es gibt Sein*" and "*es gibt Zeit.*" It would thus be necessary to think a thing, something (*Sache* and not *Ding*, a *Sache* that is not a *being*) that would be Being and time but would not be either a being or a temporal thing: "*Sein—eigne Sache, aber nichts Seiendes, Zeit—eine Sache, aber nichts Zeitliches,*" "Being—a thing in question, but not a being. Time—a thing in question, but nothing temporal." He then adds this, which we read in translation for better or worse:

> In order to get beyond the idiom and back to the matter [*Sache*], we must show how this "there is" ["*es gibt*"] can be experienced [*erfahren*] and seen [*erblicken*]. The appropriate way [*der geeignete Weg*] to get there is to explain [elucidate, localize: *erörten*] what is given [*gegeben*] in the "It gives" ["*Es gibt*"], what "Being" means, which—It gives [*das— Es gibt*]; what "time" means, which—It gives [*das—Es gibt*]. Accordingly, we try to look ahead [*vorblicken*] to the It [*Es*] which— gives [*gibt*] Being [*Sein*] and time [*Zeit*]. Thus looking ahead, we become foresighted in still another sense. We try to bring the It [*Es*] and its giving [*Geben*] into view, and capitalize the "It."[11]

And after having thus written the "It gives Being" and "It gives time," "there is Being" and "there is time," Heidegger in effect asks the question of what it is in this gift or in this "there is" that relates time to Being, conditions them, we would now say, one to the other. And he writes:

> First, we shall think [in the trace of: *nach*] Being in order to think It itself into its own element [*um es selbst in sein Eigenes zu denken*].
>
> Then, we shall think [in the trace of: *nach*] time in order to think it itself into its own element.
>
> In this way, the manner must become clear how there is, It gives [*Es gibt*] Being and how there is, It gives [*Es gibt*] time. In this giving [*Geben*; in this "*y avoir*" *qui donne*, says the French translation; in this "there Being" that gives, one might say in English], it becomes apparent [*ersichtlich*] how that giving [*Geben*] is to be determined which, as a relation [*Verhältnis*], first holds [*hält*] the two toward each other and brings them into being [*und sie er-gibt*; by producing them or obtaining them as the result of a donation, in some sort: the *es* gives Being and gives time by giving them one to the other insofar as it holds (*hält*) them together in a relation (*Verhältnis*) one to the other].[12]

In the very position of this question, in the formulation of the project or the design of thinking, namely, the "in order to" (we think "in order to" [*um . . . zu*] think Being and time in their "own element" [*in sein Eigenes, in ihr Eigenes*]), the desire to accede to the proper is already, we could say, surreptitiously ordered by Heidegger according to the dimension of "giving." And reciprocally. What would it mean to think the gift, Being, and time *properly* in that which is most proper to them or in that which is properly their own, that is, what they can give and give over to the movements of propriation, expropriation, de-propriation, or appropriation? Can one ask these questions without anticipating a thought, even a desire of the proper? A desire to accede to the property of the proper? Is this a circle? Is there any other definition of desire? In that case, how to enter into such a circle or how to get out of it? Are the entrance and the exit the only two modalities of our inscription in the circle? Is this circle itself inscribed in the interlacing of a *Geflecht* of which it forms but one figure? These are so many threads to be pursued.

The only thread that we will retain here, for the moment, is that of *play*. Whether it is a matter of Being, of time, or of their deployment in presence (*Anwesen*), the *es gibt* plays (*spielt*), says Heidegger, in the movement of the *Entbergen*, in that which frees from the withdrawal [*retrait*], the withdrawal of the withdrawal, when what is hidden shows itself or what is sheltered appears. The *play* (*Zuspiel*) also marks, works on, manifests the unity of the three dimensions of time, which is to say a fourth dimension: The "giving" of the *es gibt Zeit* belongs to the play of this "quadridimensionality," to this *properness* of time that would thus be quadridimensional. "True time [authentic time: *die eigentliche Zeit*]," says Heidegger, "is four-dimensional [*vier-dimensional*]." This fourth dimension, as Heidegger makes clear, is not a figure, it is not a manner of speaking or of counting; it is said of the thing itself, on the basis of the thing itself (*aus der Sache*) and not only "so to speak." This thing itself of time implies the play of the four and the play of the gift.

Faced with this play of *fours*, of the four, as play of the gift, one thinks of the hand dealt by this game [*la donne de ce jeu*], of the locution "ça donne" (it gives), of the French imperative "donne" that, given by grammar to be an imperative, perhaps says something other than an order, a desire, or a demand. And then one thinks of *la doña*, of the woman who has been soliciting us since the epigraph, of all the questions of language that are crossing, in German and in French, in the locutions *es gibt* and *ça donne*. Thinking of all that and the rest, we will also evoke a very fine book by Lucette Finas[13] which interlaces all these motifs: the *aléa*, the play of the four [*quatre*] and of cards [*cartes*], the verb *give*, the locution *ça donne* (for example, when it is said in French of a purulent body). All these motifs and a few others find themselves woven into a narration, into a narration of narration or into a passion of narration. We will have to recognize that the question of *récit* (narration) and of literature is at the heart of all those we are talking about now. Lucette Finas's novel knots all these threads into the absolute idiom, the effect of the absolute idiom, which is a proper name (*Donne* is a proper name in the novel), a proper name without which perhaps there would never be either a narration effect or a gift effect. Even though we do not meet Heidegger in person in this novel, it is hard to resist the impression that he is hiding behind a series of men's proper names whose initial, with its German assonance, is H.

This detour was meant first of all to remind us that the forgetting we are talking about, if it is constitutive of the gift, is no longer a category of the *psyche*. It cannot be unrelated to the forgetting of Being, in the sense in which Blanchot also says, more or less, that forgetting is another name of Being.

As the condition for a gift to be given, this forgetting must be radical not only on the part of the donee but first of all, if one can say here first of all, on the part of the donor. It is also on the part of the donor "subject" that the gift not only must not be repaid but must not be kept in memory, retained as symbol of a sacrifice, as symbolic in general. For the symbol immediately engages one in restitution. To tell the truth, the gift must not even appear or signify, consciously or unconsciously, *as* gift for the donors, whether individual or collective subjects. From the moment the gift would appear as gift, as such, as what it is, in its phenomenon, its sense, and its essence, it would be engaged in a symbolic, sacrificial, or economic structure that would annul the gift in the ritual circle of the debt. The simple intention to give, insofar as it carries the intentional meaning of the gift, suffices to make a return payment to oneself. The simple consciousness of the gift right away sends itself back the gratifying image of goodness or generosity, of the giving-being who, knowing itself to be such, recognizes itself in a circular, specular fashion, in a sort of auto-recognition, self-approval, and narcissistic gratitude.

And this is produced as soon as there is a subject, as soon as donor and donee are constituted as identical, identifiable subjects, capable of identifying themselves by keeping and naming themselves. It is even a matter, in this circle, of the movement of subjectivization, of the constitutive retention of the subject that identifies with itself. The becoming-subject then reckons with itself, it enters into the realm of the calculable as subject. That is why, if there is gift, it cannot take place between two subjects exchanging objects, things, or symbols. The question of the gift should therefore seek its place before any relation to the subject, before any conscious or unconscious relation to self of the subject—and that is indeed what happens with

Heidegger when he goes back before the determinations of Being as substantial being, subject, or object. One would even be tempted to say that a subject as such never gives or receives a gift. It is constituted, on the contrary, in view of dominating, through calculation and exchange, the mastery of this *hubris* or of this impossibility that is announced in the promise of the gift. There where there is subject and object, the gift would be excluded. A subject will never give an object to another subject. But the subject and the object are arrested effects of the gift, arrests of the gift. At the zero or infinite speed of the circle.

If the gift is annulled in the economic odyssey of the circle as soon as it appears *as* gift or as soon as it signifies *itself as* gift, there is no longer any "logic of the gift," and one may safely say that a consistent discourse on the gift becomes impossible: It misses its object and always speaks, finally, of something else. One could go so far as to say that a work as monumental as Marcel Mauss's *The Gift*[14] speaks of everything but the gift: It deals with economy, exchange, contract (*do et des*), it speaks of raising the stakes, sacrifice, gift *and* countergift—in short, everything that in the thing itself impels the gift *and* the annulment of the gift. All the gift supplements (potlatch, transgressions and excesses, surplus values, the necessity to give or give back more, returns with interest—in short, the whole sacrificial bidding war) are destined to bring about once again the circle in which they are annulled. Moreover, this figure of the circle is evoked *literally* by Mauss (literally in French since I am for the moment setting aside an essential problem of translation to which we will return). On the subject of the Kula, a kind of "grand potlatch" practiced in the Trobriand Islands and the "vehicle for busy intertribal trade [extending] over the whole of the Trobriand Islands," Mauss writes:

> Malinowski gives no translation of *kula*, which doubtless means "circle."
> Indeed it is as if all these tribes, these expeditions across the sea, these
> precious things and objects for use, these types of food and festivals,
> these services rendered of all kinds, ritual and sexual, these men and
> women,—were caught up in a *circle** following around this *circle* a *regular movement* in time and space.
> *Note: Malinowski favors the expression "*kula* ring." (Pp. 21–22;
> emphasis added)[15]

Let us take this first reference to Mauss as a pretext for indicating right away the two types of questions that will orient our reading.

1. The question of language or rather of languages. How is one to legitimate the translations thanks to which Mauss circulates and travels, identifying from one culture to another what he understands by gift, what he

calls *gift*? He does this essentially on the basis of the Latin language and of Roman law. The latter plays a singular role throughout the essay, but Mauss also takes German law into account, which is the occasion for him to remark that the "detailed study of the very rich German vocabulary of words derived from *geben* and *gaben* has not yet been made" (p. 60). This question of the idiom, as we shall see, is in itself a question of gift in a rather unusual sense that amounts to neither the gift of languages nor the gift of language.

2. The second type of question cannot be separated from the first, in its widest generality. It would amount to asking oneself in effect: What and whom is Mauss talking about in the end? What is the semantic horizon of anticipation that authorizes him to gather together or compare so many phenomena of diverse sorts, which belong to different cultures, which manifest themselves in heterogeneous languages, under the unique and supposedly identifiable category of gift, under the sign of "gift"? What remains problematic is not only the *unity* of this semantic horizon, that is, the presumed identity of a meaning that operates as general translator or equivalent, but the very existence of something like *the* gift, that is, the common referent of this sign that is itself uncertain. If what Mauss demonstrates, one way or the other, is indeed that every gift is caught in the round or the contract of usury, then not only the unity of the meaning "gift" remains doubtful but, on the hypothesis that giving would have a *meaning* and *one* meaning, it is still the possibility of an effective existence, of an effectuation or an event of the gift that seems excluded. Now, this problematic of the difference (in the sense that we evoked earlier) between "the gift exists" and "there is gift" is never, as we know, deployed or even approached by Mauss, no more than it seems to be, to my knowledge, by the anthropologists who come after him or refer to him. Questions of this type should be articulated with other questions that concern the metalinguistic or meta-ethnological conceptuality orienting this discourse, the category of totality ("total social fact"), the political, economic, and juridical ideology organizing the classification and the evaluation, for example, the one that permits Mauss, at the end (it is especially at the end that these evaluations are openly declared), to say that "segmented" societies—Indo-European societies, Roman society before the Twelve Tables, Germanic societies up to the writing of the *Edda*, Irish society up to the writing of its "chief literature"—were ones in which individuals were "less sad, less serious, less miserly, and less personal than we are. Externally at least, they were or are more generous, and more giving than we are" (p. 81).

Everything thus seems to lead us back toward the paradox or the aporia of a nuclear proposition in the form of the "if . . . then": If the gift appears or signifies itself, if it exists or if it is presently *as gift*, as what it is, then it is not, it annuls itself. Let us go to the limit: The truth of the gift (its being or its appearing such, its *as such* insofar as it guides the intentional signification or the meaning-to-say) suffices to annul the gift. The truth of the gift is equivalent to the non-gift or to the non-truth of the gift. This proposition obviously defies common sense. That is why it is caught in the impossible of a very singular double bind, the bond without bond of a bind and a non-bind. On the one hand, Mauss reminds us that there is no gift without bond, without bind, without obligation or ligature; but on the other hand, there is no gift that does not have to untie itself from obligation, from debt, contract, exchange, and thus from the bind.

But, after all, what would be a gift that fulfills the condition of the gift, namely, that it not appear as gift, that it not be, exist, signify, want-to-say as gift? A gift without wanting, without wanting-to-say, an insignificant gift, a gift without intention to give? Why would we still call that a gift? That, which is to say what?

In other words, what are we thinking when we require simultaneously of the gift that it appear and that it not appear in its essence, in what it has to be, in what it is to be, in what it will have had to be (in its *to ti en einai* or in its *quidditas*)? That it obligate and not obligate? That it be and not be that for which it is given? What does "to give" mean to say? And what does language give one to think with this word? And what does "to give" mean to say *in the case* of language, of thinking, and of meaning-to-say?

It so happens (but this "it so happens" does not name the fortuitous) that the structure of this impossible *gift* is also that of Being—that gives itself to be thought on the condition of being nothing (no present-being, no being-present)—and of time which, even in what is called its "vulgar" determination, from Aristotle to Heidegger, is always defined in the paradoxia or rather the aporia of what is without being, of what is never present or what is only scarcely and dimly. Once again let us refer to all the texts, notably those of Aristotle, that are cited in "*Ousia* and *Grammē*," beginning with the Fourth Book of the *Physics*, which says, in the exoteric phase of its discourse, *dia tôn exoterikôn logôn*, that time "is not at all or only scarcely and dimly is [*olôs ouk estin ē molis kai amudrôs*]." Such is the aporetic effect—the "what does not pass" or "what does not happen"—of time defined on the basis of the *nun*, of the now, as *peras*, limit, and as *stigmē*, the point of the instant. "Some of it has been and is not [*gegone kai ouk esti*], some of it is to be and is not yet [*mellei kai oupo estin*]. From these both infinite time [*apeiros*] and time in its incessant return [*aei lambanomenos*] are composed. But it would seem to be impossible that what is composed of things that are not should participate in being [*ousia*]."[16]

We will not analyze here the context and the situation of this proposition called exoteric. Let us take it simply as a marker in the history of an aporetics that will become law and tradition: From the moment time is apprehended on the basis of the *present* now as general form and only modifiable or modalizable in such a way that the past and the future are still presents-past and presents-to-come, this predetermination entails the aporetics of a time that is not, of a time that is what it is *without being* (*it*) [sans l'être], that is not what it is and that is what it is not, which is to be it *without being* (*it*) [*qui est de l'être* sans l'être].

If it shares this aporetic paralysis with the gift, if neither the gift nor time exist as such, then the gift that *there* can *be* [*qu'il peut* y avoir] cannot in any case *give time*, since it is nothing. If there is something that can in no case be given, it is time, since it is nothing and since in any case it does not properly belong to anyone; if certain persons or certain social classes have more time than others—and this is finally the most serious stake of political economy—it is certainly not *time itself* that they possess. But inversely, if giving implies in all rigor that one give nothing that is and that appears as such—determined thing, object, symbol—if the gift is the gift of the giving itself and nothing else, then how to give time? This idiomatic locution, "to give time," seems to mean in common usage "leave time for something, leave time to do something, to fill time with this or that." As usual, it intends less time itself and properly speaking than the temporal or what there is in time. "To give time" in this sense commonly means to give something other than time but something other that is measured by time as by its element. Beyond this historical hardening or sedimentation, perhaps the idiomatic locution "to give time" gives one at least to think—to think the singular or double condition both of the gift and of time.

What there is to give, uniquely, would be called time.

What there is *to give*, uniquely, would be called time.

What there is to give, uniquely, *would be called time.*

For finally, if the gift is another name of the impossible, we still think it, we name it, we desire it. We intend it. And this *even if* or *because* or *to the extent that* we *never* encounter it, we never know it, we never verify it, we never experience it in its present existence or in its phenomenon. The gift *itself*—we dare not say the gift *in itself*—will never be confused with the presence of its phenomenon. Perhaps there is nomination, language, thought, desire, or intention only there where there is this movement still for thinking, desiring, naming that which gives itself neither to be known, experienced, nor lived—in the sense in which presence, existence, determination regulate the economy of knowing, experiencing, and living. In this sense one can think, desire, and say only the impossible, according to the measureless measure [*mesure* sans *mesure*] of the impossible.[17] If one wants to recapture the proper element of thinking, naming, desiring, it is perhaps according to the measureless measure of this limit that it is possible, possible as relation *without* relation to the impossible. One can desire, name, think in the proper sense of these words, if there is one, *only* to the *immeasuring* extent [*dans la mesure* démesurante] that one desires, names, thinks *still* or *already*, that one still lets announce itself what nevertheless cannot *present itself* as such to experience, to knowing: in short, here *a gift that cannot make itself (a) present* [un don qui ne peut pas se faire présent]. This gap between, on the one hand, thought, language, and desire and, on the other hand, knowledge, philosophy, science, and the order of presence is also a gap between the gift and economy. This gap is not present anywhere; it resembles an empty word or a transcendental illusion. But it also gives to this structure or to this logic a form analogous to Kant's transcendental dialectic, as relation between thinking and knowing, the noumenal and the phenomenal. Perhaps this analogy will help us and perhaps it has an essential relation to the problem of "giving-time."

We are going to give ourselves over to and engage in the effort of thinking or rethinking a sort of transcendental illusion of the gift. For in order to think the gift, a *theory of the gift* is powerless by its very essence. One must engage oneself in this thinking, commit oneself to it, give it tokens of faith [*gages*], and with one's person, risk entering into the destructive circle. One must promise and swear. The effort of thinking or rethinking a sort of transcendental illusion of the gift should not be a simple reproduction of Kant's critical machinery (according to the opposition between thinking and knowing, and so forth). But neither is it a matter of rejecting that machinery as old-fashioned. In any case, we are implicated in it, in particular because of that which communicates, in this dialectic, with the problem of time on one side, that of the moral law and of practical reason on the other side. But the effort to think the groundless ground of this quasi-"transcendental illusion" should not be either—if it is going to be a matter of *thinking*—a sort of adoring and faithful abdication, a simple movement of faith in the face of that which exceeds the limits of experience, knowledge, science, economy—and even philosophy. On the contrary, it is a matter—desire beyond desire—of responding faithfully but also as rigorously as possible both to the injunction or the order of the *gift* ("give" ["*donne*"]) as well as to the injunction or the order of meaning (presence, science, knowledge): *Know* still what giving *wants to say, know how to give*, know what you want and want to say when you give, know what you intend to give, know how the gift annuls itself, commit yourself [*engage-toi*] even if commitment is the destruction of the gift by the gift, give economy its chance.

For finally, the overrunning of the circle by the gift, if there is any, does not lead to a simple, ineffable exteriority that would be transcendent and without relation. It is this exteriority that sets the circle going, it is this exteriority that puts the economy in motion. It is this exteriority that *engages* in the circle and makes it turn. If one must *render an account* (to science, to reason, to philosophy, to the economy of meaning) of the circle effects in which a gift gets annulled, this account-rendering requires that one take into account that which, while not simply belonging to the circle, engages in it and sets off its motion. What is the gift as the first mover of the circle? And how does it contract itself into a circular contract? And from what place? Since when? From whom?

That is the contract, between us, for this cycle of lectures. (Recall that Mauss's essay *The Gift* has its premises in his work and that of Davy on the contract and on sworn faith.)[18]

Even if the gift were never anything but a simulacrum, one must still render *an account* of the possibility of this simulacrum and of the desire that impels toward this simulacrum. And one must also render an account of the desire to render an account. This cannot be done against or without the *principle of reason* (*principium reddendae rationis*), even if the latter finds there its limit as well as its resource. Otherwise, why would I commit myself—making it an obligation for myself—to speak and to render an account? Whence comes the law that obligates one to give even as one renders an account of the gift? In other words, to *answer* [répondre] still for a gift that calls one beyond all responsibility? And that forbids one to forgive whoever *does not know how to give?*

"I will never forgive him the ineptitude of his calculation," concludes the narrator of "La fausse monnaie" ("Counterfeit Money"), the brief story by Baudelaire that we will read together. Was he reproaching his friend in effect for not having *known how to give?* That is one of the questions waiting for us. Here is "Counterfeit Money":

> As we were leaving the tobacconist's, my friend carefully separated his change; in the left pocket of his waistcoat he slipped small gold coins; in the right, small silver coins; in his left trouser pocket, a handful of pennies and, finally, in the right he put a silver two-franc piece that he had scrutinized with particular care.
>
> "What a singularly minute distribution!" I said to myself.
>
> We encountered a poor man who held out his cap with a trembling hand.—I know nothing more disquieting than the mute eloquence of those supplicating eyes that contain at once, for the sensitive man who knows how to read them, so much humility and so much reproach. He finds there something close to the depth of complicated feeling one sees in the tear-filled eyes of a dog being beaten.

My friend's offering was considerably larger than mine, and I said to him: "You are right; next to the pleasure of feeling surprise, there is none greater than to cause a surprise." "It was the counterfeit coin," he calmly replied as though to justify himself for his prodigality.

But into my miserable brain, always concerned with looking for noon at two o'clock (what an exhausting faculty is nature's gift to me!), there suddenly came the idea that such conduct on my friend's part was excusable only by the desire to create an event in this poor devil's life, perhaps even to learn the varied consequences, disastrous or otherwise, that a counterfeit coin in the hands of a beggar might engender. Might it not multiply into real coins? Could it not also lead him to prison? A tavern keeper, a baker, for example, was perhaps going to have him arrested as a counterfeiter or for passing counterfeit money. The counterfeit coin could just as well, perhaps, be the germ of several days' wealth for a poor little speculator. And so my fancy went its course, lending wings to my friend's mind and drawing all possible deductions from all possible hypotheses.

But the latter suddenly shattered my reverie by repeating my own words: "Yes, you are right; there is no sweeter pleasure than to surprise a man by giving him more than he hopes for."

I looked him squarely in the eyes and I was appalled to see that his eyes shone with unquestionable candor. I then saw clearly that his aim had been to do a good deed while at the same time making a good deal; to earn forty cents and the heart of God; to win paradise economically; in short, to pick up gratis the certificate of a charitable man. I could have almost forgiven him the desire for the criminal enjoyment of which a moment before I assumed him capable; I would have found something bizarre, singular in his amusing himself by compromising the poor; but I will never forgive him the ineptitude of his calculation. To be mean is never excusable, but there is some merit in knowing that one is; the most irreparable of vices is to do evil out of stupidity.[19]

From *Given Time* [1991] translation 1993.
Translated by Peggy Kamuf.

Notes

1. Madame de Maintenon's sentence is remarkable enough to have attracted the attention of the *Littré*. There are those who will be surprised, perhaps, to see me evoke the secret wife of a great king at the beginning of such a lecture. However, Madame de Maintenon seems to me to be exemplary not only because, from her position as woman and "grande dame," she poses the question of the gift, time— and the rest. She who played the role of Louis XIV's "sultan of conscience" was at

the same time—and this configuration is rarely fortuitous—an outlaw and the very figure of the law. Before she became, upon the death of the Queen, the morganatic wife of the King (and thus excluded from all noble titles and rights; the word morganatic says something of the gift and the gift of the origin: it is from low Latin *morganegiba,* gift of the morning), she had led the Sun King back to his duties as husband (by estranging him from Madame de Montespan whose protégée she had been) and as Catholic king (by restoring austerity to the court, by encouraging the persecution of the Protestants—even though she herself was raised a Calvinist—and by lending her support to the revocation of the Edict of Nantes). She who took so much trouble over what one had to *give* and *take,* over the law, over the name of the King, over legitimacy in general was also the governess of the royal bastards, a promotion she no doubt owed to the protection of Madame de Montespan. Let us stop where we should have begun: When she was a child, she experienced exile in Martinique and her father, Constant, was arrested as a counterfeiter. Everything in her life seems to bear the most austere, the most rigorous, and the most authentic stamp of counterfeit money.

2. "For if love is to give what one does not have . . ." ("La Direction de la cure," in *Ecrits* [Paris: Le Seuil, 1966], p. 618); "What is thus given to the Other to fill and which is properly what he/she does not have, since for him/her as well Being is lacking, is what is called love, but it is also hatred and ignorance" (ibid., p. 627); "This privilege of the Other thus sketches out the radical form of the gift of something which it does not have, namely, what is called its love" ("La signification du phallus," ibid., p. 691; "The Meaning of the Phallus," trans. Jacqueline Rose, *Feminine Sexuality: Jacques Lacan and the "école freudienne,"* eds. Rose and Juliet Mitchell [New York: Norton, 1985], p. 80). The symmetry of these formulae, which seem to concern love *in general,* is interrupted when the truth of this "not-having-it" appears, namely, the woman *quoad matrem* and the man *quoad castrationem* (*Encore,* vol. 20 of *Le Séminaire de Jacques Lacan,* ed. Jacques-Alain Miller [Paris: Le Seuil, 1975], p. 36), to use a later formula but one which draws together very well this whole economy. Returning, then, to the *Ecrits*:

> If it is the case that man manages to satisfy his demand for love in his relationship to the woman to the extent that the signifier of the phallus constitutes her precisely as giving in love what she does not have—conversely, his own desire for the phallus will throw up its signifier in the form of a persistent divergence towards "another woman" who can signify this phallus on several counts, whether as a virgin or a prostitute. . . . We should not, however, think that the type of infidelity which then appears to be constitutive of the masculine function is exclusive to the man. For if one looks more closely, the same redoubling is to be found in the woman, the only difference being that in her case, the Other of Love as such, that is to say, the Other as deprived of that which it gives, is difficult to perceive in the withdrawal whereby it is substituted for the being of the same man whose attributes she cherishes.

The difference of "the only difference being" organizes all the dissymmetries analyzed on this page, which, let us remember, concludes as follows: "Correlatively, one can glimpse the reason for a feature which has never been elucidated and which again gives a measure of the depth of Freud's intuition: namely, why he advances the view that there is only one libido, his text clearly indicating that he conceives of it as masculine in nature" (p. 695/84–85; trans. modified).

The expression "to give what one does not have" is found in Heidegger (in particular in "The Anaximander Fragment" ["Der Spruch des Anaximander," in *Holzwege*] but also elsewhere); [TN: This conjunction of Lacan and Heidegger is discussed more fully in a later chapter (of *Given Time*).]

3. See Jacques Derrida, "*Ousia* and *Grammē*: Note on a Note from *Being and Time*," *Margins of Philosophy*, trans. Alan Bass (Chicago: University of Chicago Press, 1982), pp. 29–67.

4. Martin Heidegger, *Being and Time*, trans. John Macquarrie and Edward Robinson (New York: Harper and Row, 1962), p. 500, n. 30; quoted in Derrida, *Margins of Philosophy*, pp. 36–38.

5. TN: We will translate *engager* variously as to involve, to commit, and rarely as to engage. Here and there we will insert the French term as a reminder that *engager*, which also commonly means to set in motion (as in "to engage a mechanism"), elicits *gage*, that is, pledge, token exchanged in an *engagement*, a promise or agreement. It marks thereby the symbolics of debt that Derrida is concerned with throughout.

6. On this subject, see Lacan's "Seminar on 'The Purloined Letter'" and the reading I proposed of it in "Le Facteur de la vérité," especially around the circle of reappropriation of the gift in the debt (*The Post Card: From Socrates to Freud and Beyond*, trans. Alan Bass [Chicago: University of Chicago Press, 1987], pp. 436ff.).

7. For example in *Feu la cendre* (Paris: Des femmes, 1987) and the other texts intersecting with it at the point where, precisely, a certain "il y a là" [there is there] intersects with the giving of the gift (pp. 57, 60ff.).

8. Of course, this unconditionality must be absolute and uncircumscribed. It must not be simply declared while in fact dependent in its turn on the condition of some context, on some proximity or family tie, be it general or specific (among human beings, for example, to the exclusion of, for example, "animals"). Can there be any gift *within the family*? But has the gift ever been thought *without the family*? As for the unconditionality evoked by Lewis Hyde in *The Gift: Imagination and the Erotic Life of Property* (New York: Vintage Books, 1983), it is explicitly limited to gifts among close friends, relatives, and most often close relatives. Which is to say that it is not what it is or claims to be: unconditional. This is what the literature on organ donation brings out. One of these studies records that the son who donates a kidney to his mother does not want any gratitude from her because she had borne him in the first place. Another who donates to his brother insists that the latter should not feel either indebted or grateful: "those who prize their closeness to the recipient," notes Hyde, "are careful to make it clear that the gift is not conditional" (p. 69). Earlier, it had been pointed out that if, in fact, something comes back, after the gift, if a restitution takes place, the gift would nevertheless cease to be a gift from the moment this return would be its "explicit condition" (p. 9).

9. See for example the *Beiträge zur Philosophie* (*Vom Ereignis*), *Gesamtausgabe* vol. 65, ed. Friedrich-Wilhelm von Herrmann (Frankfurt am Main: Klostermann, 1989). A French translation of §267 has recently been proposed by Jean Greisch, in *Rue Descartes*, an issue titled "Des Grecs" (pp. 213ff.). Beginning with the first pages of the *Vorblick*, a certain *Ereignis* is defined as the truth of Being [*die Wahrheit des Seyns*]. "L'être est l'*Ereignis* [*Das Seyn ist das Er-eignis*]" (§267, p. 470); or again: "L'être est (este, s'essencie) comme l'*Ereignis* [*Das Seyn west als Ereignis*]" (§10; p. 30).

10. We will come back to this point much later, in the second volume of this work [*Given Time*], when we approach a reading of *On Time and Being* and related texts.

11. Heidegger, *On Time and Being*, trans. Joan Stambaugh (New York: Harper and Row, 1972), p. 5.

12. Ibid.

13. *Donne* (Paris: Le Seuil, 1976).

14. *Essai sur le don* in Marcel Mauss, *Sociologie et anthropologie* (Paris: Presses Universitaires de France, 1950); *The Gift: The Form and Reason for Exchange in Archaic Societies*, trans. W. D. Halls (London: Routledge, 1990). Page references to the translation, which has occasionally been modified, will be included in parentheses in the text.

15. This circle of the "Kula Ring" is evoked at length by L. Hyde (*The Gift*, pp. 11ff.) at the beginning of a chapter that is itself titled "The Circle" and that opens with these words from Whitman: "The gift is to the giver, and comes back most to him—it cannot fail. . . ." In a later chapter, we will evoke once again the scene of the gift and the debt, not as it is studied scientifically, but rather as it is first of all assumed or denied by French sociologists. Let us note here, while citing the work of Americans who are themselves "indebted" to Mauss, that they extend this chain of the debt in a necessary and paradoxical manner. Hyde notes that Mauss's essay was the "point of departure" for all the research on exchange over the last half century. Citing as well Raymond Firth and Claude Lévi-Strauss, he recognizes a particular debt to Marshall Sahlins, notably to the chapter titled "The Spirit of the Gift" in Sahlins's *Stone Age Economics* (Chicago: University of Chicago Press, 1972) [EN: Reprinted above], which holds Mauss's *The Gift* to be a "gift," "applies a rigorous *explication de texte*" to its sources, and situates "Mauss's ideas in the history of political philosophy." "It was through Sahlins's writings," says Hyde, "that I first began to see the possibility of my own work, and I am much indebted to him" (p. xv).

16. Aristotle, *Physics* 4.10.217b–18a, in *A New Aristotle Reader*, ed. J. L. Ackrill (Princeton: Princeton University Press, 1987), p. 122.

17. On the singular modality of this "impossible," permit me to refer to *Psyché: Inventions de l'autre* (Paris: Galilée, 1987), pp. 26–59; (English translation; "Psyche: Inventions of the Other," trans. Catherine Porter in *Reading de Man Reading*, eds. Wlad Godzich and Lindsay Waters [Minneapolis: University of Minnesota Press, 1989], pp. 235–60); to *Mémoires: for Paul de Man*, trans. Cecile Lindsay, Jonathan Culler, and Eduardo Cadava (New York: Columbia University Press, 1986), p. 35ff.; and to *L'Autre Cap* (Paris: Minuit, 1991), p. 46ff. On the strange grammar of the "sans," cf. "Pas" in *Parages* (Paris: Galilée, 1986), pp. 85 ff.; on that of the "sans l'être," cf. *Dissemination*, trans. Barbara Johnson (Chicago: University of Chicago Press, 1981), p. 213.

18. See Georges Davy, *La Foi jurée: Étude sociologique du problème du contrat et de la formation du lien contractuel* (*L'Année Sociologique*, 1922), and Mauss, "Une Forme ancienne de contrat chez les Thraces," *Revue des études grecques*, no. 24 (1921): 388–397.

19. Charles Baudelaire, *Oeuvres complètes*, vol. 1, ed. Claude Pichois (Paris: Bibliothèque de la Pléïade, 1975) p. 323; *Paris Spleen*, trans. Louise Varèse (New York: New Directions, 1970), pp. 58–59; translation modified.

Sorties: Out and Out: Attacks/Ways Out/Forays

Hélène Cixous

Where is she?

Activity/passivity
Sun/Moon
Culture/Nature
Day/Night

Father/Mother
Head/Heart
Intelligible/Palpable
Logos/Pathos.

Form, convex, step, advance, semen, progress.
Matter, concave, ground—where steps are taken, holding- and dumping-ground.

Man
_____
Woman

   Always the same metaphor: we follow it, it carries us, beneath all its figures, wherever discourse is organized. If we read or speak, the same thread or double braid is leading us throughout literature, philosophy, criticism, centuries of representation and reflection.

Thought has always worked through opposition,
Speaking/Writing
Parole/Écriture
High/Low

   Through dual, hierarchical oppositions. Superior/lnferior. Myths, legends, books. Philosophical systems. Everywhere (where) ordering inter-

148

venes, where a law organizes what is thinkable by oppositions (dual, irreconcilable; or sublatable, dialectical). And all these pairs of oppositions are *couples*. Does that mean something? Is the fact that Logocentrism subjects thought—all concepts, codes and values—to a binary system, related to "the" couple, man/woman?

Nature/History
Nature/Art
Nature/Mind
Passion/Action

Theory of culture, theory of society, symbolic systems in general—art, religion, family, language—it is all developed while bringing the same schemes to light. And the movement whereby each opposition is set up to make sense is the movement through which the couple is destroyed. A universal battlefield. Each time, a war is let loose. Death is always at work.

Father/son   Relations of authority, privilege, force.
The Word/   writing   Relations: opposition, conflict, sublation, return.
Master/slave   Violence. Repression.

We see that "victory" always comes down to the same thing: things get hierarchical. Organization by hierarchy makes all conceptual organization subject to man. Male privilege, shown in the opposition between *activity* and *passivity*, which he uses to sustain himself. Traditionally, the question of sexual difference is treated by coupling it with the opposition: activity/ passivity.

There are repercussions. Consulting the history of philosophy—since philosophical discourse both orders and reproduces all thought—one notices[1] that it is marked by an absolute *constant* which orders values and which is precisely this opposition, activity/passivity.

Moreover, woman is always associated with passivity in philosophy. Whenever it is a question of woman, when one examines kinship structures, when a family model is brought into play. In fact, as soon as the question of ontology raises its head, as soon as one asks oneself "what is it?", as soon as there is intended meaning. Intention: desire, authority— examine them and you are led right back . . . to the father. It is even possible not to notice that there is no place whatsoever for woman in the calculations. Ultimately the world of "being" can function while precluding the mother. No need for a mother, as long as there is some motherliness: and it is the father, then, who acts the part, who is the mother. Either woman is passive or she does not exist. What is left of her is unthinkable, unthought. Which certainly means that she is not thought, that she does not enter into the oppositions, that she does not make a couple with the father (who makes a couple with the son).

.   .   .

The Empire of the Selfsame
(Empirically from Bad to Worse)

—For, unfortunately, Hegel isn't inventing things. What I mean is that the dialectic, its syllogistic system, the subject's going out into the other *in order to come back* to itself, this entire process, particularly described in the *Phenomenology of Mind*, is, in fact, what is commonly at work in our everyday banality. Nothing is more frightening or more ordinary than Society's functioning the way it is laid out with the perfect smoothness of Hegelian machinery, exhibited in the movement through which one passes, in three stages, from the family to the State.

A historical process dynamized by the drama of the Selfsame (*Propre*). Impossible to conceive of a desire that does not entail conflict and destruction. We are still living under the Empire of the Selfsame. The same masters dominate history from the beginning, inscribing on it the marks of their appropriating economy: history, as a story of phallocentrism, hasn't moved except to repeat itself. "With a difference," as Joyce says. Always the same, with other clothes.

Nor has Freud (who is, moreover, the heir of Hegel and Nietzsche) made anything up. All the great theorists of destiny or of human history have reproduced the most commonplace logic of desire, the one that keeps the movement toward the other staged in a patriarchal production, under Man's law.

History, history of phallocentrism, history of propriation: a single history. History of an identity: that of man's becoming recognized by the other (son or woman), reminding him that, as Hegel says, death is his master.

It is true that recognition, following the phallocentric lead, passes through a conflict the brunt of which is borne by woman; and that desire, in a world thus determined, is a desire for appropriation. This is how that logic goes:

1) Where does desire come from? From a mixture of difference and *inequality*. No movement toward, if the two terms of the couple are in a state of equality. It is always a difference of forces which results in movement. (Reasoning that is, therefore, based on "physical" laws.)

2) A little surreptitious slippage: the *sexual* difference with an *equality* of force, therefore, does not produce the movement of desire. It is *inequality* that triggers desire, as a desire—for appropriation. Without inequality, without struggle, there is inertia—death.

It is on this level of analysis (more or less conscious, depending on the supposed-masters) that what I consider to be the great masculine imposture operates:

One could, in fact, imagine that difference or inequality—if one understands by that noncoincidence, asymmetry—lead to desire without negativity, without one of the partner's succumbing: we would recognize each other in a type of exchange in which each one would keep the *other* alive and different. But in the (Hegelian) schema of recognition, there is no place for the other, for an equal other, for a whole and living woman. She must recognize and recuntnize[†] the male partner, and in the time it takes to do this, she must disappear, leaving him to gain Imaginary profit, to win Imaginary victory. The good woman, therefore, is the one who "resists" long enough for him to feel both his power over her and his desire (I mean one who "exists"), and not too much, to give him the pleasure of enjoying, without too many obstacles, the return to himself which he, grown greater—reassured in his own eyes, is making.

All women have more or less experienced this cuntditionality of masculine desire. And all its secuntdary effects. The fragility of a desire that must (pretend to) kill its object. Fantasizing rape or making the transition to the act of rape. And plenty of women, sensing what is at stake there, cuntsent to play the part of object . . .

Why did this comedy, whose final act is the master's flirtation with death, make Bataille laugh so hard, as he amused himself by pushing Hegel to the edge of the abyss that a civilized man keeps himself from falling into? This abyss that functions as a metaphor both of death and of the feminine sex.

All history is inseparable from economy in the limited sense of the word, that of a certain kind of savings. Man's return—the relationship linking him profitably to man-being, conserving it. This economy, as a law of appropriation, is a phallocentric production. The opposition appropriate/inappropriate, proper/improper, clean/unclean, mine/not mine (the valorization of the selfsame), organizes the opposition identity/difference. Everything takes place as if, in a split second, man and being had propriated each other. And as if his relationship to woman was still at play as the possibility—though threatening, of the not-proper, not-clean, not-mine: desire is inscribed as the desire to reappropriate for himself that which seems able to escape him. The (unconscious?) stratagem and violence of masculine economy consists in making sexual difference hierarchical by valorizing one of the terms of the relationship, by reaffirming what Freud calls *phallic primacy*. And the "difference" is always perceived and carried out as an opposition. Masculinity/femininity are opposed in such a way that it is male privilege that is affirmed in a movement of conflict played out in advance.

And one becomes aware that the Empire of the Selfsame is erected from a fear that, in fact, is typically masculine: the fear of expropriation, of separation, of losing the attribute. In other words, the threat of castration has an impact. Thus, there is a relationship between the problematic of the not-selfsame, not-mine (hence of desire and the urgency of reappropriation) and the constitution of a subjectivity that experiences itself only when it makes its law, its strength, and its mastery felt, and it can all be understood on the basis of masculinity because this subjectivity is structured around a loss. Which is not the case with femininity.

What does one give?

All the difference determining history's movement as property's movement is articulated between two economies that are defined in relation to the problematic of the gift.

The (political) economy of the masculine and the feminine is organized by different demands and constraints, which, as they become socialized and metaphorized, produce signs, relations of power, relationships of production and reproduction, a whole huge system of cultural inscription that is legible as masculine or feminine.

I make a point of using the *qualifiers* of sexual difference here to avoid the confusion man/masculine, woman/feminine: for there are some men who do not repress their femininity, some women who, more or less strongly, inscribe their masculinity. Difference is not distributed, of course, on the basis of socially determined "sexes." On the other hand, when I speak of political economy and libidinal economy, connecting them, I am not bringing into play the false question of origins—a story made to order for male privilege. We have to be careful not to lapse smugly or blindly into an essentialist ideological interpretation, as both Freud and Jones, for example, risked doing in their different ways. In the quarrel that brought them into conflict on the subject of feminine sexuality, both of them, starting from opposite points of view, came to support the formidable thesis of a "natural," anatomical determination of sexual difference-opposition. On that basis, both of them implicitly back phallocentrism's position of strength.

We can recall the main lines of the opposing positions: Jones (in *Early Feminine Sexuality*) in an ambiguous move attacks the Freudian theses that make woman out to be a flawed man.

For Freud:

1) The "fate" of the feminine situation is an effect of an anatomical "defect."

2) There is only one libido and it is male in essence; sexual difference is

inscribed at the beginning of the *phallic phase* that both boys and girls go through. Until that point, the girl will have been a sort of little boy: the genital organization of the infantile libido is articulated through the equivalence activity/masculinity. The vagina has not yet been "discovered."

3) Since the first object of love, for both sexes, is the mother, it is only in the boy that the love of the opposite sex is "natural."

For Jones: femininity is an autonomous "essence."

From the beginning (starting at the age of six months) the girl has a "feminine" desire for her father; analysis of the little girl's most primitive fantasies would show, in fact, that in place of the breast, which is perceived as disappointing, the penis or (by an analogical shift) an object shaped like it is desired. One is already in the chain of substitutions, which means that the child, in the series of partial objects, would come to take the place of the penis . . . for, to counter Freud, Jones obediently reenlists in Freudian territory. And overdoes it! He concludes from the equation breast-penis-child that the little girl feels a primary desire toward her father. (And the desire to have the father's child would be primary also.) He concludes that, of course, the girl has a primary love for the opposite sex as well. Therefore, she too has a right to her own Oedipus complex as a primary formation and to the threat of mutilation by the mother. In the end—a woman, that is what she is and with no anatomical defect: her clitoris is not a minipenis. Clitoral masturbation is not, as Freud claims, a masculine practice. And seeing the early fantasies, it would seem that the vagina is discovered extremely early.

In fact, by affirming that there is a specific femininity (all the while preserving orthodox theses elsewhere), Jones is still reenforcing phallocentrism under the pretext of taking femininity's side (and God's too, who, he reminds us, created them male and female!). And bisexuality disappears in the unbridged abyss separating the opponents here.

As for Freud, if one subscribes to what he says in his article on the *Disappearance of The Oedipus Complex* (1933) in which he identifies himself with Napoleon: "anatomy is destiny," one participates in condemning woman to death. And in wrapping up all of History.

It is undeniable that there are psychic consequences of the difference between the sexes. But they certainly cannot be reduced to the ones that Freudian analysis designates. Starting from the relationship of the two sexes to the Oedipus complex, the boy and the girl are steered toward a division of social roles such that women "inevitably" have a lesser productivity because they "sublimate" less than men and that symbolic activity, hence the production of culture, is the work of men.[2]

Elsewhere, Freud starts from what he calls the *anatomical* difference between the sexes. And we know how that is represented in his eyes: by the difference between having/not having the phallus. By reference to those precious parts. Starting from what will take shape as the transcendental sig-nifier with Lacan.

But *sexual difference* is not determined simply by the fantasized relation to anatomy, which depends to a great extent on catching *sight* of something, thus on the strange importance that is accorded to exteriority and to that which is specular in sexuality's development. A voyeur's theory, of course.

No, the difference, in my opinion, becomes most clearly perceived on the level of *jouissance,* inasmuch as a woman's instinctual economy cannot be identified by a man or referred to the masculine economy.

For me, the question asked of woman "What does she want?"—is a question that woman asks herself, in fact, because she is asked it. It is pre-cisely because there is so little room for her desire in society that, because of not knowing what to do with it, she ends up not knowing where to put it or if she even has it. This question conceals the most immediate and most urgent question: "How do I pleasure?" What is it—feminine *jouissance*—where does it happen, how does it inscribe itself—on the level of her body or of her unconscious? And then, how does it write itself?

One can ramble on for a long time about hypothetical prehistory and a matriarchal epoch. Or, like Bachofen,[3] one can attempt to prefigure a gynarchic society, drawing from it poetic and mythical effects, which have a powerfully subversive impact regarding the history of family and male power.

All the ways of differently thinking the history of power, property, mas-culine domination, the formation of the State, and the ideological equip-ment have some effect. But the change that is in process concerns more than just the question of "origin." There is phallocentrism. History has never produced or recorded anything else—which does not mean that this form is destinal or natural. Phallocentrism is the enemy. Of everyone. Men's loss in phallocentrism is different from but as serious as women's. And it is time to change. To invent the other history.

There is "destiny" no more than there is "nature" or "essence" as such. Rather, there are living structures that are caught and sometimes rigidly set within historicocultural limits so mixed up with the scene of History that for a long time it has been impossible (and it is still very difficult) to think or even imagine an "elsewhere." We are presently living in a transitional period—one in which it seems possible that the classic structure might be split.

It is impossible to predict what will become of sexual difference—in another time (in two or three hundred years?). But we must make no mis-take: men and women are caught up in a web of age-old cultural determina-tions that are almost unanalyzable in their complexity. One can no more speak of "woman" than of "man" without being trapped within an ideological theater where the proliferation of representations, images, reflections, myths, identifications, transform, deform, constantly change everyone's Imaginary and invalidate in advance any conceptualization.[4]

Nothing allows us to rule out the possibility of radical transformation of behaviors, mentalities, roles, political economy—whose effects on libidinal economy are unthinkable—today. Let us simultaneously imagine a general change in all the structures of training, education, supervision—hence in the structures of reproduction of ideological results. And let us imagine a real liberation of sexuality, that is to say, a transformation of each one's relationship to his or her body (and to the other body), an approximation to the vast, material, organic, sensuous universe that we are. This cannot be accomplished, of course, without political transformations that are equally radical. (Imagine!) Then "femininity" and "masculinity" would inscribe quite differently their effects of difference, their economy, their relationship to expenditure, to lack, to the gift. What today appears to be "feminine" or "masculine" would no longer amount to the same thing. No longer would the common logic of difference be organized with the opposition that remains dominant. Difference would be a bunch of new differences.

But we are still floundering—with few exceptions—in Ancient History.

The Masculine Future

There are some exceptions. There have always been those uncertain, poetic persons who have not let themselves be reduced to dummies programmed by pitiless repression of the homosexual element. Men or women: beings who are complex, mobile, open. Accepting the other sex as a component makes them much richer, more various, stronger, and—to the extent that they are mobile—very fragile. It is only in this condition that we invent. Thinkers, artists, those who create new values, "philosophers" in the mad Nietzschean manner, inventors and wreckers of concepts and forms, those who change life cannot help but be stirred by anomalies—complementary or contradictory. That doesn't mean that you have to be homosexual to create. But it does mean that there is no *invention* possible, whether it be philosophical or poetic, without there being in the inventing subject an abundance of the other, of variety: separate-people, thought-people, whole populations issuing from the unconscious, and in each suddenly animated desert, the springing up of selves one didn't know—our women, our monsters, our jackals, our Arabs, our aliases, our frights. That there is no invention of any other I, no poetry, no fiction without a certain homosexuality (the I/play of bisexuality) acting as a crystallization of my ultrasubjectivities.[5] I is this exuberant, gay, personal matter, masculine, feminine, or other where I enchants, I agonizes me. And in the concert of personalizations called I, at the same time that a certain homosexuality is repressed, symbolically, substitutively, it comes through by various signs, conduct-character, behavior-acts. And it is even more clearly seen in writing.

Thus, what is inscribed under Jean Genêt's name, in the movement of a text that divides itself, pulls itself to pieces, dismembers itself, regroups, remembers itself, is a proliferating, maternal femininity. A phantasmic meld of men, males, gentlemen, monarchs, princes, orphans, flowers, mothers, breasts gravitates about a wonderful "sun of energy"—love,—that bombards and disintegrates these ephemeral amorous anomalies so that they can be recomposed in other bodies for new passions.

She is bisexual:

What I propose here leads directly to a reconsideration of *bisexuality.* To reassert the value of bisexuality;[6] hence to snatch it from the fate classically reserved for it in which it is conceptualized as "neuter" because, as such, it would aim at warding off castration. Therefore, I shall distinguish between two bisexualities, two opposite ways of imagining the possibility and practice of bisexuality.

1) Bisexuality as a fantasy of a complete being, which replaces the fear of castration and veils sexual difference insofar as this is perceived as the mark of a mythical separation—the trace, therefore, of a dangerous and painful ability to be cut. Ovid's Hermaphrodite, less bisexual than asexual, not made up of two genders but of two halves. Hence, a fantasy of unity. Two within one, and not even two wholes.

2) To this bisexuality that melts together and effaces, wishing to avert castration, I oppose the *other bisexuality,* the one with which every subject, who is not shut up inside the spurious Phallocentric Performing Theater, sets up his or her erotic universe. Bisexuality—that is to say the location within oneself of the presence of both sexes, evident and insistent in different ways according to the individual, the nonexclusion of difference or of a sex, and starting with this "permission" one gives oneself, the multiplication of the effects of desire's inscription on every part of the body and the other body.

For historical reasons, at the present time it is woman who benefits from and opens up within this bisexuality beside itself, which does not annihilate differences but cheers them on, pursues them, adds more: in a certain way *woman is bisexual*—man having been trained to aim for glorious phallic monosexuality. By insisting on the primacy of the phallus and implementing it, phallocratic ideology has produced more than one victim. As a woman, I could be obsessed by the scepter's great shadow, and they told me: adore it, that thing you don't wield.

But at the same time, man has been given the grotesque and unenviable fate of being reduced to a single idol with clay balls. And terrified of homo-sexuality, as Freud and his followers remark. Why does man fear *being* a woman? Why this refusal *(Ablehnung)* of femininity? The question that stumps Freud. The "bare rock" of castration. For Freud, the repressed is not the other sex defeated by the dominant sex, as his friend Fliess (to whom Freud owes the theory of bisexuality) believed; what is repressed is leaning toward one's own sex.

Psychoanalysis is formed on the basis of woman and has repressed (not all that successfully) the femininity of masculine sexuality, and now the account it gives is hard to disprove.

We women, the derangers, know it only too well. But nothing compels us to deposit our lives in these lack-banks; to think that the subject is con-stituted as the last stage in a drama of bruising rehearsals; to endlessly bail out the father's religion. Because we don't desire it. We don't go round and round the supreme hole. We have no *woman*'s reason to pay allegiance to the negative. What is feminine (the poets suspected it) affirms: . . . and yes I said yes I will Yes, says Molly (in her rapture), carrying *Ulysses* with her in the direction of a new writing; I said yes, I will Yes.

To say that woman is somehow bisexual is an apparently paradoxical way of displacing and reviving the question of difference. And therefore of writ-ing as "feminine" or "masculine."

I will say: today, writing is woman's. That is not a provocation, it means that woman admits there is an other. In her becoming-woman, she has not erased the bisexuality latent in the girl as in the boy. Femininity and bisexu-ality go together, in a combination that varies according to the individual, spreading the intensity of its force differently and (depending on the moments of their history) privileging one component or another. It is much harder for man to let the other come through him. Writing is the passageway, the entrance, the exit, the dwelling place of the other in me—the other that I am and am not, that I don't know how to be, but that I feel passing, that makes me live—that tears me apart, disturbs me, changes me, who?—a feminine one, a masculine one, some?—several, some un-known, which is indeed what gives me the desire to know and from which all life soars. This peopling gives neither rest nor security, always disturbs the relationship to "reality," produces an uncertainty that gets in the way of the subject's socialization. It is distressing, it wears you out; and for men this permeability, this nonexclusion is a threat, something intolerable.

In the past, when carried to a rather spectacular degree, it was called "possession." Being possessed is not desirable for a masculine Imaginary, which would interpret it as passivity—a dangerous feminine position. It is true that a certain receptivity is "feminine." One can, of course, as History has always done, exploit feminine reception through alienation. A woman, by her opening up, is open to being "possessed," which is to say, dispossessed of herself.

But I am speaking here of femininity as keeping alive the other that is confided to her, that visits her, that she can love as other. The loving to be other, another, without its necessarily going the rout of abasing what is same, herself.

As for passivity, in excess, it is partly bound up with death. But there is a nonclosure that is not submission but confidence and comprehension; that is not an opportunity for destruction but for wonderful expansion.

Through the same opening that is her danger, she comes out of herself to go to the other, a traveler in unexplored places; she does not refuse, she approaches, not to do away with the space between, but to see it, to experience what she is not, what she is, what she can be.

Writing is working; being worked; questioning (in) the between (letting oneself be questioned) of same *and of* other without which nothing lives; undoing death's work by willing the togetherness of one-another, infinitely charged with a ceaseless exchange of one with another—not knowing one another and beginning again only from what is most distant, from self, from other, from the other within. A course that multiplies transformations by the thousands.

And that is not done without danger, without pain, without loss—of moments of self, of consciousness, of persons one has been, goes beyond, leaves. It doesn't happen without expense—of sense, time, direction.

But is that specifically feminine? It is men who have inscribed, described, theorized the paradoxical logic of an economy without reserve. This is not contradictory; it brings us back to asking about their femininity. Rare are the men able to venture onto the brink where writing, freed from law, unencumbered by moderation, exceeds phallic authority, and where the subjectivity inscribing its effects becomes feminine.

Where does difference come through in writing? If there is difference it is in the manner of spending, of valorizing the appropriated, of thinking what is not-the-same. In general, it is in the manner of thinking any "return," the relationship of capitalization, if this word "return" (*rapport*) is understood in its sense of "revenue."

Today, still, the masculine return to the Selfsame is narrower and more restricted than femininity's. It all happens as if man were more directly threatened in his being by the nonselfsame than woman. Ordinarily, this is exactly the cultural product described by psychoanalysis: someone who still has something to lose. And in the development of desire, of exchange, he is the en-grossing party: loss and expense are stuck in the commercial deal that always turns the gift into a gift-that-takes. The gift brings in a return.

Loss, at the end of a curved line, is turned into its opposite and comes back to him as profit.

But does woman escape this law of return? Can one speak of another spending? Really, there is no "free" gift. You never give something for nothing. But all the difference lies in the why and how of the gift, in the values that the gesture of giving affirms, causes to circulate; in the type of profit the giver draws from the gift and the use to which he or she puts it. Why, how, is there this difference?

When one gives, what does one give oneself?

What does he want in return—the traditional man? And she? At first what *he* wants, whether on the level of cultural or of personal exchanges, whether it is a question of capital or of affectivity (or of love, of *jouissance*)—is that he gain more masculinity: plus-value of virility, authority, power, money, or pleasure, all of which reenforce his phallocentric narcissism at the same time. Moreover, that is what society is made for—how it is made; and men can hardly get out of it. An unenviable fate they've made for themselves. A man is always proving something; he has to "show off," show up the others. Masculine profit is almost always mixed up with a success that is socially defined.

How does she give? What are her dealings with saving or squandering, reserve, life, death? She too gives *for.* She too, with open hands, gives herself—pleasure, happiness, increased value, enhanced self-image. But she doesn't try to "recover her expenses." She is able not to return to herself, never settling down, pouring out, going everywhere to the other. She does not flee extremes; she is not the being-of-the-end (the goal), but she is how-far-being-reaches.

If there is a self proper to woman, paradoxically it is her capacity to depropriate herself without self-interest: endless body, without "end," without principal "parts"; if she is a whole, it is a whole made up of parts that are wholes, not simple, partial objects but varied entirety, moving and boundless change, a cosmos where eros never stops traveling, vast astral space. She doesn't revolve around a sun that is more star than the stars.

That doesn't mean that she is undifferentiated magma; it means that she doesn't create a monarchy of her body or her desire. Let masculine sexuality gravitate around the penis, engendering this centralized body (political anatomy) under the party dictatorship. Woman does not perform on herself this regionalization that profits the couple head-sex, that only inscribes itself within frontiers. Her libido is cosmic, just as her unconscious is worldwide: her writing also can only go on and on, without ever inscribing or distinguishing contours, daring these dizzying passages in other, fleeting and passionate dwellings within him, within the hims and hers whom she inhabits just long enough to watch them, as close as possible to the unconscious from the moment they arise; to love them, as close as possible to instinctual drives, and then, further, all filled with these brief identifying hugs and kisses, she goes and goes on infinitely. She alone dares and wants to know from within where she, the one excluded, has never ceased to hear what-comes-before-language reverberating. She lets the other tongue of a thousand tongues speak—the tongue, sound without barrier or death. She refuses life nothing. Her tongue doesn't hold back but holds forth, doesn't keep in but keeps on enabling. Where the wonder of being several and turmoil is expressed, she does not protect herself against these unknown feminines; she surprises herself at seeing, being, pleasuring in her gift of changeability. I am spacious singing Flesh: onto which is grafted no one knows which I—which masculine or feminine, more or less human but above all living, because changing I.

I see her "begin." That can be written—these beginnings that never stop getting her up—can and must be written. Neither black on white nor white on black, not in this clash between paper and sign that en-graves itself there, not in this opposition of colors that stand out against each other. This is how it is:

There is a ground, it is her ground—childhood flesh, shining blood—or background, depth. A white depth, a core, unforgettable, forgotten, and this ground, covered by an infinite number of strata, layers, sheets of paper—is her sun (*sol . . . soleil*). And nothing can put it out. Feminine light doesn't come from above, doesn't fall, doesn't strike, doesn't go through. It radiates, it is a slow, sweet, difficult, absolutely unstoppable, painful rising that reaches and impregnates lands, that filters, that wells up, that finally tears open, wets and spreads apart what is dull and thick, the stolid, the volumes. Fighting off opacity from deep within. This light doesn't plant, it spawns. And I see that she looks very closely with this light and she sees the veins and nerves of matter. Which he has no need of.

Her rising: is not erection. But diffusion. Not the shaft. The vessel. Let her write! And her text knows in seeking itself that it is more than flesh and blood, dough kneading itself, rising, uprising openly with resounding, perfumed ingredients, a turbulent compound of flying colors, leafy spaces, and rivers flowing to the sea we feed.

So! Now she's her sea, he'll say to me (as he holds out to me his basin full of water from the little phallic mother he doesn't succeed in separating himself from). Seas and mothers.

But that's it—our seas are what we make them, fishy or not, impenetrable or muddled, red or black, high and rough or flat and smooth, narrow straits or shoreless, and we ourselves are sea, sands, corals, seaweeds, beaches, tides, swimmers, children, waves . . . seas and mothers.

More or less vaguely swelling like wavesurge indistinctly sea-earth-naked, and what matter made of this naked sea-rth would deter us? We all know how to finger them, mouth them. Feel them, speak them.

Heterogenous, yes, to her joyful benefit, she is erogenous; she is what is erogenous in the heterogenous; she is not attached to herself, the airborne swimmer, the thieving flyer. Stunning, extravagant, one who is dispersible, desiring and capable of other, of the other woman she will be, of the other woman she is not, of him, of you.

Woman (I) have no fear of elsewhere or of same or of other. My eyes, my tongue, my ears, my nose, my skin, my mouth, my body for (the) other, not that I desire it to stop up some hole, to overcome some flaw of mine, not because I am fatefully hounded by "feminine" jealousy, not because I am caught up in the chain of substitutions that reduces the substitutes to one ultimate object. It's all over for the stories of Tom Thumb and of the *Penisneid* that the old grandmothers whispered to us, those ogresses serving their son-fathers. Let them believe what they need to make themselves feel important—believe we are dying of envy, that we are this hole edged with penis envy; that's their age-old deal. Undeniably (we confirm this at a cost to us but also to our amusement), men are structured only for the feathering of their shafts to let us know they have a hard-on; so we will assure them (we, the motherly mistresses of their little pocket signifier) that they are something, that they still have them. It is not the penis that woman desires in the child, it is not that hot-shot piece around which every man gravitates. Except within the historical *limits* of the Ancient world, gestation doesn't come down to coincidences, to those mechanical substitutions that the unconscious of an eternally "jealous woman" puts in place, or to the *Penisneid,* or to narcissism, or to a homosexuality linked to the always-there-mother.

The relation borne to the child must also be rethought. One trend of current feminist thought tends to denounce a trap in maternity that would consist of making the mother-woman an agent who is more or less the accomplice of reproduction: capitalist, familialist, phallocentrist reproduction. An accusation and a caution that should not be turned into prohibition, into a new form of repression.

Will you, too, discounting everyone's blindness and passivity, be afraid the child might *make* a father and hence that the woman making a kid plays herself more than one dirty trick, engendering the child—the mother—the father—the family all at the same time? No, it's up to you to break the old circuits. It will be the task of woman and man to make the old relationship and all its consequences out-of-date; to think the *launching* of a new subject, into life, with defamilialization. Rather than depriving woman of a fascinating time in the life of her body just to guard against procreation's being recuperated, let's de-mater-paternalize. Let's defetishize. Let's get out of the dialectic that claims that the child is its parents' death. The child is the other but the other without violence. The other rhythm, the pure freshness, the possibles' body. Complete fragility. But vastness itself. Let's be done with repeating the litany of castration that transmits and pedigrees itself. We're not going to back up to go forward anymore. Let's not repress something as simple as wanting to live life itself. Oral drive, anal drive, vocal drive, all drives are good forces, and among them the gestational drive—just like wanting to write: a desire to live oneself within, wanting the belly, the tongue, the blood. We are not going to refuse ourselves the delights of a pregnancy, which, moreover, is always dramatized or evaded or cursed in classical texts. For if there is a specific thing repressed, that is where it is found: the taboo of the pregnant woman (which says a lot about the power that seems invested in her). It is because they have always suspected that the pregnant woman not only doubles her market value but, especially, valorizes *herself* as a *woman* in her own eyes, and undeniably takes on weight and sex. There are a thousand ways of living a pregnancy, of having or not having a relationship of another intensity with this still invisible other.

Really experiencing metamorphosis. Several, other, and unforeseeable. That cannot but inscribe in the body the good possibility of an alteration. It is not only a question of the feminine body's extra resource, this specific power to produce some thing living of which her flesh is the locus, not only a question of a transformation of rhythms, exchanges, of relationship to space, of the whole perceptive system, but also of the irreplaceable experience of those moments of stress, of the body's crises, of that work that goes on peacefully for a long time only to burst out in that surpassing moment, the time of childbirth. In which she lives as if she were larger or stronger than herself. It is also the experience of a "bond" with the other, all that comes through in the metaphor of bringing into the world. How could the woman, who has experienced the not-me within me, not have a particular relationship to the written? To writing as giving itself away (cutting itself off) from the source?

There is a bond between woman's libidinal economy—her *jouissance,* the feminine Imaginary—and her way of self-constituting a subjectivity that splits apart without regret, and without this regretlessness being the equivalent of dying, of the exhaustion described by Valéry as the Young Fate—answering herself with anomalies, without the ceaseless summoning of the authority called Ego.

Unleashed and raging, she belongs to the race of waves. She arises, she approaches, she lifts up, she reaches, covers over, washes a shore, flows embracing the cliff's least undulation, already she is another, arising again, throwing the fringed vastness of her body up high, follows herself, and covers over, uncovers, polishes, makes the stone body shine with the gentle undeserting ebbs, which return to the shoreless nonorigin, as if she recalled herself in order to come again as never before . . .

She has never "held still"; explosion, diffusion, effervescence, abundance, she takes pleasure in being boundless, outside self, outside same, far from a "center," from any capital of her "dark continent," very far from the "hearth" to which man[7] brings her so that she will tend his fire, which always threatens to go out. She watches for him, but he has to keep an eye on her; for she can be his storm as well: "will I die by a storm? Or will I go out like a light that doesn't wait to be blown out by the wind, but which dies tired and self-satisfied? . . . or: will I extinguish my own self in order not to burn down to the end?"[8] Masculine energy, with its limited oil reserves, questions itself. Whereas, the fact that feminine energy has vast resources is not without consequences—still very rarely analyzed—for exchange in general, for love-life, and for the fate created for woman's desire. Exasperating: he's afraid she "goes too far." And the irony of her fate has her either be this "nothing," which punctuates the Dora case— ("You know my wife is nothing to me")—or this too-much, too-much reversed into not-enough, the "not how it should be" that reminds her that her master is on the limited side.

She doesn't hold still, she overflows. An outpouring that can be agonizing, since she may fear, and make the other fear, endless aberration and madness in her release. Yet, vertiginous, it can also be intoxicating—as long as the personal, the permanence of identity is not fetishized—a "where-am-I," a "who-enjoys-there," a "who-I-where-delight": questions that drive reason, the principle of unity, mad, and that are not asked, that ask for no answer, that open up the space where woman is wandering, roaming (a rogue wave), flying (thieving).

This power to be errant is strength; it is also what makes her vulnerable to those who champion the Selfsame, acknowledgment, and attribution. No matter how submissive and docile she may be in relation to the masculine order, she still remains the threatening possibility of savagery, the unknown quantity in the household whole.

"Mysterious"[9]—the incalculable with which they must be counted.— Mysterious, yes—but she is blamed for that even if pleasure is derived from always wanting to expose her. And mysterious to herself, something she has been disturbed by for a long time, made to feel guilty for "not understanding herself" (taking herself in) or knowing herself (cunt-born), because all around her they valorized a "knowledge" (cunt-birth) as ordained, as a mastery, a "control" (cunt-role) (of knowings! cunt-births!) established on repression and on "capture," arrest, sub-poenis, confinement.

Writing femininity transformation:

And there is a link between the economy of femininity—the open, extravagant subjectivity, that relationship to the other in which the gift doesn't calculate its influence—and the possibility of love; and a link today between this "libido of the other" and writing.

At the present time, *defining* a feminine practice of writing is impossible with an impossibility that will continue; for this practice will never be able to be *theorized,* enclosed, coded, which does not mean it does not exist. But it will always exceed the discourse governing the phallocentric system; it takes place and will take place somewhere other than in the territories subordinated to philosophical-theoretical domination. It will not let itself think except through subjects that break automatic functions, border runners never subjugated by any authority. But one can begin to speak. Begin to point out some effects, some elements of unconscious drives, some relations of the feminine Imaginary to the Real, to writing.

What I have to say about it is also only a beginning, because right from the start these features affect me powerfully.

First I sense femininity in writing by: a privilege of *voice: writing* and *voice* are entwined and interwoven and writing's continuity/voice's rhythm take each other's breath away through interchanging, make the text gasp or form it out of suspenses and silences, make it lose its voice or rend it with cries.

In a way, feminine writing never stops reverberating from the wrench that the acquisition of speech, speaking out loud, is for her—"acquisition" that is experienced more as tearing away, dizzying flight and flinging oneself, diving. Listen to woman speak in a gathering (if she is not painfully out of breath): she doesn't "speak," she throws her trembling body into the air, she lets herself go, she flies, she goes completely into her voice, she vitally defends the "logic" of her discourse with her body; her flesh speaks true. She exposes herself. Really she makes what she thinks materialize carnally, she conveys meaning with her body. She *inscribes* what she is saying because she does not deny unconscious drives the unmanageable part they play in speech.

Her discourse, even when "theoretical" or political, is never simple or linear or "objectivized," universalized; she involves her story in history.

Every woman has known the torture of beginning to speak aloud, heart beating as if to break, occasionally falling into loss of language, ground and language slipping out from under her, because for woman speaking—even just opening her mouth—in public is something rash, a transgression.

A double anguish, for even if she transgresses, her word almost always falls on the deaf, masculine ear, which can only hear language that speaks in the masculine.

We are not culturally accustomed to speaking, throwing signs out toward a scene, employing the suitable rhetoric. Also, it is not where we find our pleasure: indeed, one pays a certain price for the use of a discourse. The logic of communication requires an economy both of signs—of signifiers—and of subjectivity. The orator is asked to unwind a thin thread, dry and taut. We like uneasiness, questioning. There is waste in what we say. We need that waste. To write is always to make allowances for superabundance and uselessness while slashing the exchange value that keeps the spoken word on its track. That is why writing is good, letting the tongue try itself out—as one attempts a caress, taking the time a phrase or a thought needs to make oneself loved, to make oneself reverberate.

It is in writing, from woman and toward woman, and in accepting the challenge of the discourse controlled by the phallus, that woman will affirm woman somewhere other than in silence, the place reserved for her in and through the Symbolic. May she get out of booby-trapped silence! And not have the margin or the harem foisted on her as her domain!

In feminine speech, as in writing, there never stops reverberating something that, having once passed through us, having imperceptibly and deeply touched us, still has the power to affect us—song, the first music of the voice of love, which every woman keeps alive.

The Voice sings from a time before law, before the Symbolic took one's breath away and reappropriated it into language under its authority of separation. The deepest, the oldest, the loveliest Visitation. Within each woman the first, nameless love is singing.

In woman there is always, more or less, something of "the mother" repairing and feeding, resisting separation, a force that does not let itself be cut off but that runs codes ragged. The relationship to childhood (the child she was, she is, she acts and makes and starts anew, and unties at the place where, as a same she even others herself), is no more cut off than is the relationship to the "mother," *as it consists of* delights and violences. Text, my body: traversed by lifting flows; listen to me, it is not a captivating, clinging "mother"; it is the equivoice that, touching you, affects you, pushes you away from your breast to come to language, that summons *your* strength; it is the rhyth-me that laughs you; the one intimately addressed who makes all metaphors, all body(?)—bodies(?)—possible and desirable, who is no more describable than god, soul, or the Other; the part of you that puts space between yourself and pushes you to inscribe your woman's style in language. Voice: milk that could go on forever. Found again. The lost mother/bitter-lost. Eternity: is voice mixed with milk.

Not the origin: she doesn't go back there. A boy's journey is the return to the native land, the *Heimweh* Freud speaks of, the nostalgia that makes man a being who tends to come back to the point of departure to appropriate it for himself and to die there. A girl's journey is farther—to the unknown, to invent.

How come this privileged relationship with voice? Because no woman piles up as many defenses against instinctual drives as a man does. You don't prop things up, you don't brick things up the way he does, you don't withdraw from pleasure so "prudently." Even if phallic mystification has contaminated good relations in general, woman is never far from the "mother" (I do not mean the role but the "mother" as no-name and as source of goods). There is always at least a little good mother milk left in her. She writes with white ink.

Voice! That, too, is launching forth and effusion without return. Exclamation, cry, breathlessness, yell, cough, vomit, music. Voice leaves. Voice loses. She leaves. She loses. And that is how she writes, as one throws a voice—forward, into the void. She goes away, she goes forward, doesn't turn back to look at her tracks. Pays no attention to herself. Running breakneck. Contrary to the self-absorbed, masculine narcissism, making sure of its image, of being seen, of seeing itself, of assembling its glories, of pocketing itself again. The reductive look, the always divided look returning, the mirror economy; he needs to love himself. But she launches forth; she seeks to love. Moreover, this is what Valéry sensed, marking his Young Fate in search of herself with ambiguity, masculine in her jealousy of herself: "seeing herself see herself," the motto of all phallocentric speculation/specularization, the motto of every Teste; and feminine in the frantic descent deeper deeper to where a voice that doesn't know itself is lost in the sea's churning.

Voice-cry. Agony—the spoken "word" exploded, blown to bits by suffering and anger, demolishing discourse: this is how she has always been heard before, ever since the time when masculine society began to push her offstage, expulsing her, plundering her. Ever since Medea, ever since Electra.

Voice: unfastening, fracas. Fire! She shoots, she shoots away. Break. From their bodies where they have been buried, shut up and at the same time forbidden to take pleasure. Women have almost everything to write about femininity: about their sexuality, that is to say, about the infinite and mobile complexity of their becoming erotic, about the lightning ignitions of such a minuscule-vast region of their body, not about destiny but about the adventure of such an urge, the voyages, crossings, advances, sudden and slow awakenings, discoveries of a formerly timid region that is just now springing up. Woman's body with a thousand and one fiery hearths, when—shattering censorship and yokes—she lets it articulate the proliferation of meanings that runs through it in every direction. It is going to take much more than language for him to make the ancient maternal tongue sound in only one groove.

We have turned away from our bodies. Shamefully we have been taught to be unaware of them, to lash them with stupid modesty; we've been tricked into a fool's bargain: each one is to love the other sex. I'll give you your body and you will give me mine. But which men give women the body that they blindly hand over to him? Why so few texts? Because there are still so few women winning back their bodies. Woman must write her body, must make up the unimpeded tongue that bursts partitions, classes, and rhetorics, orders and codes, must inundate, run through, go beyond the discourse with its last reserves, including the one of laughing off the word "silence" that has to be said, the one that, aiming for the impossible, stops dead before the word "impossible" and writes it as "end."

In body/Still more: woman is body more than man is. Because he is invited to social success, to sublimation. More body hence more writing. For a long time, still, bodily, within her body she has answered the harassment, the familial conjugal venture of domestication, the repeated attempts to castrate her. Woman, who has run her tongue ten thousand times seven times around her mouth before not speaking, either dies of it or knows her tongue and her mouth better than anyone. Now, I-woman am going to blow up the Law: a possible and inescapable explosion from now on; let it happen, right now, in language.

When "*The* Repressed" of their culture and their society come back, it is an explosive return, which is *absolutely* shattering, staggering, overturning, with a force never let loose before, on the scale of the most tremendous repressions: for at the end of the Age of the Phallus, women will have been either wiped out or heated to the highest, most violent, white-hot fire. Throughout their deafening dumb history, they have lived in dreams, embodied but still deadly silent, in silences, in voiceless rebellions.

And with what force in their fragility: "fragility," a vulnerability to match their matchless intensity. Women have not sublimated. Fortunately. They have saved their skins and their energy. They haven't worked at planning the impasse of futureless lives. They have furiously inhabited these sumptuous bodies. Those wonderful hysterics, who subjected Freud to so many voluptuous moments too shameful to mention, bombarding his mosaic statue/law of Moses with their carnal, passionate body-words, haunting him with their inaudible thundering denunciations, were more than just naked beneath their seven veils of modesty—they were dazzling. In a single word of the body they inscribed the endless vertigo of a history loosed like an arrow from all of men's history, from biblicocapitalist society. Following these yesterday's victims of torture, who anticipate the new women, no intersubjective relationship will ever be the same. It is you, Dora, you, who cannot be tamed, the poetic body, the true "mistress" of the Signifier. Before tomorrow your effectiveness will be seen to work—when your words will no longer be retracted, pointed against your own breast, but will write themselves against the other and against men's grammar. Men must not have that place for their own any more than they have us for their own.

If woman has always functioned "within" man's discourse, a signifier referring always to the opposing signifier that annihilates its particular energy, puts down or stifles its very different sounds, now it is time for her to displace this "within," explode it, overturn it, grab it, make it hers, take it in, take it into her women's mouth, bite its tongue with her women's teeth, make up her own tongue to get inside of it. And you will see how easily she will well up, from this "within" where she was hidden and dormant, to the lips where her foams will overflow.

It is not a question of appropriating their instruments, their concepts, their places for oneself or of wishing oneself in their position of mastery. Our knowing that there is a danger of identification does not mean we should give in. Leave that to the worriers, to masculine anxiety and its obsessional relationship to workings they must control—knowing "how it runs" in order to "make it run." Not taking possession to internalize or manipulate but to shoot through and smash the walls.

Feminine strength is such that while running away with syntax, breaking the famous line (just a tiny little thread, so they say) that serves men as a substitute cord, without which they can't have any fun (*jouir*), to make sure the old mother really is always behind them watching them play phallus, she goes to the impossible where she plays the other, for love, without dying of it.

De-propriation, depersonalization, because she, exasperating, immoderate, and contradictory, destroys laws, the "natural" order. She lifts the bar separating the present from the future, breaking the rigid law of individuation. Nietzsche, in *The Birth of Tragedy,* said that this is the privilege of divinatory, magical forces. What happens to the subject, to the personal pronoun, to its possessives when, suddenly, gaily daring her metamorphoses (because from her within—for a long time her world, she is in a pervasive relationship of desire with every being) she makes another way of knowing circulate? Another way of producing, of communicating, where each one is always far more than one, where her power of identification puts the same to rout.—And with the same traversing, dispersing gesture with which she becomes a feminine other, a masculine other, she breaks with explanation, interpretation, and all the authorities pinpointing localization. She forgets. She proceeds by lapse and bounds. She flies/steals.

To fly/steal is woman's gesture, to steal into language to make it fly. We have all learned flight/theft, the art with many techniques, for all the centuries we have only had access to having by stealing/flying; we have lived in a flight/theft, stealing/flying, finding the close, concealed ways-through of desire. It's not just luck if the word "voler" volleys between the "vol" of theft and the "vol" of flight, pleasuring in each and routing the sense police. It is not just luck: woman partakes of bird and burglar, just as the burglar partakes of woman and bird: hesheits [*illes*] pass, hesheits fly by, hesheits pleasure in scrambling spatial order, disorienting it, moving furniture, things, and values around, breaking in, emptying structures, turning the selfsame, the proper upside down.

What woman has not stolen? Who has not dreamed, savored, or done the thing that jams sociality? Who has not dropped a few red herrings, mocked her way around the separating bar, inscribed what makes a difference with her body, punched holes in the system of couples and positions, and with a transgression screwed up whatever is successive, chain-linked, the fence of circumfusion?

A feminine text cannot not be more than subversive: if it writes itself it is in volcanic heaving of the old "real" property crust. In ceaseless displacement. She must write herself because, when the time comes for her liberation, it is the invention of a *new, insurgent* writing that will allow her to put the breaks and indispensable changes into effect in her history. At first, individually, on two inseparable levels:—woman, writing herself, will go back to this body that has been worse than confiscated, a body replaced with a disturbing stranger, sick or dead, who so often is a bad influence, the cause and place of inhibitions. By censuring the body, breath and speech are censored at the same time.

To write—the act that will "realize" the un-censored relationship of woman to her sexuality, to her woman-being giving her back access to her own forces; that will return her goods, her pleasures, her organs, her vast bodily territories kept under seal; that will tear her out of the superegoed, over-Mosesed structure where the same position of guilt is always reserved for her (guilty of everything, every time: of having desires, of not having any; of being frigid, of being "too" hot; of not being both at once; of being too much of a mother and not enough; of nurturing and of not nurturing . . .). Write yourself: your body must make itself heard. Then the huge resources of the unconscious will burst out. Finally the inexhaustible feminine Imaginary is going to be deployed. Without gold or black dollars, our naphtha will spread values over the world, un-quoted values that will change the rules of the old game.

In the Selfsame Empire, where will the displacement's person find somewhere to lose herself, to write her not-taking-place, her permanent availability.

But somewhere else? There will be some elsewhere where the other will no longer be condemned to death. But has there ever been any elsewhere, is there any? While it is not yet "here," it is there by now—in this other place that disrupts social order, where desire makes fiction exist. Not any old fiction, for, of course, there is classical fiction caught in the oppositions of the system, and literary history has been homogeneous with phallocentric tradition, to the point of being phallocentrism-looking-at-itself, taking pleasure in repeating itself.

But I move toward something that only exists in an elsewhere, and I search in the thought that writing has uncontrollable resources. That writing is what deals with the no-deal, relates to what gives no return. That something else (what history forbids, what reality excludes or doesn't admit) can manifest itself there: some other. With the desire to keep this other alive—hence some living feminine—some difference—and some love; for example a desire, like the one that can unleash a woman, that goes all the way and does not let itself be subjugated by anything. That imposes its necessity as a value without letting itself be intimidated by cultural blackmail, the sacrosanction of social structures. That does not organize life around the threat of death; because a life that has given up can no longer call itself life.

Hence, a "place" of intransigence and of passion. A place of lucidity where no one takes what is a pretense of existence for life. Desire is clearly there like a stroke of fire, it shoots the night through with something. Lightning! that way! I don't have it wrong. Life is right here. Afterward, it's death.

Sometimes I find where to put the many-lifed being that I am. Into elsewheres opened by men who are capable of becoming woman. For the huge machine that ticks and repeats its "truth" for all these centuries has had failures, or I wouldn't be writing. There have been poets who let something different from tradition get through at any price—men able to love love; therefore, to love others, to want them; men able to think the woman who would resist destruction and constitute herself as a superb, equal, "impossible" subject, hence intolerable in the real social context. Only by breaking the codes denying her could the poet have desired that woman. Her appearance causing, if not a revolution, harrowing explosions. Sometimes, moreover, it is in the fissure made by an earthquake, when material upheaval causes radical change in things, when all structures are momentarily disoriented and a fleeting savagery sweeps order away, that the poet lets woman pass through for a brief interval. Kleist did so to the point of dying wishing that women who never lowered their heads—lover-sisters, maternal-daughters, mother-sisters—live. After it's over, as soon as the magistrates' courts are back in place, someone must pay: immediate and bloody death for these uncontrollable elements. (Only for poets, not for novelists who stick with representation. Poets because poetry exists only by taking strength from the unconscious, and the unconscious, the other country without boundaries, is where the repressed survive—women or, as Hoffmann would say, fairies.)

There was Kleist: all was passion then. Passions sweeping beyond the individual, on all levels. No more barriers. Michael Kohlhaas is wonderful, going off to war against the moral and social universe, against the political and religious stronghold, against the State because of a tariff barrier. For a tariff barrier is enough to prevent any life that thinks it is beyond being a subjugated human. One gets beyond everything with Kleist and it is not called transgression. Because passion suddenly flares up in the world where that idea does not exist.

There was that being-of-a-thousand-beings called Shakespeare. I lived all the characters of his worlds: because they are always either alive or dead, because life and death are not separated by any pretense, because all is stunningly joined to nothing, affirmation to no, because, from one to the next, there is only one kiss, one phrase of bliss or tragedy, because every place is either abyss or summit, with nothing flat, soft, temperate. There man turns back into woman, woman into man—a slaveless world: there are villains, powers of death. All the living are great, more than human.

And because compromise cannot take place on their boundless territories, and because only excessively does one venture there, those are elsewheres that put politics on trial: a universe of becoming where power and its snares can never be calmly inscribed. Through the lives profusing there, an endless, tragic struggle continues against false ideas, codes, "values," mastery's ignoble and murderous stupidity.

Kleist, Shakespeare. There are others. But I have never known an equal to such generosity. That is where I have loved. And felt I was loved. Now, from there, I will set forth my ideas about the future. Thanks to a few who were fools about life, I myself stayed alive, at the time when there was no place anywhere for the whole-me (though there was a place for little bits of me). When I wasn't writing. I was Kleist's Penthesileia, not without being Achilles, I was Antony for Cleopatra and she for him; I was also Juliet, because with Romeo I went beyond the father cult. I was Saint Teresa of Avila, that madwoman who knew a lot more than all the men. And who knew how to become a bird on the strength of loving.

Moreover, I have always been a bird. A bit vulture, a bit eagle: I have looked the sun in its face. Born several times—dead several times so that I could be reborn from my ashes; I am mysteriously related to a tree found only in Arabia. I have always practiced flight/theft, and as a thief/who-flies, I got away, flew away, moved away from lands and seas (I never crawled, burrowed, dug, trudged; but I swam a lot). And as a thief, for a long time, I inhabited Jean Genêt.

The hysterics are my sisters. As Dora, I have been all the characters she played, the ones who killed her, the ones who got shivers when she ran through them, and in the end I got away, having been Freud one day, Mrs.

Freud another, also Mr. K . . . , Mrs. K . . . —and the wound Dora inflicted on them. In 1900, I was stifled desire, its rage, its turbulent effects. I kept the merry-go-round of bourgeois-conjugal pettiness from going around without squeaking horribly. I was everything. I sent each "person"/ nobody back to his little calculations, each discourse to its lie, each cowardice to its unconscious, I said nothing but made everything known. I stole their little investments, but that's nothing. I slammed their door. I left. But I am what Dora would have been if woman's history had begun.

It is then that writing makes love other. It is itself this love. Other-Love is writing's first name.

At the beginnings of *Other-Love* there are differences. The new love dares the other, wants it, seems in flight, be-leaves, does some stealing between knowing and making up. She, the one coming from forever, doesn't stand still, she goes all over, she exchanges, she is desire-that-gives. Not shut up inside the paradox of the gift-that-takes or in the illusion of onely uniting. She enters, she betweens—she mes and thees between the other me where one is always infinitely more than one and more than me, without fearing ever to reach a limit: sensualist in our be-coming. We'll never be done with it! She runs through defensive loves, motherings and devourings. She runs her risks beyond stingy narcissism, in moving, open, transitional space. Beyond the back-to-bed of war-love that claims to represent exchange, she mocked the dynamics of Eros which is fed by hate—hate: an inheritance, a leftover, a deceiving subservience to the phallus—to love, to regard-think-seek the other in the other, to de-specularize, to de-speculate. She doesn't enter where history still works as the story of death. Still, having a present does not prevent woman's beginning the story of life elsewhere. Elsewhere, she gives. She doesn't measure what she is giving, but she gives neither false leads nor what she doesn't have. She gives cause to live, to think, to transform. That "economy" can no longer be expressed as an economic term. Wherever she loves, all the ideas of the old management are surpassed. I am for you what you want me to be at the moment in which you look at me as if you have never before seen me so: every moment. When I write, all those that we don't know we can be write themselves from me, without exclusion, without prediction, and everything that we will be calls us to the tireless, intoxicating, tender-costly-search for love. We will never lack ourselves.

From *The Newly Born Woman,* by Cixous and Catherine Clément [1975]
translation 1986.
Translated by Betsy Wing.

Notes

1. All Derrida's work traversing-detecting the history of philosophy is devoted to bringing this to light. In Plato, Hegel, and Nietzsche, the same process continues: repression, repudiation, distancing of woman; a murder that is mixed up with history as the manifestation and representation of masculine power.

†. EN: Here and elsewhere in the following few pages, Cixous's translator has chosen to acknowledge the vocal play in French of *con* (cunt) in various terms containing the syllable 'con-': *reconnaisse* (recognize/recuntnize), *conditionnalité* (conditionality/cuntditionality), *secondaires* (secondary/secuntdary), etc.

2. Freud's thesis is the following: when the Oedipus complex disappears, the *superego* becomes its heir. The moment a boy starts to feel the threat of castration, he begins to overcome the Oedipus complex, with the help of a very harsh superego. For the boy, the Oedipus complex is a primary formation—his first love object is the mother, as it is for the girl. But the girl's history is inevitably constituted under the pressure of a superego that is less harsh: because she is castrated, her superego will not be as strong. She never completely overcomes the Oedipus complex. The feminine Oedipus complex is not a primary formation. The pre-oedipal attachment to the mother entails a difficulty for the girl from which Freud says, she never recovers. It is having to change objects (to love the father) along the way—a painful conversion, which is accompanied by a supplementary renunciation: the passage from pre-oedipal sexuality to "normal" sexuality supposes the abandonment of the clitoris for the vagina. In the terms of this "destiny," women have a reduced symbolic activity: they have nothing to lose, to win, or to defend.

3. J.-J. Bachofen (1815–1887), a Swiss historian of "gynocracy," "historian" of a nonhistory. His aim is to show that the various peoples (Greek, Roman, Hebrew) have passed through an age of "gynocracy," the reign of the Mother, before arriving at patriarchy. This age can only be deduced, for it remains without history. This situation, which was humiliating for men, has been repressed, according to Bachofen's theory, and covered by historical oblivion. And he attempts (particularly in *Das Mutterrecht* [*Mother Right*] 1861) to make an archeology of the matriarchal system, which is very beautiful, beginning with a reading of the first historical texts on the level of the symptom, of what is unsaid in them. Gynocracy, he says, is organized materialism.

4. There are encoded paradigms projecting the robot couple man/woman, as seen by contemporary societies that are symptomatic of a consensus of repetition. See the UNESCO issue of 1975, which is devoted to the International Woman's Year.

5. Cixous, *Prénoms de Personne* [*Nobody's First Names*] (Paris: Editions du Seuil, 1974): "Les Comtes de Hoffmann" ["Tales of Hoffmann"], pp. 112ff.

6. See *Nouvelle Revue de Psychoanalyse* no. 7, *Bisexualité et différence des sexes* (Spring 1973).

7. The home manager, according to the definition of the English word "husband," is the "servant of the house," called the "mari."

8. Nietzsche, Aphorism 315, *The Gay Science.*

9. Is it just chance that it is something of woman, a dismembering feminine, which torments the I/Me who is not/is born only to pursue itself, split by Valéry, infinitely dispersed, never really put back together again in the Young Fate?

Women on the Market

Luce Irigaray

The society we know, our own culture, is based upon the exchange of women. Without the exchange of women, we are told, we would fall back into the anarchy (?) of the natural world, the randomness (?) of the animal kingdom. The passage into the social order, into the symbolic order, into order as such, is assured by the fact that men, or groups of men, circulate women among themselves, according to a rule known as the incest taboo.

Whatever familial form this prohibition may take in a given state of society, its signification has a much broader impact. It assures the foundation of the economic, social, and cultural order that has been ours for centuries.

Why exchange women? Because they are "scarce [commodities] . . . essential to the life of the group," the anthropologist tells us.[1] Why this characteristic of scarcity, given the biological equilibrium between male and female births? Because the "deep polygamous tendency, which exists among all men, always makes the number of available women seem insufficient. Let us add that, even if there were as many women as men, these women would not all be equally desirable . . . and that, by definition . . . , the most desirable women must form a minority."[2]

Are men all equally desirable? Do women have no tendency toward polygamy? The good anthropologist does not raise such questions. *A fortiori*: why are men not objects of exchange among women? It is because women's bodies—through their use, consumption, and circulation—provide for the condition making social life and culture possible, although they remain an unknown "infrastructure" of the elaboration of that social life and culture. The exploitation of the matter that has been sexualized female is so integral a part of our sociocultural horizon that there is no way to interpret it except within this horizon.

In still other words: all the systems of exchange that organize patriarchal societies and all the modalities of productive work that are recognized, valued, and rewarded in these societies are men's business. The production of women, signs, and commodities is always referred back to men (when a man buys a girl, he "pays" the father or the brother, not the mother . . .), and they always pass from one man to another, from one group of men to another. The work force is thus always assumed to be masculine, and "products" are objects to be used, objects of transaction among men alone.

Which means that the possibility of our social life, of our culture, depends upon a ho(m)mo-sexual monopoly? The law that orders our society is the exclusive valorization of men's needs/desires, of exchanges among men. What the anthropologist calls the passage from nature to culture thus amounts to the institution of the reign of hom(m)o-sexuality [*hom(m)o-sexualité*†]. Not in an "immediate" practice, but in its "social" mediation. From this point on, patriarchal societies might be interpreted as societies functioning in the mode of "semblance." The value of symbolic and imaginary productions is superimposed upon, and even substituted for, the value of relations of material, natural, and corporal (re)production.

In this new matrix of History, in which man begets man as his own likeness, wives, daughters, and sisters have value only in that they serve as the possibility of, and potential benefit in, relations among men. The use of and traffic in women subtend and uphold the reign of masculine hom(m)o-sexuality, even while they maintain that hom(m)o-sexuality in speculations, mirror games, identifications, and more or less rivalrous appropriations, which defer its real practice. Reigning everywhere, although prohibited in practice, hom(m)o-sexuality is played out through the bodies of women, matter, or sign, and heterosexuality has been up to now just an alibi for the smooth workings of man's relations with himself, of relations among men. Whose "sociocultural endogamy" excludes the participation of that other, so foreign to the social order: woman. Exogamy doubtless requires that one leave one's family, tribe, or clan, in order to make alliances. All the same, it does not tolerate marriage with populations that are too far away, too far removed from the prevailing cultural rules. A sociocultural endogamy would thus forbid commerce with women. Men make commerce of them, but they do not enter into any exchanges with them. Is this perhaps all the more true because exogamy is an economic issue, perhaps even subtends economy as such? The exchange of women as goods accompanies and stimulates exchanges of other "wealth" among groups of men. The economy— in both the narrow and the broad sense—that is in place in our societies thus requires that women lend themselves to alienation in consumption, and to exchanges in which they do not participate, and that men be exempt from being used and circulated like commodities.

◻

Marx's analysis of commodities as the elementary form of capitalist wealth can thus be understood as an interpretation of the status of woman in so-called patriarchal societies. The organization of such societies, and the operation of the symbolic system on which this organization is based—a symbolic system whose instrument and representative is the proper name:

the name of the father, the name of God—contain in a nuclear form the developments that Marx defines as characteristic of a capitalist regime: the submission of "nature" to a "labor" on the part of men who thus constitute "nature" as use value and exchange value; the division of labor among private producer-owners who exchange their women-commodities among themselves, but also among producers and exploiters or exploitees of the social order; the standardization of women according to proper names that determine their equivalences; a tendency to accumulate wealth, that is, a tendency for the representatives of the most "proper" names— the leaders—to capitalize more women than the others; a progression of the social work of the symbolic toward greater and greater abstraction; and so forth.

To be sure, the means of production have evolved, new techniques have been developed, but it does seem that as soon as the father-man was assured of his reproductive power and had marked his products with his name, that is, from the very origin of private property and the patriarchal family, social exploitation occurred. In other words, all the social regimes of "History" are based upon the exploitation of one "class" of producers, namely, women. Whose reproductive use value (reproductive of children and of the labor force) and whose constitution as exchange value underwrite the symbolic order as such, without any compensation in kind going to them for that "work." For such compensation would imply a double system of exchange, that is, a shattering of the monopolization of the proper name (and of what it signifies as appropriative power) by father-men.

Thus the social body would be redistributed into producer-subjects no longer functioning as commodities because they provided the standard of value for commodities, and into commodity-objects that ensured the circulation of exchange without participating in it as subjects.

Let us now reconsider a few points[3] in Marx's analysis of value that seem to describe the social status of women.

Wealth amounts to a subordination of the use of things to their accumulation. Then would the way women are used matter less than their number? The possession of a woman is certainly indispensable to man for the reproductive use value that she represents; but what he desires is to have them all. To "accumulate" them, to be able to count off his conquests, seductions, possessions, both sequentially and cumulatively, as measure or standard(s).

All but one? For if the series could be closed, value might well lie, as Marx says, in the relation among them rather than in the relation to a standard that remains external to them—whether gold or phallus.

The use made of women is thus of less value than their appropriation one by one. And their "usefulness" is not what counts the most. Woman's price is not determined by the "properties" of her body—although her body constitutes the *material* support of that price.

But when women are exchanged, woman's body must be treated as an *abstraction.* The exchange operation cannot take place in terms of some intrinsic, immanent value of the commodity. It can only come about when two objects—two women—are in a relation of equality with a third term that is neither the one nor the other. It is thus not as "women" that they are exchanged, but as women reduced to some common feature—their current price in gold, or phalluses—and of which they would represent a plus or minus quantity. Not a plus or a minus of feminine qualities, obviously. Since these qualities are abandoned in the long run to the needs of the consumer, *woman has value on the market by virtue of one single quality: that of being a product of man's "labor."*

On this basis, each one looks exactly like every other. They all have the same phantom-like reality. Metamorphosed in identical sublimations, samples of the same indistinguishable work, all these objects now manifest just one thing, namely, that in their production a force of human labor has been expended, that labor has accumulated in them. In their role as crystals of that common social substance, they are deemed to have value.

As commodities, women are thus two things at once: utilitarian objects and bearers of value. "They manifest themselves therefore as commodities, or have the form of commodities, only in so far as they have two forms, a physical or natural form, and a value form" (p. 55).

But "the reality of the value of commodities differs in this respect from Dame Quickly, that we don't know 'where to have it'" (ibid.). *Woman, object of exchange, differs from woman, use value, in that one doesn't know how to take (hold of) her,* for since "the value of commodities is the very opposite of the coarse materiality of their substance, not an atom of matter enters into its composition. Turn and examine a single commodity, by itself, as we will. Yet in so far as it remains an object of value, it seems impossible to grasp it" (ibid.). The value of a woman always escapes: black continent, hole in the symbolic, breach in discourse. . . . It is only in the operation of exchange among women that something of this—something enigmatic, to be sure—can be felt. *Woman thus has value only in that she can be exchanged.* In the passage from one to the other, something else finally exists beside the possible utility of the "coarseness" of her body. But this value is not found, is not recaptured, in her. It is only her measurement against a third term that remains external to her, and that makes it possible to compare her with another woman, that permits her to have a relation to another commodity in terms of an equivalence that remains foreign to both.

Women-as-commodities are thus subject to a schism that divides them into the categories of usefulness and exchange value; into matter-body and an envelope that is precious but impenetrable, ungraspable, and not suscepti- ble to appropriation by women themselves; into private use and social use.

In order to have a *relative value,* a commodity has to be confronted with another commodity that serves as its equivalent. Its value is never found to lie within itself. And the fact that it is worth more or less is not its own doing but comes from that to which it may be equivalent. Its value is tran- scendent to itself, *super-natural, ek-static.*

In other words, for the commodity, there is no mirror that copies it so that it may be at once itself and its "own" reflection. One commodity cannot be mirrored in another, as man is mirrored in his fellow man. For when we are dealing with commodities the self-same, mirrored, is not "its" own like- ness, contains nothing of its properties, its qualities, its "skin and hair." The likeness here is only a measure expressing the *fabricated* character of the commodity, its trans-formation by man's (social, symbolic) "labor." The mirror that envelops and paralyzes the commodity specularizes, specu- lates (on) man's "labor." *Commodities, women, are a mirror of value of and for man.* In order to serve as such, they give up their bodies to men as the supporting material of specularization, of speculation. They yield to him their natural and social value as a locus of imprints, marks, and mirage of his activity.

Commodities among themselves are thus not equal, nor alike, nor dif- ferent. They only become so when they are compared by and for man. And *the prosopopoeia of the relation of commodities among themselves is a projec- tion* through which producers-exchangers make them reenact before their eyes their operations of specula(riza)tion. Forgetting that in order to reflect (oneself), to speculate (oneself), it is necessary to be a "subject," and that matter can serve as a support for speculation but cannot itself speculate in any way.

Thus, starting with the simplest relation of equivalence between com- modities, starting with the possible exchange of women, the entire enigma of the money form—of the phallic function—is implied. That is, the appro- priation-disappropriation by man, for man, of nature and its productive forces, insofar as a certain mirror now divides and travesties both nature and labor. Man endows the commodities he produces with a narcissism that blurs the seriousness of utility, of use. Desire, as soon as there is exchange, "perverts" need. But that perversion will be attributed to commodities and to their alleged relations. Whereas they can have no relationships except from the perspective of speculating third parties.

The economy of exchange—of desire—is man's business. For two reasons: the exchange takes place between masculine subjects, and it requires a *plus-value* added to the body of the commodity, a supplement which gives it a valuable form. That supplement will be found, Marx writes, in another commodity, whose use value becomes, from that point on, a standard of value.

But that surplus-value enjoyed by one of the commodities might vary: "just as many a man strutting about in a gorgeous uniform counts for more than when in mufti" (p. 60). Or just as "*A*, for instance, cannot be 'your majesty' to *B*, unless at the same time majesty in *B*'s eyes assume the bodily form of *A*, and, what is more, with every new father of the people, changes its features, hair, and many other things besides" (ibid.). Commodities— "things" produced—would thus have the respect due the uniform, majesty, paternal authority. And even God. "The fact that it is value, is made manifest by its equality with the coat, just as the sheep's nature of a Christian is shown in his resemblance to the Lamb of God" (ibid.).

Commodities thus share in the cult of the father, and never stop striving to resemble, to copy, the one who is his representative. It is from that resemblance, from that imitation of what represents paternal authority, that commodities draw their value—for men. But it is upon commodities that the producers-exchangers bring to bear this power play. "We see, then, all that our analysis of the value of commodities has already told us, is told us by the linen itself, so soon as it comes into communication with another commodity, the coat. Only it betrays its thoughts in that language with which alone it is familiar, the language of commodities. In order to tell us that its own value is created by labor in its abstract character of human labor, it says that the coat, in so far as it is worth as much as the linen, and therefore is value, consists of the same labor as the linen. In order to inform us that its sublime reality as value is not the same as its buckram body, it says that value has the appearance of a coat, and consequently that so far as the linen is value, it and the coat are as like as two peas. We may here remark, that the language of commodities has, besides Hebrew, many other more or less correct dialects. The German '*werthsein,*' to be worth, for instance, expresses in a less striking manner than the Romance verbs '*valere,*' '*valer,*' '*valoir,*' that the equating of commodity B to commodity A, is commodity A's own mode of expressing its value. Paris vaut bien une messe" (pp. 60–61).

So commodities speak. To be sure, mostly dialects and patois, languages hard for "subjects" to understand. The important thing is that they be preoccupied with their respective values, that their remarks confirm the exchangers' plans for them.

The body of a commodity thus becomes, for another such commodity, a mirror of its value. Contingent upon a bodily supplement. A supplement opposed to use value, a supplement representing the commodity's supernatural quality (an imprint that is purely social in nature), a supplement completely different from the body itself, and from its properties, a supplement that nevertheless exists only on condition that one commodity agrees to relate itself to another considered as equivalent: "For instance, one man is king only because other men stand in the relation of subjects to him" (p. 66, n. 1).

This supplement of equivalency translates concrete work into abstract work. In other words, in order to be able to incorporate itself into a mirror of value, it is necessary that the work itself reflect only its property of human labor: that the body of a commodity be nothing more than the materialization of an abstract human labor. That is, that it have no more body, matter, nature, but that it be objectivization, a crystallization as visible object, of man's activity.

In order to become equivalent, a commodity changes bodies. A super-natural, metaphysical origin is substituted for its material origin. Thus its body becomes a transparent body, *pure phenomenality of value.* But this transparency constitutes a supplement to the material opacity of the commodity.

Once again there is a schism between the two. Two sides, two poles, nature and society are divided, like the perceptible and the intelligible, matter and form, the empirical and the transcendental . . . The commodity, like the sign, suffers from metaphysical dichotomies. Its value, its truth, lies in the social element. But this social element is added on to its nature, to its matter, and the social subordinates it as a lesser value, indeed as nonvalue. Participation in society requires that the body submit itself to a specularization, a speculation, that transforms it into a value-bearing object, a standardized sign, an exchangeable signifier, a "likeness" with reference to an authoritative model. *A commodity—a woman—is divided into two irreconcilable "bodies":* her "natural" body and her socially valued, exchangeable body, which is a particularly mimetic expression of masculine values. No doubt these values also express "nature," that is, the expenditure of physical force. But this latter—essentially masculine, moreover—serves for the fabrication, the transformation, the technicization of natural productions. And it is this *super*-natural property that comes to constitute the value of the product. Analyzing value in this way, Marx exposes the meta-physical character of social operations.

The commodity is thus a dual entity as soon as its value comes to possess a phenomenal form of its own, distinct from its natural form: that of exchange value. And it never possesses this form if it is considered in isolation. A commodity has this phenomenal form added on to its nature only in relation to another commodity.

As among signs, value appears only when a relationship has been established. It remains the case that the establishment of relationships cannot be accomplished by the commodities themselves, but depends upon the operation of two exchangers. The exchange value of two signs, two commodities, two women, is a representation of the needs/desires of consumer-exchanger subjects: in no way is it the "property" of the signs/articles/women themselves. At the most, the commodities—or rather the relationships among them—are the material alibi for the desire for relations among men. To this end, the commodity is disinvested of its body and reclothed in a form that makes it suitable for exchange among men.

But, in this value-bearing form, the desire for that exchange, and the reflection of his own value and that of his fellow man that man seeks in it, are ek-stasized. In that suspension in the commodity of the relationship among men, producer-consumer-exchanger subjects are alienated. In order that they might "bear" and support that alienation, commodities for their part have always been dispossessed of their specific value. On this basis, one may affirm that the value of the commodity takes on *indifferently* any given form of use value. The price of the articles, in fact, no longer comes from *their* natural form, from *their* bodies, *their* language, but from the fact that they mirror the need/desire for exchanges among men. To do this, the commodity obviously cannot exist alone, but there is no such thing as a commodity, either, so long as there are not *at least two men* to make an exchange. In order for a product—a woman?— to have value, two men, at least, have to invest (in) her.

The general equivalent of a commodity no longer functions as a commodity itself. A preeminent mirror, transcending the world of merchandise, it guarantees the possibility of universal exchange among commodities. Each commodity may become equivalent to every other from the viewpoint of that sublime standard, but the fact that the judgment of their value depends upon some transcendental element renders them provisionally incapable of being directly exchanged for each other. They are exchanged by means of the general equivalent—as Christians love each other in God, to borrow a theological metaphor dear to Marx.

That ek-static reference separates them radically from each other. *An abstract and universal value preserves them from use and exchange among themselves.* They are, as it were, transformed into value-invested idealities. Their concrete forms, their specific qualities, and all the possibilities of "real" relations with them or among them are reduced to their common character as products of man's labor and desire.

We must emphasize also that *the general equivalent,* since it is no longer a commodity, *is no longer useful. The standard as such is exempt from use.*

Though a commodity may at first sight appear to be "a very trivial thing, and easily understood, . . . it is, in reality, a very queer thing, abounding in metaphysical subtleties and theological niceties" (p. 81). No doubt, "so far as it is a value in use, there is nothing mysterious about it. . . . But, so soon as [a wooden table, for example] steps forth as a commodity, it is changed into something transcendent. It not only stands with its feet on the ground, but, in relation to all other commodities, it stands on its head, and evolves out of its wooden brain grotesque ideas, far more wonderful than 'table-turning' ever was" (pp. 81–82).

"The mystical character of commodities does not originate, therefore, in their use value. Just as little does it proceed from the nature of the determining factors of value. For, in the first place, however varied the useful kinds of labor, or productive activities, may be, it is a physiological fact, that they are functions of the human organism" (p. 82), which, for Marx, does not seem to constitute a mystery in any way . . . The material contribution and support of bodies in societal operations pose no problems for him, except as production and expenditure of energy.

Where, then, does the enigmatic character of the product of labor come from, as soon as this product takes on the form of a commodity? It comes, obviously, from that form itself. *Then where does the enigmatic character of women come from?* Or even that of their supposed relations among themselves? Obviously, from the "form" of the needs/desires of man, needs/desires that women bring to light although men do not recognize them in that form. That form, those women, are always enveloped, veiled.

In any case, "the existence of things *qua* commodities, and the value relation between the products of labor which stamps them as commodities, have absolutely no connection with their physical properties and with the material relations arising there-from. [With commodities] it is a definite social relation between men, that assumes, in their eyes, the fantastic form of a relation between things" (p. 83). *This phenomenon has no analogy except in the reli-*

gious world. "In that world the productions of the human brain appear as independent beings endowed with life, and entering into relation both with one another and the human race. So it is in the world of commodities with the products of men's hands" (ibid.). Hence the fetishism attached to these products of labor as soon as they present themselves as commodities.

Hence *women's role as fetish-objects,* inasmuch as, in exchanges, they are the manifestation and the circulation of a power of the Phallus, establishing relationships of men with each other?

�«▣»

Hence the following remarks:

On value.

It represents the equivalent of labor force, of an expenditure of energy, of toil. In order to be measured, these latter must be *abstracted* from all immediately natural qualities, from any concrete individual. A process of generalization and of universalization imposes itself in the operation of social exchanges. Hence the reduction of man to a "concept"—that of his labor force—and the reduction of his product to an "object," the visible, material correlative of that concept.

The characteristics of "sexual pleasure" corresponding to such a social state are thus the following: its productivity, but one that is necessarily laborious, even painful; its abstract form; its need/desire to crystallize in a transcendental element of wealth the standard of all value; its need for a material support where the relation of appropriation to and of that standard is measured; its exchange relationships—always rivalrous—among men alone, and so on.

Are not these modalities the ones that might define the economy of (so-called) masculine sexuality? And is libido not another name for the abstraction of "energy" in a productive power? For the work of nature? Another name for the desire to accumulate goods? Another name for the subordination of the specific qualities of bodies to a—neutral?—power that aims above all to transform them in order to possess them? Does pleasure, for masculine sexuality, consist in anything other than the appropriation of nature, in the desire to make it (re)produce, and in exchanges of its/these products with other members of society? An essentially economic pleasure.

Thus the following question: *what needs/desires of (so-called) masculine sexuality have presided over the evolution of a certain social order,* from its primitive form, private property, to its developed form, capital? But also: *to*

what extent are these needs/desires the effect of a social mechanism, in part
autonomous, that produces them as such?

On the status of women in such a social order.

   What makes such an order possible, what assures its foundation, is thus
the exchange of women. The circulation of women among men is what
establishes the operations of society, at least of patriarchal society. Whose
presuppositions include the following: the appropriation of nature by man;
the transformation of nature according to "human" criteria, defined by
men alone; the submission of nature to labor and technology; the reduction of its material, corporeal, perceptible qualities to man's practical concrete activity; the equality of women among themselves, but in terms of
laws of equivalence that remain external to them; the constitution of
women as "objects" that emblematize the materialization of relations
among men, and so on.

   In such a social order, women thus represent a natural value and a social
value. Their "development" lies in the passage from one to the other. But
this passage never takes place simply.

   As *mother, woman remains on the side of* (re)productive *nature* and,
because of this, man can never fully transcend his relation to the "natural."
His social existence, his economic structures, and his sexuality are always
tied to the work of nature: these structures thus always remain at the level
of the earliest appropriation, that of the constitution of nature as landed
property, and of the earliest labor, which is agricultural. But this relationship to productive nature, an insurmountable one, has to be denied so that
relations among men may prevail. This means that mothers, reproductive
instruments marked with the name of the father and enclosed in his house,
must be private property, excluded from exchange. The *incest taboo* represents this refusal to allow productive nature to enter into exchanges among
men. As both natural value and use value, mothers cannot circulate in the
form of commodities without threatening the very existence of the social
order. Mothers are essential to its (re)production (particularly inasmuch as
they are [re]productive of children and of the labor force: through maternity, child-rearing, and domestic maintenance in general). Their responsibility is to maintain the social order without intervening so as to change it.
Their products are legal tender in that order, moreover, only if they are
marked with the name of the father, only if they are recognized within his
law: that is, only insofar as they are appropriated by him. Society is the

place where man engenders himself, where man produces himself as man, where man is born into "human," "super-natural" existence.

The virginal woman, on the other hand, is pure exchange value. She is nothing but the possibility, the place, the sign of relations among men. In and of herself, she does not exist: she is a simple envelope veiling what is really at stake in social exchange. In this sense, her natural body disappears into its representative function. *Red blood* remains on the mother's side, but it has no price, as such, in the social order; woman, for her part, as medium of exchange, is no longer anything but *semblance*. The ritualized passage from woman to mother is accomplished by the *violation of an envelope*: the hymen, which has taken on the value of *taboo*, the taboo of virginity. Once deflowered, woman is relegated to the status of use value, to her entrapment in private property; she is removed from exchange among men.

The *prostitute* remains to be considered. Explicitly condemned by the social order, she is implicitly tolerated. No doubt because the break between usage and exchange is, in her case, less clear-cut? In her case, the qualities of woman's body are "useful." However, these qualities have "value" only because they have already been appropriated by a man, and because they serve as the locus of relations—hidden ones—between men. Prostitution amounts to *usage that is exchanged*. Usage that is not merely potential: it has already been realized. The woman's body is valuable because it has already been used. In the extreme case, the more it has served, the more it is worth. Not because its natural assets have been put to use this way, but, on the contrary, because its nature has been "used up," and has become once again no more than a vehicle for relations among men.

Mother, virgin, prostitute: these are the social roles imposed on women. The characteristics of (so-called) feminine sexuality derive from them: the valorization of reproduction and nursing; faithfulness; modesty, ignorance of and even lack of interest in sexual pleasure; a passive acceptance of men's "activity"; seductiveness, in order to arouse the consumers' desire while offering herself as its material support without getting pleasure herself . . . *Neither as mother nor as virgin nor as prostitute has woman any right to her own pleasure.*

Of course the theoreticians of sexuality are sometimes astonished by women's frigidity. But, according to them, this frigidity is explained more by an impotence inherent to feminine "nature" than by the submission of that nature to a certain type of society. However, *what is required of a "normal" feminine sexuality is oddly evocative of the characteristics of the status of a commodity.* With references to and rejections of the "natural"—physiological and organic nature, and so on—that are equally ambiguous.

And, in addition:

—just as nature has to be subjected to man in order to become a commodity, so, it appears, does "the development of a normal woman." A development that amounts, for the feminine, to subordination to the forms and laws of masculine activity. The rejection of the mother—imputed to woman—would find its "cause" here;

—just as, in commodities, natural utility is overridden by the exchange function, so the properties of a woman's body have to be suppressed and subordinated to the exigencies of its transformation into an object of circulation among men;

—just as a commodity has no mirror it can use to reflect itself, so woman serves as reflection, as image of and for man but lacks specific qualities of her own. Her value-invested form amounts to what man inscribes in and on its matter: that is, her body;

—just as commodities cannot make exchanges among themselves without the intervention of a subject that measures them against a standard, so it is with women. Distinguished, divided, separated, classified as like and unlike, according to whether they have been judged exchangeable. In themselves, among themselves, they are amorphous and confused: natural body, maternal body, doubtless useful to the consumer, but without any possible identity or communicable value;

—just as commodities, despite their resistance, become more or less autonomous repositories for the value of human work, so, as mirrors of and for man, women more or less unwittingly come to represent the danger of a disappropriation of masculine power: the phallic mirage;

—just as a commodity finds the expression of its value in an equivalent—in the last analysis, a general one—that necessarily remains external to it, so woman derives her price from her relation to the male sex, constituted as a transcendental value: the phallus. And indeed the enigma of "value" lies in the most elementary relation among commodities. Among women. For, uprooted from their "nature," they no longer relate to each other except in terms of what they represent in men's desire, and according to the "forms" that this imposes upon them. Among themselves, they are separated by his speculations.

This means that the division of "labor"—sexual labor in particular—requires that woman maintain in her own body the material substratum of the object of desire, but that she herself never have access to desire. The economy of desire of exchange—is man's business. And that economy subjects women to a schism that is necessary to symbolic operations: red blood/semblance; body/value-invested envelope; matter/medium of exchange; (re)productive nature/fabricated femininity . . . That schism—characteristic of all speaking nature, someone will surely object—is experienced by women without any possible profit to them. And without any way for them to transcend it. They are not even "conscious" of it. The symbolic system that cuts them in two this way is in no way appropriate to them. In them, "semblance" remains external, foreign to "nature." *Socially*, they are "objects" for and among men and furthermore they cannot do anything but mimic a "language" that they have not produced; *naturally*, they remain amorphous, suffering from drives without any possible representatives or representations. For them, the transformation of the natural into the social does not take place, except to the extent that they function as components of private property, or as commodities.

Characteristics of this social order

This type of social system can be interpreted as *the practical realization of the meta-physical.* As the *practical destiny* of the meta-physical, it would also represent its *most fully realized form.* Operating in such a way, moreover, that subjects themselves, being implicated in it through and through, being produced in it as concepts, would lack the means to analyze it. Except in an after-the-fact way whose delays are yet to be fully measured . . .

This practical realization of the meta-physical has as its founding operation the appropriation of woman's body by the father or his substitutes. It is marked by women's submission to a system of general equivalents, the proper name representing the father's monopoly of power. It is from this standardization that women receive their value, as they pass from the state of nature to the status of social object. This trans-formation of women's bodies into use values and exchange values inaugurates the symbolic order. But that order depends upon a *nearly pure added value.* Women, animals endowed with speech like men, assure the possibility of the use and circulation of the symbolic without being recipients of it. Their nonaccess to the symbolic is what has established the social order. Putting men in touch with each other, in relations among themselves, women only fulfill this role by relinquishing their right to speech and even to animality. No longer in the natural order, not yet in the social order that they nonetheless maintain, women are the symptom of the exploitation of individuals by a society that remunerates them only partially, or even not at all, for their "work." Unless subordination to a system that utilizes you and oppresses you should be considered as sufficient compensation. . . ? Unless the fact that women are branded with the proper name—of the "father"—should be viewed as the symbolic payment awarded them for sustaining the social order with their bodies?

But by submitting women's bodies to a general equivalent, to a transcendent, super-natural value, men have drawn the social structure into an ever greater process of abstraction, to the point where they themselves are produced in it as pure concepts: having surmounted all their "perceptible" qualities and individual differences, they are finally reduced to the average productivity of their labor. The power of this practical economy of the meta-physical comes from the fact that "physiological" energy is transformed into abstract value without the mediation of an intelligible elaboration. No individual subject can be credited any longer with bringing about this transformation. It is only after the fact that the subject might possibly be able to analyze his determination as such by the social structure. And even then it is not certain that his love of gold would not make him give up everything else before he would renounce the cult of this fetish. "The saver thus sacrifices to this fetish all the penchants of his flesh. No one takes the gospel of renunciation more seriously than he."

Fortunately—if we may say so—women/commodities would remain, as simple "objects" of transaction among men. Their situation of specific exploitation in exchange operations—sexual exchange, and economic, social, and cultural exchanges in general—might lead them to offer a new critique of the political economy. *A critique that would no longer avoid that of discourse, and more generally of the symbolic system, in which it is realized.* Which would lead to interpreting in a different way the impact of symbolic social labor in the analysis of relations of production.

For, without the exploitation of women, what would become of the social order? What modifications would it undergo if women left behind their condition as commodities—subject to being produced, consumed, valorized, circulated, and so on, by men alone—and took part in elaborating and carrying out exchanges? Not by reproducing, by copying, the "phallocratic" models that have the force of law today, but by socializing in a different way the relation to nature, matter, the body, language, and desire.

From *This Sex Which Is Not One* [1977] translation 1985.
Translated by Catherine Porter, with Carolyn Burke.

Notes

This text was originally published as "Le marché des femmes," in *Sessualità e politica* (Milan: Feltrinelli, 1978).

1. Claude Lévi-Strauss, *The Elementary Structures of Kinship* (*Les Structures élémentaires de la Parenté*, 1949, rev. 1967), trans. James Harle Bell, John Richard von Sturmer, and Rodney Needham (Boston: Beacon Press, 1969), p. 36.

2. Ibid., p. 38.

†. EN: Irigaray's neologism plays on the French '*homo*' ('same') and '*homme*' ('man'), drawing attention to the tendency in psychoanalysis and elsewhere to frame "homosexuality" in terms of a male desire for the same.

3. These notes constitute a statement of points that will be developed in a subsequent chapter [of *This Sex Which Is Not One*]. All the quotations in the remainder of this chapter are excerpted from Marx's *Capital*, section 1, chapter 1. (The page numbers given in the text refer to the Modern Library edition, trans. Samuel Moore and Edward Aveling, ed. Frederick Engels, rev. Ernest Untermann [New York: Modern Library, 1906].) Will it be objected that this interpretation is analogical by nature? I accept the question, on condition that it be addressed also, and in the first place, to Marx's analysis of commodities. Did not Aristotle, a "great thinker" according to Marx, determine the relation of form to matter by analogy with the relation between masculine and feminine? Returning to the question of the difference between the sexes would amount instead, then, to going back through analogism.

Selections from *The Logic of Practice*

Pierre Bourdieu

The Work of Time

So long as one only considers practices which, like rituals, derive some of their most important properties from the fact that they are "detotalized" by their unfolding in succession, one is liable to neglect those properties of practice that detemporalizing science has least chance of reconstituting, namely the properties it owes to the fact that it is constructed in time, that time gives it its form, as the order of a succession, and therefore its direction and meaning. This is true of all practices which, like gift exchange or the joust of honor, are defined, at least in the eyes of the agents, as irreversible oriented sequences of relatively unpredictable acts. It will be recalled that, in opposition to the ordinary representation and to the famous analysis by Marcel Mauss, whom he accuses of placing himself at the level of a "phenomenology" of gift exchange, Lévi-Strauss holds that science must break with native experience and the native theory of that experience and postulate that "the primary, fundamental phenomenon is exchange itself, which gets split up into discrete operations in social life" (Lévi-Strauss 1987: 47), in other words, that the "automatic laws" of the cycle of reciprocity are the unconscious principle of the obligation to give, the obligation to return a gift and the obligation to receive (1987: 43). In postulating that the objective model, obtained by reducing the polythetic to the nomothetic, the detotalized, irreversible succession to the perfectly reversible totality, is the immanent law of practices, the invisible principle of the movements observed, the analyst reduces the agents to the status of automata or inert bodies moved by obscure mechanisms toward ends of which they are unaware. "Cycles of reciprocity," mechanical interlockings of obligatory practices, exist only for the absolute gaze of the omniscient, omnipresent spectator, who, thanks to his knowledge of the social mechanics, is able to be present at the different stages of the "cycle." In reality, the gift may remain unreciprocated, when one obliges an ungrateful person; it may be rejected as an insult, inasmuch as it asserts or demands the possibility of reciprocity, and therefore of recognition.[1] Quite apart from the trouble-makers who call into question the game itself and its apparently flawless mechanism (like the man the Kabyles call *amahbul*), even when the agents' dispositions are as perfectly harmonized as possible and when the sequence of actions and reactions seems entirely predictable from outside, uncertainty remains as to the outcome of the interaction until the whole sequence is completed. The most ordinary and even the seemingly most routine exchanges of ordinary life, like the "little gifts" that "bind friendship," presuppose an improvisation, and therefore a constant uncertainty, which, as we say, make all their *charm*, and hence all their social efficacy.

Little presents, which are halfway between "gratuitous" gifts (*elmaatar*, the unrequited gift, "like a mother's milk," or *thikchi*, a thing given without recompense) and the most rigorously forced gifts (*elahdya* or *lehna*), must be of modest value and hence easy to give and easy to match ("it's nothing," as we say); but they must be frequent and in a sense continuous, which implies that they must function within the logic of the "surprise" or the "spontaneous gesture" rather than according to the mechanism of ritual. These presents intended to maintain the everyday order of social intercourse almost always consist of a dish of cooked food, couscous (with a piece of cheese, when they mark a cow's first milk), and follow the course of minor family celebrations—the third or seventh day after a birth, a baby's first tooth or first steps, a boy's first haircut, first visit to the market or first fast. Linked to events in the life-cycle of mankind or the earth, they involve those wishing to share their joy, and those who share in it, in what is nothing less than a fertility rite: when the dish that contained the gift is taken back, it always contains, "for good luck" (*el fal*), what is sometimes called *thiririth* (from *er*, give back), that is to say, a little wheat, a little semolina (never barley, a female plant and a symbol of frailty) or, preferably, some dried vegetables, chick peas, lentils, etc., called *ajedjig* (flower), given "so that the boy [the pretext for the exchange] will flower" into manhood. These ordinary gifts (which include some of those called *tharzefth*, which are visiting presents) are clearly opposed to the extra-ordinary gifts, *elkhir*, *elahdya* or *lehna*, given for the major festivals called *thimeghriwin* (sing. *thameghra*)—weddings, births, circumcisions—and *a fortiori* to *lwaada*, the obligatory gift to a holy man. Indeed, little gifts between relatives and friends are opposed to the present of money and eggs which is given by affines remote in both space and genealogy, and also in time—since they are seen only rarely, on the "great occasions"—and the magnitude and solemnity of which makes it a kind of controlled challenge, in the same way that marriages within the lineage or neighborhood, so frequent that they pass unnoticed, are opposed to the more prestigious but infinitely more hazardous extra-ordinary marriages between different villages or tribes, sometimes intended to set the seal on alliances or reconciliations and always marked by solemn ceremonies.

The simple possibility that things might proceed otherwise than as laid down by the "mechanical laws" of the "cycle of reciprocity" is sufficient to change the whole experience of practice and, by the same token, its logic. The shift from the highest probability to absolute certainty is a qualitative leap out of proportion to the numerical difference. The uncertainty which has an objective basis in the probabilistic logic of social laws is sufficient to modify not only the experience of practice, but practice itself, for example by encouraging strategies aimed at avoiding the most probable outcome. To reintroduce uncertainty is to reintroduce time, with its rhythm, its orientation and its irreversibility, substituting the dialectic of strategies for the mechanics of the model, but without falling over into the imaginary anthropology of "rational actor" theories.

The *ars inveniendi* is an *ars combinatoria*. And one can construct a relatively simple generative model which makes it possible to give an account of the logic of practice, that is, to generate—on paper—the universe of practices (conducts of honor, acts of exchange) really observed, which impress both by their inexhaustible diversity and their apparent necessity, without resorting to the imaginary "file of prefabricated representations," as Jakobson (1956) puts it, that would enable one to "choose" the conduct appropriate to each situation. Thus, to account for all the observed conducts of honor, and only those, one simply needs a fundamental principle, that of equality in honor, which, although it is never explicitly posited as an axiom of all ethical operations, seems to orient practices, because the sense of honor gives practical mastery of it. The exchange of honor, like every exchange (of gifts, words, etc.) is defined as such—in opposition to the unilateral violence of aggression—that is, as implying the possibility of a continuation, a reply, a riposte, a return gift, inasmuch as it contains recognition of the partner (to whom, in the particular case, it accords equality in honor).[2] The challenge, as such, calls for a riposte, and is therefore addressed to a man deemed capable of playing the game of honor, and of playing it well: the challenge confers honor. The converse of this principle of reciprocity is that only a challenge issued by a man equal in honor deserves to be taken up. The act of honor is completely constituted as such only by the riposte, which implies recognition of the challenge as an act of honor and of its author as a man of honor. The fundamental principle and its converse imply in turn that a man who enters into an exchange of honor (by issuing or taking up a challenge) with someone who is not his equal in honor dishonors himself. By challenging a superior, he risks a snub, which would cast the dishonor back on himself; by challenging an inferior or taking up his challenge, he dishonors himself. Thus *elbahadla*, total humiliation, rebounds on to the man who misuses his advantages and humiliates his adversary to excess rather than letting him "cover himself in shame." Conversely, *elbahadla* would recoil on a man who imprudently stooped to take up a senseless challenge, whereas, by declining to riposte, he leaves his presumptuous challenger to bear the full weight of his arbitrary act.[3]

We thus have a very simple diagram:

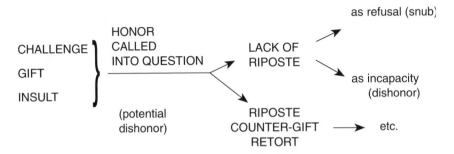

This generative model which reduces exchange to a series of successive choices performed on the basis of a small number of principles with the aid of a simple combinatory formula, and which makes it possible to give a very economical account of an infinity of particular cases of exchanges phenomenally as different as exchanges of gifts, words, or challenges, reproduces, in its own order, the functioning of *habitus* and the logic of practice that proceeds through series of irreversible choices, made under pressure and often involving heavy stakes (sometimes life itself, as in the exchanges of honor or in magic) in response to other choices obeying the same logic.[4]

Similarly, it is sufficient to use a few principles of very general application obtained by combining the fundamental schemes of the mythico-ritual world-view (day/night, male/female, inside/outside, etc.) that constitute the sacred as such, with the logic of social exchanges (the principle of isotimy [EN: equality in honor] and its corollaries), in order to account for all the clauses of all the customary laws collected by the ethnographic tradition and even to have the means of producing the corpus of all possible acts of jurisprudence conforming to the "sense of equity" in its Kabyle form.[5] It is these schemes, hardly ever stated as such in practice,[6] that make it possible to assess the seriousness of a theft by taking into account all the circumstances (place and time) of its commission, within the logic of *h'aram*, opposing the house (or mosque), as sacred places, to all other places, night to day, feastdays to ordinary days, etc. Other things being equal, a more severe sanction will be attached to the first term in each opposition (with, at one extreme, theft committed by night from a house, a sacrilegious violation of *h'aram* which makes it an offence against honor, and at the other extreme theft by day in a distant field). These practical principles are only stated in exceptional cases, in which the very nature of the object stolen requires that they be suspended. For example, the *qanun* of Ighil Imoula provides that "he who steals a mule, ox or cow, by force or trickery shall pay 50 reals to the *djemaa* and pay the owner the value of the stolen animal, whether the theft be by night or by day, from inside or outside a house, and whether the animals belong to the householder or someone else" (Hanoteau and Letourneux 1873: vol. III, 338). The same basic schemes, always functioning in the practical state, apply in cases of assault. There are the same oppositions between the house and other places (the murder of an intruder caught in one's house entails no sanction, being a legitimate response to a violation of *h'urma*), between night and day, feastdays and ordinary days, together with variations according to the socially recognized status of aggressor and victim (man/woman, adult/child) and the weapons or methods used (treachery—in sleep for example—or man-to-man combat) and the degree of commission of the act (mere threats or actual violence).

But the specificity of the practical logic that generates an infinity of practices adapted to situations that are always different, on the basis of schemes so generally and automatically applied that they are only exceptionally converted into explicit principles, is revealed by the fact that the customary laws of different groups (villages or tribes) exhibit variations in the seriousness of the punishments assigned to the same offence. This vagueness and uncertainty, which are understandable when the same implicit schemes are being implemented, would be eliminated from a series of acts of jurisprudence produced by applying a single explicit code, expressly produced in a law-making operation designed to provide for all possible cases of transgression and capable of serving as a basis for homogeneous and constant, that is, predictable and calculable, acts of jurisprudence. Practical logic, based on a system of objectively coherent generative and organizing schemes, functioning in the practical state as an often imprecise but systematic principle of selection, has neither the rigor nor the constancy that characterize logical logic, which can deduce rational action from the explicit, explicitly controlled and systematized principles of an axiomatics (qualities which would also be those of practical logic if it were deduced from the model constructed to account for it). This is why practical logic manifests itself in a kind of stylistic unity which, though immediately perceptible, has none of the strict, regular coherence of the concerted products of a plan.

By producing externally, in objectivity, in the form of explicit principles, that which guides practices from inside, theoretical analysis makes possible a conscious awareness, a transmutation (materialized in the diagram) of the scheme into a representation which gives symbolic mastery of the practical principles that practical sense enacts either without representing them or while giving itself only partial or inadequate representations of them. Just as the teaching of tennis, the violin, chess, dancing or boxing extracts a series of discrete positions, steps or moves, from practices that integrate all these artificially isolated elementary units of behavior into the unity of an organized, oriented practice, so informants tend to present either general norms (always accompanied by exceptions) or remarkable "moves,"[7] because they cannot appropriate theoretically the practical matrix from which these moves can be generated and which they possess only in practice, "in so far as they are what they are," as Plato puts it. Perhaps the subtlest pitfall lies in the fact that agents readily resort to the ambiguous vocabulary of the rule, the language of grammar, morality and law, to explain a social practice which obeys quite different principles. They thus conceal, even from themselves, the true nature of their practical mastery as learned ignorance (*docta ignorantia*), that is, a mode of practical knowledge that does not contain knowledge of its own principles. Native theories are in fact dangerous not so much because they lead research towards illusory explanations, but rather because they bring quite superfluous reinforcement to the theory of practice that is inherent in the objectivist approach to practices, which, having extracted from the *opus operatum* the supposed principles of its production, sets them up as norms governing practices (with phrases like "honor requires . . . ," "propriety demands . . . ," "custom insists . . . ," etc.).

The pedagogic work of inculcation—together with institutionalization, which is always accompanied by a degree of objectification in discourse (especially in law, designed to prevent or punish the misfirings of socialization) or in some other symbolic medium (ritual symbols or instruments, etc.)—is one of the major occasions for formulating and converting practical schemes into explicit norms. It is probably no accident that the question of the relationship between the *habitus* and the "rule" is brought to light with the historical appearance of a specialized, explicit action of inculcation. As is suggested by a reading of Plato's *Meno,* the emergence of institutionalized education is accompanied by a crisis of diffuse education which moves directly from practice to practice without passing through discourse. Excellence (that is, practical mastery in its accomplished form) has ceased to exist once people start asking whether it can be taught, as soon as they seek to base "correct" practice on rules extracted, for the purposes of transmission, as in all academicisms, from the practices of earlier periods or their products. The new masters can safely challenge the *kaloi kagathoi,* who are unable to bring to the level of discourse what they have learned *apo tou automatou,* no one knows how, and possess "in so far as they are what they are"; but the upholders of old-style education have no difficulty in devaluing a knowledge which, like that of the *mathonthes,* the men of knowledge, bears the marks of having been taught. This is no doubt because the "deviation" that is denounced in the term *academicism* is inherent in every attempt to make explicit and codify a practice that is not based on knowledge of the real principles of that practice. For example, research by some educationalists (such as René Deleplace) who have endeavored to rationalize the teaching of sporting or artistic activities by trying to favor conscious awareness of the mechanisms really at work in these practices, shows that, if it fails to be based on a formal model making explicit the principles which practical sense (or more precisely, the "feel for the game" or tactical intelligence) masters in the practical state and which are acquired practically through mimeticism, the teaching of sport has to fall back on rules and even formulae, and focus its attention on typical phases ("moves"). It thus runs the risk of often producing dysfunctional dispositions because it cannot provide an adequate view of the practice as a whole (for example, in rugby, training draws attention to the links between team-mates instead of giving priority to the relationship with the opposing side, from which successful teamwork derives).

It becomes clearer why that "semi-learned" production, the rule, is the obstacle *par excellence* to the construction of an adequate theory of practice. By spuriously occupying the place of two fundamental notions, the theoretical matrix and the practical matrix, it makes it impossible to raise the question of their relationship. The abstract model that has to be constructed (for example, to account for the practices of honor) is completely valid only if it is presented for what it is, a theoretical artefact totally alien to practice—although a rational pedagogy can make it serve practical functions by enabling someone who possesses its practical equivalent to really appropriate the principles of his practice, either in order to bring them to their full realization or in order to try to free himself from them. The motor of the whole dialectic of challenge and riposte, gift and counter-gift, is not an abstract axiomatics but the sense of honor, a disposition inculcated by all early education and constantly demanded and reinforced by the group, and inscribed in the postures and gestures of the body (in a way of using the body or the gaze, a way of talking, eating or walking) as in the automatisms of language and thought, through which a man asserts himself as a real, manly man.[8] This practical sense, which does not burden itself with rules or principles (except in cases of misfiring or failure), still less with calculations or deductions, which are in any case excluded by the urgency of action "which brooks no delay," is what makes it possible to appreciate the meaning of the situation instantly, at a glance, in the heat of the action, and to produce at once the opportune response.[9] Only this kind of acquired mastery, functioning with the automatic reliability of an instinct, can make it possible to respond instantaneously to all the uncertain and ambiguous situations of practice. For example, one can imagine the mastery of the taxonomies and the art of playing on them that are presupposed by imposing the absence of riposte as a mark of disdain when the difference between the antagonists is not very marked and when contempt can be suspected of concealing evasion. In this case, as is shown by the transgressions of the "wise men" (*imusnawen*) who violate the official rule in the name of a higher law (cf. Mammeri and Bourdieu 1978), it is not simply a question of acting, but of commanding belief, immediately, by imposing simultaneously a response and a definition of the situation capable of getting it recognized as the only legitimate one. This requires a very exact knowledge of one's own symbolic value, the value socially accorded to one's opponent, and the probable meaning of conduct which depends first of all on the judgment that others make of it and its author.

Everything combines to show that correct use of the model, which presupposes separation, requires one to move beyond the ritual alternatives of separation and participation and to develop the theory of the logic of practice as practical participation in a game, *illusio,* and, correlatively, the theory of theoretical separation and the distance it presupposes and produces. This theory, which has nothing in common with participation in practical experience, is what makes it possible to avoid the theoretical errors that are usually encouraged by descriptions of practice. To be persuaded of the need to use this theory of practice (and of theory) as the basis for a methodical control of all scientific practice, one has to return to the canonical example of gift exchange, in which the objectivist view, which substitutes the objective model of the cycle of reciprocity for the experiential succession of gifts, is particularly clearly opposed to the subjectivist view. The former privileges practice as seen from outside, timelessly, rather than as it is lived and enacted in an experience which is summarily relegated to the state of pure appearance.

To stop short at the objectivist truth of the gift, that is, the model, is to set aside the question of the relationship between the so-called objective truth, that of the observer, and the truth that can hardly be called subjective, since it represents the collective and even official definition of the subjective experience of the exchange; it is to ignore the fact that the agents practice as irreversible a sequence of actions that the observer constitutes as reversible. Knowing the detemporalizing effect of the "objective" gaze and the relationship that links practice to time, one is forced to ask if it is appropriate to choose between the objectively reversible and quasi-mechanical cycle that the observer's external, totalizing apprehension produces and the no less objectively irreversible and relatively unpredictable succession that the agents produce by their practice, that is, by the series of irreversible choices in and through which they temporalize themselves. To be truly objective, an analysis of exchange of gifts, words, or challenges must allow for the fact that, far from unfolding mechanically, the series of acts which, apprehended from outside and after the event, appears as a cycle of reciprocity, presupposes a continuous creation and may be interrupted at any stage; and that each of the inaugural acts that sets it up is always liable to fall flat and so, for lack of a response, to be stripped retrospectively of its intentional meaning (the subjective truth of the gift can, as has been seen, only be realized in the counter-gift which consecrates it as such). Thus, even if reciprocity is the "objective" truth of the discrete acts that ordinary experience knows in discrete form and associates with the idea of a gift, it is perhaps not the whole truth of a practice that could not exist if its subjective truth coincided perfectly with its "objective" truth.

In every society it may be observed that, if it is not to constitute an insult, the counter-gift must be deferred and different, because the immediate return of an exactly identical object clearly amounts to a refusal. Thus gift exchange is opposed to swapping, which, like the theoretical model of the cycle of reciprocity, telescopes gift and counter-gift into the same instant. It is also opposed to lending, in which the return of the loan, explicitly guaranteed by a legal act, is in a sense already performed at the very moment when a contract is drawn up ensuring the predictability and calculability of the acts it prescribes. The difference, and particularly the delay which the "monothetic" model obliterates, must be brought into the model not, as Lévi-Strauss suggests, out of a "phenomenological" concern to restore the lived experience of the practice of exchange, but because the functioning of gift exchange presupposes individual and collective misrecognition of the truth of the objective "mechanism" of the exchange, a truth which an immediate response brutally exposes. The interval between gift and counter-gift is what allows a relation of exchange that is always liable to appear as irreversible, that is, both forced and self-interested, to be seen as reversible. "Overmuch eagerness to discharge one's obligations," said La Rochefoucauld, "is a form of ingratitude." To betray one's haste to be free of an obligation one has incurred, and thus to reveal too overtly one's desire to pay off services rendered or gifts received, to be quits, is to denounce the initial gift retrospectively as motivated by the intention of obliging one.

It is all a matter of style, which means in this case timing and choice of occasions; the same act—giving, giving in return, offering one's services, paying a visit, etc.—can have completely different meanings at different times, coming as it may at the right or wrong moment, opportunely or inopportunely. The reason is that the lapse of time that separates the gift from the counter-gift is what allows the deliberate oversight, the collectively maintained and approved self-deception, without which the exchange could not function. Gift exchange is one of the social games that cannot be played unless the players refuse to acknowledge the objective truth of the game, the very truth that objective analysis brings to light, and unless they are predisposed to contribute, with their efforts, their marks of care and attention, and their time, to the production of collective misrecognition. Everything takes place as if the agents' strategies, and especially those that play on the tempo of action, or, in interaction, with the interval between actions, were organized with a view to disguising from themselves and from others the truth of their practice, which the anthropologist brutally reveals simply by substituting the interchangeable moments of a reversible sequence for practices performed in time and in their own time.

To abolish the interval is also to abolish strategy. The period interposed which must be neither too short (as is clearly seen in gift exchange) nor too long (especially in the exchange of revenge-murders), is quite the opposite of the inert gap of time, the time-lag, which the objectivist model makes of it. Until he has given back, the receiver is "obliged," expected to show his gratitude towards his benefactor or at least to show regard for him, go easy on him, pull his punches, lest he be accused of ingratitude and stand condemned by "what people say," which decides the meaning of his actions. The man who has not avenged a murder, not bought back his land acquired by a rival family, not married off his daughters in time, sees his capital diminished from day to day by passing time—unless he is capable of transforming forced delay into strategic deferment. To put off revenge or the return of a gift can be a way of keeping one's partner-opponent in the dark about one's intentions; the moment for the counterstrike becomes impossible to determine, like the really evil moment in the ill-omened periods of the ritual calendar, when the curve turns up and when lack of response ceases to be negligence and turns into disdainful refusal. Delay is also a way of exacting the deferential conduct that is required so long as relations are not broken off. It makes sense within this logic that a man whose daughter is asked for in marriage must reply as quickly as possible if he intends to refuse, lest he seem to be taking advantage of the situation and offend the suitor, whereas if he intends to agree he is free to delay his answer as long as he can, so as to maintain his situational advantage, which he will lose as soon as he gives his consent. Everything takes place as if the ritualization of interactions had the paradoxical effect of giving time its full social efficacy, which is never more active than when nothing is going on, except time. "Time," we say, "is working for him"; the opposite can also be true.

Thus time derives its efficacy from the state of the structure of relations within which it comes into play; which does not mean that the model of this structure can leave it out of account. When the unfolding of the action is heavily ritualized, as in the dialectic of offence (assault on *h'aram*) and vengeance, where failure to respond, even when presented as disdain, is ruled out, there is still room for strategies that consist in playing with the time, or rather the tempo, of the action, by delaying revenge so as to use a capital of provocations received or conflicts suspended, with its charge of potential revenge and conflict, as an instrument of power based on the capacity to take the initiative in reopening or suspending hostilities. This is true, *a fortiori*, of all the less strictly regulated occasions which offer unlimited scope for strategies exploiting the opportunities for manipulating the pace of the action—holding back or putting off, maintaining suspense or expectancy, or on the other hand, hurrying, hustling, surprising, stealing a march, not to mention the art of ostentatiously giving time ("devoting one's time to someone") or withholding it ("no time to spare"). We know, for example, how much advantage the holder of a transmissible power can derive from the art of delaying transmission and keeping others in the dark as to his ultimate intentions. Nor should one forget all the strategies intended simply to neutralize the action of time and ensure the continuity of interpersonal relations, making continuity out of discontinuity, as mathematicians do, through infinite addition of the infinitely small, in the form, for example, of tiny gestures and acts of "thoughtfulness" or the "little gifts" that are said to "bind in friendship" ("O gift—*thunticht*—you won't make me rich but you are the bond of friendship").

This takes us a long way from the objectivist model and the mechanical interlocking of pre-set actions that is commonly associated with the notion of ritual. Only a virtuoso with a perfect mastery of his "art of living" can play on all the resources inherent in the ambiguities and indeterminacies of behaviors and situations so as to produce the actions appropriate in each case, to do at the right moment that of which people will say "There was nothing else to be done," and to do it the right way. We are a long way, too, from norms and rules. Doubtless there are slips, mistakes and moments of clumsiness to be observed here as elsewhere—and also grammarians of decorum able to say (and elegantly, too) what it is elegant to do and say; but they never presume to encompass in a catalogue of recurrent situations and appropriate conduct the "art" of the necessary improvisation that defines excellence. The temporal structure of practice functions here as a screen preventing totalization. The interval inserted between the gift and the counter-gift is an instrument of denial which allows a subjective truth and a quite opposite objective truth to coexist, in both individual experience and the common judgment.[10] It is the curse of objectivism that, here as in all cases where it confronts collective belief, it can only establish, with great difficulty, truths that are not so much unknown as repressed;[11] and that it cannot include, in the model it produces to account for practice, the individual or collective, private or official, subjective illusion against which it has had to win its truth, in other words the *illusio*, belief, and the conditions of production and functioning of this collective denial.

The relationship between the objectivist model and the *habitus*, between the theoretical schema and the scheme of practical sense (which is shadowed by practical rules, partial and imperfect statements of the principles), is thus complicated by a third term, the official norm and the native theory which redouble at the level of discourse, and so reinforce, the repression of the "objective" (that is, objectivist) truth that is inscribed in the very structure of practice and, as such, is part of the full truth of practice. Inculcation is never so perfect that a society can entirely dispense with all explicit statement, even in cases where, as in Kabylia, the objectification of the generative schemes in a grammar of practices, a written code of conduct, is limited to the absolute minimum. Official representations, which, as well as customary rules, include gnomic poems, sayings, proverbs every kind of objectification of the schemes of perception and action in words, things or practices (that is, as much in the vocabulary of honor or kinship, with the model of marriage that it implies, as in ritual acts or objects), have a dialectical relationship with the dispositions that are expressed through them and which they help to produce and reinforce. *Habitus* are spontaneously inclined to recognize all the expressions in which they recognize themselves, because they are spontaneously inclined to produce them—in particular all the exemplary products of the most conforming *habitus* which have been selected and preserved by the *habitus* of successive generations and which are invested with the intrinsic force of objectification and with the authority attached to every publicly authorized realization of the *habitus*.

The specific force of official representations is that they institute the principles of a practical relation to the natural and social world in words, objects, practices and especially in collective, public events, such as the major rituals, deputations and solemn processions (the Greeks called them *theories* . . .), of which our processions, rallies and demonstrations, in which the group presents itself as such, in its volume and structure, are the secularized form. These ritual manifestations are also representations, theatrical performances, shows, that stage and present the whole group, which is thus constituted as the spectator of a visible representation of what is not so much a representation of the natural and social world, a "world-view," as a practical, tacit relationship to the things of the world. Officialization is the process whereby the group (or those who dominate it) teaches itself and masks from itself its own truth, binds itself by a public profession which sanctions and imposes what it utters, tacitly defining the limits of the thinkable and the unthinkable and so contributing to the maintenance of the social order from which it derives its power.[12] It follows that the intrinsic difficulty of any explicit statement of the logic of practice is intensified by the obstacle of the whole set of authorized representations in which the group is willing to recognize itself.[13]

Objectivist critique is justified in questioning the official definition of practices and uncovering the real determinants hidden under the proclaimed motivations. The brutally materialist reduction which describes values as collectively misrecognized, and so recognized, interests, and which points out, with Max Weber, that the official rule determines practice only when there is more to be gained by obeying than by disobeying it, always has a salutary effect of demystification. But it must not lead one to forget that the official definition of reality is part of a full definition of social reality and that this imaginary anthropology has very real effects.

One is right to refuse to credit the rule with the efficacy that legalism ascribes to it, but it must not be forgotten that there is an interest in "toeing the line" which can be the basis of strategies aimed at regularizing the agent's situation, putting him in the right, in a sense beating the group at its own game by presenting his interests in the misrecognizable guise of the values recognized by the group. Strategies directly oriented towards primary profit (for example, the social capital accruing from an advantageous marriage) are often accompanied by second-degree strategies aimed at giving apparent satisfaction to the demands of the official rule, so combining the satisfactions of interest with the prestige or respect which almost universally reward actions apparently motivated by respect for the rule. There is nothing that groups demand more insistently and reward more generously than this conspicuous reverence for what they claim to revere.[14]

Strategies aimed at producing practices "according to the rules" are one among other types of officialization strategy, aimed at transmuting "egoistic," private, particular interests (notions which can only be defined in the relationship between a social unit and the unit which encompasses it at a higher level) into "disinterested," collective, publicly avowable, legitimate interests. In the absence of constituted political institutions endowed with the *de facto* monopoly of legitimate violence, specifically political action can only be exerted through the officialization effect. It therefore presupposes competence (in the sense of the capacity socially granted to an authority) which is essential, especially in moments of crisis when collective judgment hesitates, in order to manipulate the collective definition of the situation so as to bring it closer to the official definition and to mobilize the largest possible group by solemnizing and universalizing a private incident (for example, by presenting an insult to a particular woman as an assault on the *h'urma* of the whole group); or to demobilize it by disowning the person directly concerned and reducing him to the status of a private individual so devoid of reason that he seeks to impose his private reason (*idiôtès* in Greek, *amahbul* in Kabyle).

When, as in ancient Kabylia, there is no judicial apparatus endowed with the monopoly of physical or even symbolic violence, the precepts of custom can carry some weight only to the extent that they are skillfully manipulated by the holders of authority within the clan (the "guarantors" or "wise men") in such a way as to "reactivate" dispositions capable of reproducing them. The assembly does not function like a tribunal pronouncing verdicts by reference to a pre-existing code but as an arbitration or family council that seeks to reconcile the adversaries' points of view and bring them to accept a settlement. Thus the functioning of the system presupposes the orchestration of *habitus*, since the arbitrator's decision can only be implemented with the consent of the "offending" party (failing which, the plaintiff can only resort to force) and will not be accepted unless it conforms to the "sense of equity" and is imposed in forms recognized by the "sense of honor." And it is clear that means of symbolic coercion such as the curse ("A man who carries off dung spread out on the market-stalls shall be fined 50 douros and a curse shall be pronounced on him that will make him an *amengur* [he will die without an heir]," Article XC of the *qanun* of Adni, reported by Boulifa 1913: 15-27) or banishment owe their efficacy to the objective complicity, the belief, of those whom they constrain.

Politics is the arena *par excellence* of officialization strategies. In their endeavors to draw the group's delegation to themselves and to withdraw it from their competitors, the agents competing for political power can only implement ritual strategies and strategic rituals, aimed at the symbolic universalization of private interests or the symbolic appropriation of official interests.[15] This is why all kinds of official representations, especially those that are objectified in language in the form of sayings, proverbs and gnomic poems, are among the most hotly contested stakes in their struggles. To appropriate the "sayings of the tribe" is to appropriate the power to act on the group by appropriating the power the group exerts over itself through its official language. The principle of the magical efficacy of this performative language which makes what it states, magically instituting what it says in constituent statements, does not lie, as some people think, in the language itself, but in the group that authorizes and recognizes it and, with it, authorizes and recognizes itself.

Thus objectivism falls short of objectivity by failing to integrate into its account of reality the representation of reality against which it has had to construct its "objective" representation, but which, when it is backed by the unanimity of the group, realizes the most indisputable form of objectivity. Gift exchange is the paradigm of all the operations through which symbolic alchemy produces the reality-denying reality that the collective consciousness aims at as a collectively produced, sustained and maintained misrecognition of the "objective" truth. The official truth produced by the collective work of euphemization, an elementary form of the work of objectification which eventually leads to the legal definition of acceptable behavior, is not only the group's means of saving its "spiritualistic point of honor." It also has a practical efficacy, for, even if it were belied by the practice of everyone, like a grammatical rule to which every case proved an exception, it would still remain a true description of such practices as are intended to be acceptable. The ethic of honor bears down on each agent with the weight of all the other agents; and the disenchantment that leads to the progressive unveiling of repressed meanings and functions can only result from a collapse of the social conditions of the cross-censorship that each agent may suffer reluctantly but without ceasing to impose it on others, and from the ensuing crisis of collective denial.

Urbanization, which brings together groups with different traditions and weakens the reciprocal controls (and even before urbanization, the generalization of monetary exchanges and the introduction of wage labor), results in the collapse of the collectively maintained and therefore entirely real fiction of the religion of honor. For example, trust is replaced by credit—*talq*—which was previously cursed or despised (as is shown by the insult "credit face!"—the face of a man who is so constantly humiliated that he has ceased to feel dishonor, or the fact that repudiation with restitution, the greatest offence imaginable, is called *berru natalq*). The doxic relation to the world is the most visible manifestation of the effect that occurs whenever the practices of the group show very little dispersion (a J-curve) and when each member helps to impose on all the others, willy-nilly, the same constraint that they impose on him. The idea of breaking this kind of circular control, which could only be cast off by a collective raising of consciousness and a collective contract, is excluded by the very logic of the unanimity effect, which is quite irreducible to an effect of imitation or fashion. (Contrary to what was supposed by theories of the original contract, only a contract can free a group from the contract-less constraint of social mechanisms that is sanctioned by *laissez-faire*.) The fact that the primary belief of strongly integrated communities is the product of the serial constraint that the group applies to itself (which may be suffered with great impatience, as was the case with religious control in village communities, but without ever being able to spark off a revolt that could call them into question) perhaps explains why breaks (for example, in religious practice) often take a sudden, collective form, with circular control losing its efficacy as soon as there is a glimpse of the real possibility of breaking it.

Symbolic Capital

The theoretical construction which retrospectively projects the counter-gift into the project of the gift does not only have the effect of producing mechanical sequences of obligatory acts from the risky but necessary improvisation of everyday strategies—strategies which owe their infinite complexity to the fact that the giver's undeclared calculation has to reckon with the receiver's undeclared calculation, and hence satisfy his expectations without appearing to know what they are. In the same operation, it removes the conditions of possibility of the institutionally organized and guaranteed misrecognition that is the basis of gift exchange and, perhaps, of all the symbolic labor aimed at transmuting the inevitable and inevitably interested relations imposed by kinship, neighborhood or work, into elective relations of reciprocity, through the sincere fiction of a disinterested exchange, and, more profoundly, at transforming arbitrary relations of exploitation (of woman by man, younger brother by elder brother, the young by the elders) into durable relations, grounded in nature. In the work of reproducing established relations—feasts, ceremonies, exchange of gifts, visits or courtesies and, above all, marriages—which is no less vital to the existence of the group than the reproduction of the economic bases of its existence, the labor required to conceal the function of the exchanges is as important as the labor needed to perform this function.[1] If it is true that the lapse of time interposed is what enables the gift or counter-gift to be seen as inaugural acts of generosity, without a past or a future, that is, without calculation, then it is clear that by reducing the polythetic to the monothetic, objectivism destroys the reality of all practices which, like gift exchange, tend or pretend to put the law of self-interest into abeyance. Because it protracts and so disguises the transaction that a rational contract would telescope into an instant, gift exchange is, if not the only mode of circulation of goods that is practiced, at least the only one that can be fully recognized in societies that deny "the true ground of their life," as Lukács puts it; and also the only way of setting up durable relations of reciprocity—and domination—with the interposed time representing the beginnings of institutionalized obligation.

Economism is a form of ethnocentrism. Treating pre-capitalist economies, in Marx's phrase, "as the Fathers of the Church treated the religions which preceded Christianity," it applies to them categories, methods (economic accountancy, for example) or concepts (such as the notions of interest, investment or capital) which are the historical product of capitalism and which induce a radical transformation of their object, similar to the historical transformation from which they arose. Economism recognizes no other form of interest than that which capitalism has produced, through a kind of real operation of abstraction, by setting up a universe of relations between man and man based, as Marx says, on "callous cash payment" and more generally by favoring the creation of relatively autonomous fields, capable of establishing their own axiomatics (through the fundamental tautology "business is business," on which "the economy" is based). It can therefore find no place in its analyses, still less in its calculations, for any form of "non-economic" interest. It is as if economic calculation had been able to appropriate the territory objectively assigned to the remorseless logic of what Marx calls "naked self-interest," only by relinquishing an island of the "sacred," miraculously spared by the "icy waters of egoistic calculation," the refuge of what has no price because it has too much or too little. But, above all, it can make nothing of universes that have not performed such a dissociation and so have, as it were, an economy in itself and not for itself. Thus, any partial or total objectification of the archaic economy that does not include a theory of the subjective relation of misrecognition which agents adapted to this economy maintain with its "objective" (that is, objectivist) truth, succumbs to the most subtle and most irreproachable form of ethnocentrism. It is the same error as that incurred when one forgets that the constitution of art as art is inseparable from the constitution of a relatively autonomous artistic field, and treats as aesthetic certain "primitive" or "folk" practices which cannot see themselves in this way.

Everything takes place as if the specificity of the "archaic" economy lay in the fact that economic activity cannot explicitly recognize the economic ends in relation to which it is objectively oriented. The "idolatry of nature" which makes it impossible to think of nature as raw material and, conse-quently, to see human activity as labor, that is, as man's struggle against nature, combines with the systematic emphasis on the symbolic aspect of the acts and relations of production to prevent the economy from being grasped as an economy, that is, as a system governed by the laws of inter-ested calculation, competition or exploitation.

By reducing this economy to its "objective" reality, economism annihi-lates the specificity located precisely in the socially maintained discrepancy between the "objective" reality and the social representation of production and exchange. It is no accident that the vocabulary of the archaic economy is entirely made up of double-sided notions that are condemned to disinte-grate in the very history of the economy, because, owing to their duality, the social relations that they designate represent unstable structures which inevitably split in two as soon as the social mechanisms sustaining them are weakened (see Benveniste 1973). Thus, to take an extreme example, *rah-nia*, a contract by which the borrower grants the lender the usufruct of some of his land for the duration of the loan, and which is regarded as the worst form of usury when it leads to dispossession, differs only in the nature of the social relation between the two parties, and thus in the detailed terms of the agreement, from the aid granted to a distressed relative so as to save him from selling land which, even when the owner is still allowed to use it, constitutes a kind of security on the loan.[2] As Mauss (1966: 52) says:

> It was precisely the Greeks and Romans who, possibly following the Northern and Western Semites, drew the distinction between personal rights and real rights, separated purchases from gifts and exchanges, dis-sociated moral obligations from contracts, and, above all, conceived of the difference between ritual, rights and interests. By a genuine, great and venerable revolution, they passed beyond the excessively hazardous, costly and elaborate gift economy, which was encumbered with personal considerations, incompatible with the development of the market, trade and production, and, in a word, uneconomic.

The historical situations in which the artificially maintained structures of the good-faith economy break up and make way for the clear, economical (as opposed to expensive) concepts of the economy of undisguised self-interest, reveal the cost of operating an economy which, by its refusal to rec-ognize and declare itself as such, is forced to devote almost as much ingenuity and energy to disguising the truth of economic acts as it expends in performing them. For example, a much esteemed Kabyle mason, who had learned his trade in France, caused a scandal, around 1955, by going home when his work was finished without eating the meal traditionally given in the mason's honor when a house is built, and then demanding, in addition to the price of his day's work (1,000 francs), a bonus of 200 francs in lieu of the meal. His demand for the cash equivalent of the meal was a sacrilegious reversal of the formula used in symbolic alchemy to transmute labor and its price into unsolicited gifts, and it thus exposed the device most commonly used to keep up appearances through a collectively produced make-believe. As an act of exchange setting the seal on alliances ("I set the wheatcake and the salt between us"), the final meal at the time of the *thiwizi* of harvest or house-building naturally became a rite of alliance intended to transfigure an interested transaction retrospectively into a generous exchange (like the vendor's gifts to the purchaser which often rounded off the most tenacious haggling). The subterfuges sometimes used to minimize the cost of the meals at the end of the *thiwizi* (for example, only inviting the leading representatives of each group, or one man per family), a departure from the principles which still paid lip-service to their legitimacy, were viewed with the greatest indulgence, but the reaction could only be scandal and shock when a man took it upon himself to declare that the meal had a cash equivalent, thus betraying the best-kept and worst-kept of secrets (since everyone kept it), and breaking the law of silence that guaranteed the complicity of collective bad faith in the economy of "good faith."

The good-faith economy, based on a set of mechanisms tending to limit and disguise the play of (narrowly) "economic" interest and calculation, calls forth the strange incarnation of *homo economicus* known as *buniya* (or *bab niya*), the man of good faith (*niya* or *thiâuggants*, from *aâggun*, the child still unable to speak, as opposed to *thah'raymith*, calculating intelligence). The man of good faith would not think of selling certain fresh food products—milk, butter, cheese, vegetables, fruit—but always distributes them among his friends or neighbors. He practices no exchanges involving money and all his relations are based on complete trust. Unlike the shady dealer, he has recourse to none of the guarantees (witnesses, security, written documents) with which commercial transactions are surrounded. The closer the individuals and groups are in genealogy, the easier it is to reach agreements (and therefore the more frequent they are) and the more they are entrusted to good faith. Conversely, as the relationship becomes more impersonal, that is, as one moves out from the relation between brothers to that between virtual strangers (people from different villages), so a transaction is less and less likely to be established at all but it can, and increasingly does, become more purely "economic," i.e., closer to its economic truth, and the interested calculation which is never absent from the most generous exchange (in which both parties count themselves satisfied, and therefore count) can be more and more openly revealed.[3]

Friendly transactions between kinsmen and affines are to market transactions as ritual war is to total war. The "goods or beasts of the fellah" are traditionally opposed to the "goods or beasts of the market," and informants will talk endlessly of the tricks and frauds that are commonplace in the "big markets," that is to say, in exchanges with strangers. There are endless tales of mules that run off as soon as the purchaser has got them home, oxen made to look fatter by rubbing them with a plant that makes them swell (*adhris*), purchasers who band together to force prices down. The incarnation of economic war is the shady dealer, who fears neither God nor man. Men avoid buying animals from him, and from any total stranger. As one informant said, for straightforward goods, like land, it is the thing to be bought that determines the buyer's decision; for problematic goods, such as beasts of burden and especially mules, it is the choice of seller that decides, and at least an effort is made to substitute a personalized relationship for a totally impersonal, anonymous relationship. Every intermediate stage can be found, from transactions based on complete distrust, such as that between the peasant and the shady dealer, who cannot demand or obtain guarantees because he cannot guarantee the quality of his wares or find guarantors, to the exchange of honor which can dispense with conditions and rely entirely on the good faith of the "contracting parties." But in the great majority of transactions the notions of buyer and seller tend to be dissolved in the network of middlemen and guarantors who aim to turn the purely economic relationship into a genealogically based and guaranteed relationship. Marriage itself is no exception: it is almost always set up between families already linked by a whole network of previous exchanges, underwriting the specific new agreement. It is significant that in the first phase of the very complex negotiations that lead to the marriage agreement, the two families bring in prestigious kinsmen or affines as "guarantors." The symbolic capital thus displayed serves both to strengthen their hand in the bargaining and to underwrite the agreement once it is concluded.

The true nature of production is no less repressed than the true nature of circulation. The indignant comments provoked by the heretical behavior of peasants who have departed from traditional ways draw attention to the mechanisms which inclined the peasant to maintain an enchanted relationship with the land and made it impossible for him to see his toil as labor. "It's sacrilege, they have profaned the earth. They have done away with fear (*elhiba*). Nothing intimidates them or stops them. They turn everything upside down, I'm sure they will end up ploughing in *lakhrif* (the fig season) if they are in a hurry and if they feel like spending *lah'lal* (the licit period for ploughing) doing something else, or in *rbiâ* (spring) if they've been too lazy in *lah'lal*. It's all the same to them." Everything in the peasant's practice actualizes, in a different mode, the objective intention revealed in ritual. The land is never treated as raw material to be exploited, but always as the object of respect mingled with fear (*elhiba*). It will "settle its scores," they say, and take revenge for bad treatment it receives from a hasty or clumsy farmer. The accomplished peasant "presents" himself to the land with the stance befitting one man meeting another, face to face, with the attitude of trusting familiarity he would show a respected kinsman. During ploughing, he would not think of delegating the task of leading the team, and the only task he leaves for his "clients" (*ichikran*) is that of breaking up the soil behind the plough. "The elders used to say that to plough properly, you had to be the master of the land. The young men were left out of it. It would have been an insult to the land to 'present' it (*qabel*) with men one would not dare present to other men." "It is the man who faces other men," says a proverb, "who must face the earth."

To take up Hesiod's opposition between *ponos* and *ergon*, the peasant does not, strictly, work, he "takes pains." "Give to the earth and the earth will give to you," says a proverb. This can be taken to mean that, in accordance with the logic of gift exchange, nature gives her fruits only to those who bring her their toil as a tribute. The heretical behavior of those who leave to the young the task of "opening the earth and ploughing into it the wealth of the new year" provokes the older peasants to express the principle of the relationship between men and the land, which could remain unformulated so long as it was taken for granted: "The earth no longer gives because we give it nothing. We openly mock the earth and it is only right that it should pay us back with lies." A self-respecting man should always be busy doing something: if he cannot find anything to do, "at least he can carve his spoon." Activity is as much a duty of communal life as an economic imperative. What is valued is activity for its own sake, regardless of its strictly economic function, inasmuch as it is seen as appropriate to the specific function of the person who performs it.

There is strong disapproval of individuals who are no use to their family or their group, "dead men whom God has drawn from living men," in the words of a verse of the Koran often applied to them, and who "cannot pull their weight." To remain idle, especially when one belongs to a great family, is to shirk the duties and tasks that are an inseparable part of belonging to the group. So a man who has been out of farming for some time, because he has emigrated or been ill, is quickly found a place in the cycle of work and the circuit of the exchange of services. The group has the right to demand of each of its members that he should have an occupation, however unproductive or even purely symbolic. A peasant who provides idlers with an opportunity to work on his land is universally approved because he gives these marginal individuals a chance to integrate themselves into the group by doing their duty as men.

The distinction between productive and non-productive, or profitable and non-profitable work, is unknown. It would destroy the *raison d'être* of the countless minor tasks intended to assist nature in its labor. No one would think of assessing the technical efficiency or economic usefulness of these inseparably technical and ritual acts, the peasant's version, so to speak, of art for art's sake, such as fencing the fields, pruning the trees, protecting the new shoots from animals, or "visiting" (*asafqadh*) and watching over the fields, not to mention practices generally regarded as rites, such as actions intended to expel evil (*as'ifedh*) or to mark the coming of spring; or of all the social acts which the application of alien categories would define as unproductive, such as the tasks that fall to the head of the family as the representative and leader of the group—co-ordinating the work, speaking in the men's assembly, bargaining in the market, reading in the mosque.[4] "If the peasant were to count," runs a proverb, "he would not sow." Perhaps this implies that the relationship between work and its product is not really unknown, but socially repressed, because the productivity of labor is so low that the peasant must refrain from counting his time and measuring (as Marx does, reasoning here as an objectivist agronomist) the disparity between the working period and the production period, which is also the consumption period, in order to preserve the meaningfulness of his work; or—and this is only an apparent contradiction—that in a world in which scarcity of time is so rare and scarcity of goods so great, his best and only course is to spend his time without counting it, to squander the one thing that exists in abundance.[5]

In short, "pains" are to labor as the gift is to trade (an activity for which, as Benveniste points out, the Indo-European languages had no name). The discovery of labor presupposes the constitution of the common ground of production, that is, the disenchanting of a natural world reduced to its economic dimension alone. Ceasing to be the tribute paid to a necessary order, activity can be directed towards an exclusively economic goal, the one that money, henceforward the measure of all things, starkly designates. This means the end of the primal undifferentiatedness which made possible the play of individual and collective misrecognition. Measured by the yardstick of monetary profit, the most sacred activities find themselves constituted negatively as symbolic, that is, in a sense the word sometimes receives, as lacking concrete, material effect, in a word, gratuitous, that is, disinterested but also useless.

In an economy which is defined by the refusal to recognize the "objective" truth of "economic" practices, that is, the law of "naked self-interest" and egoistic calculation, even "economic" capital cannot act unless it succeeds in being recognized through a conversion that can render unrecognizable the true principle of its efficacy. Symbolic capital is this denied capital, recognized as legitimate, that is, misrecognized as capital (recognition, acknowledgment, in the sense of gratitude aroused by benefits can be one of the foundations of this recognition) which, along with religious capital (see Bourdieu 1971), is perhaps the only possible form of accumulation when economic capital is not recognized.

Whatever conscious or unconscious efforts are made to regulate the routine of the ordinary course of events through ritual stereotyping and to reduce crises by producing them symbolically or ritualizing them as soon as they arise, the archaic economy cannot escape the opposition between ordinary and extra-ordinary occasions, between regular needs, which can be satisfied by the domestic community, and the exceptional needs, both material and symbolic, for goods and services, which arise in special circumstances— economic crisis, political conflict or simply the urgency of agricultural work—and which require the voluntary assistance of a more extended group. The strategy of accumulating the capital of honor and prestige which produces a clientele as much as it is produced by it, therefore provides the optimum solution to the problem that would arise from continuously maintaining the whole of the labor force that is needed during the working period (which is necessarily very short, because of the rigors of the climate and the weakness of the technical resources: "The harvest is like lightning"—*lerzaq am lebraq*; "When it's a bad year, there are always too many mouths to feed; when it's a good year, there are never enough hands to do the work"). It enables the great families to marshal the maximum workforce during the working period while minimizing consumption. This vital assistance provided in brief moments of great urgency is obtained at low cost since it will be rewarded either in the form of labor, but outside the period of intense activity, or in other forms, protection, the loan of animals, etc.

One is entitled to see this as a disguised form of purchase of labor power or a covert exaction of corvées, but only on condition that the analysis holds together what holds together in the object, namely the double reality of intrinsically equivocal, ambiguous practices. This is the pitfall awaiting all those whom a naively dualistic representation of the relationship between the "native" economy and the "native" representation of the economy leads into the self-mystifying demystifications of a reduced and reductive materialism. The complete truth of this appropriation of services lies in the fact that it can *only* take place in the disguise of *thiwizi*, voluntary assistance which is also a corvée and is thus a voluntary corvée and forced assistance, and that, to use a geometrical metaphor, it presupposes a double half-rotation returning to the starting-point, that is, a conversion of material capital into symbolic capital itself reconvertible into material capital.

In reality, *thiwizi* mainly benefits the richest farmers and also the *t'aleb* (whose land is ploughed and sown collectively). The poor need no help with their harvest. But *thiwizi* can also help a poor man in the case of the building of a house (for the transporting of beams and stones). Ostracism is a terrible sanction and is more than symbolic: owing to the limited technical resources, many activities would be impossible without the help of the group (for example, house-building, with stones to be carried, or the transporting of mill-wheels, which used to mobilize forty men in shifts for several days). Moreover, in this economy of insecurity, a capital of services rendered and gifts bestowed is the best and indeed only safeguard against the "thousand contingencies," on which, as Marx observes, depends the maintenance or loss of working conditions, from the accident that causes the loss of an animal to the bad weather that destroys the crops.

As well as the additional labor-power which it provides at the times of greatest need, symbolic capital procures all that is referred to under the term *nesba,* that is, the network of affines and relationships that is held through the set of commitments and debts of honor, rights and duties accumulated over the successive generations, and which can be mobilized in extra-ordinary circumstances. Economic and symbolic capital are so inextricably intertwined that the display of material and symbolic strength represented by prestigious affines is in itself likely to bring in material profits, in a good-faith economy in which good repute constitutes the best if not the only, economic guarantee.[6] It is clear why the great families never miss an opportunity to organize exhibitions of symbolic capital—processions of kinsmen and allies which solemnize the pilgrim's departure or return, the bride's escort, measured by the number of "rifles" and the intensity of the salutes fired in the couple's honor, prestigious gifts, like the sheep given for a wedding, the witnesses and guarantors who can be mobilized at any time and any place, to attest the good faith of a transaction or to strengthen the hand of the lineage in negotiating a marriage and solemnize the contract.

Symbolic capital is valid even in the market. A man may enhance his prestige by making a purchase at an exorbitant price, for the sake of his point of honor, just to "show he could do it"; but he may also take pride in having managed to conclude a deal without laying out a penny in cash, either by mobilizing a number of guarantors, or, even better, by virtue of the credit and the capital of trust that stems from a reputation for honor as well as wealth. Because of the trust they enjoy and the capital of social relations they have accumulated, those who are said to "be able to come back with the whole market, even if they went out empty-handed," can afford to "go to market with only their faces, their names and their honor for money" and even "to bid whether they have money on them or not." The collective judgment which makes the "market man" (*argaz nasuq*) is a total judgment on the total man which, like such judgments in all societies, involves the ultimate values and takes into account—at least as much as wealth and solvency—the qualities strictly attached to the person, those which "can neither be borrowed or lent."[7]

When one knows that symbolic capital is credit, but in the broadest sense, a kind of advance, a credence, that only the group's belief can grant those who give it the best symbolic and material guarantees, it can be seen that the exhibition of symbolic capital (which is always very expensive in material terms) is one of the mechanisms which (no doubt universally) make capital go to capital.

So it is by drawing up a comprehensive balance-sheet of symbolic profits, without forgetting the undifferentiatedness of the symbolic and the material components of a family's wealth, that it becomes possible to grasp the economic rationality of conduct which economism dismisses as absurd. For example, the decision to buy a second yoke of oxen after the harvest, on the grounds that they are needed for treading out the grain—which is a way of making it known that the crop has been plentiful—only to have to sell them again for lack of fodder, before the autumn ploughing, when they would technically be necessary, seems economically aberrant only if one forgets all the material and symbolic profit accruing from this (albeit fictitious) enhancement of the family's symbolic capital in the late-summer period when marriages are negotiated. The perfect rationality of this strategy of bluff lies in the fact that marriage is the occasion for an (in the widest sense) economic circulation which cannot be seen purely in terms of material goods. The circulation of immediately perceptible material goods, such as the bridewealth, disguises the total circulation, actual or potential, of indissolubly material and symbolic goods of which they are only the aspect that is visible to the eye of *homo economicus*. The amount of the bridewealth would not justify the hard bargaining that takes place over it if it did not take on a symbolic value of the greatest importance, by manifesting unequivocally the value of a family's products on the matrimonial market, as well as the capacity of its spokesmen to get the best price for their products through their bargaining skills.[8] Thus the profits that a group is likely to derive from this total transaction increase with its material and especially its symbolic patrimony, or, in the language of banking, with the "credit of renown" that it can command. This "credit-worthiness," which depends on the capacity of the group's point of honor to ensure the invulnerability of its honor, is an undivided whole, indissolubly uniting the quantity and quality of its goods and the quantity and quality of the men capable of turning them to good account. It is what enables the group, especially through marriage, to acquire prestigious affines (wealth in the form of "rifles," measured not only by the number of men but also their quality, their point of honor) and defines the group's capacity to preserve its land and its honor, particularly the honor of its women, in short, the capital of material and symbolic strength which can actually be mobilized, for market transactions, contests of honor or work on the land.

The interest at stake in the conducts of honor is one for which economism has no name and which has to be called symbolic, although it is such as to inspire actions that are very directly material. Just as there are professions, like law and medicine, whose practitioners must be "above all suspicion," so a family has a vital interest in keeping its capital of honor, its credit of honorability, safe from suspicion. The hypersensitivity to the slightest slur or innuendo (*thasalqubth*), and the multiplicity of strategies designed to belie or avert them, can be explained by the fact that symbolic capital is less easily measured and counted than land or livestock, and that the group, ultimately the only source of credit, will readily withdraw it and direct its suspicions at even the strongest, as if, in matters of honor, as in land, one man's wealth made others that much poorer.

The defence of "symbolic" capital can thus lead to "economically" ruinous conduct. This is the case when, on the basis of a socially accepted definition of the symbolic patrimony, a piece of land takes on a symbolic value disproportionate to its technical, "economic" qualities, those that render the closest, best kept, most "productive" fields, those most accessible to the women (by private paths, *thikhurad-jiyin*), more valuable in the eyes of an ordinary purchaser. When land that has been in the family for a long time and is therefore strongly associated with the name of the family falls into the hands of strangers, buying it back becomes a matter of honor, akin to avenging an offence, and it may reach an exorbitant price. This price is purely theoretical in most cases, since, within this logic, the symbolic profits of the challenge are greater than the material profits that would accrue from cynical (hence reprehensible) exploitation of the situation. The new owners are as determined to hold on to the land, especially if its acquisition is sufficiently recent to remain a challenge, as the others are to buy it back and take revenge for the affront to the *h'urma* of their land. It may happen that a third group will step in with a higher bid, thus challenging not the seller, who only profits from the competition, but the "legitimate" owners.

Only a partial and reductive, and therefore inconsistent, materialism can fail to see that strategies whose object is to conserve or enhance the symbolic capital of the group (like blood vengeance or marriage) are dictated by interests no less vital than inheritance or marriage strategies. The interest leading an agent to defend his symbolic capital is inseparable from tacit adherence, inculcated in the earliest years of life and reinforced by all subsequent experience, to the axiomatics objectively inscribed in the regularities of the (in the broad sense) economic order, an original investment which constitutes a given type of goods as worthy of being pursued and conserved. The objective harmony between the agents' dispositions (here, their propensity and capacity to play the game of honor) and the objective regularities of which they are the product, means that membership of this economic cosmos implies unconditional recognition of the stakes which, by its very existence, it presents as self-evident, that is, misrecognition of the arbitrariness of the value it confers on them. This primary belief is the basis of the investments and over-investments (in both the economic and psychoanalytic senses) which, through the ensuing competition and scarcity, cannot fail to reinforce the well-grounded illusion that the value of the goods it designates as desirable is in the nature of things, just as interest in these goods is in the nature of men.

Modes of Domination

The theory of strictly economic practices is a particular case of a general theory of the economy of practices. Even when they give every appearance of disinterestedness because they escape the logic of "economic" interest (in the narrow sense) and are oriented towards non-material stakes that are not easily quantified, as in "pre-capitalist" societies or in the cultural sphere of capitalist societies, practices never cease to comply with an economic logic. The correspondences which are established between the circulation of land sold and bought back, revenge killings "lent" and "redeemed," or women given and received in marriage, in other words between the different kinds of capital and the corresponding modes of circulation, require us to abandon the economic/non-economic dichotomy which makes it impossible to see the science of "economic" practices as a particular case of a science capable of treating all practices, including those that are experienced as disinterested or gratuitous, and therefore freed from the "economy," as economic practices aimed at maximizing material or symbolic profit. The capital accumulated by groups, which can be regarded as the energy of social physics,[1] can exist in different kinds (in the Kabyle case, these are the capital of fighting strength, linked to the capacity for mobilization and therefore to the number of men and their readiness to fight; "economic" capital, in the form of land, livestock and labor force, this too being linked to the capacity for mobilization; and the symbolic capital accruing from successful use of the other kinds of capital). Although they are subject to strict laws of equivalence and are therefore mutually convertible, each of these kinds of capital produces its specific effects only in specific conditions. But the existence of symbolic capital, that is, of "material" capital misrecognized and thus recognized, though it does not invalidate the analogy between capital and energy, does remind us that social science is not a social physics; that the acts of cognition that are implied in misrecognition and recognition are part of social reality and that the socially constituted subjectivity that produces them belongs to objective reality.

An unbroken progression leads from the symmetry of gift exchange to the asymmetry of the conspicuous redistribution that is the basis of the constitution of political authority. As one moves away from perfect reciprocity, which assumes a relative equality of economic situation, the proportion of counter-services that are provided in the typically symbolic form of gratitude, homage, respect, obligations or moral debts necessarily increases. If they had been aware of this continuity, those who, like Karl Polanyi and Marshall D.

Sahlins, have realized the decisive role of redistribution in establishing political authority and in the functioning of the tribal economy (in which the
accumulation-redistribution circuit fulfills a similar function to that of the
State and public finances) would no doubt also have observed the central
operation of this process, namely the conversion of economic capital into
symbolic capital, which produces relations of dependence that have an economic basis but are disguised under a veil of moral relations. In focusing
solely on the particular case of exchanges designed to consecrate symmetrical
relations, or solely on the economic effect of asymmetrical exchanges, one is
liable to forget the effect produced by the circular circulation in which symbolic added-value is generated, namely the legitimation of the arbitrary,
when the circulation covers an asymmetrical power relationship.

. . .

While there are ample grounds for re-emphasizing these negative conditions of the privileged or exclusive recourse to the symbolic forms of
power, it must not be forgotten that they no more account for the logic of
symbolic violence than the absence of the lightning rod or the electric tele-
graph, which Marx refers to in a famous passage in the introduction to the
Grundrisse, can be used to explain Jupiter or Hermes, in other words the
internal logic of Greek mythology. To go further, one has to take seriously
the representation that the agents offer of the economy of their own practice when this is most opposed to its "economic" truth. The chief is
indeed, in Malinowski's phrase, "a tribal banker" who accumulates food
only to lavish it on others and so build up a capital of obligations and debts
that will be repaid in the form of homage, respect, loyalty and, when the
occasion arises, work and services, which may be the basis of new accumulation of material goods. But the analogy must not mislead us: processes of
circular circulation such as the levying of a tribute followed by a redistribution apparently leading back to the point of departure would be perfectly
absurd if they did not have the effect of transmuting the nature of the
social relationship among the agents or groups involved. Everywhere they
are observed, these consecration cycles perform the fundamental operation
of social alchemy, the transformation of arbitrary relations into legitimate
relations, *de facto* differences into officially recognized distinctions.

A rich man is "rich in order to give to the poor."[2] This saying is an
exemplary expression of the practical denial of interest which, like Freud's
Verneinung, makes it possible to satisfy interest but only in a (disinterested)
form tending to show that it is not being satisfied (the "lifting of repression" implying no "acceptance of the repressed"). A man possesses in order
to give. But he also possesses by giving. A gift that is not returned can
become a debt, a lasting obligation; and the only recognized power—

recognition, personal loyalty or prestige—is the one that is obtained by giving. In such a universe, there are only two ways of getting and keeping a lasting hold over someone: debts and gifts, the overtly economic obliga-tions imposed by the usurer,[3] or the moral obligations and emotional attachments created and maintained by the generous gift, in short, overt violence or symbolic violence, censored, euphemized, that is, misrecogniz-able, recognized violence. The "way of giving," the manner, the forms, are what separate a gift from straight exchange, moral obligation from eco-nomic obligation. To "observe the formalities" is to make the way of behaving and the external forms of the action a practical denial of the con-tent of the action and of the potential violence it can conceal.[4] There is a clear connection between these two forms of violence, which exist in the same social formation and sometimes in the same relationship: when domi-nation can only be exerted in its elementary form, from person to person, it takes place overtly and has to be disguised under the veil of enchanted relations, the official model of which is presented by relations between kinsmen; in short, to be socially recognized, it must be misrecognized. If the pre-capitalist economy is the site *par excellence* of symbolic violence, this is because the only way that relations of domination can be set up within it, maintained or restored, is through strategies which, if they are not to destroy themselves by revealing their true nature, must be disguised, transfigured, in a word, euphemized. The censorship that this economy imposes on the overt manifestation of violence, especially in its crudely economic form, means that interests can only be satisfied on condition that they be disguised in and by the very strategies aimed at satisfying them.

So it would be wrong to see a contradiction in the fact that violence is here both more present and more masked.[5] Because the pre-capitalist economy cannot count on the implacable, hidden violence of objective mechanisms which enable the dominant to limit themselves to reproduc-tion strategies (often purely negative ones), it resorts simultaneously to forms of domination which may strike the modern observer as more brutal, more primitive, more barbarous, and at the same time as gentler, more humane, more respectful of persons.[6] This coexistence of overt physical or economic violence and the most refined symbolic violence is found in all the institutions characteristic of this economy and at the very heart of each social relation. It is present in both the debt and the gift, which, despite their apparent opposition, can each provide the basis of dependence and even servitude, as well as solidarity, depending on the strategies they serve (Moses Finley [1965] shows that a debt that was sometimes set up to cre-ate a situation of slavery could also serve to create relations of solidarity between equals). This essential ambiguity of all the institutions that mod-ern taxonomies would incline one to treat as "economic" is evidence that the opposing strategies that may coexist, as in the master-*khammes* ["a kind of sharecropper who received only a very small share of the crop, usually a fifth, with local variants"] relationship, are alternative, interchangeable ways of fulfilling the same function: the "choice" between overt violence and gentle violence depends on the state of the power relations between the two parties and the integration and ethical integrity of the group that arbitrates. So long as overt violence, that of the usurer or the ruthless master, is collectively disapproved of and is liable to provoke either a violent riposte or the flight of the victim—that is, in both cases, for lack of any legal recourse the destruction of the very relationship that was to be exploited—symbolic violence, gentle, invisible violence, unrecognized as such, chosen as much as undergone, that of trust, obligation, personal loyalty, hospitality, gifts, debts, piety, in a word, of all the virtues honored by the ethic of honor, presents itself as the most economical mode of domination because it best corresponds to the economy of the system.

. . .

The harder it is to exercise direct domination, and the more it is disapproved of, the more likely it is that gentle, disguised forms of domination will be seen as the only possible way of exercising domination and exploitation. It would be as fallacious to identify this essentially two-sided economy with its official truth as it would be to reduce it to its "objective" truth, seeing mutual aid as a corvée, the *khammes* as a kind of slave, and so on. "Economic" capital can here only work in the euphemized form of symbolic capital. This conversion of capital which is the condition of its efficacy is in no way automatic. As well as a perfect knowledge of the logic of the economy of denial, it requires constant labor in the form of the care and attention devoted to making and maintaining relations; and also major investments, both material and symbolic—political aid against attack, theft, offences and insults, and economic aid, which can be costly, especially in times of scarcity. It also requires the (sincere) disposition to give things that are more personal, and therefore more precious than goods or money, because, as the saying goes, they can "neither be lent nor borrowed," such as time[7]—the time that has to be taken to do things "that are not forgotten," because they are done properly, at the proper time, marks of "attention," friendly "gestures," acts of "kindness." If authority is always seen as a property of the person—*fides*, as Benveniste (1973: 84ff.) points out, is not "trust" but "the inherent quality of a person who inspires trust and is exercised in the form of protective authority over those who entrust themselves to him"—it is because gentle violence requires those who exercise it to pay a *personal* price.

. . .

In short, in the absence of an officially declared and institutionally guaranteed delegation, personal authority can only be lastingly maintained through actions that reassert it practically through their compliance with the values recognized by the group.[8] The "great" can least afford to take liberties with the official norms and they have to pay for their outstanding value with exemplary conformity to the values of the group. Until a system of mechanisms automatically ensuring the reproduction of the established order is constituted, the dominant agents cannot be content with letting the system that they dominate follow its own course in order to exercise durable domination; they have to work directly, daily, personally, to produce and reproduce conditions of domination which even then are never entirely certain. Because they cannot be satisfied with appropriating the profits of a social machine which has not yet developed the power of self-perpetuation, they are obliged to resort to the elementary forms of domination, in other words the direct domination of one person over another, the limiting case of which is appropriation of persons, that is, slavery. They cannot appropriate the labor, services, goods, homage and respect of others without "winning" them personally, "tying" them, in short, creating a bond between persons. The transformation of any given kind of capital into symbolic capital, a legitimate possession grounded in the nature of its possessor, is the fundamental operation of social alchemy (the paradigm of which is gift exchange). It always presupposes a form of labor, a visible (if not necessarily conspicuous) expenditure of time, money and energy, a redistribution that is necessary in order to secure recognition of the prevailing distribution, in the form of the recognition granted by the person who receives to the person who, being better placed in the distribution, is in a position to give, a recognition of a debt which is also a recognition of value.

Thus, contrary to simplistic uses of the distinction between infrastructure and superstructure,[9] the social mechanisms that ensure the production of compliant *habitus* are, here as elsewhere, an integral part of the conditions of reproduction of the social order and of the productive apparatus itself, which could not function without the dispositions that the group inculcates and continuously reinforces and which exclude, as *unthinkable,* practices which the disenchanted economy of "naked self-interest" presents as legitimate and even self-evident. But the particularly important role played by the *habitus* and its strategies in setting up and perpetuating durable relations of domination is once again an effect of the structure of the field. Because it does not offer the institutional conditions for the accumulation of economic or cultural capital (which it even expressly discourages through a censorship forcing agents to resort to euphemized forms of power and violence), this economic order is such that strategies oriented towards the accumulation of symbolic capital, which are found in all social formations, are here the most rational ones, since they are the most effective strategies within the constraints of this universe. The principle of the pertinent differences between the modes of domination lies in the degree of objectification of capital. Social formations in which relations of domination are made, unmade and remade in and through personal interactions contrast with those in which such relations are mediated by objective, institutionalized mechanisms such as the "self-regulating market," the educational system or the legal apparatus, where they have the permanence and opacity of things and lie beyond the reach of individual consciousness and power.

The opposition between, on the one hand, universes of social relations that do not contain within themselves the principle of their own reproduction and have to be kept up by nothing less than a process of continuous creation, and on the other hand, a social world carried along by its *vis insita* which frees agents from this endless work of creating or restoring social relations, is directly expressed in the history or prehistory of social thought. "In Hobbes' view," writes Durkheim (1960: 136), "the social order is generated by an act of will and sustained by an act of will that must be constantly renewed."[10] And there is every reason to think that the break with this artificialist vision, which is the precondition for scientific apprehension, could not be made before the constitution, in reality, of objective mechanisms like the self-regulating market which, as Polanyi points out, was intrinsically conducive to belief in determinism.[11]

Objectification in institutions guarantees the permanence and cumulativity of material and symbolic acquisitions which can then subsist without the agents having to recreate them continuously and in their entirety by deliberate action. But, because the profits provided by these institutions are subject to differential appropriation, objectification also and inseparably tends to ensure the reproduction of the structure of the distribution of capital which, in its various kinds, is the precondition for such appropriation, and, in so doing, it tends to reproduce the structure of relations of domination and dependence.

Paradoxically, it is precisely because there exist relatively autonomous fields, functioning in accordance with rigorous mechanisms capable of imposing their necessity on the agents, that those who are in a position to command these mechanisms and appropriate the material or symbolic profits accruing from their functioning are able to dispense with strategies aimed expressly and directly at the domination of individuals. The saving is a real one, because strategies designed to establish or maintain lasting relations of personal dependence are, as we have seen, extremely costly, with the result that the means eat up the end and the actions necessary to ensure the continuation of power themselves help to weaken it. Might has to be expended to produce rights, and a great deal of it may be used up in this way. [12]

The point of honor is politics in the pure state. It inclines agents to accumulate material riches that do not have their justification "in themselves," that is, in their "economic" or "technical" function, and which, in extreme cases, may be totally useless, like the objects exchanged in a number of archaic economies, but which are valued as means of manifesting power, as symbolic capital tending to contribute to its own reproduction, that is, to the reproduction and legitimation of the prevailing hierarchies. In such a context, the accumulation of material wealth is simply one means among others of accumulating symbolic power—the power to secure recognition of power. What might be called demonstrative expenditure (as opposed to "productive" expenditure, which is why it is called "gratuitous" or "symbolic") represents, like any other visible expenditure of the signs of wealth that are recognized in a given social formation, a kind of legitimizing self-affirmation through which power makes itself known and recognized. By asserting itself visibly and publicly, securing acceptance of its right to visibility, as opposed to all the occult, hidden, secret, shameful and therefore censored powers (such as those of malign magic), this power awards itself a rudimentary form of institutionalization by officializing itself. But only full institutionalization makes it possible, if not to dispense completely with "demonstration," at least to cease depending on it completely in order to secure the belief and obedience of others and to mobilize their labor power or fighting strength. And there is every reason to think that, as in the case of feudalism according to Georges Duby, the accumulation of "economic" capital becomes possible once symbolic capital can be reproduced durably and cheaply so that the political war for rank, distinction and pre-eminence can be pursued by other, more "economical" means. In place of the relationships between persons indissociable from the functions they fulfill, which they can perpetuate only at direct personal cost, institutionalization sets up strictly established, legally guaranteed relations between recognized positions, defined by their rank in a relatively autonomous space, distinct from and independent of their actual and potential occupants, themselves defined by *entitlements* which, like titles of nobility, property titles or educational qualifications (*titres*), authorize them to occupy these positions.[13] As opposed to personal authority, which can neither be delegated nor bequeathed, the title, as a measure of rank or order, that is, as a formal instrument of evaluation of agents' positions in a distribution, makes it possible to set up quasi-perfect relations of commensurability (or equivalence) among agents defined as aspiring to the appropriation of a particular class of goods—real estate, precedence, offices, privileges—and these goods, which are themselves classified. Thus the relations among agents can be durably settled as regards their legitimate order of access to these goods and to the groups defined by exclusive ownership of these goods.

Thus, for example, by giving the same value to all holders of the same certificate, thereby making them interchangeable, the educational system minimizes the obstacles to the free circulation of cultural capital which result from its being incorporated in particular individuals (without, however, destroying the profits associated with the charismatic ideology of the irreplaceable individual).[14] It makes it possible to relate all qualification-holders (and also, negatively, all unqualified individuals) to a single standard, thereby setting up a unified market for all cultural capacities and guaranteeing the convertibility into money of the cultural capital acquired at a given cost in time and labor. Educational qualifications, like money, have a conventional, fixed value which, being guaranteed by law, is freed from local limitations (in contrast to academically uncertified cultural capital) and temporal fluctuations: the cultural capital which they in a sense guarantee once and for all does not constantly need to be proved. The objectification performed by certificates, diplomas and, more generally, all forms of "credentials" ("a written proof of qualification that confers credit or authority") is inseparable from the objectification that law produces by defining permanent positions which are independent of the biological individuals they call for and which may be occupied by agents who are biologically different but interchangeable in respect of the qualifications they hold. From then on, relations of power and dependence are no longer established directly between individuals; they are set up, in objectivity, among institutions, that is, among socially guaranteed qualifications and socially defined positions, and through them, among the social mechanisms that produce and guarantee both the social value of the qualifications and the distribution of these social attributes among biological individuals.

Law does no more than symbolically consecrate—by recording it in a form that renders it both eternal and universal—the structure of power relations among the groups and the classes that is produced and guaranteed practically by the functioning of these mechanisms. For example, it records and legitimates the distinction between the function and the person, between power and its holder, together with the relationship that obtains at a particular moment between qualifications and posts (depending on the bargaining power of the sellers and buyers of qualified, that is, scholastically guaranteed, labor power), a relationship that is materialized in a particular distribution of the material and symbolic profits assigned to holders (or non-holders) of qualifications. Law thus adds its specific symbolic force to the action of the whole set of mechanisms which render it superfluous constantly to reassert power relations through the overt use of force.

The effect of legitimation of the established order is thus not solely the work of the mechanisms traditionally regarded as belonging to the order of ideology, such as law. The system of cultural goods production and the system producing the producers also fulfill ideological functions, as a by-product, through the very logic of their functioning, owing to the fact that the mechanisms through which they contribute to the reproduction of the social order and the permanence of the relations of domination remain hidden. As I have shown elsewhere, the educational system helps to provide the dominant class with a "theodicy of its own privilege" not so much through the ideologies it produces or inculcates, but rather through the practical justification of the established order that it supplies by masking—under the overt connection that it guarantees, between qualifications and jobs—the relationship, which it surreptitiously records, under cover of formal equality, between the qualifications obtained and inherited cultural capital. The most successful ideological effects are the ones that have no need of words, but only of *laissez-faire* and complicitous silence.

It follows, incidentally, that any analysis of ideologies in the narrow sense of "legitimizing discourses" which fails to include an analysis of the corresponding institutional mechanisms is liable to be no more than a contribution to the efficacy of those ideologies. This is true of all internal (semiological) analyses of political, educational, religious or aesthetic ideologies which forget that the political function of these ideologies may in some cases be reduced to the effect of displacement and diversion, dissimulation, and legitimation, which they produce by reproducing the effects of the objective mechanisms, through their oversights and omissions, in their deliberately or involuntarily complicitous silences. This is true, for example, of the charismatic (or meritocratic) ideology, a particular form of the giving of "gifts," which explains differential access to qualifications by reference to the inequality of innate "gifts," thereby reinforcing the effect of the mechanisms that mask the relationship between qualifications obtained and inherited cultural capital.

If it is true that symbolic violence is the gentle, disguised form which violence takes when overt violence is impossible, it is understandable that symbolic forms of domination should have progressively withered away as objective mechanisms came to be constituted which, in rendering the work of euphemization superfluous, tended to produce the "disenchanted" dispositions that their development demanded.[15] It is equally clear why the development of the capacity for subversion and critique that the most brutal forms of "economic" exploitation have aroused, and the uncovering of the ideological and practical effects of the mechanisms ensuring the reproduction of the relations of domination, should bring about a return to modes of accumulation based on the conversion of economic capital into symbolic capital, with all the forms of legitimizing redistribution, public ("social" policies) and private (financing of "disinterested" foundations, donations to hospitals, academic and cultural institutions, etc.), through which the dominant groups secure a capital of "credit" which seems to owe nothing to the logic of exploitation;[16] or the thesaurization of luxury goods attesting to the taste and distinction of their possessor. The denial of the economy and of economic interest which, in pre-capitalist societies, was exerted first in the very area of "economic" transactions, from which it had to be expelled in order for "the economy" to be constituted as such, thus finds its favored refuge in the domain of art and "culture," the site of pure consumption—of money, of course, but also of time. This island of the sacred, ostentatiously opposed to the profane, everyday world of production, a sanctuary for gratuitous, disinterested activity, offers, like theology in other periods, an imaginary anthropology obtained by denial of all the negations really performed by the "economy."

From *The Logic of Practice* [1980] translation 1990.
Translated by Richard Nice.

Notes

The Work of Time

1. "Don't be offended at me for making this offer. . . . I am so thoroughly conscious of counting for nothing in your eyes, that you can even take money from me. You can't take offence at a gift from me" (Dostoyevsky 1966: 44).

2. A gift always contains a more or less disguised challenge. "He has put him to shame," the Moroccan Berbers used to say, according to Marcy (1941), apropos of the challenge-gift (*thawsa*) which marked the great occasions. It can be seen that the logic of challenge and riposte is the limit towards which gift exchange moves when generous exchange tends towards an "overwhelming" generosity.

3. Though presented here in deductive form, these propositions were not produced by deduction, as can be seen from the successive versions of the analysis: the first, published in 1965, was still very close to the native, i.e., official, representation; the second, published in 1972, was based on a series of case-studies and presented the model put forward here, but in a less economical form.

4. Rites of possession or exorcism and all magical struggles show, through this limiting case, that magical acts are "logical" operations performed in situations of life-and-death urgency. The "magical stereotyping" that Weber refers to is probably due in part to the fact that mistakes have grave consequences.

5. The statements contained in the customary law of a particular clan or village represent only a very small proportion of the universe of possible acts of jurisprudence, and if one adds to them the statements produced from the principles to be found in the customs of other groups, this still gives only a limited idea of the full possibilities.

6. The *qanun* of each clan (or village) essentially consists of a list of specific misdemeanors each followed by the corresponding fine. The principles from which these consecrated acts of jurisprudence are produced are left implicit. For example, the *qanun* of Agouni-n-Tesellent, a village of the At Akbil tribe, includes, in a total of 249 clauses, 219 "repressive laws" (in Durkheim's sense), i.e., 88 per cent, as

against 25 "restitutory" laws, i.e., 10 per cent, and only 5 clauses concerning the foundations of the political system.

7. All sorts of examples of this will be seen in the analyses below, such as *elba-hadla*, excessive humiliation, in the exchanges of honor, or marriage with the parallel cousin in matrimonial exchanges.

8. The verb *qabel,* which several informants offer as a kind of concentrated expression of all the values of honor, in fact brings all these levels together, since it designates all at once bodily postures (standing up straight, facing up to someone, looking him in the eyes), recognized virtues (like the art of receiving an honored guest, or knowing how to confront others, for better or worse, by looking them straight in the face), and mythico-ritual categories (facing the east, the light, the future).

9. If practice is content with a partial or discontinuous logic and a "satisficing or limited rationality," this is not because, as has been noted, recourse to empirical procedures or tried and tested decision-making principles enables it to save the costs of information gathering and analysis (cf. Simon 1954). It is also because the saving in logic resulting from intuitive, rule-of-thumb decisions implies a saving in time, which, even in economic choices, is no small matter when one remembers that the characteristic of practice is that it operates in emergency conditions and that the best decision in the world is worthless when it comes too late, after the opportunity or the ritual moment. (Analysts and experimenters forget this when they proceed as if an agent involved in the action could pause to decipher without risking the practical sanction of his delay.)

10. Sayings that exalt generosity, the supreme virtue of the man of honor, coexist with proverbs betraying the temptation to calculate: "A gift is a misfortune," says one of them, and another: "A present is a chicken and the recompense a camel." Playing on the word *lehna,* which means both "present" and "peace," and on *elahdya* which means 'present', the Kabyles also say: "You who bring us peace (a present), leave us in peace," "Leave us in peace (*lahna*) with your present (*elahdya*)," or "The best present is peace."

11. This is true, for example, of all research on the cult of art and culture. The sociology that brings to light the "objective" truth must expect to see the self-evidences that it supplies (I am thinking, for example, of the relationship between educational level and visits to art galleries established in *L'Amour de l'art* [Bourdieu 1966]) countered by a denial (in Freud's sense) which is only the defensive form of ordinary gainsaying. This must lead it to integrate into its theoretical construction the illusion, that is, the belief, that it has had to combat, and the objectification of the conditions of its production and functioning. (This is what I have tried to do in my work subsequent to *L'Amour de l'art* on the conditions of production of the belief in the value of the work of art.)

12. The effect of symbolic imposition that official representation intrinsically exerts is intensified by a deeper effect when semi-learned grammar, a normative description, is (differentially) taught by a specific institution and so becomes the basis of a cultivated *habitus.* Thus, in a class society, the legitimate linguistic *habitus* presupposes objectification (more precisely, thesaurization and formalization by grammarians) and inculcation, by the family and the educational system, of the system of rules (the grammar) resulting from this objectification. In this case, as in the field of art and, more generally, of learned ["high"—trans.] culture, it is the semi-learned ["middle-brow"] norm (grammar, scholastic categories of perception, appreciation and expression, etc.) which, incorporated (in the form of "culture"),

becomes the principle of the production and understanding of practices and discourses. It follows that relations to high culture (and formal language) are objectively defined by the degree of incorporation of the legitimate norm. The ease of those who, with a precocious and deep command of the learned grammar of practices and discourses, are so manifestly in line with its demands that they can allow themselves the liberties with the rule that defines excellence, is opposed to the tension and pretension of those whose strict conformity to the rule reveals that they are limited to execution of the rule, not to mention those who, whatever they do, cannot fall into line with rules that are made against them.

13. Those who are designated to speak about the group on behalf of the group, the authorized spokesmen to whom the anthropologist is first referred (men rather than women, respected middle-aged or old men rather than young or marginal men), offer a discourse in line with the view that the group wants to give and have of itself, emphasizing (especially to an outsider) values (e.g., those of honor) rather than interests, rules rather than strategies, etc.

14. Between the agent whom the "excellence" of practice naturally complying with the official rule predisposes to serve as a delegate and spokesman and the agent who, not content with breaking the rules of the game, does nothing to hide or extenuate his transgressions, there is a recognized place for the agent who, by offering the appearances or the intention of conformity, i.e., recognition, to the rule he can neither observe nor refuse, contributes to the official existence of the rule.

15. Competition for official power is restricted to men; women can only compete for a power that always remains unofficial. Men have the whole social order and the whole official institution working for them, starting with mythico-ritual and genealogical structures, which, by reducing the opposition between the official and the private to the opposition between the outside and the inside, and therefore between the male and the female, establish a systematic hierarchization assigning female interventions to a shadowy, clandestine or, at best, unofficial existence. Even when women hold the real power, as is often the case, at least in matrimonial matters, they can only exercise it fully so long as they leave the appearances, the official manifestation, of power to men. Women can have a degree of power only if they are willing to make do with the unofficial power of the *éminence grise*, a dominated power which can only be exerted by proxy, covered by an official authority, so that it still serves the authority it makes use of.

Symbolic Capital

1. To convince oneself this is so, one only has to remember the tradition of "confraternity" within the medical profession. No doctor ever pays a fellow doctor a fee. Instead, he has to find him a present, without necessarily knowing what he wants or needs, not worth too much more or too much less than the price of the consultation, but also not coming too close, because that would amount to stating the price of the service, thereby giving away the self-interested fiction that it was free.

2. "You've saved me from having to sell" is what a man says in such cases to the lender who prevents land falling into the hands of a stranger, by means of a sort of fictitious sale (he gives the money while allowing the owner the continued use of his land).

3. The reluctance to use formal guarantees increases with the social proximity of the parties and with the solemnity of the guarantees invoked. Similarly, the share of the loss that the partners agree to bear when an animal suffers an accident varies

greatly depending on the relationship between them. A man who has lent an animal to a very close relative will minimize his partner's responsibility.

4. This distinction (like the related distinction that Marx makes between labor time—here, the time devoted to ploughing and harvesting—and productive time—which, as well as the labor time, includes the nine months between ploughing and sowing) has been imposed by the effects of the economic domination linked to colonization and more especially by the generalization of monetary exchange. The awareness of unemployment, measured by the discrepancy between the fact of declaring oneself "in work" and the real activity in the days preceding the survey, varies with the degree of penetration of the capitalist economy and the associated dispositions (see Bourdieu 1979: 57).

5. Since the price of time rises as productivity rises (and with it the quantity of goods offered for consumption, and hence consumption itself, which also takes time), time becomes scarcer as the scarcity of goods declines. Squandering of goods can even become the only way of saving time which is now more valuable than the goods that could be saved if time were devoted to maintenance, repair, etc. (see Becker 1965). This is no doubt one of the bases of the contrast in attitudes to time that has often been observed.

6. It has to be borne in mind that the distinction between economic capital and symbolic capital is the product of the application of a principle of differentiation alien to the universe to which it is applied and that it can only grasp the undifferentiatedness of these two states of capital in the form of their perfect convertibility.

7. A man who seeks to belie his reputation as a "house man" (*argaz ukhamis*—as opposed to the "market man") is put in his place with: "Since you're only a *thakwath* man, stay a *thakwath* man!" (*thakwath* designates the alcove in the wall of the house, used to hide the small, typically feminine objects which must not be left on view, spoons, rags, weaving tools, etc.).

8. Proof that what is at stake in marriage strategies is not reducible to the bridewealth alone is provided by history, which, here too, has dissociated the symbolic and the material aspects of transactions. In being reduced to its purely monetary value, the bridewealth has been dispossessed, even in the agents' own eyes, of its significance as a symbolic rating, and the debates that used to take place about it, having been reduced to the level of haggling, come to be seen as shameful.

Modes of Domination

1. Although he draws no real conclusions from it, Bertrand Russell (1938: 12–14) expresses very well an intuition of the analogy between energy and power which could serve as the basis for a unification of social science: "Like energy, power has many forms, such as wealth, armaments, civil authority, influence or opinion. No one of these can be regarded as subordinate to any other, and there is no one form from which the others are derivative. The attempt to treat one form of power, say wealth, in isolation, can only be partially successful, just as the study of one form of energy will be defective at certain points, unless other forms are taken into account. Wealth may result from military power or from influence over opinion, just as either of these may result from wealth." And he goes on to define the programme for a science of the conversions of the different forms of social energy: "Power, like energy, must be regarded as continually moving from any one of its forms into any other, and it should be the business of social science to seek the laws of such transformations."

2. Wealth, a gift God makes to man so that he can relieve the poverty of others, chiefly implies duties. The belief in immanent justice, which governs a number of practices (such as collective oath-taking), no doubt helps to turn generosity into a sacrifice that will merit in return the blessing of generosity. "A generous man is a friend of God" ("the two worlds belong to him"); "Eat, you who are used to feeding others"; "Lord, give unto me that I may give" (only a saint can give without owning).

3. Usurers are universally despised and some of them, fearing ostracism, prefer to grant their debtors extra time (e.g., until the next olive harvest) rather than force them to sell land in order to pay.

4. Archaic societies devote more time and effort to "form," because their refusal to recognize self-evidences such as the "business is business" or "time is money" on which the unaesthetic life-style of the "harried leisure classes" in so-called advanced societies is based, imposes a stronger censorship of personal interest. So it is understandable why these societies offer connoisseurs of beautiful forms the enchanting spectacle of a life-style conducted as art for art's sake.

5. Benveniste's history of the vocabulary of Indo-European institutions charts the linguistic milestones in the process of unveiling and disenchantment which leads from physical or symbolic violence to "economic" law, from ransom (of a prisoner) to purchase, from the prize (for a notable action) to wages, from moral recognition to the recognition of debts, from worthiness to credit-worthiness, and from moral obligation to the court order (Benveniste 1973: 159-84).

6. The question of the relative value of the different modes of domination—a question raised, at least implicitly, by Rousseauistic evocations of primitive paradises or Americanocentric disquisitions on "modernization"—is totally meaningless and can only give rise to necessarily interminable debates on the advantages and disadvantages of "before" and "after," the only interest of which lies in the revelation of the writer's own social fantasies, i.e., his unanalyzed relationship to his own society. As in all comparisons of one system with another, it is possible *ad infinitum* to contrast partial representations of the two systems (e.g., enchantment versus disenchantment) differing in their affective coloring and ethical connotations depending on which of them is taken as a standpoint. The only legitimate object of comparison is each system considered as a system, and this precludes any evaluation other than that implied *in fact* in the immanent logic of its evolution.

7. A man who fails to "give others the time he owes them" is reproached in terms like these: "You've only just arrived, and now you're off again." "Are you leaving us? We've only just sat down . . . We've hardly spoken."

8. The marabouts are in a different position, because they wield an institutionally delegated authority as members of a respected body of "religious officials" and because they maintain a separate status for themselves. They do this by practicing fairly strict endogamy and a whole set of traditions specific to themselves, such as confining their women to the house. The fact remains that these men who, as the saying goes, "like mountain torrents, grow great in stormy times," cannot derive profit from their quasi-institutionalized role as mediators unless their knowledge of the traditions and of the persons involved gives the means of exerting a symbolic authority which only exists by virtue of direct delegation by the group. The marabouts are most often simply the loophole, the "door," as the Kabyles say, that enables groups in conflict to compromise without losing face.

9. Thinking in terms of "instances" owes its almost inevitable social success to the fact that, as is shown by the most elementary analysis of usages, it makes it pos-

sible to mobilize all the reassuring symbolism of architecture for classificatory and apparently explanatory purposes, with "structure" of course, and therefore "infrastructure" and "superstructure," but also "base," "basis," "ground," "foundations," not forgetting Gurvitch's inimitable "floors" (*paliers*) (in depth . . .).

10. The analogy with Descartes's theory of continuous creation is perfect. And when Leibniz criticized a conception of God condemned to move the world "as a carpenter moves his axe or as a miller drives his millstone by diverting water towards the wheel" (1939: 92), and put forward, in place of the Cartesian universe, which cannot subsist without unremitting divine attention, a physical world endowed with a *vis propria,* he was initiating the critique—which did not find full expression until much later (in Hegel's Introduction to the *Philosophy of Right*)—of all forms of the refusal to acknowledge that the social world has a "nature," that is, an immanent necessity.

11. The existence of mechanisms capable of ensuring the reproduction of the political order, without any express intervention, in turn induces acceptance of a restricted definition of politics and of the practices oriented towards acquisition or conservation of power, which tacitly excludes the competition for control over the mechanisms of reproduction. Thus, when social science takes as its main object the sphere of legitimate politics, as what is called "political science" now does, it uncritically accepts the pre-constructed object that reality imposes on it.

12. It has often been pointed out that the logic that makes the redistribution of goods the *sine qua non* of the perpetuation of power tends to slow down or prevent the primitive accumulation of economic capital and the emergence of division into classes (see for example Wolf 1959: 216).

13. A social history of the notion of the "title," of which the title of nobility or the educational qualification (*titre scolaire*) are particular cases, would have to show the social conditions and the effects of the shift from personal authority (e.g., the *gratia*—esteem, influence—of the Romans) to the institutionalized title, in other words from honor to *jus honorum.* Thus, in Rome, the use of titles (such as *eques Romanus*) defining a *dignitas,* an officially recognized position within the State (as distinct from a purely personal quality) was, like the use of *insignia,* progressively subjected to detailed control by custom or law (see Nicolet 1966: 236–41).

14. Educational qualifications, a measure of rank, indicating an agent's position in the structure of the distribution of cultural capital, are socially perceived as guaranteeing possession of a particular quantity of cultural capital.

15. In the ideological struggle among the groups (age groups, the sexes, etc.) or the social classes for the power to define reality, symbolic violence, a misrecognized and thus recognized violence, is held in check by the awakening of awareness of arbitrariness ("consciousness-raising"), which deprives the dominant of part of their symbolic strength by sweeping away misrecognition.

16. It was not a sociologist but a group of American businessmen who conceived the "bank-account theory" of public relations: "It necessitates making regular and frequent deposits in the Bank of Public Good-Will, so that valid checks can be drawn on this account when it is desirable" (quoted by MacKean 1944). See also Gable (1953: 262) on the different ways in which the National Association of Manufacturers tries to influence the general public, teachers, churchmen, women's club leaders, farmers' leaders, etc., and H. A. Turner (1958) on the way in which "an organization elevates itself in the esteem of the general public and conditions their attitudes so that a state of public opinion will be created in which the public will almost automatically respond with favor to the programs desired by the group."

Works Cited

Becker, G. S. 1965. "A Theory of the Allocation of Time." *Economic Journal* 75: 493–517.

Benveniste, Émile. 1973. *Indo-European Language and Society*. London: Faber.

Boulifa, S. 1913. *Méthode de langue kabyle. Étude linguistique et sociologique sur la Kabylie du Djurdjura*. Algiers: Jourdan.

Bourdieu, Pierre. 1966. *L'Amour de l'art*. Paris: Éditions de Minuit.

———. 1971. "Genèse et structure du champ religieux." *Revue française de sociologie* 12: 295–334.

———. 1979. "The Sense of Honour." In *Algeria 1960*. Cambridge: Cambridge University Press and Paris: Éditions de la Maison des Sciences de l'Homme.

Dostoyevsky, Fyodor. 1966. "The Gambler." In *The Gambler, Bobok, A Nasty Story*. Harmondsworth: Penguin.

Durkheim, Émile. 1960. *Montesquieu and Rousseau: Forerunners of Sociology*. Trans. Ralph Manheim. Ann Arbor: University of Michigan Press.

Finley, Moses. 1965. "La servitude pour dettes." *Revue d'histoire du droit française et étranger*. 4th series, 43: 159–84.

Gable, R. W. 1953. "Influential Lobby or Kiss of Death?" *Journal of Politics* 15, 2.

Hanoteau, A., and A. Letourneux. 1873. *La Kabylie et les coutumes kabyles*. Paris: Imprimerie nationale.

Jakobson, Roman. 1956. *Fundamentals of Language*. The Hague: Mouton.

Leibniz, G. W. 1939. "De Ipsa Natura." In *Opuscula Philosophica Selecta*. Paris: Boivin.

Lévi-Strauss, Claude. 1987. *Introduction to the Work of Marcel Mauss*. Trans. Felicity Baker. London: Routledge and Kegan Paul. (First French edition: 1950.)

MacKean, Dayton. 1944. *Party and Pressure Politics*. New York: Houghton Mifflin.

Mammeri, M., and P. Bourdieu. 1978. "Dialogue sur la poésie oral en Kabylie." *Actes de la recherche en sciences sociales* 23: 51–66.

Marcy, Georges. 1941. "*Les vestiges de la parente maternelle en droit coutumier berbère et le régime des successions touarègues*." *Revue Africaine* 85: 187–211.

Marx, Karl. 1973. *Grundrisse*. Harmondsworth: Penguin.

Mauss, Marcel. 1966. *The Gift*. London: Cohen and West.

Nicolet, Claude. 1966. *L'Ordre équestre à l'époque républicaine*. Vol. 1. Paris: Édition de Boccard.

Russell, Bertrand. 1938. *Power: A New Social Analysis*. London: Allen & Unwin.

Simon, H. 1954. "A Behavioral Theory of Rational Choice." *Quarterly Journal of Economics* 69: 99–118.

Turner, H. A. 1958. "How Pressure Groups Operate." *Annals of the American Academy of Political and Social Science* 319: 63–72.

Wolf, Eric. 1959. *Sons of the Shaking Earth*. Chicago: University of Chicago Press.

Marginalia—
Some Additional Notes on the Gift

Pierre Bourdieu

The analysis of gifts that I put forward in *Outline of a Theory of Practice* and *The Logic of Practice* (which, to avoid repetitions, I will assume to be known) departs from previous theories, in particular the phenomenological and structuralist ones, on three fundamental points: it makes room for time, or more precisely, for the time lag between gift and counter-gift, and for uncertainty; it brings in a theory of the agent and of action that makes the dispositions constituting the *habitus,* rather than consciousness or intention, the basis of practices; and it relates gift exchange to a quite specific logic, that of the economy of symbolic goods and the specific belief (*illusio*) that underlies it.

The major characteristic of the experience of the gift is, without doubt, its ambiguity. On the one hand, it is experienced (or intended) as a refusal of self-interest and egoistic calculation, and an exaltation of generosity—a gratuitous, unrequited gift. On the other hand, it never entirely excludes awareness of the logic of exchange or even confession of the repressed impulses or, intermittently, the denunciation of another, denied, truth of generous exchange—its constraining and costly character ("a gift is a misfortune," the Kabyles say). This leads to the question of the *dual truth* of the gift and of the social conditions that make possible what can be described (somewhat inadequately) as an individual and collective self-deception,[†] the very one which Marcel Mauss refers to in one of the most profound sentences that an anthropologist has ever written: "Society always pays itself in the counterfeit coin of its dream."

The model I have put forward takes note of and accounts for the gap between the two truths and, in parallel with this, between the vision that Lévi-Strauss, thinking of Mauss, calls "phenomenological,"[1] and the structural or structuralist approach. It is the lapse of time between the gift and the counter-gift that makes it possible to mask the contradiction between the experienced (or desired) truth of the gift as a generous, gratuitous, unrequited act, and the truth that emerges from the model, which makes it a stage in a relationship of exchange that transcends singular acts of exchange. In other words, the interval that makes it possible to experience the objective exchange as a discontinuous series of free and generous acts is what makes gift exchange viable and acceptable by facilitating and favoring self-deception, a lie told to oneself, as the condition of the coexistence of recognition and misrecognition of the logic of the exchange.

But it is clear that individual self-deception is only possible because it is supported by collective self-deception. The gift is one of those social acts whose social logic cannot become "common knowledge," as economists put it (information is called common knowledge when everyone knows that everyone else knows . . . that everyone has it). More precisely, it is a common knowledge that cannot be made public, an "open secret" which cannot become public knowledge, an official truth, publicly proclaimed (like the great mottos of the Republic, for example). This collective self-deception is only possible because the *repression* from which it arises (whose phenomenological condition of possibility is indeed the lapse of time) is inscribed, as an *illusio*, at the foundation of the economy of symbolic goods, the anti-economic economy (in the restricted modern sense of "economic") that is based on denial (*Verneinung*) of interest and calculation. More precisely, it is based on a collective labor devoted to maintaining misrecognition with a view to perpetuating collective faith in the value of the universal that is simply a form of individual and collective bad faith (in the Sartrean sense of lying to oneself) and on a permanent investment in institutions that, like gift exchange, produce and reproduce trust in the fact that trust, i.e., generosity, private or civic virtue, will be rewarded. No one is really unaware of the logic of exchange (it constantly surfaces in explicit form, when for example someone wonders whether a present will be judged sufficient), but no one fails to comply with the rule of the game which is to act as if one did not know the rule. We might coin the term "common miscognition" [EN: in English in original]†† to designate this game in which everyone knows—and does not want to know—that everyone knows—and does not want to know—the true nature of the exchange.

If social agents can appear as both deceiving and deceived, if they can appear to deceive others and deceive themselves about their (generous) "intentions," this is because their deception (which can also be said, in a sense, to deceive no one) is sure to encounter the complicity both of the direct addressees of their act and of third parties who observe it. All of them have always been immersed in a social universe in which gift exchange is *instituted* in the form of an economy of symbolic goods. This quite distinctive economy is based both on specific objective structures and on internalized, embodied structures, *dispositions*, which the former presuppose and which they produce by providing the conditions for their realization.

Concretely, this means that the gift as a generous act is only possible for social agents who have acquired—in social universes in which they are expected, recognized, and rewarded—generous dispositions adjusted to the objective structures of an economy capable of providing rewards (not only in the form of counter-gifts) and recognition, in other words a *market*, if such an apparently reductive term is permitted. This economy of symbolic goods presents itself, like every economy, in the form of a system of objective probabilities of profit (positive or negative), or, to use Marcel Mauss's phrase, a set of "collective expectations" that can be counted on and that have to be reckoned with.[2] In such a social universe, the giver knows that his generous act has every chance of being recognized as such (rather than being seen as a naiveté or an absurdity) and of obtaining recognition (in the form of a counter-gift or gratitude) from the beneficiary; in particular because all the other agents operating in that world and shaped by its necessity also expect things to be so.

In other words, at the basis of generous action, the inaugural gift in a series of gifts, there is not the conscious intention (calculating or not) of an isolated individual but the *disposition* of the *habitus,* which is generosity and which tends, without explicit and express intention, toward the conservation and increase of symbolic capital. Like the sense of honor (which can be the starting point for a series of murders), this disposition is acquired by being deliberately taught (as in the case of the young nobleman discussed by Norbert Elias: when the son brings back, intact and unused, the purse of gold coins his father had given him, the father throws it out of the window), or through early and prolonged exposure to social worlds in which it is the undisputed law of behavior. For someone endowed with dispositions attuned to the logic of the economy of symbolic goods, generous conduct is not the product of a choice made by free will, a free decision made at the end of a deliberation that allows for the possibility of behaving differently; it presents itself as "the only thing to do."[3]

Only if one puts into parentheses the *institution*—and the labor, especially the pedagogic labor, of which it is the product—and forgets that both the giver and the receiver are prepared, by the whole labor of socialization, to enter into generous exchange without intention or calculation of profit, to know and recognize the gift for what it is, i.e., in its twofold truth, can one bring up the subtle and insoluble paradoxes of a casuistic ethic. If one adopts the standpoint of a philosophy of mind, by asking about the intentional meaning of the gift, and if one performs a kind of "examination of conscience" worthy of the Byzantine *salos* who feared that his most saintly actions might be inspired by the symbolic profits associated with saintliness[4]—by wondering whether the gift, conceived as the free decision of an isolated individual, is a real gift, is really a gift, or (which amounts to the same thing) whether it conforms to the essence of a gift—then this is indeed sufficient to raise insuperable antinomies (a gift is really a gift only if neither the giver nor the receiver sees it as such) that force one to conclude that a gratuitous gift is impossible. But if some writers can go so far as to say that the intention of giving destroys the gift, cancelling it out as a gift, i.e., as a disinterested act, this is because, succumbing to a particularly acute form of what J. L. Austin called the "scholastic bias" and the intellectualist error that accompanies it, they are seeing the two agents involved in the gift as calculators who assign themselves the subjective project of doing what they are objectively doing, according to Lévi-Strauss's model, an exchange obeying the logic of reciprocity. To put it another way, such an analysis puts into the minds of the agents the model that science has had to construct in order to account for their practice (here, the model of gift exchange). This amounts to producing a kind of theoretical monster, impossible in practice—the self-destructive experience of a generous, gratuitous gift that contains the conscious aim of obtaining the counter-gift (which is posited as a possible outcome, a contingent future).[5]

It is not possible to reach an adequate understanding of the gift without leaving behind both the philosophy of mind that makes a conscious intention the principle of every action and the economism that knows no other economy than that of rational calculation and interest reduced to economic interest.

Among the consequences of the process through which the economic field was constituted as such, one of the most pernicious, from the point of view of knowledge, is the tacit acceptance of a certain number of principles of di-vision, the emergence of which is correlative with the social construction of the economic field as a separate field (on the basis of the axiom "business is business"), as the opposition between passions and interests; these principles, which, because they impose themselves, unexamined, on all those who are immersed, from birth, in the "icy waters" of the economic economy, tend to govern the science of economics, which itself sprang from that separation.[6]

The gift economy, in contrast to the economy where equivalent values are exchanged, is based on a denial of the economic (in the narrow sense), a refusal of the logic of the maximization of economic profit, i.e., of the spirit of calculation and the exclusive pursuit of material (as opposed to symbolic) interest, a refusal which is inscribed in the objectivity of institutions and in dispositions. It is organized with a view to the accumulation of symbolic capital (a capital of recognition, honor, nobility, etc.) that is brought about in particular through the transmutation of economic capital achieved through the alchemy of symbolic exchanges (exchange of gifts, words, challenges and ripostes, women, etc.) and only available to agents endowed with dispositions adjusted to the logic of "disinterestedness" (dispositions that can culminate in the "supreme sacrifice," the one that consists in "giving one's life," preferring death to dishonor, or, in the context of the modern State, "dying for the fatherland").

The economy of equal exchange is the product of a symbolic revolution that took place progressively, in European societies, with, for example, all the incremental processes of unveiling and "disambiguation" of which the "vocabulary of Indo-European institutions," analyzed by Benveniste, conserves the trace, and which led from ransom—of a prisoner—to purchase; from the prize—for a notable action—to the wage; from moral recognition (gratitude) to recognizance; from belief to credit; from moral obligation to legally enforceable agreement. This "great and venerable revolution," as Mauss called it, was able to break away from the gift economy, which, he observes, "was ultimately, at the time, anti-economic," only by progressively suspending the collective denial of the economic foundations of human existence (except in certain reserved sectors: religion, art, the family), so making possible the emergence of pure interest and the generalization of calculation and the spirit of calculation (assisted by the invention of wage labor and the use of money). The possibility that then opens up of subjecting every kind of activity to the logic of calculation ("in business there's no room for sentiment") tends to legitimate this, so to speak, official cynicism that is particularly flaunted in law (for example, with contracts providing for the most pessimistic and disreputable eventualities) and in economic theory (which, at the beginning, helped to create this economy, just as jurists' treatises on the State helped to create the State). This economy, which turns out to be remarkably economical since, in particular, it makes it possible to dispense with the effects of the ambiguity of practices and the "transaction costs" that weigh so heavily on the economy of symbolic goods (one only has to think of the difference between a personalized gift, which becomes a personal message, and a check for the equivalent amount), leads to the legitimation of the use of calculation even in the most sacred areas (the prayer wheel) and the generalization of the *calculating disposition*, the perfect antithesis of the generous disposition, which comes hand in hand with the development of an economic and social order characterized, as Weber puts it, by calculability and predictability.

The particular difficulty we have in thinking about gifts is due to the fact that as the gift economy has tended to shrink to an island in the ocean of the equivalent-exchange economy, its meaning has changed (the tendency of some colonial ethnography to see it as no more than a form of credit being simply the limiting case of the propensity to ethnocentric reduction, the effects of which are still to be seen in the most reflexive-seeming analyses). Within an economic universe based on the opposition between passion and interest (or *amour fou* and the marriage of convenience), between things that are free and things that have a price tag, the gift loses its real meaning as an act situated beyond the opposition between constraint and freedom, individual choice and collective pressure, disinterestedness and self-interest and becomes a simple rational investment strategy directed toward the accumulation of social capital, with institutions such as public relations and company gifts, or a kind of ethical feat that is impossible to achieve because it is measured against the ideal of the true gift, understood as a perfectly gratuitous and gracious act performed without obligation or expectation, without reason or goal, for nothing.

If one is really to break away from the ethnocentric vision that underlies the questions of economism, one would have to examine how the logic of gift exchange leads to the establishment of durable relationships that economic theories based on an ahistorical anthropology cannot comprehend. It is remarkable that economists who rediscover the gift[7] forget, as ever, to pose the question of the economic conditions of these "anti-economic" acts (in the narrow sense of "economic") and ignore the specific logic of the economy of symbolic exchanges that makes them possible. Thus, to explain "how cooperation can arise" between individuals who are presumed to be (by nature) egoistic, "how reciprocity gives rise to cooperation" between individuals who are held—*ex hypothesi*—to be "motivated by their self-interest alone," the "economics of conventions," an empty intersection between economics and sociology, can only invoke "convention," a conceptual artifact that no doubt owes its success among economists to the fact that, like Tycho Brahé's attempt to salvage the Ptolemaic model of the universe with conceptual patchwork, it avoids a radical change of paradigm ("a regularity is a convention if everyone complies with it and expects others to do the same"; "a convention is the result of an inner deliberation, balancing rules of moral action against instrumental rules of action"). This ad hoc invention cannot really account for social cohesion, either in gift economies—where it is never based entirely upon the orchestration of *habitus* but always makes room for elementary forms of contract—or in equal-exchange economies, where, although it depends heavily on the constraints of contract, it is also based to a large extent on the orchestration of *habitus* and on an adjustment between the objective structures and the cognitive structures (or dispositions) that ensures the concordance of individual anticipations and the convergence of "collective expectations."

The ambiguity of an economy oriented toward the accumulation of symbolic capital lies in the fact that communication, unduly privileged by the structuralist approach, is one of the channels of domination. The gift is expressed in the language of obligation. It is obligatory, it creates obligations, it obliges; it sets up a legitimate domination. Among other reasons, this is because it brings in the factor of time, by defining the interval between gift and counter-gift (or murder and revenge) as a collective expectation of the counter-gift or gratitude or, more clearly, as recognized, legitimate domination, submission that is accepted or loved. This is put well by La Rochefoucauld, whose position at the transitional point between the equal-exchange economy and the gift economy gives him (like Pascal) an extreme lucidity about the subtleties of symbolic exchange, of which structuralist ethnology is unaware: "Overmuch eagerness to discharge an obligation is a kind of ingratitude." Eagerness, normally a sign of submission, is here a sign of impatience with dependence, and therefore virtually an ingratitude, because of the haste it expresses, a haste to acquit a debt, to be quits, to be free to quit (without being forced, like some *khammès* in Kabyle society, into shameful flight), to shed an obligation, a recognition of debt. It is a haste to reduce the gap of time that distinguishes the generous exchange of gifts from the harsh exchange of equivalents and that means one is bound so long as one feels bound to respond; a haste to cancel out the obligation that takes effect with the initial act of generosity and can only grow as recognition of debt, which can always be acquitted, turns into internalized gratitude, incorporated recognition, inscribed in the body itself in the form of passion, love, submission, respect for an unrepayable and, as people often say, eternal debt. Symbolic power relations are power relations that are set up and perpetuated through knowledge and recognition, which does not mean through intentional acts of consciousness. In order for symbolic domination to be set up, the dominated have to share with the dominant the schemes of perception and appreciation through which they are perceived by them and through which they perceive them; they have to see themselves as they are seen. In other words, their knowledge and recognition have to be rooted in practical dispositions of acceptance and submission, which, because they do not pass through deliberation and decision, escape the dilemma of consent or constraint.

Here we are at the heart of the alchemical transmutation that is the basis of symbolic power, a power that is created, accumulated, and perpetuated through communication, symbolic exchange. Because it brings matters to the level of knowledge and recognition (which implies that it can only occur between agents capable of communicating and understanding each other, therefore endowed with the same cognitive schemes and inclined to communicate and consequently to recognize each other as legitimate interlocutors, equal in honor, to be "on speaking terms"), communication converts brute power relations, which are always uncertain and liable to be suspended, into durable relations of symbolic power through which a person is bound and feels bound. It transfigures economic capital into symbolic capital, economic domination (of the rich over the poor, master over servant, man over woman, adults over children, etc.) into personal dependence (paternalism, etc.), even devotion, filial piety or love. Generosity is possessive, and perhaps all the more so when, as in affective exchanges (between parents and children, or even between lovers), it is and appears most sincerely generous.[8]

Here too, time plays a decisive role. The inaugural act that institutes communication (by addressing words, offering a gift, issuing an invitation or a challenge, etc.) always entails a kind of intrusion or even a calling into question (hence the interrogative precautions that tend to accompany it, as Bally observed—"If I may be so bold as to . . ."). In addition, it always inevitably contains the potentiality of a bond, an obligation. It is true that, contrary to what the structuralists' mechanical model would suggest, it implies uncertainty and therefore a temporal opening: one can always choose not to reply to the interpellation, invitation, or challenge or not to reply immediately, to defer and to leave the other party in expectation. But non-response is still a response, and it is not so easy to shrug off the initial calling into question, which acts as a kind of *fatum*, a destiny. The meaning of a positive response—repartee, counter-gift, riposte—is no doubt unequivocal as an affirmation and recognition of equality in honor (*isotimia*) that can be taken as the starting point for a long series of exchanges; by contrast, absence of response is essentially ambiguous and can always be interpreted, by the initiator or by others, either as a refusal to respond and a kind of snub or as an evasion attributable to impotence or cowardice, entailing dishonor.

But the uncertainty, even anxiety, linked to anticipation of the destiny effect would not be so strong (especially for the dominated party, the woman, for example, in the relationship of seduction) if the relationship of communication that is set up did not always contain the potentiality of a relation of domination. The exotic character of the objects to which analyses of exchange have been applied, such as potlatch, has caused it to be forgotten that the seemingly most gratuitous and least costly relations of exchange, such as expressions of concern, kindness, consideration or advice, not to mention acts of generosity that cannot be repaid, such as charity, when they are set up in conditions of lasting asymmetry (in particular because they link people separated by an economic or social gulf too great to be bridged) and when they exclude the possibility of an equivalent in return, the very hope of an active reciprocity, which is the condition of possibility of genuine autonomy, is likely to create lasting relations of dependence, variants (euphemized by subjectivation) of enslavement for debt in archaic societies. For they tend to become inscribed in the body itself in the form of belief, trust, affection, and passion, and any attempt to transform them through consciousness and will comes up against the stubborn resistance of affects and the tenacious injunctions of guilt.

Although there is apparently every difference in the world between them, the structuralist ethnologist who makes exchange the creative principle of the social bond and the neomarginalist economist who desperately seeks the specifically economic principles of cooperation between agents reduced to the state of isolated atoms are united in ignoring the economic and social conditions in which historical agents are produced and reproduced, endowed (through their upbringing) with durable dispositions that make them able and inclined to enter into exchanges, equal or unequal, that give rise to durable relations of dependence. Whether it is the *philia* that, in the ideal vision at least, governs domestic relations, or the trust accorded to a person or an institution (a well-reputed trademark, for example), these relations of "trust" or "credit" are not necessarily grounded in and set up by rational economic calculation (as is sometimes supposed by those who seek to explain the trust placed in long-established companies by the length of the critical tests they have had to overcome), and they can always be ascribed to the durable domination that symbolic violence secures.

One would need to analyze here all the forms of necessarily ostentatious *redistribution* through which individuals (almost always the richest ones, naturally, as with the Greek munificence ["evergetism"] analyzed by Paul Veyne, or royal or princely largesse) or institutions, companies (with their great foundations) or the State itself tend to set up asymmetrical relations of dependence of recognition/gratitude[9] based on the credit granted to beneficence. One would also need to analyze the long process through which symbolic power, the accumulation of which initially benefited one individual, as in potlatch, slowly ceases to be the basis of personal power (through the personal approval of a clientele, distribution of gifts, livings, honors, grace, and favors, as in the period of absolute monarchy) and becomes the basis of bureaucratic, impersonal state authority, through the bureaucratic redistribution that, although in principle it obeys the rule, "the State makes no presents" (to private individuals), never completely excludes—with corruption—forms of personal appropriation and patronage.

Thus, through redistribution, taxation enters into a cycle of symbolic production in which economic capital is transformed into symbolic capital. As in potlatch, redistribution is necessary in order to secure the recognition of the distribution. While, as the official reading insists, it obviously tends to correct the inequalities of the distribution, it also and more importantly tends to produce recognition of the legitimacy of the State.

What is underlined through gift exchange, the counterfeit coin of generosity in which society pays itself, the collective hypocrisy in and through which it pays tribute to its dream of virtue and disinterestedness, is the fact that virtue is a political matter, that it is not and cannot be abandoned, with no other resource than a vague "deontology," to the singular, isolated efforts of individual minds and wills or the examinations of conscience of a confessor's casuistics. At a time when, to make it easier to "blame the victims," there is a greater tendency than ever to pose political problems in moral terms, the cult of individual success, preferably economic, which has accompanied the expansion of neoliberalism, and whose most ardent advocates are found among some devotees of socialism, masks the need for collective investment in institutions that produce the economic and social conditions for virtue, or, to put it another way, that cause the civic virtues of disinterestedness and devotion—a gift to the group—to be encouraged and rewarded by the group. The purely speculative and typically scholastic question of whether generosity and disinterestedness are possible should give way to the political question of the means that have to be implemented in order to create universes in which, as in gift economies, people have an interest in disinterestedness and generosity, or, rather, are durably disposed to respect these universally respected forms of respect for the universal.

January 1996
Translated by Richard Nice for this volume.

Notes

†. EN: Throughout his original French text, Bourdieu uses the English terms "self-deception," "common knowledge," and "public knowledge."

1. This "phenomenology" is very imperfect since it fails to grasp both the ambiguity and the temporal dimension of the gift. On what Lévi-Strauss means by "phenomenology" or "phenomenological," see his "Introduction à l'oeuvre de Marcel Mauss" in M. Mauss, *Sociologie et anthropologie* (Paris: Presses Universitaires de France, 1950), p. xxxv (see above, p. 53): "a purely phenomenological datum on which analysis has no hold"; p. xxxviii (see above, p. 55): "The whole theory thus demands the existence of a structure of which *experience* offers only the fragments, the scattered moments, or rather the elements"; p. xxxix (see above, pp. 55–56): where Lévi-Strauss criticizes Mauss for taking over a kind of spontaneous theory of the gift, the native theory of *hau*, "the conscious form in which the people of a given society (. . .) have apprehended an unconscious necessity, the reason of which lies elsewhere."

††. EN: Bourdieu's decision to use the English "common miscognition" plays both on the discussion of "common knowledge" above and the translator's rendering of *méconnaissance* as "misrecognition."

2. Cf. M. Mauss, *Oeuvres*, Vol. 2 (Paris: Éditions de Minuit, 1974), p. 117: "We are together in society in order to expect, together, this or that result."

3. To all those who look to the "prisoner's dilemma" for the basis of all strategies of cooperation, I would suggest that they imagine it involving not interchangeable strangers but members of the same family in a house on fire. By this I mean that in the reality of existence, the economic and social conditions that have to be fulfilled for a logical exercise of this type to be possible never are fulfilled.

4. Cf. G. Dagron, "L'Homme sans honneur ou le saint scandaleux," *Annales ESC* (juillet–août 1990): 929–39.

5. Through the question of the true gift, the gift that is truly a gift (like, elsewhere, the question of the true observance of the rule, which requires one to go beyond the rule), Jacques Derrida formulates in new terms the old Kantian question of duty and the possibility of detecting some "secret impulse of amour-propre" behind the greatest sacrifice, the one that is supposed to be performed out of pure duty when it is only performed in a way that "conforms to duty" (on the—true—gift as "duty beyond duty," "law," and "necessity without obligation," see J. Derrida, *Donner le temps. 1. La fausse monnaie* [Paris: Galilée, 1991], p. 197). As soon as every generous action that springs from a generous disposition is rejected as merely "conforming to generosity," inevitably one denies the possibility of disinterested action, just as Kant, in the name of a similar philosophy of mind or intention, cannot conceive of a single action conforming to duty that cannot be suspected of obeying "pathological" determinations (cf. J. Derrida, *Passions* [Paris: Galilée, 1993], pp. 87–9).

6. On the separation that occurred, in the 17th and 18th centuries, between passions and interests or exclusively economic motives, see A. Hirschman, *The Passions and the Interests* (Princeton: Princeton University Press, 1977). It is probably because they accept (not always realizing it) this *historically founded* opposition, explicitly stated in Pareto's founding distinction between logical actions and nonlogical actions, "residues" or "derivations," that economists tend to specialize in analysis of behavior motivated by interest alone: "Many economists," wrote P. A. Samuelson, "would separate economics from sociology upon the basis of rational or irrational behavior" (*Foundations of Economic Analysis*, Cambridge, MA: Harvard University Press, 1947, p. 90).

7. Cf. P. Batifoulier, L. Cordonnier, Y. Zenou, "L'emprunt de la théorie économique à la tradition sociologique, le cas du don contre-don," *Revue économique* 5 (septembre 1992): 917–46.

8. The crises of the gift economy, which are always particularly tragic, coincide with the breaking of enchantment that reduces the logic of symbolic exchange to the order of economic exchange ("After all we've done for you . . .").

9. TN: The French word *reconnaissance* conveniently means both.

Part Four

◘

ANGLO-AMERICAN
INTERVENTIONS

Bataille, Gift Giving, and the Cold War

Allan Stoekl

In recent years the question of "general economy" has come to be associated with the primarily philosophical question of a general writing.[1] This was not at all the case in the immediate postwar period: the review *Critique,* founded in 1946 and in its early years edited by Georges Bataille, for example, was concerned to a great extent with questions of expenditure and conservation as these questions cut across the logic of capitalist and state socialist economies. Contributors such as Bataille, François Perroux, Georges Ambrosino, and Jean Piel all posed questions having to do with excess and loss in modern economies, societies, and even nature. Only later, in the 1960s, was the question of "general economy" reoriented away from society and the material effects of excess, most notably by Derrida. This aspect of the intellectual climate of the immediate postwar period, then, remains poorly understood, and yet Bataille's appropriation of the Maussian problematic of the gift, starting already in 1932 with "The Notion of Expenditure," has been widely noted.[2]

A book length study would clearly be needed to do justice to the problems raised by the early contributors to *Critique.* My goal here is more modest: to consider the implications, for Bataille, of the end of history for the dominant modern economies of the United States and the Soviet Union. This will entail a consideration of the final chapters of *The Accursed Share* ([1949] 1988), a collection of essays that Bataille had originally published in *Critique.* Above all, I want to stress the importance of the notion of a general economy, of gift giving "without return," as a social and cultural effect. Is it possible, in the post–cold war context, to think of gift giving in these terms, as Bataille did in the early cold war context? Or must we think of it exclusively as a general writing, a primarily literary and philosophical problematic that excuses us from having to think about modern economies and their implications for the social—and the sacred?

By the end of World War II, many thinkers had turned to the question of the "end of history." In Communist circles, it was all straightforward: one foresaw a long and arduous but finally successful struggle against capitalism and the triumph of some system that guaranteed the preeminence of the proletariat as the conscience of history, the definitive establishment of a classless society, and so on. But the non-Communist left also became obsessed with the question. In the United States it took the form of the "end of ideology"; the end of history was nothing less than the demise of the very model that European (and a few U.S.) Communists held to be the real end: ideas as a mode of action, the justification of means by ends, the very possibility of a unitary and homogeneous movement, and end, of history.[3] Somewhere between or outside these two extremes are figures of the left in France like Alexandre Kojève and Georges Bataille.

Kojève, the noted commentator of Hegel (his lectures on Hegel at the École pratique des Hautes Études did much to revive interest in Hegel in the 1930s), finally published his lectures from the thirties in 1947: this work, the *Introduction à la lecture de Hegel*, contained some very interesting footnotes added at the time of publication, and even after (the last, and perhaps most important one, dates from the second edition published in 1959).

The problem was one that must have bedeviled Kojève every time he spoke before an audience: What form would the end of history take? What could we expect after all the wars have been fought, and nothing more of substance, of real historical significance, can or will happen? The body of Kojève's text, the commentary itself, offers little: we know that a universal and homogeneous State will codify and guarantee the transparency of human relations—that is, equality, in the form of the recognition on the part of each citizen of the desire of every other citizen—the desire, in fact, to be recognized as a free, desiring citizen.[4] If this definition sounds like a tautology, well, that's precisely the problem. It doesn't offer us a lot in the way of concrete detail. Each person will find his or her freedom in and through the institutions and activities of the State; all acts will derive their meaning through this activity; no acts can be exterior to the functioning of the State. (One finds a savage parody of this bureaucratic model in the 1948 novel *Le Très Haut*, by Maurice Blanchot.) But what will people *do* in the Kojèvian future? The Communists could at least supply a kind of naive mythology, an iconographic future of workers and farmers cooperating and smiling.

In one footnote, Kojève notes that "Man" himself will die. This is not a heroic, Nietzschean/Foucauldian death that posits a fracturing and multiplicity of drives and power. Rather it is simply the recognition that with nothing more to do in history, Man will cease to be, since He was constituted through his labor, which is inseparable from Time. Man will die and Time will end; the Wise Man, the *Sage* (i.e., Hegel and/or Kojève himself), whose writing comprehends this movement and end, will die as a "person"; since the writing of his Book, his Wisdom, is completed, it too will end. It will not disappear though, but it will exist only in a book; it will no longer be temporally elaborated. Kojève writes: "The end of History is the *death* of Man properly speaking. After this death there remains: 1) Living bodies having a human form, but lacking Spirit, in other words lacking Time or creative power; 2) a Spirit that exists empirically, but in the form of a not living, inorganic reality: as a Book which, not even being an animal life, no longer has anything to do with Time. The relation between the Wise Man and his Book is thus rigorously analogous to that of Man and his *death*" (ILH, 388, note).[5] The *Sage*, Hegel or Kojève, will be nothing more than wood pulp, in other words; that collaborator of the Wise Man, on the other hand, the agent of change, Napoleon or Stalin, will cease to exist, since his violent labors are at an end. His unreflected actions, only an adjunct to the Concept of the Wise Man before, will now be totally superfluous.

This doesn't seem to get us far. Since labor and Time are at an end, even the Book, History's knowledge and consciousness of itself, is over and done with. It is no longer a process, so it must be simply paper and ink. It cannot be a text that is read and interpreted, because that process would itself always imply a change in emphasis, a difference as to knowledge, a modification. But the Spirit cannot be modifiable, for it is definitive; therefore the Book will not be read in any sense that we could give that word. The Book will simply be there, an object. We are back, but with a difference, to the raw matter, the element of nature, that the slave faced, and transformed, at the beginning of his historical labor.

So much for the Book—what then of Man? According to a footnote added in 1947, Man too is dead, and his future life will therefore be that of animals. This is only logical: if Man is nothing other than historical labor and consciousness, at the end of labor and consciousness there will be no more Man. There will be a return, but on a higher level, to the animality, the mere physical experience, against which Man revolted when the first "Master" risked his life before a rival. Kojève writes: "'The definitive annihilation of Man properly so-called' also means the definitive disappearance of human Discourse (*Logos*) in the strict sense. Animals of the species *Homo sapiens* would react by conditioned reflexes to vocal signals of sign 'language,' and thus their so-called 'discourses' would be like what is supposed to be the 'language of bees'" (IRH, 160). Later, in 1959, Kojève adds another note, this time revising his previous assertion: now he claims that, at the end of History, Man will not become an animal; instead, labor, and presumably some version of Time will continue. But since there will be nothing more to do—no paradigms to create, revolutions to make, etc.— man's labor will be purely formal. Life at the end of History, in other words, will come to resemble the purely formal Japanese ceremonies that consume much energy (tea ceremonies) and even life (Kamikaze raids), that demonstrate great expertise, but in the end, accomplish nothing. Posthistorical people will be dandies.

But, we should note, the emphasis placed on dandyism opens the way, in

Kojève, for gift giving. The world of mutual recognition in transparency is, one could say, one of adequacy: each "person" is fully recognized by the other. Kojève's version of the Hegelian Book could evidently never be given away, made a gift: it was, instead, a kind of absolutely terminal Spirit, necessary yet unread: solid matter whose existence alone somehow counted. The Kojèvian Book could not be read because it was finished: it was therefore closed to the inevitable vagaries of reading or interpretation, loss, and dissemination.[6] Dandyism, however, introduces the arbitrary, the gratuitous, the pointless, the excessive. Pure unread matter is not a gift—who could even accept it, or return it "with interest"?—but the purely formal, dandified object is. The latter implies not a relation of equality and transparency, but one of confrontation, defiance, one-upsmanship, extravagance.

Kojève saw this "Japanese" dandyism as resolutely minor. It was only what remained after the end, nothing more than the hastily jotted answer to the question "what will remain after . . . ?" It is the solution, the future, yet paradoxically it is of no interest in itself.

Bataille, on the other hand, focuses on the importance of the gift at the end of history. But the figure of the dandy, reassuring perhaps to Kojève because in principle it represents political and social stasis, because it "does nothing," is replaced in Bataille by the madman, the lover—and by U.S. State power and the Marshall Plan.

It's in this context, I think, that Georges Bataille's postwar "take" on Stalinism and the end of history must be grasped. The last chapters of *The Accursed Share* make clear that Bataille is working the same turf as Kojève: how can we think about history and its end, given the realities of the blocs—the Soviets on the one hand, the Americans on the other? Bataille does not dismiss Stalin as a throwback, or an irrelevancy, a soon to be surpassed principle of historical completion (as does Kojève). For him, in a strange way, the Soviet Communists are necessary to an end of history in which life will be characterized by an immense, State-sponsored potlatch, or gift-giving ceremony.

For Bataille, Soviet Communism is the rigorous death not of Man, but of the bourgeois individual: the worker works not for personal gain, but for the strengthening and development of the State. The individual's needs are thus thoroughly subordinated to those of the State: just as troublesome individuals, those who think for themselves, are routinely liquidated, so too the "needs" of the individual, and his or her possibilities of accumulation, are severely curtailed. The Soviet industrial plan, for example, stresses not the production of consumer goods, but the reinvestment of wealth into the means of production. Useless, in other words, individual expenditure is kept to an absolute minimum: wealth instead always goes to strengthening the means of the production of more wealth. It is as close as the world has ever come to a "closed economy," not in principle but in fact.

Bataille explicitly ties this absolute subordination of means to ends, of individual to State, to a Hegelian perspective. And it answers Kojève's question: Will man become an animal at the end of history, or a dandy? For Bataille neither; he will be wholly subordinated to the workings, and larger self-consciousness, of the State itself. Bataille writes:

> [the Soviet Union] gives the state the preponderant and definitive place that Hegel gave it. Man as defined by the Hegelian idea is not an individual, but the state. The individual has died in it, has been absorbed into the higher reality and into the service of the state; in a wider sense, the "man of the state" is the sea into which flows the river of history. Insofar as he participates in the state, man leaves both animality and individuality behind him: He is no longer separate from universal reality. Every isolable part of the world refers to the totality, but the supreme authority of the world state can only refer to itself. (151-52)[7]

Such a productivist State will of course be an expansionist one. It will constantly annex other countries, other workers, until every nation on earth is a "Soviet Republic" and every citizen a worker in that State. This version of the end of history posits not the end of labor and Time, but its apotheosis. Man is neither an animal nor an individualist dandy; he is a pure worker. His being is nothing but work.

Bataille opposes to this model the American one. Here the problem is not insufficient productive capacity, but excess. Bataille presents the Marshall Plan as the solution not only to an immediate dilemma—the postwar collapse of Europe due to an insufficiency of capital reserves and productive capacity—but to a larger, posthistorical one. If the Soviet model is one of conservation and recuperation, the American is one of expenditure without return, *dépense*. The Americans, after all, seek no immediate gain, no conventional profit. Through the Marshall Plan they are spending like the Tlingit chiefs of the American Northwest, without, in principle at least, any thought for the future, any plans for later construction or return.

Now the interesting thing in all this, besides the strange conjunction of a prewar proto-surrealism with a postwar championing of U.S. power, is Bataille's retention of an emphasis on the State and State power. Only a fairly centralized State can marshal the resources and control the self-interest of individual capitalists, so that large amounts of wealth can be given away. Once again, in other words, what might be called "the individual" is subordinated to a larger strategy of the State. Man is still a creature of the

State, in other words, as in Kojève's reading of Hegel; only now, instead of an animal or a dandy, Man is a worker whose "crystalized labor," whose wealth, is not to be reinvested and conserved by the State, but is to be given away. The ultimate posthistorical consciousness, once again, will be that of a State, this time a relatively tolerant and benign U.S. one, but one that nevertheless has borrowed certain centralizing features from the Soviet model.

Thus Bataille can write of "self-consciousness," not of the worker, but of the State itself. But pure self-consciousness, in his view, is not of a thing—for that thing will always be *other* than consciousness—but of consciousness itself. The State, by spending without return, focuses not on the future, on something other than the here and now, on some goal toward which one works, and for which one conserves, but exclusively on the present. The State's activity, here, is inseparable from the consciousness of the atheistic mystic, who focuses not on any god or myth, but on nothingness itself. Bataille writes: "It is a question of arriving at the moment when consciousness will cease to be a consciousness of *something*; in other words, of becoming conscious of the decisive meaning of an instant in which increase (the acquisition of *something*) will resolve into expenditure; and this will be precisely *self-consciousness*, that is, a consciousness that henceforth has *nothing as its object*" (190). Bataille adds in a note to this last sentence: "Nothing but pure interiority, which is not a thing" (footnote 21, 197).

Individual self-consciousness, in other words, will be subordinated to a giant mystical State self-consciousness at the end of History. Even stranger is the notion that this State activity will itself be dependent on the action of the Soviets. For without Soviet pressure, there would have been no Marshall Plan, no *dépense* on a massive scale and hence, in principle at least, no State atheistic mysticism. Bataille writes:

> In a paradoxical way, the situation is governed by the fact that without the salutary fear of the Soviets (or some analogous threat), there would be no Marshall Plan. The truth is that the diplomacy of the Kremlin holds the key to the American coffers. Paradoxically, the tension it maintains in the world is what determines the latter's movements. Such assertions could easily slip into absurdity, but one can say that without the USSR, without the politics of tension it adheres to, the capitalist world could not be certain of avoiding paralysis. This truth dominates current developments. (183–84)

It seems as if we have returned to a kind of master/slave dialectic, with the Soviets playing the slave—hell bent on productive labor, attempting to wrest consciousness and thus mastery from a master who can only spend and destroy—and with the Americans playing the master, willing to risk their wealth in the face of death (or nuclear destruction) in order to be recognized as having the superior economic system. But the Americans are, perhaps more than the "master," in this scenario, the sovereign, in the Bataillean sense of the word; their spending is not logically prior to the useful labor, and history, of the slave, but logically posterior to it. It is they who now possess the definitive consciousness, and not the slave. They have collectively attained the self-consciousness of the mystic, and in addition, at least through Bataille's own text, they recognize the necessity of the Soviet challenge for their spending and their mysticism. In this way too the moment of recognition, so often seemingly missing in Bataille, but so central to Kojève's Hegel, makes a surprising return; it is not so much the master who is "recognized" by the slave now, his humanity affirmed, but rather the Bataillean sovereign who recognizes the Soviet "slave," who affirms the latter's profound necessity and human labor. The sovereign in this sense does not at all "go beyond" the slave, as the slave had gone beyond, or mastered, the master. The sovereign in his recognition transgresses—but that transgression necessarily implies an interdiction, the moment of the necessity of an affirmation of the slave's conservation and deferring.

To what extent, then, would the Soviet challenge have to be invented, if it did not exist? Bataille's *The Accursed Share* seems like a classic cold war document, attempting, as it does, to elaborate a rationale for a political and economic policy of capitalist nations in the face of Communism. But at the same time Bataille does not at all want to valorize the "bourgeois individual," as do so many apologists for the existing order. True to his intellectual roots in the avant-garde of the twenties and thirties, he sees this "human person" as a symptom of cultural decadence, doomed and irrelevant. Instead he appropriates the subjugation of the individual to the State from the Hegelian-Kojèvian tradition and in this way evinces a certain sympathy for the Soviet model. How else could the vast changes be brought about in the Russian economy, he asks, if not through the necessary but cruel subordination of individual needs and desires to those of the nation? In this way Bataille's book is not at all a cold war document, in the sense that it does not pose the problem of the containment and eventual, albeit problematic, defeat of the Soviet Union. Rather it recognizes the kinship of the U.S. system with that of the Soviets—the individual has been subordinated in both—and it also affirms the necessity of the pressure the Soviets bring to bear.

In this way *The Accursed Share*, written at the dawn of the cold war, is already a post-cold war document, and it anticipates in many ways the kind of postmodern positions that have only come to seem significant in the gap left by the demise of the great struggle of modern ideologies that characterized the cold war. By the end of Bataille's last chapter, on the Marshall Plan, we see that the Soviet threat is less historical or political than it is logical; there will always have to be some moment of resistance, the refusal to spend, in order for sufficient accumulation to take place so that spending can occur. True, Bataille sees a terrible risk of war and nuclear annihilation, but that possibility is only a measure of the extent to which people do not and cannot conceive of the necessity of each system to the other, the Soviets offering State centralization and planning, plus, of course, conservation and deferring of consumer expenditure, as an alternative to the American model, and the Americans offering a glorious and blind "spending without return" as an alternative to the Soviet model.

At the end of the cold war, this model can still be seen as being perfectly valid; but it is irrelevant where the pressure to spend comes from—it matters little whether it comes from the "inside" or the "outside." The Americans have certainly always had an inner superego commanding them to save and reinvest—although this Protestant heritage, of late, seems to be becoming weaker and weaker, as the U.S. moves to an economy that places emphasis almost exclusively on consumer expenditure and military waste (one element Bataille hoped would be eradicated from any model of nonproductive expenditure). And the Japanese, the successors, no doubt, to Bataille's fantasmatic Soviets as the prime reinvestors and conservers of the planet, are urged by the Americans to spend a little more, throw away more money on frivolous consumer goods, and indulge in modern-day Marshall Plan giveaways throughout the world. (The Japanese argue, of course, that the Americans should spend less and reinvest more.) So Bataille's breakdown of nations according to whether or not they indulge (unconsciously, for the most part) in a contemporary version of potlatch may still have a certain validity in a post–cold war world; both sides, polemically at least, would like to see the other move toward an ideal state in which the "other" is internalized, and the thrifty, deferring portion is always perfectly doubled by the spendthrift, orgiastic one. Polemically, at least, the Japanese and Americans today, if we believe each one's propaganda about the other, want to see (again, in the ideal Other) the definitive balance between conservation and expenditure. But it's always the *other one* who should bring it off.

Each nation flatters the other, seeing it—and not so much itself—as the ideal bearer of the posthistorical message. Now the pressure of resistance to spending, or conserving, is supposed to come from the inside rather than the outside. The system itself poses the resistance. It's interesting to note, though, that Bataille's message has never gotten across in the sense that modern economies are still seen as based on necessity and utility; the U.S.

economy, with its Marshall Plans and consumer spending, always portrays that expenditure as only useful to the maintenance of a healthy economy.[8] Bataille's polemical gesture goes in exactly the opposite direction; for him expenditure made sense not as an adjunct to conservation but as a gesture inevitably tied to, and leading to, an intellectual and moral potlatch inseparable from a kind of vast, collective, atheistic mystical experience, as far removed as possible from the pseudo-pragmatism inherent in U.S. economic discourse. In Bataille's version, of course, we see a vestige of French republican social science, and in particular Durkheim, who associated collective experience with states of religious exaltation.

The posthistorical cold war "take" put forward by Bataille becomes instead a posthistorical and postmodern one when we realize that the resistant moment of conservation is essentially an internal one. The resistance is posed by the system itself and is overcome repetitiously through the inner transgression of signs. Bataille's mystic, whether "individual" or "collective" it finally hardly matters, gains "self-consciousness" at the end of history through the recognition that all other-directed "investment" only distracts from a full reflective knowledge. But that inherently conserving knowledge is itself only the erasure of knowledge, since it knows only the void of itself when it is not focused on other things—when, precisely, it is focused on nothing, the *rien* of the inner state. There will be, then, a constant sliding, as *the* model of knowledge, labor, coherency, and conservation, determined and imposed from within, is inevitably and repetitiously "gone beyond," not in the direction of a new synthesis or externalized state of being, but in the direction of a nothing. This, finally, may not be that different from Kojève's take on the "end." For Kojève's dandy, the state of conservation was also a limit determined and imposed, but also transgressed from within; Kojève's Japanese (if not the real Japanese), with their exquisite ceremonies, still labored and produced, but did so only in order to destroy; their productions had no meaning beyond or outside of themselves. The tea ceremony, No theatre, etc., refer to nothing beyond their formal arrangements of signs; they are, in this sense, an arbitrary collection of scenarios and fictions. The labor and knowledge they entail is a cancellation of the necessity and determinate significance of utility. Once again, at the end of history, signs are volatilized and fictionalized, as they point to their own nothingness. Kojève and Bataille meet as the figures of the dandy and the mystic come together at the end of the cold war. What at first may seem to be a radical opposition—Kojève's minor key expenditure (dandyism) and Bataille's major (U.S. State power, the Marshall Plan) are now united—both in the end are functions of the same profound posthistorical opposition between conservation and expenditure, sense and show.

Perhaps the next stage of the post–cold war era will be the recognition, on the part of the Americans, that by internalizing the moment of absolute recuperation—what used to be externalized in the "Soviet threat"—they will also have subordinated it; the U.S. will not be a commanding presence, but a mere function inevitably secondary to a larger, "inner" function, expenditure as the self-consciousness of "pure interiority," which, as Bataille reminds us, is "not a thing." At this point hard headed U.S. economic thought will become indistinguishable from the writings of the most exalted mystics.[9] Perhaps.

The end of the cold war perhaps means the end of the massive U.S. "gift giving" that Bataille valued so strongly. Instead of a confrontation of "blocs," however, we now see the splintering of countries, resurgent nationalism, and civil war. The very notion of centralized and monocultural State authority seems to have become, in the years since 1989, much less tenable. What then of a Bataillean state-sponsored gift giving and mysticism—have they completely lost whatever sense they might once have had? Perhaps. But in the absence of cold war camps, and in the absence (so far at least) of huge nationalist-fascist states, we are left with a multiplicity of micro-nationalisms battling it out in the ruins. This vision of posthistory may recall the decay depicted in Blanchot's *Le Très-Haut* more than it does Bataille's industrialized, collective *dépense*. But with the end of the cold war, Bataille's prewar critique of fascist expenditure becomes more important than ever. The fascist too mistakes the nothing of gift giving, the heterogeneity of expenditure, for the superiority of culture, and the heroism of personalized will.[10]

Cruelty, it seems, has returned to the post–cold war era, in a new but familiar guise. Bataille himself (writing of the rigors of Soviet industrial development) remarked that "all renunciation of the present in favor of the future is cruel."[11] This might apply to the radical *elimination* of gift giving practiced by the Soviets, but also, in another context, to the internalized moment of necessary conservation inherent in any fruitful activity. But if the post–cold war and the posthistorical are congruent, does that then mean that cruelty, like negativity as depicted in Bataille's letter to Kojève of 1937,[12] will be "out of a job," and will nevertheless continue to circulate? Are cruelty and the negativity of labor, the deferring of pleasure in the moment of conservation, intimately tied? If so, will the "nothing" of Bataille's economist/mystic always entail a series of "inner" civil wars? Within the collective? Within the individual? (And is the individual even an option?) Nationalisms may come and go, but the cruelty of the inevitable deferring of generalized gift giving may be with us for good.

Notes

1. The founding document of this tendency is Jacques Derrida's "From Restricted to General Economy: A Hegelianism without Reserve," in *Writing and Difference*, trans. Alan Bass (Chicago: University of Chicago Press, 1978), pp. 251–77.

2. "The Notion of Expenditure" has been translated in Georges Bataille, *Visions of Excess: Selected Writings, 1927-1939*, ed. Allan Stoekl, trans. Allan Stoekl with Carl R. Lovitt and Donald M. Leslie Jr. (Minneapolis: University of Minnesota Press, 1985), pp. 116–29.

3. See Daniel Bell, *The End of Ideology: On the Exhaustion of Political Ideas in the Fifties* (Glencoe, IL: Free Press, 1960).

4. On the question of desire in Kojève, see Judith Butler, *Subjects of Desire: Hegelian Reflections in Postwar France* (New York: Columbia University Press, 1987), pp. 63–78.

5. Unfortunately, when citing Kojève's work on Hegel one is constrained to quote from two different editions. The English translation, *Introduction to the Reading of Hegel*, ed. Allan Bloom and trans. J. H. Nichols Jr. (New York: Basic Books, 1969), and hereafter cited as IRH, contains only part of the larger French edition. So, for the parts not deemed worthy of inclusion by Bloom, one must cite the French: *Introduction à la lecture de Hegel* (Paris: Gallimard, collection "Tel," 1980), hereafter ILH. (Note also that the pagination of the French "Tel" edition is different from that of the original Gallimard edition of 1947.) All translations from the French are my own.

6. Perhaps the Kojèvian/Hegelian Book would have the status of the official "meter," which is never actually used to measure anything but is kept in some museum or institute in Paris as a guarantee of all other "meters."

7. Page references are to Georges Bataille's *The Accursed Share: An Essay on General Economy, Vol 1: Consumption*, trans. Robert Hurley (New York: Zone Books, 1988).

8. Americans, it seems, are afraid, above all, of people who don't *work*. The only entitlement program that can be safely challenged in today's political climate is "welfare," even though the latter involves sums of money that are insignificant when compared to the entitlements that benefit primarily the middle class or the rich—i.e., people who are seen to "work," or to have "worked" in the past.

9. Bataille, at the end of *The Accursed Share*, notes his intellectual kinship with the projects, throughout history, of mystics (footnote 22, p. 197).

10. For Bataille's critique of the fascist appropriation of what he calls "heterogeneity," see the 1933–34 essay "The Psychological Structure of Fascism," in *Visions of Excess*, pp. 137–60.

11. See Bataille, *Oeuvres Complètes*, vol. 8 (Paris: Gallimard, 1976), p. 318.

12. Bataille's letter to Kojève of 1937 is available in English as "Letter to Blank, Instructor of a Course on Hegel," in *Guilty*, trans. Bruce Boone (Venice, CA: Lapis Press, 1988), pp. 123–25.

What Goes Around Comes Around: Derrida and Levinas on the Economy of the Gift and the Gift of Genealogy

Robert Bernasconi

I

In "Force of Law," Derrida distinguishes between two styles of deconstruction: "One takes on the demonstrative and apparently ahistorical allure of logico-formal paradoxes. The other, more historical or more anamnesic, seems to proceed through readings of texts, meticulous interpretations and genealogies."[1] Derrida would surely be the first to insist that these styles, especially insofar as they can be used to characterize his own texts, represent only the dominant tendency in each case. Deconstruction interweaves the two styles. There was a time, perhaps, when the meticulous readings of texts predominated, but recently the exploration of aporias has been given greater prominence. Derrida's account of the logic of the gift is one of the best examples of interest in logico-formal paradoxes. It provides a good setting in which to examine the very real tension between the "apparently ahistorical" and the "more historical, more anamnesic" as it works itself out in the difference between the two styles.[2]

The aporia of the gift as Derrida presents it takes the following form: if what defines the gift is its difference from the object of exchange, then any form of reciprocity or return to the giver destroys the gift precisely by turning it into an object of exchange. There is, therefore, a problem of how one accepts a gift, a question of whether one can even receive a gift without destroying it *qua* gift. It is not only that an exchange of gifts is, on these terms, strictly speaking not an act of giving. Even gratitude returns the gift to the giver and compromises its gratuitous character. Even to refuse it, is to acknowledge it and so, in a sense, give a return. The problem is still more acute in the case of the giver: how can the giver not be aware of giving? Insofar as the giver is conscious of doing something good in giving, is not its gratuitous character compromised? This leads Derrida to ask if the conditions of possibility of the gift are not the conditions of its impossibility.

Although Derrida explores this aporia in a number of different places, his most sustained discussion of it is to be found in *Given Time. 1. Counterfeit Money*. In this text both styles of deconstruction are operative across the close reading of Baudelaire's "La fausse monnaie" and the accompanying exploration of the logic of the gift with special reference to Marcel Mauss's *The Gift*.[3] However, what makes *Given Time* especially interesting in this regard is the fact that it also includes some historical remarks that Derrida considers necessary background for his reading. These do not constitute a genealogy and the most that could be said is that the pages on the "determined place" of the beggar "in a social, politico-economic, and symbolic typology," especially with the extracts from certain pages of Foucault, provide the materials that would be necessary for a genealogy.[4] In this paper, I want to pose the question of how genealogy combines with the close reading of texts and the exploration of logico-formal paradoxes. Does it merely help their elaboration? Or can it also threaten in its historicality the status of a paradox that is presented as ahistorical? I will pursue these questions through an examination of almsgiving, particularly as it developed within early modern Europe, and I will juxtapose Derrida's account of the gift with that found in Levinas. Reference to Levinas seems particularly appropriate in this context, not only because the topic of almsgiving is very much within the orbit of Levinasian ethics, but also because Derrida seems to suggest that something like genealogy is lacking from Levinas's ethics, even and especially in the very naming of it as ethics.[5]

Levinas is mentioned by name in *Given Time* only once and then only as part of a quotation from Marion (DT 73n; GT 52n), but he is undoubtedly a central figure for an appreciation of Derrida's development of the logic of the gift. Among the most important of the texts in which Derrida explores this logic is "At this very moment in this work here I am," a text which was not only *about* Levinas's work in some sense, but also a gift to him, insofar as it was first published in a collection of essays dedicated to his writings entitled *Textes pour Emmanuel Levinas*.[6] The essay exemplifies the logic it seeks to expose. Derrida returns Levinas's texts to him in a way that Levinas could never recognize: this is Derrida's way of accepting the gift of Levinas's writings in the way that seems best designed to minimize the betrayal of the gift—by being ungrateful, by refusing to accept the gift of Levinas's texts as they are, by not taking them as *given*. Derrida claims that the non-responsive response was already expounded by Levinas in "The Trace of the Other" and in "Meaning and Sense." Levinas writes there that "the Work thought through all the way requires a radical generosity of the movement which in the Same goes toward the Other. It consequently requires an *ingratitude* of the other."[7] Nevertheless, closer examination of the texts suggests that there is a difference in the way that

Levinas and Derrida develop this logic. The most immediate difference is that Levinas does not present the problem in terms of the gift, but in terms of work.[8] How important is that difference? Does Levinas recognize the aporia of the gift? How does he negotiate it?

In "The Trace of the Other," Levinas describes work in terms of a "departure without return." Nevertheless, he says that this is not to be equated with "pure expenditure" or "pure loss" in what is a possible reference to Bataille (DEHH 191; TO 349). Paradoxically, pure expenditure would be as much tied to the notion of a goal as are the good works of someone seeking to acquire merit: "beneath the apparent gratuity of his action, both he who chases after merits and the nihilist agent forthwith takes himself as the goal." If gratitude compromises the movement of the same to the Other, any conception of a goal does so at least as readily. Hence the work loses its "absolute goodness" if it is justified by reference to a projected end. For Levinas, the only way in which this structure of subordination to thought is avoided is if the agent renounces being the contemporary of the outcome of the action "in a time *without me*" (DEHH 192; TO 349). In other words, the work is a "passage to the time of the other." It takes place "in an eschatology without hope for oneself, an eschatology of liberation from my own time." In "The Trace of the Other," Levinas affirms the possibility that sacrifice meets this condition,[9] just as in *Totality and Infinity* he locates this structure in fecundity. "Fecundity engendering fecundity accomplishes goodness: above and beyond the sacrifice that imposes a gift, the gift of the power of giving, the conception of the child."[10] Levinas emphasizes the importance of this passage by remarking that desire as transcendence, with which *Totality and Infinity* begins, is accomplished in the "engendering Desire" of fecundity.[11]

In *Totality and Infinity* Levinas argues that the encounter with the Other that puts me in question and so "puts an end to power" is

> positively produced as the possession of a world I can bestow as a gift on the Other—that is, as a presence before the face. For the presence before a face, my orientation toward the Other, can lose the avidity proper to the gaze only by turning into generosity, incapable of approaching the other with empty hands. (TeI 21; TI 50)

For Levinas, it seems, the Other puts in question my possessions, just as the Other puts in question my right to exist. So, in "The Trace of the Other," he writes: "The relationship with another puts me into question, empties me of myself, and does not let off emptying me—uncovering for me ever new resources. I did not know myself so rich, but I have no longer any right to keep anything" (DEHH 193; TO 350–351). This analysis was already prepared for in *Totality and Infinity* when Levinas insists in the context of his discussion of habitation and dwelling that "I must know how *to give* what I possess" (TeI 145; TI 171). The possibility of giving lies in the face of the Other who, because he or she comes not just from outside but from above, calls me into question and solicits giving.[12] Or, more precisely, in the face of the Other I find myself no longer so attached to my possessions.[13] I am ready to "put out funds at a loss." This last phrase is found in "The Trace of the Other" as Levinas's explanation of the Greek word "liturgy" (*leitourgiai*), with which he identifies ethics (DEHH 192; TO 350). Ethics is gratuitous. But is it possible?

Although Levinas recognizes the problem that gives rise to the aporia of the gift, it does not lead him to judge the gift impossible. In fact, his reflections on work are introduced in "The Trace of the Other" precisely as a response to the question of whether one can identify a heteronomous experience that cannot be converted into a category. He finds the answer in goodness and in "the works without which goodness is but a dream without transcendence, a pure wish (*blosser Wunsch*), as Kant put it" (DEHH 190–191; TO 348). It would seem, therefore, that Levinas's interest in the work—or the gift—is precisely in their possibility. However, that does not mean that Levinas and Derrida are as resolutely opposed as this would suggest. It is not the case that Derrida is trying to rule out or exclude that on which Levinas relies. Derrida is in fact better understood as expressing in more dramatic terms what follows from what Levinas says in "The Trace of the Other" and which Levinas confirms elsewhere, that the gift is impossible within the order of being and occurs only as an "interruption" of that order. So Levinas would have no difficulty underwriting the formula that Derrida employs to summarize the structural paradoxes of the gift at the end of *Given Time*; the formula's use of the "without" and its appeal to Plato's account of the good that Levinas has been using since *Existence and Existents* to name the subject matter of his thinking, seems designed to show the proximity of the two thinkers. Derrida writes that what is at stake is "the gift as remaining (*restance*) without memory, without permanence and consistency, without substance or subsistence; at stake is this rest that is, without being (it), beyond Being, *epekeina tes ousias*" (DT 187; GT 147).[14] The logic of the "without" (*sans*) that both Levinas and Derrida share is an interruptive logic in which what interrupts the order of being is "impossible, unthinkable, unsayable" from within that realm.[15] When Levinas writes that "the gift *is not*" (EM 25; AM 15), he is saying that the gift is not an event in being. Exchange, circulation and rationality are interrupted by the gift (DT 197; GT 156). The pure gift, if

there is any, must be a gift without obligation or duty, in order to differentiate it from exchange. The question now becomes that of how Levinas and
Derrida both think this interruption of the order of being from beyond
being to which the "without" points.[16] The way in which Derrida's
account of the interruption might still be thought of as a challenge to
Levinas's account can best be illustrated by taking up the discussion of
almsgiving that provides the central example of giving in *Given Time*.

II

In *Given Time* Derrida acknowledges the necessity of examining the discourse of alms and begging, although he excuses himself from undertaking
a full detailed analysis of it (DT 174; GT 137). However, the few pages
that Derrida devotes to the topic raise many of the important questions
suggested by an examination of that discourse: the contrast between the
beggar who *in principle* produces nothing and the beggar's role of symbolic mediation in a sacrificial structure, where the giving of alms does
indeed fulfill a regulated and regulating function (DT 170–75; GT
134–38); the way that the incorporation of the beggar without assimilation
assures an identity by exclusion (DT 171; GT 135); the different situations
for beggars before the age of industrial capitalism from that which they
found later (DT 173; GT 136), and so on. Derrida's point is that almsgiving is never found independently of the "economy of alms" (DT 180; GT
142); the beggar is always encountered within a specific social context.
"The regularity of this social irregularity each time reinscribes begging and
alms in a sacrificial structure" (DT 174; GT 137). Because almsgiving is
always governed by a certain "institutional regularity," almsgiving is not
gratuitous. It is bound (*liée*) by moral, legal or religious obligations (DT
175; GT 137).[17]

It is clear that the problematic posed by Derrida in *Given Time* goes to
the heart of the Levinasian conception of ethics as asymmetrical. One
could even understand Derrida's remarks about almsgiving as a response to
a rare mention by Levinas of the beggar. In "Enigma and Phenomenon"
the trace is expounded in terms of the nakedness of a face that interrupts
order without receiving a meaning from the context interrupted because it
was already "ab-solute" (DEHH 207–8; CP 65). "In this solicitation that
does not have the effrontery to solicit and is non-audacity, in this beggar's
solicitation, expression does not participate in the order from which it tears
itself, but thus precisely faces and confronts in a face, approaches and disturbs absolutely" (DEHH 208; CP 65. Trans. modified). In response to
this passage, Derrida could be understood as saying in *Given Time* that the
encounter with the beggar is never pure; it is always contaminated by the

"economy of alms." Derrida, perhaps recalling "Violence and Metaphysics," also says that violence is the condition of the gift (DT 186; GT 147), but even here the difference between Levinas and Derrida is not so apparent as it might seem at first. Derrida also focuses on what he takes to be a formal trait, independent of these historical details: "By reason of the disorder with which they seem to interrupt the economic order of the same, beggars can signify the absolute demand of the other, the inextinguishable appeal, the unquenchable thirst for the gift" (DT 174; GT 137). This seems to be in line with Levinas's account. Derrida's gift without exchange would be like, for example, Levinas's saying without a said (AE 58–61; OB 45–48). There is no saying without a said. It is to that extent impossible. Saying always arises within a linguistic context. But it also interrupts that order, albeit it is readily reinscribed within it, just as is the case with the gift. The difference between Levinas and Derrida now falls on the fact that, unlike Levinas, Derrida judges it worthwhile to examine the discourse of alms and of begging in a kind of genealogy, just as he judges it appropriate to quote extensively from Marcel Mauss's classic study, *The Gift*, to show the system of exchange operating universally. These additions would seem to give the advantage to Derrida. They give his account a historical concreteness that is apparently lacking in Levinas. In the next two sections I will examine, first, Derrida's use of Mauss and, then, his appeal to genealogy, with a view to the question of whether these additions do not render his account more problematic than he seems to realize.

III

What is Derrida's basis for saying that "for there to be a gift, there must be no reciprocity, return, exchange, countergift, or debt" (DT 24; GT 12)? Derrida ascribes it to language: it is what the word "gift" means, or has come to mean, at least in certain languages. On this basis Derrida seeks to depart "in a peremptory and distinct fashion" from "the metaphysics of the gift" that has "*quite rightly and justifiably*, treated *together*, as a system, the gift and the debt, the gift and the cycle of restitution, the gift and the loan, the gift and credit . . ." (DT 25; GT 13). Marcel Mauss's *The Gift* exemplifies this metaphysics. What Mauss describes as gift was, as he himself readily admits, the circulation of gifts, where it belongs to "the nature of the gift in the end to bring its own reward" (D 199; G 34). If the gift is as Derrida describes it, then Mauss discusses everything but the gift (DT 39; GT 24). By focusing on exchange, Mauss departs from the logic of the gift and so, according to Derrida, "a consistent discourse on the gift becomes impossible."

Derrida has another objection to Mauss. Derrida starts from the familiar observation that Mauss insists on drawing some moral conclusions from his

study. For example, Mauss wants a return to the custom of "noble expenditure," of which the Greek *leitourgiai* is an example (D 262; G 66). But
Derrida's criticism is more far-reaching than the standard objection when
he observes that "Mauss's discourse is oriented by an ethics and a politics
that tend to valorize the generosity of the giving-being" (DT 64; GT 44).
But does the valorization of generosity not belong to the meaning of
the gift in our language? Does not Derrida's willingness to question that
aspect of its meaning not compromise his reliance on language as a source
for the aporia?[18]

However, the most striking feature of Derrida's method in *Given Time*
is his silence about Mauss's methodological procedures. Even the paradox
that Mauss translated the materials at his disposal into a language that
allegedly incorporates the logic of the gift that is nowhere reflected in
Mauss's survey is not subjected to scrutiny. If Mauss's subsumption of the
diverse practices he studies under the restricted connotations of the term
"gift" was questionable even to Mauss himself (D 267; G 70), one would
have expected Derrida to have known that his readers would be at least
equally suspicious about his imposition of the logic of the gift on very
diverse cultural practices and would want an examination of the evidence
for its applicability. Those readers would also have expected that Derrida
would have made some attempt to expose the operation by which Mauss
applied the logic of Western metaphysics with its oppositions and hierarchies to cultures that proceed differently.[19] Perhaps Derrida intends in the
projected continuation of *Given Time* to examine Mauss's own methodological reflections and the questions posed by Lévi-Strauss in his "Introduction to the Work of Marcel Mauss."[20] It seems likely that Derrida will
do so because he quotes extensively from Mauss but does relatively little
with it, as if setting the scene for a subsequent volume. But it is nevertheless something of a surprise to find Derrida referring to Gloria Goodwin
Raheja's *The Poison in the Gift* without recognizing explicitly the extent to
which it challenges not only Mauss's interpretations and his use of his
materials but also goes to the heart of Mauss's study. She shows that in
Pahansu, a village on the Hindi-speaking region of Northern India the *dān*
are not to be reciprocated in any way by exchange of goods or services and
that the recipient has the obligation to accept. However, Derrida simply
calls *The Poison in the Gift* an "interesting discussion of Mauss on the subject of the gift and the (non-reciprocal) reception of the *dān*" without further comment (DT 54n; GT 36n). Not only does Derrida fail to take the
opportunity to distance himself from Mauss's insistence on universal structures, he leaves unclear his relation to the empirical evidence from which
those universal structures are supposedly drawn by Mauss. If Derrida's

reading of Mauss is dominated by his interest in the ahistorical paradox apparently at the expense of the specificity of the evidence, does the genealogy fare any better?

IV

In terms of that question, the beginning of *Given Time* could not be more promising. Derrida frames his study of the impossibility of the gift with a supposition, "an intention-to-give: Some 'one' wants or desires to give" (DT 23; GT 11). Derrida's account of the gift, in *Given Time* at least, is firmly rooted to this presupposition: "The simple intention to give, insofar as it carries the intentional meaning of the gift, suffices to make a return payment to oneself" (DT 38; GT 23). This suggests that particular attention would be given by Derrida to the ethics of intention but it does not really happen. Derrida does not even ask, when reading Mauss's *The Gift*, whether intention is universally given the same importance.

In fact, the genealogical analysis of almsgiving in *Given Time* is still relatively undeveloped as a genealogy. Derrida has more often advised others to engage in genealogical inquiry than he has engaged in it himself. For a fuller sense of what Derrida has come to mean by genealogy, we must turn to the 1992 essay "Donner la mort" for guidance.[21] "Donner la mort" is an enigmatic phrase; it evokes both suicide and the sacrifice of dying for the other, as well as the economy of the gift (DM 19; GD 10). For his elaboration of genealogy, Derrida relies largely on Jan Patočka's "Is technological civilization a civilization in decline, and why?"[22] Patočka's brief essay offers in broad strokes a reexamination of the history of Europe in terms of the orgiastic, Platonic, and Christian mysteries. Not since the early days of deconstruction, when Derrida relied heavily on Heidegger's account of Western metaphysics in terms of Being as presence, has he been so drawn to the big picture. Derrida reads Patočka as offering not just a genealogy of responsibility *in* Europe, but also a genealogy of responsibility *as* Europe. According to Derrida, Patočka's essay deconstructs the history of this responsibility by underlining the heterogeneity of the mystery of the sacred and responsibility (DM 52; GD 48–49). On the very first page of his essay, Derrida refers this heterogeneity to Levinas, thinking no doubt of Levinas's distinction between the sacred and the saintly (DM 11; GD 1).[23] At this level, Derrida, without in any way equating Levinas's project with Patočka's, brings them together so as to explore the question of unequal responsibility. What makes responsibility unequal to itself is the fact that "one is never responsible enough." This arises not just because one is finite, but also because responsibility exhibits a contradictory movement. One not only responds in one's irreplaceable singularity for what one does, says, and gives, but one also, inasmuch as one is good, forgets or effaces the origin of one's giving (DM 55; GD 51). Derrida claims that Patočka does not develop the aporia in this way, although it has to be said that Patočka does recognize a certain opposition between Plato's idea of the good and the Christian idea of a goodness forgetful of itself (EH 115–16). In any event, the terms in which the aporia is developed are much more reminiscent of Levinas than Patočka, leaving one with the impression that it is almost as if Derrida wants to give to Levinas, not the genealogy he needs precisely, but at least an indication of the kind of genealogy he needs.

But does Derrida succeed, here or elsewhere, in interweaving the two styles of deconstruction that he sets out in "Force of Law"? The problem can be illustrated by juxtaposing "Donner la mort" and "Passions." In a long note in *Passions*, Derrida takes up, with reference to debt, the aporetic analysis of duty that in the main body of the text he had already explicated in terms of politeness. Utilizing the logic of the "without," he poses the question, "But is there a duty without debt?"[24] The question is important insofar as the ethicity of ethics is measured against "an unlimited, incalculable or uncalculating giving, without any possible reappropriation" (PO 75; POO 26). Underlining the way in which the logic of the "without" is an interruptive logic, Derrida describes this duty that does not prescribe anything as "a discrete and silent break with culture and language" (PO 76; POO 26). This is a position that echoes some of Levinas's remarks on culture (HH 54–56; CP 100–102). But is the "feeling" that tells Derrida that "pure morality must exceed all calculation, conscious or unconscious, of restitution or reappropriation" (PO 75; POO 26), really culturally indeterminate?

Recalling "Donner la mort," this "feeling" is surely not unrelated to the biblical demand not to do one's alms before men, because one would already have had one's reward (Matthew 6:1). At the same time it stands opposed to the Greek understanding of goodness, thereby already setting up the conflict that conditions and perhaps even constitutes the aporia. For the Greeks, not just the manifestation of a quality but also a reputation for it, seems to have been an essential component of that quality. This was especially true in respect to goodness and the excellences. Goodness was not a quality that resides in someone, so much as a function of one's status or public estimation, even after one's death.[25] However, the biblical text not only insists that one should do one's alms in secret in disregard of what others might think. It also evokes the secret and prescribes that when giving alms the left hand should not know what the right hand is doing.[26] Derrida cites this phrase in "Donner la mort" as part of a long meditation on the secret introduced in relation to Kierkegaard's allusion to Matthew 6:4, 6, and 18 (DM 95, 101; GD 101, 108).[27] Derrida's initial concern is to address the question of the return that, according to the biblical text, one will receive in heaven:

> 3. But when thou doest alms, let not thy left hand know what thy right hand doeth:
> 4. That thine alms may be in secret: and thy Father which seeth in secret himself shall reward thee openly.

On the one hand, Derrida recognizes here a displacement, a "mutation in the history of the secret" (DM 94; GD 100): "the end of secrecy, but it is also the beginning of the paradox of the secret as irreducible in its interiority" (DM 95; GD 100). On the other hand, Derrida allows that if there is a new economy, it breaks with exchange as simple reciprocity. It is not clear from the context whether Derrida would put the same weight on the phrase "origin of the paradox" that I am doing, but it is readily apparent that he is locating the aporia within a specific history.[28] Nevertheless, Derrida was quite explicit in "Passions" that the contradiction that he there isolated within the concept of politeness—"It is impolite to be merely polite, to be polite out of politeness"—is cross-cultural, and, presumably, transhistorical also: "For whatever cultural tradition [it] is linked to (Western or otherwise), the hypothesis about politeness and the sharp determination of this value relates to what enjoins us to go beyond rules, norms, and hence ritual" (PO 24; POO 9). It seems that the genealogical account threatens to undercut the ahistorical account. At very least, one would want to hear more from Derrida as to how these apparently rival analyses are to be reconciled. The two styles of deconstruction have given rise to two contradictory conclusions that could not be entertained at the same time without further deconstruction.

If Levinas is not faced with the same problem that I have found in Derrida, this is because he seems to locate the aporia specifically within the relation between Western philosophy and what interrupts it. So, when Levinas in *Totality and Infinity* sets out the distinction between need and desire, which provides the basis for his exposition of the radical ingratitude required by the work, he is clear that the order of goodness that it opened went "beyond the rules of formal logic" (TeI 77; TI 104). The imposition of what Levinas calls formal logic tends to reduce desire to a form of exchange. The difficulty of thinking asymmetry without reducing it to symmetry arises from the tendency within the tradition of philosophy that began with Parmenides to impose unity on multiplicity (TeI 76; TI 102). Although in *Totality and Infinity* Levinas merely suggests that this reflects only one of the paths offered by Greek metaphysics, in subsequent texts he sometimes identifies the alternative as a specifically Judaic wisdom. Indeed, in "The Trace of the Other," in the context of the discussion of work as a movement from the same to the other without return, Levinas writes: "To the myth of Ulysses returning to Ithaca, we wish to oppose the story of Abraham who leaves his fatherland forever for a yet unknown land, and forbids his servant to even bring back his son to the point of departure" (DEHH 191; TO 348). This leads Derrida to ask in "Violence and Metaphysics" if the theme of the return is so unhebraic (ED 228n; WD 320). In the fifth section, I shall pose the related question of whether breaking the circularity of exchange is so ungreek. Aristotle's discussion of the gift, and particularly of the *leitourgiai*, is especially revealing because it takes place in a context in which intentions have not yet become the decisive issue.

V

In *Given Time* (DT 177; GT 139), Derrida refers to the discussion of magnanimity in Book IV of Aristotle's *Nicomachean Ethics* (henceforth NE), but the account of friendship in Books VIII and IX is more relevant to Levinas's discussion, and perhaps Derrida's also.[29] It might seem at first as if Aristotle's account runs entirely counter to the one I have been exploring. Aristotle is concerned with the difficulty of maintaining friendship between partners who are unequal or who contribute an unequal share. He recognizes the positive side of reciprocity as opposed to asymmetry. His initial model of perfect friendship is one in which one party receives from the other similar benefits to those he or she has contributed (NE 1156b 32–35). It is because of passages like this that Aristotle has been associated with a "morality of the *mediocritas* and of the happy medium," which is in fact Derrida's phrase for describing Mauss's preference for exchange over the excess of generosity exemplified by the pure gift, where the best becomes dangerous or threatening to the system (DT 88; GT 65). Nevertheless, Aristotle does recognize a certain asymmetry in the relation. Friendship consists more in loving than in being loved (NE 1159a 27). In friendships based on virtue, each competes with the other to give rather than to receive, and the one who outdoes the other does not complain (NE 1162b 5–13).

In friendships based on utility, if one gives to a friend, one expects to receive an equivalent or greater return as though it had not been a gift but a loan (NE 1162b 21–34). Similarly, a base friend is one who is always seeking his or her advantage, like one who seeks to avoid their proper share of the *leitourgiai* (NE 1167b 9–13). In such cases, there will often be disputes as to the value of a service rendered, disputes not easily resolved because of the possible difference between the benefit to the recipient and the cost to the doer, especially in unequal friendships (NE 1162a 10–15). By contrast, in friendships based on virtue there are no such complaints and the measure of the benefit of the gift to the recipient is not the gift itself, but the *proairesis* of the giver (NE 1163a 21–24). Aristotle is not to be understood as saying that it is the thought behind the gift that counts, at least not in the way that this idiom is usually understood. He is not referring the gift to the intention in giving, even though *proairesis* is usually translated as "intention" in this context. The *proairesis* is not to be judged separately from the inherent value of what is given, as if it was enough to mean well. The phrase would appear to mean that if one's *proairesis* is noble (*kalon*), then one seeks to give more and without measuring this more by reference to what has been received. In other words, the gift, like the friendship from which it derives, has the character of an excess (*huperbole*) such that it cannot be measured by any calculation of its value. Aristotle is not unaware of the threat that calculating might eventually come into play. That is why he still finds his model in the case where each of the two friends, while vying to give more, happen by some lucky accident to hit on an equal exchange. But where that does not arise or is not possible, *proairesis* is the appropriate measure. Aristotle recommends *proairesis* as the principle for the payment of philosophy lessons, as also of one's debt to the gods and to one's parents, where we must simply make such return as is in our power (NE 1164b 32–1165a 64). It is clear that this again cannot be reduced simply to a matter of intentions as they are conceived by the ethics of intentions (cf. also Eudemian Ethics 1243a 32–1243b 14).

If Derrida in *Given Time* refers to Aristotle's discussion of magnanimity, rather than to his discussion of friendship, it is perhaps because in Book IV, Aristotle describes some of the difficulties of receiving a gift. The magnanimous person is

> the sort of person who does good but is ashamed when he receives it; for doing good is proper to the superior person, and receiving it to the inferior. He returns more than he has received; for in this way the original giver will be repaid, and will also have incurred a new debt to him, and will be the beneficiary.[30] (NE 1124b 10–13)

This shows an understanding of the problems that arise from the logic of exchange, but it does not amount to an aporia. Aristotle is concerned to show the difficulties that arise from asymmetry, but he does not show any recognition that the asymmetry of the gift might be impossible. In the books on friendship he asks why the benefactor loves the beneficiary more than the benefactor is loved in return. His explanation is that that happens when giving amounts to a kind of making (*poiesis*) (NE 1167b 16–1168a 10). In the friendship that surpasses exchange and is measured, by contrast, by *proairesis*, the problem does not arise. Although this is a very different problem from the one that concerns Derrida, it does help to diagnose one element of Derrida's aporia in the form of a certain conceptuality that interferes with the thought of the gift. One can speculate that, insofar as the philosophical tradition has relied on intellectual resources drawn from the experience of *poiesis*, giving as a *praxis* has been reduced to *poiesis* and thus to exchange.[31] The dominance of *poiesis* contributes to the structures Levinas in *Totality and Infinity* describes as formal logic.

But the particular form of the aporia developed by Levinas and Derrida relies on a conception of the relation of goodness and intentions that was unknown to Aristotle. We have already seen from "The Trace of the Other" that Levinas is firmly rooted in the tradition in which goodness has to hide from itself. He repeats the same thought elsewhere: "The just who know themselves to be just are no longer just. The first and last condition of the just is that their justice remains clandestine to them."[32] That there are dominant forms of thought that force asymmetry into symmetry, desire into need, alterity into the same, the gift into exchange, does not yet impose the aporia in its full force. These forces only become overwhelming with the additional requirement that goodness remains hidden.

This helps explain why in "Meaning and Sense" Levinas appeals to the Greek liturgies. Aristotle contrasts the *leitourgiai*, the public or religious services performed at one's own cost, unfavorably with friendship, on the grounds that in friendship one's benefits serve as a kind of repayment of one's contribution (NE 1163a 28–31. Also *Eudemian Ethics* 1242b 16–21). It is tempting to view Levinas's decision to identify the gratuitous work of *leitourgiai* with ethics as his ignorance of Greek social practices. The liturgies were not voluntary but were duties required of the richer citizens by law. There was even an appeals system by which one could challenge one's assignment.[33] They were also often useless, or virtually useless, at least according to Aristotle.[34] However, many would voluntarily accept additional service. It is true that, in so doing, they often expected the appreciation of the people. Lysias, defending a client from the charge of the embezzlement of public funds, pleaded for acquittal on the grounds that he had gone beyond what was required of him by the *leitourgiai* in fulfilling his obligations to the public.[35] But perhaps what draws Levinas to the liturgies is the fact that they are embedded within a social context that rendered them almost ordinary. They did not draw attention to themselves and were surrounded by a certain ambiguity: a *leitourgiai* might be imposed or might

be voluntary, just as it might be performed in order to establish a good reputation or be gratuitous. Above all, it was not judged by reference to the
motivation of the one performing it. Because it is in the context of the discussion of the gift that Levinas seeks to free the discussion of goodness from
both an account of the triumph of goodness and an insistence on good
intentions, it is perhaps not accidental that he turned as if nostalgically to
Greece for one of his more concrete examples of the ethical, even though he
associates the ethical preeminently with Judaism. One wonders if the aporia
is not perhaps best understood as the result of combining two distinct traditions that have never been fully reconciled. And is this not because there has
been insufficient interest in exposing their differences? Perhaps Derrida and
Levinas both have such profound recognition of the aporia of the gift,
because their thought is governed by the Jew-Greek relation.

Derrida, for all his interest in history and social context, does not see the
Greek tradition as one tradition among others. The power and the unforeseeable resources of the Greek *logos* are such that whatever encounters the
Greek tradition from the outside is immediately appropriated or assimilated
to it. However, this has more of the status of a dogma than a working
hypothesis to be tested. Derrida still relies on the consensus that philosophy is essentially Greek, even as he acknowledges that which is irreducible
to it.[36] It is Derrida's faith in the Greek *logos* that makes it possible for him
to declare that the aporia of the gift is universal, even as he locates its origin
in the juxtaposition of the Greek with the Judeo-Christian.

Levinas, by contrast, while acknowledging a certain lack of limits to the
Greek language, is nevertheless quite explicit about the limits of Greek wisdom, to which he increasingly opposes Judaic wisdom. For him, Greek wisdom is characterized by a reciprocity, a symmetry, a return, that runs
counter to the directionality of Judaism. That is why he can characterize
the difference between exchange and the work or gift as the difference
between Ulysses and Abraham. And yet, when seeking to illustrate ethics as
"putting out of funds at a loss," he chooses a Greek example, the *leitourgiai*. Levinas wants the excess to be preeminently Judaic but knows that it
need not be. It is no surprise that the demand to give without falling prey
to what in the aporia resists giving should display itself, at least once in his
works, in the form of a certain nostalgia for Greek practices conducted in
ignorance of the problem. However, if Levinas does not face the question
of whether his account of the interruption is universal in its status as
opposed to arising within the specific structure of the surpassing of Greek
wisdom by Judaic wisdom, it is perhaps only because he devalues everything other than the Greek and the Jewish and does so quite explicitly. He
does not seem to hold back from making universal claims. To that extent

the difference between Levinas and Derrida here is not as pronounced as I have made it. But this paper is not ultimately an argument about them, so much as an argument about the need for further genealogical investigations to avoid some of the mystifications that a lack of historical awareness produces. At the same time, I have tried to present the issue in such a way as to draw attention to the most obvious dangers of such genealogical investigations insofar as they are understood to be confined to an alleged linearity of the West. They all too readily leave intact the West's tendency to declare its universality by devaluing, excluding, appropriating, or assimilating its other.[37]

Notes

1. "Force of Law: The 'Mystical Foundation of Authority,'" trans. Mary Quaintance, *Cardozo Law Review* 11, 5–6 (July/Aug. 1990): 959. Henceforth FL.

2. For some more general reflections on aporias, see Jacques Derrida, "Apories: Mourir-s'attendre aux limites de la vérité," in *Le Passage des frontières* (Paris: Galilée, 1994), esp. pp. 313–17; trans. Thomas Dutoit, *Aporias* (Stanford: Stanford University Press, 1993), esp. pp. 11–21.

3. Marcel Mauss, "Essai sur le don," *Sociologie et Anthropologie* (Paris: Presses Universitaires de France, 1991), pp. 143–279; trans. Ian Cunnison, *The Gift* (New York: Norton, 1967). Henceforth D and G respectively.

4. Jacques Derrida, *Donner le temps. 1. La fausse monnaie* (Paris: Galilée, 1991), pp. 170–74; trans. Peggy Kamuf, *Given Time. 1. Counterfeit Money* (Chicago: University of Chicago Press, 1993), pp. 134–37. Henceforth DT and GT respectively. The fact that this is only Part One raises the possibility, of course, that subsequent parts will answer some of the questions posed in this essay, or even show their inappropriateness. For that reason, much of what is said here is only provisional.

5. Jacques Derrida and Pierre-Jean Labarière, *Altérités* (Paris: Osiris, 1986), p. 71.

6. Jacques Derrida, "En ce moment même dans cet ouvrage me voici," *Textes pour Emmanuel Levinas*, ed. François Laruelle (Paris: Jean-Michel Place, 1980), pp. 21–60; trans. Ruben Berezdivin "At this very moment in this work here I am," in *Re-Reading Levinas*, eds. Robert Bernasconi and Simon Critchley (Bloomington: Indiana University Press, 1991), pp. 11–48. Henceforth EM and AM respectively. I expand on this reading of Derrida's essay in "Skepticism in the Face of Philosophy" in *Re-Reading Levinas*, pp. 149–61.

7. The text is cited by Derrida at EM 22; AM 13. It is found in two places in Levinas's works. "La signification et le sens," *Humanisme de l'autre homme* (Montpellier: Fata Morgana, 1977), p. 41; trans. Alphonso Lingis, "Meaning and Sense," in *Collected Philosophical Papers* (Dordrecht: Martinus Nijhoff, 1987), p. 92. Henceforth HH and CP respectively. Also Levinas, "La trace de l'autre," *En découvrant l'existence avec Husserl et Heidegger* (Paris: Vrin, 1967), p. 191; trans. Alphonso Lingis, "The Trace of the Other," in *Deconstruction in Context*, ed. Mark Taylor (Chicago: University of Chicago Press, 1986), p. 349. Henceforth DEHH and TO respectively.

8. Another difference, whose importance will emerge later, is that Derrida insists

on specifying what Levinas, at most, only implies: that giving should be "beyond acknowledgment (*au'delà de la reconnaissance*)" (EM 24; AM 14).

9. "The Trace of the Other" suggests that "perhaps the possibility of sacrifice" provides confirmation of the analysis whereas "Meaning and Sense" reads "at least (*du moins*) the possibility of sacrifice" (HH 42–43; CP 92). The fact that Levinas points to sacrifice rather than to the gift is another indication that his interests are different from those of Derrida, who quickly dismisses sacrifice as an exchange that still hopes for some benefit (cf. DT 174; GT 137). Derrida thereby sides with Mauss who says that "sacrificial destruction implies giving something that is to be repaid" (D 167; G 14) and against Bataille for whom the spectacular destruction of wealth without possible response was the ideal form of wealth. In 1933, in "The Notion of Expenditure," Bataille attributes this idea to Mauss, but he subsequently seems to have recognized that it runs counter to the general direction of Mauss's account and takes it as his own. Georges Bataille, "La notion de dépense," *Oeuvres Complètes* vol. 1 (Paris: Gallimard, 1970), p. 309; trans. Allan Stoekl, "The Notion of Expenditure," in *Visions of Excess* (Minneapolis: University of Minnesota Press, 1985), p. 121. Compare Georges Bataille, *The Accursed Share Vol. 1,* trans. Robert Hurley (New York: Zone Books, 1988), p. 70.

10. Emmanuel Levinas, *Totalité et Infini* (The Hague: Martinus Nijhoff, 1961), p. 247; trans. Alphonso Lingis, *Totality and Infinity* (Pittsburgh: Duquesne University Press, 1969), p. 269. Henceforth TeI and TI respectively.

11. The importance of this step, which took Levinas "Beyond the Face," as Section IV is entitled, has been neglected, perhaps in part because Levinas's text is so highly gender specific, with its focus on paternity and filiality. The discussion of maternity in *Otherwise than being* seems to present itself as a correction of these analyses that perhaps are still too dominated by a conception of identity across fecundity (TeI 244–45; TI 267), which the notion of substitution based on maternity and vulnerability challenges. *Autrement qu'être ou au-delà de l'essence* (The Hague: Martinus Nijhoff, 1974), p. 135; trans. Alphonso Lingis, *Otherwise than being or beyond essence* (The Hague: Martinus Nijhoff, 1981), p. 106. Henceforth AE and OB respectively.

12. Levinas subsequently extends his analysis of the conditions of giving to include "incarnation" (AE 139; OB 109). See also *Hors sujet* (Montpellier: Fata Morgana, 1987), pp. 56–57; trans. Michael B. Smith, *Outside the Subject* (Stanford: Stanford University Press, 1993), p. 39.

13. Although in *Totality and Infinity* and "The Trace of the Other" the Other questions my right to possessions, this does not deny the painfulness of giving that is emphasized by Levinas later. See AE 93–94; OB 74.

14. Derrida expresses his concerns about the Platonic formula in "Comment ne pas parler. Dénégations," in *Psyché* (Paris: Galilée, 1987), pp. 563–66; trans. Ken Frieden, "How to Avoid Speaking: Denials," in *Derrida and Negative Theology,* eds. Harold Coward and Toby Foshay (Albany: State University of New York, 1992), pp. 101–3.

15. Jacques Derrida, *L'écriture et la différence* (Paris: Seuil, 1967), p. 168; trans. Alan Bass, *Writing and Difference* (Chicago: University of Chicago Press, 1978), p. 114. Henceforth ED and WD respectively.

16. Derrida similarly writes in "Force of Law": "This 'idea of justice' seems to me to be irreducible in its affirmative character, in its demand of gift without exchange, without circulation, without recognition or gratitude, without economic

circulation, without calculation and without rule, without reason and without rationality" (FL 965). I have discussed the logic of the "without" at greater length in "The Ethics of Suspicion," *Research in Phenomenology* 20 (1990): 3–18.

17. For my own provisional contribution to the task of writing this genealogy, see "The Poor Box and the Changing Face of Charity in Early Modern Europe," *Acta Institutionis Philosophiae et Aestheticae* 10 (1992): 33–54.

18. The valorization of the gift is somewhat mitigated by the ambiguity that Derrida emphasizes whereby "gift" can also mean poison, as in German.

19. See Michèle H. Richman, *Reading Georges Bataille: Beyond the Gift* (Baltimore: Johns Hopkins University Press, 1982), p. 11.

20. Derrida had already given that text a certain prominence in "Structure, Sign and Play in the Discourse of the Human Sciences" where totalization and history were already at issue. See ED 423–28; WD 289–93.

21. Jacques Derrida, "Donner la mort," in *L'éthique du don. Jacques Derrida et la pensée du don*, ed. Jean-Michel Rabaté and Michael Wetzel (Paris: Métailié-Transition, 1992), pp. 11–108; trans. David Wills, *The Gift of Death* (Chicago: University of Chicago Press, 1995). Henceforth DM and GD respectively. Derrida announces his interest in genealogy in *Of Grammatology* but does not say much more than that "the question of genealogy exceeds by far the possibilities that are at present given for its elaboration." Jacques Derrida, *De la grammatologie* (Paris: Minuit, 1967), pp. 149 and 26; trans. Gayatri Chakravorty Spivak, *Of Grammatology* (Baltimore: Johns Hopkins University Press, 1976), pp. 101 and 14.

22. Jan Patočka, "La civilisation technique est-elle une civilisation de déclin, et pourquoi?" in *Essais hérétiques*, trans. Erika Abrams (Paris: Verdier, 1981), pp. 105–27. Henceforth EH.

23. For the distinction, see Emmanuel Levinas, *Du sacré au saint* (Paris: Minuit, 1977), pp. 89–90; trans. Annette Aronowicz, *Nine Talmudic Readings* (Bloomington: Indiana University Press, 1990), p. 141.

24. Jacques Derrida, *Passions. "L'offrande oblique"* (Paris: Galilée, 1993), p. 76; trans. David Wood, "Passions: 'An Oblique Offering,'" in *Derrida: A Critical Reader*, ed. David Wood (Oxford: Blackwell, 1992), p. 26. Henceforth PO and POO respectively.

25. Kenneth J. Dover, *Greek Popular Morality in the Time of Plato and Aristotle* (Oxford: Basil Blackwell, 1974), p. 235.

26. For the philosophical issues, see further G. W. F. Hegel, "Der Geist des Christentums und sein Schicksal," in *Frühe Schriften*, *Werke* 1 (Frankfurt: Suhrkamp, 1974), pp. 331–32; trans. T. M. Knox, "The Spirit of Christianity," in *Early Theological Writings* (Philadelphia: University of Pennsylvania Press, 1971), p. 219. See also Hannah Arendt, *The Human Condition* (Chicago: University of Chicago Press, 1958), p. 74. Patočka read Arendt, as does Derrida.

27. Søren Kierkegaard, *Fear and Trembling*, trans. H. V. Kong and E. H. Kong (Princeton: Princeton University Press, 1983), p. 120.

28. In "Donner la mort" Derrida also cites the passage that says that for a man to look on a woman with lust is for him already to have committed adultery in his heart (Matthew 5:28). It is a passage that later was central to the development of the ethics of intention that, as I showed earlier, plays a crucial role in giving the aporia of the gift the form that it has in *Given Time*.

29. It should be recalled that Derrida introduced his discussion of friendship with a saying Montaigne attributed to Aristotle, "O my friends, there is no friend."

Derrida, "The Politics of Friendship," *Journal of Philosophy* 85, 11 (1988): 632–44.

30. Aristotle, *Nicomachean Ethics*, trans. Terence Irwin (Indianapolis: Hackett, 1985).

31. For the framework underlying this hypothesis, see my "The Fate of the Distinction Between *Praxis* and *Poiesis*," in *Heidegger in Question* (Atlantic Highlands: Humanities Press, 1993), pp. 2–24.

32. Emmanuel Levinas, "Transcendance et Hauteur," *Bulletin de la Société française de philosophie* 54 (1962): 96.

33. R. K. Sinclair, *Democracy and Participation in Athens* (Cambridge: Cambridge University Press, 1988), p. 64.

34. Aristotle in his *Politics* advises against continuing with many of the *leitourgiai* for that reason, 1309a 18–22 and 1320b 1–5.

35. Lysias, "Speech XXI: Defence Against a Charge of Taking Bribes," trans. W. R. M. Lamb in *Lysias* (Cambridge, MA: Harvard University Press, 1976), pp. 474–89.

36. Jacques Derrida, "Nous autres Grecs," in *Nos Grecs et leurs modernes* (Paris: Seuil, 1992), p. 263.

37. Earlier versions of this paper were given to the Department of Comparative Literature at SUNY-Buffalo in April 1994 and to the Canadian Society for Hermeneutics and Postmodern Thought in June 1994. At the risk of invoking the aporia of the gift, I am grateful to the participants on both occasions for their helpful comments.

The Metaphysics of Presents: Nietzsche's Gift, the Debt to Emerson, Heidegger's Values

Gary Shapiro

> Setting prices, determining values, contriving equivalences, exchanging
> —these preoccupied the earliest thinking of man to so great an extent
> that in a certain sense they constitute thinking *as such* . . .
>
> Nietzsche, *Toward a Genealogy of Morals,* II, 8

In the Preface to *Ecce Homo,* Nietzsche says that with *Zarathustra* he has "given mankind the greatest present (*Geschenk*) that has been made to it so far."[1] I propose to take Nietzsche's talk of the gift seriously, not only with respect to his claim about *Zarathustra* but also in so far as that book itself involves a discourse of the gift. Most obviously in the first part of that text, the gift is never far away; it is announced at the beginning and eventually becomes the subject of a chapter "On the Gift-Giving Virtue" ("*Von der schenckenden Tugend*"). The question of the gift is internal to the text of *Zarathustra.* What is it to be a gift, to be a giver, to be a receiver—these are questions that arise throughout the book (a gift for all and none). Giving and everything associated with it are clearly thematized and problematized within the text. For example (but it is more than an example), in the series of economic speeches in which he weighs and measures the "three evils"— sex, the lust to rule and selfishness—Zarathustra considers each of these both in the "evil" form in which it is conventionally stigmatized and the transvalued form in which it appears to him after his return home, the return in which he now finds his own language. Of the lust to rule (*Herrschsucht*), he says

> The lust to rule—but who would call it *lust* [*Sucht*] when what is high longs downward for power? Verily, there is nothing diseased or lustful in such longing and condescending. That the lonely heights should not remain lonely and self-sufficient eternally; that the mountain should descend to the low plains—oh, who were to find the right name for such

longing? "Gift-giving virtue"—thus Zarathustra once named the unnameable. (*Z*, 208, *4*, 238)[2]

As we will see, Nietzsche's attempt (through Zarathustra) to name the unnameable will become more intelligible both by exploring his debt to Emerson and by considering Heidegger's critique of the supposed commitment to a metaphysics of values that he finds in Nietzsche's thought.

I. The Unnameable

Why is this virtue "unnameable"? Marcel Mauss says something similar in his *Essay on the Gift*. Mauss argues that gift-giving, exchange and potlatch are totalistic phenomena of archaic cultures that cannot be understood in terms of the individualistic and economistic categories of modern rationality. The practices connected with the gift, its exchange and circulation are unnameable within a social and economic order assuming the priority of private accumulation and possession; in such a context the gift is an occasional matter, an exception reserved for holidays and special events rather than the very nerve of communal life.

Gift-giving is unnameable from the perspective of the market; recall that it is the crowd in the marketplace to whom Zarathustra first attempts to give his gifts, and they can understand neither him nor the practice and discourse within which such giving is possible. If gift-giving should be named, as it is by the Kwakiutl or the Melanesians, for example, then our own moral categories treating of property and individuality would be put in question. Such groups typically have "only a single word to cover buy and sell, borrow and lend . . . Concepts which we like to put in opposition—freedom and obligation; generosity, liberality, luxury on the one hand and saving, interest, austerity on the other—are not exact and it would be well to put them to the test."[3] Mauss says something that recalls Zarathustra's equation of *Herrschsucht* and *schenkende Tugend*, observing that "Even the destruction of wealth does not correspond to the complete disinterestedness which one might expect." Despite the appearance of mad, frenzied destruction, of "wasteful expenditure," these activities are not disinterested: "Between vassals and chiefs, between vassals and their henchmen, the hierarchy is established by means of these gifts. To give is to show one's superiority . . . To accept without returning is to face subordination. . . ."[4]

The complexity of gift-giving is already announced and enacted at the beginning of *Thus Spoke Zarathustra*. In the generalized economy of gift-giving the gift is "for all and none," so it is put into circulation, and eventually it passes through the entire social world; but it is destined to be a permanent possession for none (in gift-giving societies the corresponding status may be marked by the complete wasting, destruction or expenditure of the object in question). In the *Vorrede*, Zarathustra's first speech is to the sun, whom he personifies and praises for his *schenkende Tugend*: "You great star, what would your happiness be had you not those for whom you shine?" And Zarathustra too is overfull: "Behold, I am weary of my wisdom, like a bee that has gathered too much honey; I need hands outstretched to receive it."

"I would give away and distribute (*verschenken und austeilen*), until the wise among men find joy once again in their folly, and the poor in their riches" (*Z*, 39; *4*, 11). *Verschenken und austeilen*: these name the processes of expenditure that constitute Zarathustra's *Untergehen* among men. And at the same time that he praises the sun, who always gives and never receives, he names the deficiency, the vice that corresponds to the gift-giving virtue: "So bless me then, you quiet eye that can look upon an all-too-great-happiness without envy [*Neid*]!" Envy, we learn later (for example, in "On the Tree on the Mountainside"), is a disease of the eye, the evil eye that characterizes the economic stance of the resentful who practice a morality of good and evil. When Zarathustra confesses to envy in "The Night Song," it is a complex, paradoxical envy of the receiver by the giver; he longs to surrender his blazing light in order to accept another's gifts.

Those who live alone exist in a precarious and sensitive relation to the modalities of giving and receiving exemplified by the extremes of the quiet or the evil eye. The evil eye would destroy a good thing or another's happiness not in a spirit of festive expenditure and not to take possession of it for oneself but simply to free itself from the pain it is caused by that good or by the happiness of another.[5] Zarathustra's first contact, after his solitary silence, is with a hermit who recognizes him by the purity of his eyes: "Yes, I recognize Zarathustra. His eye is pure and no disgust lurks about his mouth." In Zarathustra's first conversational exchange, the subject is the varieties of exchange itself. *Why* does Zarathustra go down to men, to "sleepers," demands the hermit. Zarathustra's initial answer is "I love man," but the hermit easily replies that love of man is precisely *his* reason for having retreated into solitude: man is unworthy of love, love of man would be fatal for him. Zarathustra's self-correction is speedy: "Did I speak of love? I bring men a gift [*ein Geschenk*]" (*Z*, 40; *4*, 13).

In this contrast between love and gift-giving, perhaps the most obvious implication is that the gift is always ambiguous; it may not be, and perhaps never is, the correlate of a purely disinterested act of bestowing. The gift places the recipient under an obligation burdensome in proportion to its value. Zarathustra's entire exchange with the hermit articulates these ambiguities of the gift-relationship. And of course as an *exchange* it also exemplifies these very same ambiguities, for Zarathustra is a speaker and what he has to give are his words.

> "Give them nothing!" said the saint. "Rather take something off them and bear it with them—that will please them best; if only it be pleasing to you! And if you want to give to them, give no more than alms, and let them beg for that!"
> "No," answered Zarathustra. "I give no alms. I am not poor enough for that."

Zarathustra replies to the hermit's suggestion that he make men beg for alms. That would be a kind of poverty, for it would presuppose that one did not have the strength and riches for a fuller exchange. The hermit knows that Zarathustra's entrance into society will be difficult. If he has treasures (*Schätze*) to give he must beware of men's wariness in accepting them, for they are "mistrustful of hermits" and will more readily see them as thieves than as benefactors. Gifts and exchange are expected; they form the very principle of sociality when there is some tie or ongoing communication among people. The outsider will be feared as a thief. How should we understand the encounter of the two hermits, Zarathustra on his way down to man, and the saint who, as he explains himself, praises God by "singing, crying, laughing, and humming" in the forest? And despite the hermit's apparent self-sufficiency he expects something from Zarathustra for he asks "what do you bring us as a gift?" However, Zarathustra is all discretion and leaves quickly so as not to take anything from this hermit who has yet to hear that God is dead. By echoing the simplest question of the child to a parent returning from a trip—"what did you bring me?"— the hermit shows how difficult it is to be truly isolated. The gift economy is ready to be activated at any time. And Zarathustra observes at least one principle of hospitality by discreetly refusing to disillusion his host. In this exchange words are skillfully deployed to insure that the balance remains what it was before the encounter.

II. Emerson and Nietzsche on the Gift-giving Virtue

Giving and receiving are both fraught with danger. *Die schenkende Tugend*, like other virtues, requires courage. Nietzsche read this in Emerson. Certainly a careful reading of the latter's "Gifts" would both help to alter the still popular picture of Emerson as a cheery and superficial sage (humming to God in the forest) and would demonstrate the ground of the elective affinity Nietzsche discovered with the American philosopher. Emerson writes that

> The law of benefits is a difficult channel, which requires careful sailing,
> or rude boats. It is not the office of a man to receive gifts. How dare
> you give them? We wish to be self-sustained. We do not quite forgive a
> giver. The hand that feeds us is in some danger of being bitten. We can
> receive anything from love, for that is a way of receiving it from our-
> selves; but not from any one who assumes to bestow.[6]

For Emerson both giving and receiving entail risks and are capable of multiple forms of perversion and degradation. Giving itself is degraded when
one substitutes a commodity expressly designed to be given for the true
gift. Emerson admonishes us that "Rings and other jewels are not gifts, but
apologies for gifts. The only gift is a portion of thyself. Thou must bleed
for me." He seems to recognize that gift-giving is seen by both giver and
recipient as a sign of power, or of the *Herrschsucht* which for Nietzsche is
its other name. So, for example, "[y]ou cannot give anything to a magnanimous person. After you have served him he at once puts you in debt by his
magnanimity."[7] Gift-giving risks undermining the masks, as Nietzsche calls
them, that are necessary for our protection. In giving a gift one undertakes
the hermeneutical project of discovering what is appropriate to the true
character of the recipient. If I fail to interpret him properly, he will feel that
some violence or degradation has been done; but if the donor succeeds in
reading the heart of the donee the latter may feel that his private space has
been invaded and his very joy at the gift will confirm the donor in his interpretation of the man behind the mask. Some of the bi- or multi-valence of
giving is apparent in Nietzsche's notes from the time of the composition
of *Zarathustra*:

> It's more than a matter of giving: it's also a matter of creating and vio-
> lence [*Vergewaltigen*]!
> The essential thought of the second solitude (beginning of III)
> Our "gifts" [*Geschenke*] are dangerous (*10*, 512)[8]

And in a note entitled "Plan for *Zarathustra* III," he writes ". . . giving
[*das Schenken*] transforms itself—from giving [*Geben*] arose the practice of
forcing someone to receive [*Zwang-zum-Nehmen*]" (*10*, 516). In the next
sentence Nietzsche writes of "the tyranny of the artist," suggesting that in
his giving there is also a withholding and a violent imposition.

Perhaps a large part of the substance of the debt that Nietzsche often
expresses to Emerson is a complex of themes drawn from economic
thought, taken in the most comprehensive sense: debt, gifts, compensation, squandering and the like. The external signs of indebtedness have

often been noted. Nietzsche's notes for *The Gay Science* and for *Thus Spoke Zarathustra* are full of references to Emerson and citations from his *Essays*. Very often the same notebook entry will contain such references along with specific plans for one of these books. Let us explore one of these sketches for it suggests something of the economies of friendship, the gift and the state.

> Zarathustra recognizes that he is also not there for his friends "Who are my friends?" Neither for the people, nor for individuals. *Neither for the many nor for the few! Friendship is to be overcome! Signs* of self-overcoming at the beginning of III.
> Emerson p. 426 description of the wise man. (*10*, 512)

The passage from Emerson's essay "Politics" articulates themes that are recognizable in the published text of *Zarathustra* III.[9] There Zarathustra's long homecoming is portrayed, as he progressively takes his leave of various forms of social and political life with which he first became engaged in going down to men after a ten years' solitude and then in a second sojourn after a dream came to warn him that his teaching was in danger. When Zarathustra the wise finally comes home to himself he rejoices that he no longer needs to speak the distorting language of the crowd (in "The Homecoming") and he struggles silently with his most abysmal thought, after which he breaks out into a series of songs for which there is no audience of friends or spectators. Of the wise man Emerson says that "he has no personal friends" because he has "the spell to draw the prayer and piety of all men unto him," a formula that could describe the way in which the higher men seek out Zarathustra in the last part of Nietzsche's book. The wise man is portrayed as beyond the contractual requirements of the state and the money economy. His "presence" to men takes the form of presents: His relation to men is angelic; his memory is myrrh to them; his presence, frankincense and flowers. In the next few sentences Emerson adds that Malthus and Ricardo, that is, the theorists of political economy, have no way of recording or even suspecting the existence of the "presence" of character. As angelic the wise man is a gift, a luminous visitation. Emerson discusses the nature of this gift in his essay on that subject. Although his advice there that "Flowers and Fruits are always fit presents" may sound like a simpering cliché, the reason adduced is one that shows a rigorous economic logic:

> flowers, because they are a proud assertion that a ray of beauty outvalues all the utilities of the world . . . Fruits are acceptable gifts, because they

are the flower of commodities, and admit of fantastic values being attached to them.[10]

In the same essay, however, Emerson notes that once we give gifts of a more specific nature by which we aim at discerning or matching the particular character of our friends, we enter into a risky business in which the receiver may feel offended either by our failure to understand him or by our having understood him all too well.

Consider the economic thought of Emerson's essay "Compensation" which develops what could be thought of as a general economy of life. The essay begins by arguing against the conventional religious view that there is no justice in this life but that there is an appropriate compensation in the next one. This amounts to a needless doubling of the world, generated by the resentment of those who think that they see the wicked prosper while their own virtue goes unrewarded. It also seems to suggest that the rewards of the virtuous life are simply those things like stocks and champagne that are denied to the poor in this world. Here Emerson provides an account of the creation of a fictitious secondary world resembling the one that Nietzsche gives in the first essay of *Toward a Genealogy of Morals*. It's also suggested that it is possible to affirm this world in all its variety, with its circulation of credits and debits, without reference to anything beyond or outside it: "Being is the vast affirmative, excluding negation, self-balanced and swallowing up all relations, parts and times within itself." What's most remarkable however in the economic doctrine of "Compensation" is Emerson's prescription of what appears to be an inversion of the debtor/creditor analogy as it applies to man and God:

> Put God in your debt. Every stroke shall be repaid. The longer payment
> is withholden, the better for you; for compound interest on compound
> interest is the rate and usage of this exchequer.[11]

The Christian view, as Nietzsche argues in the second essay of *Toward a Genealogy of Morals* is that we owe an immeasurable debt to God, one that could not possibly be repaid. God's grace through Christ is equivalent to writing off a bad debt, but it is a forgiveness that leaves the debtors with the feeling that the debt could not possibly have been repaid through their own efforts. In *The Gay Science* Nietzsche is quoting from Emerson's "Gifts" when he says:

> *Frankincense.*—Buddha says: "Do not flatter your benefactors." Repeat
> this saying in a Christian church: right away it clears the air of every-
> thing Christian. (§142; *3*, 489)[12]

When Zarathustra replies to the hermit "I give no alms. For that I am not poor enough," we can take him to be commenting on such a completely asymmetric relationship of giver and receiver. When one gives alms, for which one expects no return whatsoever, one humiliates the objects of one's charity by placing them in a situation that emphasizes their impotence and incapacity. Zarathustra's remark says, in effect, that the need to establish such an asymmetry is itself a form of poverty, for one who was rich, strong and overflowing would take delight in the contest and circulation of gift-exchange. The call to "Put God in your debt" is the principle of an economy of excess in which one is willing to compete with the wealthiest. Zarathustra's first speech begins by taking the constantly giving sun as his model; the sun gives to excess, but it also provokes responses in the form of growth, flowering and energy.

Zarathustra gives his own discourse on "*Die schenkende Tugend*" when he leaves his disciples (at the end of *Z* I) after the series of speeches he's given in the town called the Motley Cow. In this ceremonial summing up the master takes leave of his disciples and asks them to take leave of him. But not before accepting a farewell gift on this occasion for symbolic exchange. It is "a staff on whose golden handle a serpent coiled around the sun." The golden globe is, I suggest, the ball that Zarathustra threw out in his previous discourse "On Free Death" to open up a game with his disciples. Death, he said, should be a consummation, a festival, a gift for the living. It would be the ultimate expenditure, the blessing given to those who squander themselves. "Verily, Zarathustra had a goal; he threw his ball: now you, my friends, are the heirs of my goal; to you I throw my golden ball" (*Z*, 99; *4*, 95). The postponement of Zarathustra's death is linked to gift-giving and exchange. Before he can die, leaving the disciples in his debt, they return the golden ball, luring their teacher into a game of catch.

Through the gift of the staff, the disciples throw the ball back into Zarathustra's court. It's an appropriate gift for a wanderer and a mountain-climber and the design exhibits careful thought. The teacher shows his delight by putting it to immediate use, leaning on it. He keeps the ball in play and the gift in circulation by interpreting it in order to explain the gift-giving virtue. As Michel Serres says "a ball is not an ordinary object, for it is what it is only if a subject holds it. Over there, on the ground, it is nothing; it is stupid . . . The ball is the quasi-object and quasi-subject by which I am a subject, that is to say, sub-mitted."[13] This back and forth play of the ball, a play that allows us to become subjects, was also the theme of Freud's meditations on play and the repetition compulsion. These ball games can be attempts to master the threat of absence and death by producing a *fort/da* pattern that the subject initiates and sustains.

In the interpretation that Zarathustra tosses back to his disciples he explains that gold has the highest value because it is "uncommon and use-less and shining and mellow in luster" (*Z*, 100; *4*, 97). It is an image of the highest virtue, a parable or metaphor (*Gleichniss*) of the elevation of body and spirit. And just as the disciples had interpreted him through their gift, so he interprets them in his commentary on it: "You thirst to become sacri-fices and gifts yourselves; and that is why you thirst to heap up all riches in your soul . . . You compel all things to come to you and into you, that they may flow back from your fountain as gifts of your love" (*Z*, 100; *4*, 98).

We can distinguish two moments of gift-giving that are only implicitly distinct in the thought of an anthropologist like Mauss. There is a stabiliz-ing dimension, in which a regular series of exchanges and expectations is produced and legitimated. But there is also the dangerous, transgressive aspect, as in the violence of the potlatch, with its valorization of waste, destruction, and expenditure. The first of these is surreptitiously identified as the whole of the practice in Mauss's nostalgic hope for a rebirth of com-munalism in modern society out of the spirit of the gift. Georges Bataille's notion of expenditure, taking its cue from the radicalism of the potlatch, stands in contrast to such utopianism. The second form, which Zarathustra attributes to the disciples, can be seen as the *Umwertung* of the first. In his hermeneutic speech on the meaning of the staff, Zarathustra constructs a proportional metaphor: gold is to the gift-giving virtue as mind and virtue are to the body. This is a classical trope. Before Aristotle had praised the proportional metaphor, Plato had deployed a complex form of it in his story about the sun and the good. Yet Zarathustra's version, again focusing on a golden globe, rejects the Platonic notion of the sun as self-sufficient. If the final term in traditional philosophy and theology is the Good or God, understood as sheer presence, the final term here is the radiant body; but it is not the body as indestructible energy source, but the body that, as Zarathustra tells us, "poetizes and raves and flutters with broken wings" (*Z*, 60; *4*, 36).[14] These are forms of expenditure, of giving as squandering. Zarathustra has transformed the ritualistic scene of giving a gift to an esteemed teacher into an occasion for praise of an unrestricted giving, what Bataille would call *dépense*.

In the second part of the discourse on the gift-giving virtue, Zarathustra commands "let the value of all things be posited newly by you!" (*Z*, 100; *4*, 100). The language of value that Nietzsche so often invokes, in contexts ranging from this one to the project of *Umwertung* itself, is more than the mere residue of the Platonic and metaphysical tradition. Value and valua-tion are set within the context of expenditure and passionate squandering. In the third section of the discourse, Zarathustra admonishes the young men to "lose me and find yourselves." Isn't this also a squandering of his disciples, a willingness to let them be dispersed and disseminated rather than identifying them as his intellectual progeny or property? Later Zarathustra will squander or "waste" the higher men assembled at his cave by simply blowing them away.

III. Heidegger on Values, Nietzsche on Transvaluation

This is perhaps the time to reflect a bit more closely on Heidegger's critical and polemical account of what could be called in the broadest sense Nietzsche's economic philosophy, that is his understanding of value, valuation, revaluation and allied concepts. It's well known that Heidegger sees this entire dimension of Nietzsche's thought as the tragic fulfillment of Western metaphysics. As he says toward the end of the *Introduction to Metaphysics*:

> What seems more plausible than to take Plato's ideas in the sense of values and to interpret the being of *das Seiende* from the standpoint of value? . . .
>
> *At bottom* this being [of values] meant neither more nor less than the presence of something already there, though not in so vulgar and handy a sense as tables and chairs . . .
>
> How stubbornly the idea of values ingrained itself in the nineteenth century can be seen from the fact that even Nietzsche, and precisely he, never departed from this perspective . . . His entanglement in the thicket of the idea of values, his failure to understand its questionable origin, is the reason why Nietzsche did not attain to the true center of philosophy.[15]

In his lectures on Nietzsche, Heidegger tells us that it was Nietzsche who put the word value "into circulation." As Heidegger would no doubt agree, the claim that the word could be put "into circulation" presupposes that there was already a functioning economy of exchange in which the value of key words and ideas can rise and fall.

Now the burden of Heidegger's polemic against thinking in terms of values is fairly clear: values, like the will to power, are one more expression of the demand for presence that has constituted the *hybris* of philosophy since Plato. In his Nietzsche book, Heidegger's most extended discussion of values and transvaluation takes place in the section called "European Nihilism." He devotes several chapters to the analysis of a rather long note, number 12, from *The Will to Power* entitled "Decline of the Cosmological Values." Heidegger pointedly rejects an approach to reading Nietzsche on the question of value that was followed by academic philosophers who produced philosophies and phenomenologies of value. For these misguided scholars

> Values themselves appeared to be things in themselves, which one might arrange into "systems." Although tacitly rejecting Nietzsche's philosophy, one rummaged through Nietzsche's writings, especially *Zarathustra*, for such values. Then, "more scientifically" than the "unscientific philosopher-poet" Nietzsche, one organized them into an "ethics of value."[16]

So Heidegger wants to situate his own reading between the false economy of a scientific, systematic study of values that takes them as presences and the arbitrary, disordered, and therefore wasteful activity of simply reading through the fragments of *The Will to Power* in the editors' order. That those fragments are Nietzsche's own excess and waste, many of which he had consigned to the garbage, adds a certain piquancy to Heidegger's concern for sound, fundamental principles of good business and efficient housekeeping.

The fragment itself, number 12, begins by identifying three factors that contribute to the development of what Nietzsche calls "nihilism as a psychological state." The first of these considerations is introduced as follows:

> Nihilism, then, is the recognition of the long *squandering* [*Vergeudung*] of strength, the agony of the "in vain," the insecurity, the lack of any opportunity to recuperate and to regain tranquillity—being ashamed of oneself, as if one had *deceived* oneself all too long . . .

Nietzsche says that one form of nihilism arises when human beings see that they have *squandered* themselves in such ways that recuperation is no longer possible. That is, it has been supposed that becoming has a goal, and that human actions have specific goals, which may contribute to the larger ones. But "now one grasps the fact that becoming aims at *nothing* and achieves *nothing* . . ." It's the way the reader of Nietzsche might feel after years of poring over the published works, the *Nachlass*, the letters and the personal testimony, only to discover that there was no final insight here, no central concept, no totalistic system, no perspective of all perspectives. One would feel that time, eyesight, money and intellectual energy had been *squandered*. Now in discussing the fragment, Heidegger acutely distinguishes many of the uses of "value" and its derivatives and affiliates. He succeeds in articulating the way that this notion *circulates* in Nietzsche's text. But he has nothing to say about *squandering* as such, even though Nietzsche emphasizes the word and says that its recognition is the first occasion of a certain sort of nihilism—the process by which the highest values devalue themselves and which is the necessary presupposition of an *Umwertung aller Werthe*. We may be reminded here of that absence of commentary, documented in Derrida's *Spurs*, on the phrase "*sie wird Weib*" in Heidegger's performance of *Twilight of the Idols*. Perhaps there is some relation between squandering and becoming woman that would lead to their neglect in Heidegger's bravura close readings.

Squandering, as we have seen already, is thematized in *Zarathustra*'s economic discourse. To the men in the marketplace Zarathustra says "I love him whose soul squanders itself, who wants no thanks and returns none; for he always gives away and does not want to preserve himself." And at the beginning of the fourth part he describes himself as a squanderer. Having just deceived his animals with the ruse that he is going off to perform the honey-sacrifice, he asks:

> Why sacrifice? I squander what is given to me, I a squanderer with a thousand hands: how could I call that sacrificing? (*Z*, 252, *4*, 296)

Clearly squandering (*Verschwenden* or *Vergeudung*) has at least a double value in Nietzsche's texts. From the nihilistic standpoint analyzed in *The Will to Power* 12, squandering is seen as a loss that weakens and exhausts the agent; the recognition of that waste leads to the belief that everything is in vain. Yet Zarathustra's uses of *Verschwenden* and similar terms suggest the Dionysiac joy in destruction, expenditure, and *dépense* which inspired Bataille.

Heidegger does not consider the possibility that a transvaluation of values might also involve rethinking the associations of squandering. Yet while he omits any discussion of this notion, he is careful to emphasize Nietzsche's use of an economic language in the fragment analyzed, especially such terms as "invest" and "withdraw," so that Nietzsche's account of how values are attributed to things and then denied of them begins to sound like the buying and selling of stocks. The bottom line of Heidegger's reading of the fragment on nihilism, and of Nietzsche's general understanding of nihilism, is that that understanding is itself nihilistic because it arises from "valuative thought" (*Wertgedanken*).[17] Yet Heidegger's reading is forced and narrow. In the fragment in question Nietzsche never commits himself to a discourse of value *except* insofar as he is reproducing the point of view of nihilism. It is nihilism for which the world finally "seems *valueless*" after the invested values have been withdrawn. It is "nihilism as a psychological state" that Nietzsche aims at explicating; and in order to do so he impersonates the nihilist who reckons up his profits and losses. Should we then conclude the following with Heidegger?

> There are "results" only where there is reckoning and calculation. In fact Nietzsche's train of thought, as nihilistic, is reckoning [*Rechnen*] . . . To reckon psychologically means to appraise everything on the basis of value and to calculate value on the basis of the fundamental value, will to power—to figure how and to what extent "values" can be evaluated in accord with will to power and so prove valid.[18]

And Heidegger goes on to claim that "the will to power is the object and the subject of a metaphysics thoroughly dominated by valuative thinking."[19] In line with such a reading he places the greatest weight on such phrases as "Principles of a New Valuation" which appear in Nietzsche's notebooks and he understands the project of transvaluation as essentially a reversal of the hierarchy of values rather than construing it (as one might) as a transformation of valuative thinking.

Now it might be supposed that the poetic mode of Nietzsche's "greatest gift" lends itself to an archaicizing tendency in which scraps and memories of premonetary cultures are introduced as part of the fantasmatic time and place of Zarathustra's speeches. But consider then some of the earliest and most fundamental themes of *Beyond Good and Evil*, which Nietzsche describes as the no-saying companion piece to *Zarathustra*. The first chapter is entitled "Of the Prejudices of Philosophers." It is true that Nietzsche opens that chapter by asking what the *value* of truth is, but he immediately demonstrates that such a question must be uncanny in every respect; to take it seriously is to call each of its terms into question. It is an abyssal question, such that once thoughtfully asked we are at a loss to say "Which of us is Oedipus here? Which is the Sphinx?" (§1). One asks about the value of truth here not because value is the last word, retaining its meaning (its value) throughout the uncanny experience of questioning, but because it is a first word, a strategic way of unsettling the unreflective position that truth is of unquestioned value, that we know the value of truth and the truth of value. In the next section Nietzsche claims that "The fundamental belief of metaphysicians is the belief in opposite values" (§2). The true and the false, the real and the apparent, being and becoming: these binary distinctions and more are interrogated and deconstructed in the text that follows. It is, however, not only the belief in "opposites" which is in question, but that in "opposite *values*." Nietzsche then would be questioning the principle according to which, for example, if the value of reality rose the value of appearance would have to fall. But he is also questioning whether the opposition reality/appearance is a helpful or illuminating way of thinking. And, finally, he may also be asking whether there is some other form of value thinking, free of the metaphysical prejudice of opposite values. I suggest that his most coherent and perspicuous strategy is one that would either put the concept of value in question (for what are values that do not admit of opposites?) or that would lead to rethinking it in such a way that it would be radically different from our customary conception of value (for one thing, Nietzsche implies that this would be a non-metaphysical conception of value). In part of his sermon on *die schenkende Tugend,* Zarathustra says: "Truly such a bestowing love must become a robber of all values" (*"Wahrlich, zum Räuber an allen Werthen muss solche schenkende Liebe werden"*). Values then are not the sorts of things that remain constant, in place, or present; the gift-giving virtue can seize and transform them. This is not a discourse of values but an injunction against the primacy of values.

In one sense Heidegger is right in warning us against constructing a "scientific" system of values by rummaging around in *Thus Spoke Zarathustra*. We can anticipate that such systems will have difficulties comprehending the praise of squandering. Although Heidegger does not name these systematizers of value, we could think of Nicolai Hartmann's *Ethics,* published in 1926, which does indeed offer a systematic account of the realm of values. And Hartmann could plausibly be accused of having "rummaged" in *Thus Spoke Zarathustra* for some of these values. For he calls one of his three "self-sufficient virtues" *die schenkende Tugend,* acknowledging that it was without a name until Nietzsche attempted to define it.[20] Yet Hartmann does not explore the uncanny dimension of that "naming the unnameable." For Hartmann *die schenkende Tugend* has to do with what he calls "spiritual gifts"; the law of giving and taking that pertains to such gifts is distinct from that which governs material goods, for he who bestows such gifts is in no way diminished by them. ("Radiant virtue" in the English translation has a tendency to steer us away from the ambivalences of the gift.) Hartmann sees *die schenkende Tugend* as a vast overflowing, a scattering of seeds broadcast (he cites the parable of the sower). Everything about this virtue is admirable and positive; the man who exemplifies it glows like the sun. In the presence of those with this creative genius "all hearts are opened. No one goes away from them except laden with gifts, yet no one can say what he has received."[21] Hartmann enthusiastically endorses Nietzsche's figure of the sun and his praise of uselessness. Yet there is no hint of the ambivalence that one finds in Nietzsche or Emerson in this analysis. Hartmann speaks of this virtue as a "virtue without sacrifice," because "the imparter simply overflows."[22] Zarathustra, however, had told his disciples that they desired to be sacrifices, to spend themselves. And although Hartmann repeats the images of dissemination found in *Zarathustra* (such virtue is like "wind-scattered pollen") he omits any reference to episodes like "The Night Song" in which the giver confesses his limits and his envy of those who receive.[23] And while Hartmann devotes much laborious inquiry into the question of what order of priority obtains among the many values of his phenomenological ethics, he does not seem to have taken seriously Zarathustra's claim that *die schenkende Tugend* is first in the order of rank, or to put it in another fashion, that virtue precedes value. Nor does he have a place for Zarathustra's declarations that *die schenkende Tugend* is a robber of all values and that it is identical with the lust to rule.

We can understand Heidegger's dismissing such procedures and sympathize with his turning to Nietzsche himself, who put the idea of value "into circulation." At the same time we must note the determined way in which Heidegger seeks to show a line of descent from Nietzschean value-thinking to quasi-scientific theories of value or, worse, various thoughtless forms of value-relativism.

We also wish that Heidegger's exploration of the sense of "*es gibt*" could have been enriched by a consideration of the giving and receiving, squandering and sacrificing, spending and expending in *Zarathustra*. Presumably Heidegger would include Nietzsche among those he accuses of a naïve understanding, a thoughtless use of language in "*es gibt.*" No one in the Plato to Nietzsche tradition, Heidegger suggests, has heard the *gift* and the *giving* in "the given." The charge would seem to hold against the dominant tendencies in English language philosophy, although we might want to note some countervailing currents in eccentrics like Emerson and Thoreau (whose *Walden* begins with a long chapter on "Economy"). The Heideggerian account of *es gibt* is bound up with his diagnosis of the metaphysics of presence. Perhaps that metaphysics is already inscribed in our language when we speak of *presenting* something to someone, of making her a *present*. The given, we suppose, is present, just as the gift is a present. Heidegger warned against such a reading of his own "*es gibt.*" In *Being and Time* he had written "Only so long as Dasein is, is there [*gibt es*] Being."[24] In the *Letter on Humanism* there is this clarification: "To be sure. It means that only so long as the lighting of Being comes to pass does Being convey itself to man. But the fact that the *Da*, the lighting as the truth of Being itself, comes to pass is the dispensation of Being itself . . . The sentence does not say that Being is the product of man."[25] That is, it does not say that man produces the presence of Being, as if through the presence of his consciousness.

Heidegger would like us to listen to his language, to take what he has given us in the appropriate way, to be sensitive to his gift. Yet (as Heidegger also knows) to attend to the speaking of language would be to realize that when something is given there is always the possibility that something is held back and the gift that is sent may always fail to reach the one for whom it is destined. If there is giving there is also receiving; gifts may be gratefully acknowledged, accepted only with reservations as the workings of a dominating power, or rejected and scorned by an evil, envious eye. Nietzsche indicates all of these possibilities by means of the complex protocols that accompany the presentation of the great gift of *Zarathustra*. And he does not fail to make use of the possibilities of this sort lurking in the German language in which *Gabe* can be either a gift or a dose and in which *Gift*, which now means poison, once had the sense of our English "gift" or "present." In this light we might read one of Nietzsche's notes from the period of *Zarathustra*'s composition: "'*Es gibt sich*': *sagt eure Bequemlichkeit? Nein, es nimmt sich und wird immer sich nehmen.*" "Does your laziness say 'It gives itself?' No, it is taken and it will always be taken" (*10*, 497). Here Nietzsche seems to respond to the same metaphysical and linguistic naïvete that Heidegger identifies. And he suggests not only that we should hear the giving in the given but that along with the giving there must also be a taking. There is a play of giving and receiving, of presenting and withholding, of presence and absence. In *Zarathustra* this note is taken up and transformed within one of the speeches "Of the Virtue that Makes Small":

> *"Es gibt sich"—das ist auch eine Lehre von Ergebung. Aber ich sage euch, ihr Behaglichen: es nimmt sich und wird immer mehr noch von euch nehmen!*
>
> "It is given"—that is also a doctrine of submission. But I tell you, you comfortable people: *it is taken,* and will be taken more and more from you!

The two forms of the saying vary from the more general, one might say the ontological, to the economic and the hortatory. In German "*es gibt sich*" suggests a certain confidence or expectation, a reliance that things will continue to be given. This is a tone that can also be found in many of Heidegger's discussions of the *es gibt*. Comfort and assurance must be placed in an economy in which their fragility becomes obvious. The "present" is nothing but a moment in such an economy; Nietzsche's coinage "*es nimmt sich*" is a criticism of the metaphysics of presence *avant la lettre*.

Jacques Derrida has already pointed to the obliquity in Heidegger's reading of Nietzsche that circles around property and the gift. In *Spurs* he says:

it is not from an onto-phenomenological or semantico-hermeneutic interrogation that property [*propre*] is to be derived. For the question of the truth of being is not *capable* of the question of property. On the contrary, it falls short of the undecidable exchange of more into less.[26]

And Derrida warns us that we ought not to dispense with "the critical resources of the ontological question" as raised by Heidegger in order to assume that we *know* what property and all of its affiliates "propriation, exchange, give, take, debit, price, etc." are. These are significant remarks for the reading of *Zarathustra*, to the extent that it is these very words and thoughts that are thematized and problematized there. On one level this text with its talk of gift-giving, revenge, envy, squandering and sacrifice may appear to take place on a pre-critical level in which many of the contents of a pre-industrial folk psychology seem to have been incorporated into a poetic production. Yet if we listen to Derrida's warning not to assume that we know what such contents are, we might be open to a reading of Nietzsche that is more responsive to his dangerous and risky gift. Incidentally, it may be worth noting that Mauss had in his way, and at a lesser level of generality, said something similar in his *Essay on the Gift* fifty years before Derrida's *Spurs*. The latter statement—a truly Socratic confession of ignorance—says of the structuralist investigations of recent years what Mauss had said of positivist ethnography and ethnocentric popular views of social practices. Namely, they assume too much, thinking that the laws of property are accessible to us when we hardly know what property is. If these warnings are right, then it may be said that we have hardly begun to read *Thus Spoke Zarathustra* if we do not know what gifts are—gifts, for example such as the one that Zarathustra was carrying down the mountain, the present passed to him in secret by the little old woman, or the gift that Nietzsche addressed to humanity. These *presents* are as difficult for us to understand as *presence* itself, and for much the same reasons.[27]

Notes

1. Friedrich Nietzsche, *Ecce Homo*, trans. Walter Kaufmann (New York: Random House, 1968), p. 219.

2. References to *Z* are to Friedrich Nietzsche, *Thus Spoke Zarathustra*, trans. R. J. Hollingdale (New York: Penguin, 1961); references of the form *1* are to volumes of Friedrich Nietzsche, *Kritische Studienausgabe*, eds. Giorgio Colli and Mazzino Montinari (Berlin: de Gruyter, 1980).

3. Marcel Mauss, *The Gift: Forms and Functions of Exchange in Archaic Societies*, trans. Ian Cunnison (New York: Norton, 1967), pp. 31, 70.

4. Ibid., p. 72.

5. On the concept of envy and the evil eye, see my "Nietzsche on Envy," *International Studies in Philosophy* (1983): 269–76.

6. Ralph Waldo Emerson, "Gifts" in *Essays and Lectures* (New York, 1983), p. 536. EN: Seeabove p. 26.

7. Ibid., p. 537. EN: Reprinted above, p. 27.

8. This same notebook page (*10*, 512) contains a citation from Emerson that Nietzsche employs to sketch Zarathustra's posing of the question, "Who are my friends?"

9. Emerson, "Politics," in *Essays and Lectures*, pp. 567–68.

10. Ibid., p. 535.

11. Ibid., p. 300. On Emerson's economic thought, see Richard A. Grusin. "'Put God in Your Debt': Emerson's Economy of Expenditure," *PMLA* (January 1988): 35–44. Discussions of Nietzsche's reading of and use of Emerson are to be found in Eduard Baumgarten, *Das Vorbild Emersons im Werk und Leben Nietzsches* (Heidelberg: C. Winter, 1957); Stanley Hubbard, *Nietzsche und Emerson* (Basel: Verlag für Recht und Gesellschaft, 1958); Walter Kaufmann, "Translator's Introduction," Friedrich Nietzsche, *The Gay Science* (New York: Random House, 1974), pp. 7–13.

12. In "Gifts," Emerson writes: "It is a very onerous business, this of being served, and the debtor naturally wishes to give you a slap. A golden text for these gentlemen is that which I so admire in the Buddhist who never thanks, and who says, 'Do not flatter your benefactors'" (*Essays and Lectures*, p. 532).

13. Michel Serres, *The Parasite*, trans. Lawrence R. Schehr (Baltimore: Johns Hopkins University Press, 1982), pp. 225, 227.

14. Cf. also my discussion of the metaphorics of this chapter in *Nietzschean Narratives* (Bloomington: Indiana University Press, 1989), pp.53–59.

15. Martin Heidegger, *An Introduction to Metaphysics*, trans. Ralph Manheim (New York: Anchor, 1961), pp. 166–67.

16. Martin Heidegger, *Nietzsche, Volume IV: Nihilism*, trans. Frank A. Capuzzi and ed. David Farrell Krell (New York: Harper and Row, 1982), p. 59.

17. Ibid., p. 22.

18. Ibid., p. 48.

19. Ibid., p. 53.

20. Nicolai Hartmann, *Ethics, Volume II: Moral Values*, trans. Stanton Coit (New York: Macmillan, 1932), pp. 332–40.

21. Ibid., p. 336.

22. Ibid., pp. 334–35.

23. Ibid., p. 338.

24. Martin Heidegger, *Sein und Zeit*, (Tübingen: Niemeyer, 1984), p. 212.

25. Martin Heidegger, *Basic Writings*, ed. David Farrell Krell (New York: Harper and Row, 1977), p. 216.

26. Jacques Derrida, *Spurs: Nietzsche's Styles*, trans. Barbara Harlow (Chicago: University of Chicago Press, 1979), pp. 111, 113.

27. This essay is a shorter and slightly revised version of the chapter "On Presents and Presence: The Gift in *Thus Spoke Zarathustra*," in *Alcyone: Nietzsche on Gifts, Noise, and Women* (Albany: State University of New York Press, 1991); see also my essay "Debts Due and Overdue: Beginnings of Philosophy in Nietzsche, Heidegger, and Anaximander," in Richard Schacht, ed. *Nietzsche, Genealogy, Morality* (Berkeley: University of California Press, 1994) for a discussion of related themes in Nietzsche's and Heidegger's readings of the saying of Anaximander.

Partners and Consumers: Making Relations Visible

Marilyn Strathern

At the 1990 meetings for the British Association for the Advancement of Science, an experimental embryologist expounded an expert's view to a lay audience.[1] Martin Johnson was concerned to demonstrate the continuity of biological process. A person's birth begins with primitive gametes laid down when one's parents were embryos in the grandparental womb. Subsequent development depends not only on genetic coding but on extragenetic influences that operate on chromosomes from the start; these include stimulation from material enveloping the egg,[2] as well as nutritive and other effects derived from placenta and uterus.

It was a powerful origin story,[3] especially in the context of current legislative decisions with respect to the Human Fertilization and Embryology Act (1990). Here, however, the problem has been to formulate discontinuities between developmental phases. The House of Commons decided that research on human embryos is permissible up to fourteen days, by which time, among other things, the pre-embryonic material is now discernably divided into those cells that will form the future embryo-fetus and those that will form the placenta. The Secretary for Health was reported as saying that status as an individual could begin only at the stage where cells could be differentiated.[4] Yet while biology appeared to provide an index,[5] the further problem of personhood raised the same notion of continuous process. Another member of the Commons pointed out: "It is a very difficult matter to say at what stage do you have a citizen, a human being. At various stages fresh rights are acquired."[6] Rights can only be acquired of course, in this view, if there is an individual person to bear them.[7]

Here are experts informing lay persons (the BAAS talk), experts informing experts (the Secretary for Health is briefed on what the fourteen-day stage means), and lay persons (Members of Parliament) turning expert in making legislative decisions. An anthropologist might wish to bracket all of them lay insofar as they promote a common view of the person that, in his/her eyes, must have the status of a folk model. For the anthropological expert, "person" is an analytic construct whose utility is evinced through cross-cultural comparison. One draws, as always, from one's culture of origin, but to be an expert in anthropology is to demonstrate simultaneously the cultural origins of one's analytic constructs and their cross-cultural applicability.

A person cannot in this sense be seen without the mediation of analysis. Yet those who discuss the potential personhood of the embryo implicitly contest such an appropriation of the concept. Visual representations of first the division of cells and then the human form as it takes shape regularly accompany not just talks designed to popularize the findings of science but attempts to make vivid the political issues at stake.[8] Indeed, a flurry of fascination/repulsion was created by the Society for the Protection of the Unborn Children which in April (while the Act was still in debate) sent all 650 MPs a life-sized model of a twenty-week-old fetus. This parody of the ubiquitous free gift was intended to mobilize a parallel concern over the limit for legal abortions. The plastic fetus lifted out from a sectional womb,[9] and its message was clear. One can "see" a (potential) person, and a person is known by its individuality. Individuality in turn means a naturally entire and free-standing entity: the claim was that at twenty weeks a fetus is a viable whole.

Between the anthropologist as expert and the layperson with his or her folk model lies more than an epistemological issue over what is usefully designated a "person"; there is an ontological issue over the nature of the category. The anthropologist is dealing with a category that refers to certain analytical constructions. The laity may argue over what they see and what they call it but take for granted that the category refers to persons existing as visible and substantial entities. So while it may be hard to tell when a person begins, and while the law may have to define the stages at which rights accrue, it seems self-evident that the subject of these debates is a concrete human being. The anthropologist is not, of course, untouched by this cultural certitude.

Now for "person" one could write "gift." That concept was drawn into anthropology from various domains of Western or Euro-American discourse (economy, theology, and so forth) though its most notable proponents made out of the indigenous connotation of presentations voluntarily made an analytical category that also included the social fact of obligation. The point is that the concept of gift seemed readily applicable to self-evident and concrete "gifts." The term trailed a reassuring visualism. One could "see" gift exchange because one could see the gifts, the things that people exchanged with one another. It also trailed a concern, as Panoff, Parry, and others have noted, with individual autonomy (voluntarism) and interpersonal relations measured by degrees of interestedness (altruism).[10]

As an anthropologist I am crippled, so to speak, by expertise—by the desire to appropriate the category "gift" in a special way, insofar as those negotiations of relationships known as gift exchange in Melanesia have a character whose uniqueness I would be reluctant to relinquish. I say crippled to the extent that this position appears to set up barriers. Blind: I do not believe the evidence of my eyes, that one will recognize a gift when one sees it. Constricted: I cannot stride across the world map looking for gifts at all times and places. The wrong color: monochrome rather than polychrome, for exhilarating as the company of other disciplines can be, I lose appropriative capability, feel very lay in the presence of other expertise. Other knowledge does not necessarily repair deficiencies in one's own. Not something that concerns Melanesians, one should add for they borrow from foreigners all the time, including the most intimate powers of reproduction.

Melanesians borrow origin stories, wealth, and—as in the area I know best (Mount Hagen)—the expertise by which to organize their religion and their future. One clan takes from another its means of life. Indeed, exchanges surrounding the transfer of reproductive potential are intrinsic to the constitution of identity. From a clan's point of view, foreign wives are drawn to them by virtue of bridewealth, and such items of wealth are themselves considered to have reproductive potential. Pigs create pigs and money creates money, as shell valuables also reproduce themselves, an idea given visible form in the iconography that developed with the influx of pearlshells into the Hagen area at the time of contact. Shells for circulation in gift exchange were mounted on resin boards vividly colored with red ochre. The whole appeared a free-standing entity. But it was not an image of one. Rather than plastic molding a visible homunculus, the child/embryo in its netbag/womb was indicated in the abstract by the curvature of the shell crescent, and the resin molded a container around it.[11]

Personalized Commodities?

In taking off from some of the expert discourse of Melanesian anthropology, I confine myself to certain issues in the understanding of gifts, namely those concerned with reproduction and the life cycle. It is arguable that all Melanesian gift exchanges are "reproductive," but I make a more restricted point. The reason is to provide an approximation of the indigenous Euro-American understanding of gifts as "transactions within a moral economy, which [make] possible the extended reproduction of social relations."[12] This account ignores those aspects of the Melanesian gift that have seemed most strange to the twentieth-century Westerner (competition and the political striving for prestige), in order to focus on the apparently familiar (the celebration of kinship).

From the perspective of the Papua New Guinea Highlands, of the kind that Lederman has described for Mendi,[13] I thus appear to privilege one nexus of gifting (kinship-based) over another (clan-based). Or, more accurately, to evoke one type of sociality, for it is also arguable that each set of relations transforms the moral base of the other. But my interest is not in the relative moralities of exchanges.[14] It is in whether Melanesian gifting can illuminate the very idea of there being part-societies ("moral economies") that "typically consist of small worlds of personal relationships that are the emotional core of every individual's social experiences" (*GE* 15).

Whatever parallels might be useful for earlier European materials,[15] in the late twentieth century any understandings of such part-societies must in turn be put into their specific Euro-American context: consumer culture. Cheal himself goes on to give a consumerist definition of sociality. Everywhere (he says) people live out their lives in small worlds; the primitive (he says) because the societies were small, the modern because people "prefer to inhabit intimate life worlds" (*GE* 15)[!].[16] Now recent anthropological discussion of the gift has turned, among other things, on the analytic advantage of distinguishing gift-based economies from commodity-based ones. Gregory has been notable here,[17] and while his arguments explicated the contrast between gifts and commodities in terms of production, they have also opened up the question of consumption. In the formula he adopts, it is through consumption that things are drawn into the reproduction of persons, and reproduction can be understood as a process of personification. But consumption as a universal analytic is one thing. I take my own cue from the further fact that we live in a self-advertised "consumer" culture.

A consumer culture is a culture, one might say, of personalization. And to Euro-Americans, gift-giving seems a highly personalized form of transaction. After all, it was the person in the gift that attracted anthropological attention to the concept in the first place. But whether useful parallels can be drawn between the personalizations of consumerism and the personifications of Melanesian gift exchange remains to be seen.

Free-standing Entities

The notorious individualism of Western culture has always seemed an abstraction of the state or of the market economy that lies athwart those concrete persons we recognize in interactions with others. No one is really an isolate. This was a point the embryologist wanted to get across, and for which he offered biological reasoning.

Johnson was concerned to demonstrate the influence of the environment in all stages of fetal development. Its significance for him lies in its contribution to the identity of the emergent individual: personal identity is the outcome not just of a unique genetic combination but of a unique history of continuous development which affects the way genetic factors themselves take effect. The organism is a finite and discrete entity; the process is continuous. Thus, he opined, an individual is always in interaction with its environment. This provoked a comment from the gynecologist Modell who observed that, as far as the embryo is concerned, the environment is immediately the mother and the mother is *another person*. Among other things, the embryo undergoes the effects of the parent's changing perceptions of it.

The point slid by without much comment. What I see in that interchange is more than a dispute among experts, for it barely registered as a dispute. It epitomized the simultaneous delineation of a hegemonic model (of personhood) and the possibility of contesting it, somewhat parallel to the manner in which anthropologists have extricated the idea of gift from hegemonic understandings in Western culture in order to contest either the application of these understandings to non-Western cultures or the dominance of the model in people's lives.[18] Modell's mild intervention sounded, in fact, almost like a version of critiques well rehearsed through the contested notion of rights in abortion debates. The right of the mother against the right of the child presents a contest of alternatives.[19] However, I wish to make a different kind of contest appear.

Johnson's idea of the individual person doubly defined by genetic programming and by environmental factors seems a solution to the old nature/nurture debate: we have, so to speak, put the individual back into its "environment," in much the same way as social scientists are perpetually putting individuals back into "society." This is an individualism that gives full recognition to the context in which persons flourish, and we may read off from the image of the embryo an image of the individual person in a responsive, interactive, and creative mode with the external world. Indeed, it is colloquial English to speak of an individual's "relationship" to its environment as we do of an individual's "relationship" to society.

But what a bizarre coupling! The whole person is held to be a substantial and visible entity. The environment, on the other hand, like society, is regularly construed as existing in the abstract, for it cannot be seen as a whole.[20] We may concretize the environment through examples of its parts, as uterus or as trees and mountains, as we may concretize society through referring to groups and institutions. But there was more to Johnson's purpose. He wished to convey how it is potentially *everything* beyond the individual person that may influence that unique person and help make it what it is. The forces that continuously shape us are always, as he comments elsewhere, both genetic and epigenetic, and "epigenetic" is the biologist's catchall "for everything else besides the genes."[21] I would add that this makes the latter of a different order from the former precisely insofar as they are imagined, hypothetically and thus abstractly, as infinite. "Myriad" is his word; the environment consists in this view of the sum of all the factors that might have an effect.

The view against which Johnson argues would hold that the whole and finite individual is determined largely by its genetic programming. But rather than contest, perhaps we should see analogy between the conceptualizations here. Suppose the concept of the genetic program were analogous to that of the individual, then the concept of epigenetic forces would appear analogous to that of environment/society. In turn, the relationship between genetic and epigenetic forces that Johnson postulates would be seen to miniaturize or replicate commonsense understandings of that between individual organism and enveloping world. And the interest of Modell's remark would be in the way it cut across the analogies. For she displaced the image of a (finite, concrete) person contextualized by an (infinite, abstract) society/environment with another image: the exterior world imagined as another (finite, concrete) person.

She thus gave voice to a capability that also rests in English: of imagining a world that does not imagine such abstractions for itself, where sociality impinges in the presence of other persons. English speakers readily enough personify the agency of "society" or even "environment," though they would be hard put to think of these entities as persons. Yet that is exactly the way in which they might imagine that Melanesians imagine the world beyond themselves.[22] What contains the child is indeed "another person," whether that other person is the mother, or the clan that nurtures its progeny, or the land that nurtures the clan and receives a fertilizing counterpart in the burial of the placenta. This other person may be regarded as the cause or origin of the effective agency of those it contains.[23]

When Euro-Americans think of more than one person, they are faced with the disjunction of unique individuals and overcome this in the notion that individuals "relate" to one another. What lies between them are relationships, so that society may be thought of as the totality of made relationships. That relationships are made further supposes that what are linked are persons as individual subjects or agents who engage in their making: "[i]nterpersonal dependence is everywhere [!] the result of socially constructed ties between human agents" (*GE* 11). The idea of persons in the plural evokes, then, the image of the interactions between them, in turn the immediate social environment for any one of them.

It is because society is likened to an environment that it is possible for Euro-Americans to think of individual persons as relating not to other persons but to society as such, and to think of relations as after the fact of the individual's personhood rather than integral to it. Or so the folk model goes. Anthropologists, for their part, have captured the category of person to stand for subjects understood analytically in the context of social relations with others. In the particular way she/he looks to making "society" visible,[24] the anthropologist would be scandalized at the idea of a nonrelation definition of persons.

The analytical necessity appears to have been given by just such societies as are found in Melanesia. Indeed, the anthropological experience may be that in such societies everything is relational. Certainly Melanesians constantly refer to the acts and thoughts of other persons. But if they seemingly situate themselves in a world full of what we call "social relationships," such relationships do not link individuals. Rather, the fact of relating forms a background sociality to people's existence, out of which people work to make specific relationships appear.[25] Relations are thus integral to the person or, in Wagner's formulation,[26] persons may be understood fractally: their dimensionality cannot be expressed in whole numbers. The fractal person is an entity with relationships integrally implied. Any scale of social activity mobilizes the same dimensionality of person/relation.

There is no axiomatic evaluation of intimacy or closeness here. On the contrary, people work to create divisions between themselves. For in the activation of relations people make explicit what differentiates them.[27] One may put it that it is the relationship between them that separates donor from recipient or mother from child. Persons are detached, not as individuals from the background of society or environment, but from other persons. However, detachment is never final, and the process is constantly recreated in people's dealings with one another. To thus be in a state of division with respect to others renders the Melanesian person dividual.

Persons are not conceptualized, therefore, as free-standing. A Hagen clan is composed of its agnates and those foreigners detached from other clans who will give birth to its children; a woman contains the child that grows through the acts of a man; shells are mounted on the breast. One person may "carry" another, as the origin or cause of its existence and acts. An implicate field of persons is thus imagined in the division or dispersal of bodies or body parts.[28] From their viewpoint, Western Euro-Americans cannot readily think of bodies and body parts as the substance of people's interactions. They can imagine objects flowing between persons "as though" they "symbolized" body parts, but for them to discover that a shell is like a fetus in a womb is simply to uncover an image, a metaphorical statement about (say) fertility. So let me return to the embryologist's address and to a moment when he seemed at a loss for a metaphor.

During his presentation, Johnson flashed on the screen a picture of twin babies with their common placenta between them. The three were genetically identical, he briefly observed. Three what? One may fill in the silence, that of course they were not three persons, for only the twins, not the placenta, would grow into autonomous subjects. The placenta is regarded as a source of support, at once part of the fetus and part of the fetus's environment, yet only through detachment from it is the individual person made;[29] the picture included the cut cords and the scissors that cut them. Not at all how the Melanesian 'Are'Are of Malaita in the Solomon Islands would see it. There the placenta both remains part of the person and, in becoming detached at birth, is treated as another person. Detachment is conceptualized as a separation of (dividual) persons from one another.

De Coppet describes how the placenta is buried in ancestral land, linking the living person to a network of ancestral funeral sites and returning to source two vital parts of personal substance.[30] It is planted like a dead taro that has lost its living stem (the baby); taro denotes "body." The 'Are'Are placenta is also referred to as the baby's pig, an allusion to animate "breath." (What the placenta lacks is a third part, the ancestral "image" that adults assume when they die naturally, that is, are killed by their own ancestors; the unimaged placenta is buried somewhat after the manner of an unimaged murder victim.) Pig and taro assure the vitality of the living child; it is also expected that scavenging pigs will eat the buried placenta and that taro will grow there. The land that nourishes the food that nourishes the child is also constituted of what constitutes the living person and is a cause of its life. 'Are'Are personify the land, territorialize the person. When one understands how the land owns people, de Coppet was told,[31] one can understand how people own land.

This relationship to the land is not quite the same as the English-speaking conceptualization of a (concrete) person's relationship to the (abstract) environment/society. For the 'Are'Are person (land) thereby *enters into an exchange* with the land (person). If your placenta has been buried, "it proves that, in return for your life, through the land, you have given back the share of 'body' and 'breath' which must rejoin the universal circulation."[32]

It is for such a world as this, where persons' actions always seem to be caused by or elicited by other "persons," that the borrowed concept of the gift captures what a Westerner would sense as a pervasive sociality. It seems just the formula to emphasize the personal nature of interpersonal relations. Perhaps that is because gifts in turn typify a sector of Western culture which seemingly parallels the pervasive sociality of Melanesian life: the close interpersonal relations of kinship and friendship. Here one gives and takes on an intimate basis. Yet the appearance of similarity is, inevitably, misleading. Euro-American intimacy is signaled by two constructs peculiar to it, altruism and voluntarism.

Altruism: Donors and Partners

Advances in reproductive medicine that have highlighted artificial mechanisms to assist procreation have also heightened certain Western perceptions of the interaction between procreating partners. Thus in the context of discussing artificial insemination by donor Sissa recalls the assumption "that semen is donated, the uterus only loaned."[33] That paternity should in addition be thought a matter of opinion, maternity a matter of fact, turns not on the certainty about donation but on certainty about social identity. It is because semen has the appearance of a (visible) detachable bodily substance that it seems alienable. Because it is alienable, its source may be in doubt. Both the substantial nature of semen and the asymmetry of the relationship between semen and uterus (individual and environment) present an inverse of the supposition found in Aristotle, that semen provided form and maternal blood the substance of the child. The potency of semen in this ancient view was that it was efficacious in the way a craftsman's activities were efficacious; it had an activating force on female blood but did not contribute particles of matter to the embryo. The movement of the male body, the act of donation, constituted the male part in procreation.[34]

Sissa draws the inevitable parallel with the Trobriands, between the multiple fathering made possible by insemination by donor and the fact (as she puts it) that the Trobriand child has two fathers, one whose semen molds somatic identity and one (the mother's brother) who defines the kin group to which the child belongs. Yet the parallel is a poor one, since the social identity of the Trobriand father is integral to his somatic role, whereas in the case of DI knowing the father's identity is both optional and after the fact of the donation. Donation linking a person to a source of genetic endowment does not necessarily link the person to another person. Indeed, twentieth-century people who talk of semen "donation" treat it as a substance that will fertilize the maternal egg *whether or not* its identity is known. This is the crux. Semen is potentially alienable (from the body), I suggest, because of the possibility of its being produced without being elicited by another person. This is, in turn, a general conceptual possibility, regardless of whether or not DI is at issue, captured in its visual representation as a detachable substance.[35] DI adds the further conceptual possibility that conception need not be accompanied by bodily movement; movement is only required to produce the semen. Sissa points out that Aristotle's emphasis on the transcendent and nonsubstantial aspect of the semen led him to assert it could never be frozen, whereas twentieth-century people keep frozen specimens in banks for future use.

Nonetheless, the new reproductive technologies have repaired some of the asymmetry, for it would seem that "egg donation" has passed into the lay imagination as a process analogous to semen donation.[36] Anonymity may or may not be preserved. In the case of maternal surrogacy, however, a partnership of a kind has to be set up between the commissioning couple and the surrogate mother. People talk crudely of womb-renting, or more delicately of the gift of life.[37]

Donation is here conceptualized in two ways. On the one hand it may simply involve an act of bodily emission intended for an anonymous recipient; on the other hand it may involve a relationship between donors and recipients as partners in a single enterprise. This corresponds to the double conceptualization of sociality in consumer culture, as much a matter of an individual's relationship to society in the abstract as of interaction between concrete persons.

The terminology of donation and gift is seemingly encouraged by clinical and other experts by virtue of this double evocatory power. It evokes the charitable altruism of blood and organ donors; it also evokes the intimate altruism of transactions that typify personal relations outside the market. (1) Organ donors can give anonymously because human organs are regarded as anonymous: kidneys differ in physical condition rather than social identity.[38] Such organs or materials as can be excised or secreted from the body become freestanding entities. So although semen carries formative genetic material that will contribute to a person's identity, it is also possible to think of contributing one's part to a general supply. Donation here carries connotations of the charitable gesture, the personal sacrifice for the public good, a gift to society. (2) Alternatively, sometimes in the case of egg donation and certainly of willingness to carry a child, altruism may be embedded in specific relations. A partnership is created between donor and recipient. An egg donated from a close relative can thus be regarded as belonging to a relationship that already exists, an expression of love. The carrying mother, related or not, is regarded as sacrificing comfort and ease in order to enable others to have children; because of the nature of her labor and the attempt to protect such acts from commercial exploitation, as in the case of charity the language of gift-giving becomes the language of altruism.

But do these gestures and does this language constitute a gift economy? Cheal has argued exactly this in examining the nexus of present-giving among friends and relatives, as at Christmas and birthdays, in suburban Canada (see GE). Gifts indicate community membership (the reproduction of social status) as well as relations of intimacy. In either case, they symbolize the central values of a "love culture," he argues, whether the love is generally or specifically directed. We encounter here the same double: gifts for society and gifts for persons. Cheal introduces a further distinction between the immediate society of the moral economy (his "small world," the real community) and the further society of the political economy. Gifts make gestures of altruism within, it would seem, the near society, whereas the far society is seen as a realm of commerce. It is in their immediate circles that persons "make" relationships as they "make" love, and community-giving is a diffuse, impersonal version of intimacy-giving.

While I would dispute neither the evocation of emotions and (society-near) relational behavior among friends and relatives nor the way this mobilizes conventions distinct from those that regulate other (society-far) areas of life, I add one comment: *the circulation of gifts does not create distinct kinds of persons.* "Gifts" (presents) are free-standing entities just like commodities, alienable, as Cheal says. Indeed the person who purchases a present to give to a friend simply puts in reverse the same process which makes it possible for him/her to donate body substance to a blood bank, cadaver to science. An anonymously-produced object becomes part of a store on which others draw. Preserving the social anonymity of market goods is of course fundamental to the supposition that goods are available for all. That such goods can be appropriated by the consumer and fashioned to the ends of personal identity[39]—the wrapped present, the exhibited taste—is part of the cultural interpretation of consumption as consumerism.[40]

While they may express personal identity, *goods do not have to be made into gifts* in order to do so. Gifts between persons can make statements about relationships, yet a relationship is not necessary to the creation of identity. The analogy with reproductive process is evident: genetic identity does not imply a social relationship.

As I understand it, what Euro-Americans call gifts in late twentieth-century consumer culture, whether body substance or merchandise, are regarded as extensions of the self insofar as they carry the expression of sentiments. Sentiments are commonly expressed toward other persons, but they may equally well be directed to abstract entities such as "society." For sentiments emanate outwards from the person, *whether or not they are "received" by specific others.* They thus appear as the person would like to appear, autonomous, charitable. Sentiment is supposed to have positive connotations in the same way as near relations are supposed to be benign, and presents carry positive overtones of sociability and affection. Hence Cheal's closeted language of community and intimacy.

Indeed, the kinds of presents Cheal describes are like the "goods" of classical economy: objects of desire. It is individuals, he observes, who give and receive goods and who reproduce their relations with others, though they do so, I would add, from their own vantage point (of desire). Cheal himself offers a comparison (*GE* 10); he takes the free disposition of items as distinguishing the gift in the moral economy of suburban Canada from those reciprocities allegedly described by Gregory that put people into a state of (his term not Gregory's) bondage.[41] It is the alienability of the former that confers freedom. The sentiment such items express springs from within the individual person, and it is the flow of sentiment (the ideology of love) that makes relationships. As a consequence Euro-American gift-giving really only works as a sign of personal commitment if it is also a sign of benign feeling. Benign feeling in turn is presented as an attribute of the small-scale, with its dialectic of intimacy and community. This confident equation of the small-scale with the interpersonal is, to say the least, an interesting cultural comment on the dimensions of persons.

Where the cycling of gifts among kin effects the procreation and regeneration of relationships, this can comprise activity of a cosmic order. Consider the Melanesian Sabarl on the eastern tip of the Massim archipelago.[42] Not only is this tiny dialect group of fewer than a thousand people able to account for the beginning of time, their gift exchanges are of universal dimensions. No part-societies here; the entire system of production, distribution, and consumption is a process of personification "that converts food and objects and people into other people."[43] And society does not exist apart from other people; rather, persons are of global dimensions, sociality integral to them. This is made evident by their parentage. A person is forever a dependant with respect to his or her father's clan, with whom he/she is involved in a lifetime of exchanges. Dependency is conceptualized in terms of specific relations: a member of the father's clan acts as a designated "father" to the eternal "child" whom he "feeds," an activity that lasts from conception till burial when it must be stopped.[44] In this matrilineal society, paternal kin are keepers of mortality and the father's donations have effect (only) for as long as the child lives. This is no more nor less "bondage" than one might say one is a slave to life or, in Aristotle's terms, a victim of paternal motility.

The partner in such exchanges is always another and specific person. Gifts are never free-standing: they have value because they are attached to one social source ("father") in being destined for another ("child") and, whether they originate in labor or in other transactions, carry identity. Yet when all such encounters are interpersonal encounters, they convey no special connotations of intimacy. Nor of altruism as a source of benign feeling.

The Western notion of persons being contained by their environment/society is indeed significant here, though not quite for Johnson's reasons. It enables Euro-Americans to think of the gift as altruistic by the conceivable analogy of a gesture toward exactly such abstract entities.[45] Altruistic gestures toward other persons are invariably tempered by the aftereffect of realizing that one's own self-interest must be bound up somewhere, if only in maintaining one's (social) environment. Conversely, it is possible to think of gifts as voluntarily given despite social pressure and obligation precisely because they conventionally typify those relations that are made through the spontaneous emission of emotions.

Voluntarism: Recipients and Consumers

Consumer culture, it would seem, springs from the perpetual emanations of desire held to radiate from each individual person. This wellspring is like the bottomless pit of need that Euro-Americans are also supposed to suffer, such as the celebrated biological need for women to have children—a "drive to reproduce."[46] In meeting need and desire, the individual person expresses the essential self. A rhetoric of accumulation is thus bound to the voluntarism of individual effort. One might remark that the constant necessity for the individual to implement his or her subjectivity has its own coercive force.

If there is a similarity between the coercions of gift-giving in Melanesia and late-twentieth-century consumerism, then we may indeed find its echo in the desire/drive/need for the individual to act as a free agent. With two differences. One, that on the Melanesian side the need is located not in the agent but in those "other persons" who cause the agent to act. Two, that Melanesian accumulation is tempered by the fact that acts, like relations, work to substitutive effect. Relations are not perpetually "made." Rather, relations are either made to appear or appear in their making; every new relationship displaces a former one. Each gift is a substitution for a previous gift. One extracts from another what one has had extracted from oneself. Thus de Coppet points to the chain of transformations that constitute the common task on which 'Are'Are society is based. An endless process of perpetual dissolution by which "objects, animals, persons, or elements of persons" change continuous decay into life.[47]

As elsewhere in Austronesian-speaking Melanesia,[48] a death divides survivors into mourners (feast givers) and workers (who bury the deceased and are feasted). In 'Are'Are each side makes a pile of food, topped with money, which reconstitutes the dead person. Not only do both piles incorporate food items from the other, the two piles are then exchanged. They replace the deceased with a composition both of the relations once integral to him or her, and of his or her basic elements, "body" (taro and coconut), "breath" (pork), and "image" (money). These replacements enable the deceased's body/breath to be consumed, later themselves replaced by a further display composed entirely of money. First the workers take charge of it, then reassemble it for the mourners (the deceased's family) to dispose of; the latter return all the wealth received in the course of the funeral and thereby complete the final element, the ancestor's image.[49] The new ancestor is now accessible to his living descendants.

De Coppet refers to "replacement" rather than substitution,[50] which for him carries too many resonances of displacing one individual object by another. Yet, as we have seen, what are also replaced are not just the elements that compose an individual but the relationships of which the person is composed. A relationship is "replaced" through the substitution of a counterpart. The point is explicit in Battaglia's account of Sabarl mortuary ritual, where the actions of mourning and burial mobilize the respective maternal and paternal kin of the deceased. That person is visibly reconstituted in the assembling of funeral foods (sago pudding) and wealth (axe blades), simultaneously semen and bones being returned by maternal kin to the paternal.

These are gifts of life. Life is given in the necessity to consume the deceased as a physical presence and thus release the future—the ancestor to future descendants—from present relationships. As a consequence, the relations that composed and supported the deceased must be made finally visible. Most importantly, in the course of the funeral feasts, relations between maternal and paternal kin appear in the division between donors and recipients. The "father" makes a final presentation of axe blades; maternal kin then substitute for these blades of their own and hand back the items with increment. But more than this. Food and valuables are composed into an image of the deceased before being given to the paternal kin. The Sabarl deceased is thus rendered into a form at once visible (in the abstract) and dissoluble (in its substance): its components can be consumed or dissipated. "[P]eople consume other people."[51] The dead die because the link between persons out of which the person was born is dissolved.

Insofar as one might imagine elements of this exchange sequence as involving the transfer of gifts, the obligation to receive cannot be reduced to the enactment of any one particular exchange. For the person to die, relationships must be undone. And once the person has died, paternal kin on Sabarl can no more avoid being the recipients of funeral gifts than the maternal body in Western discourse can avoid bearing a child.

Sabarl recipients are also consumers: that is, they turn these things (food, valuables) into their own bodies (to be eaten, distributed). Similarly de Coppet suggests that 'Are'Are life is dominated by the fact that it is one's own kin who have the ultimate right to consume one, body and breath being thereby absorbed back into body and breath to be available for future generations. The capacity to consume is thus the capacity to substitute future relations for past ones. It depends on a double receptivity—to reabsorb parts of oneself and to be open to the (body) parts of others. The difference between death and life is the absence or presence of such relationships with "other" persons.

The Melanesian recipient of a gift who puts wealth into the recesses of a house, as a clan contains the external sources of its fertility within, is literally "consuming" the gift. But the vitalizing power of the gift lies in the fact that it derives from an exogenous source. One attaches and contains the parts of specific others, for the process of attachment and detachment is the motility that signals life. Actions are registered (fractally) in the actions of other persons, each person's acts being thereby replaced, reconstituted, in new and even foreign persons/forms. Thus is the living person personified.

By contrast, the latter-day Euro-American consumer draws from an impersonal domain, such as the market, goods that, in being turned into expressions of self-identity, become personalized. The exercise of choice is crucial; choice creates consumption as a subjective act. To evince subjectivity is to evince life. One may even appear to exercise "more" subjectivity in some situations/relationships than in others. This rather bizarre notion—that ideally one ought always to act as a subject but cannot always do so—is symbolized in the special domain of interpersonal relations.

The Euro-American person is presented, then, as a potentially free-standing and whole entity (an individual subject or agent) contained within an abstract impersonal matrix which may include other persons but also includes other things as its context (environment/society). And this is the image of the consumer. Consumer choice is thinkable, I would suggest, precisely insofar as "everything else" is held to lie beyond the fetus/embryo/person: *anything consumed by that person comes from the outside*, whether or not the source is other persons. For generative power lies in the individual person's own desire for experience. Desire and experience: the principal dimensions of the consumer's relationship with his/her environment. And the field is infinite; it consists of the sum of all the possibilities that may be sampled. Satisfied from without, the impetus is held to spring from within.[52] While individual desires may be stimulated by the outside world—advertising, marketing, and so forth—that in turn is supposed to be oriented to the consumer's wants.

Whereas the Melanesian capacity to receive has to be nurtured in and elicited from a partner, sometimes to the point of coercion, the twentieth-century consumer is depicted as having infinite appetite. Above all, the consumer is a consumer of experience and thus of him/her self. Perhaps it is against the compulsion of appetite, the coercion of having to choose, the prescriptiveness of subjective self-reference, that the possibility of unbidden goods and unanticipated experiences presents itself as exotic. The "free gift."

My assertions have no doubt resisted certain commonsense formulations (one cannot see a gift) only to substitute others (we know what a consumer is). And to suggest that the issues which the concept of the gift trails through anthropological accounts—a relational view of the person, altruism, voluntarism—have to be understood in terms of its culture of origin is hardly original. But perhaps the particular substitution I mention here has interest. Given the part that so-called gift exchange plays in the reproduction of persons in Melanesia, it was not inapposite to consider the new language of gifting that accompanies the propagation of late-twentieth-century reproductive technologies. There we discover the Euro-American person as a free-standing entity interacting with its environment, a figure missing from the twentieth-century Melanesian pantheon. The first question to ask, then, is what kind of person the Melanesian gift reproduces.

The double orientation of gifts in consumer culture presupposes two kinds of relationships: an individual person's interpersonal relations with others and an individual person's relations with society. Melanesian gifts on the other hand presuppose two kinds of persons, partners divided by their transaction: paternal from maternal kin, fetus from placenta, clansmen from the ground they cultivate, descendants from ancestors. Gifts may come from an outside source, but that source is hardly imagined as beyond persons in the way the talents and the riches of the world seemingly come from God in Davis's sixteenth-century France.[53] For even where the other person is imagined as a deity or spirit or as the very land itself, the Melanesian act of giving that divides recipient from donor presupposes a partnering of finite identities. By contrast, the gift capable of extending a personalized self into a potentially infinite universe turns the person into a potential recipient of everything.

Late twentieth-century and Euro-American, the embryo visualized as a homunculus is a consumer in the making. For the consumer actualizes his or her relationship with society/the environment in its own body process. This prompts a second question: whether gift-giving in a consumer culture contests the coercive nature of this relationship or is another example of it.

From *New Literary History,* 1991.

Notes

This was initially presented to the conference on *The Gift and Its Transformations,* organized by Natalie Davis, Rena Lederman, and Ronald Sharp, National Humanities Center, N.C., November 1990. I am most grateful for comments from the participants. I should add that I have retained the original mode of address, since the paper was written for a multidisciplinary audience.

1. See also Martin Johnson, "Did I Begin?" *New Scientist*, 9 December 1989, pp. 39–42. The BAAS meetings are intended to present scientific investigations and discoveries to the public. The debate, *Human Embryo Research: What are the Issues?*, was organized by the Ciba Foundation.

2. The early conceptus is dependent on the developmental history of the egg in the mother, which provides "a mature physical and biochemical entity within which the whole complex process" of early development operates (Johnson, "Did I Begin?" p. 40), an interaction quite distinct from the egg's genetic contribution to the conceptus.

3. See Sarah Franklin, "Making Sense of Missed Conceptions: Anthropological Perspectives on Unexplained Fertility," a paper presented to the 152nd Annual Meeting of the British Association for the Advancement of Science (Swansea, 1990).

4. See Martin Linton and Nikki Knewstub, "MPs Give Overwhelming Backing to Medical Research on Embryos," *The Guardian*, 24 April 1990, p. 6.

5. To the lay person. To the embryologist, "Biology does not tell us that a line should or should not be drawn" (Johnson, "Did I Begin?" p. 41). It is the job of legislation to draw the lines.

6. Linton and Knewstub, p. 6.

7. See Gordon Dunstan, "The Moral Status of the Human Embryo," in *Philosophical Ethics in Reproductive Medicine*, eds. David R. Bromham, Maureen E. Dalton, and Jennifer C. Jackson (Manchester: Manchester University Press, 1990), p. 6.

8. See Rosaline Pollack Petchesky, "Foetal Images: The Power of Visual Culture in the Politics of Reproduction," in *Reproductive Technologies: Gender, Motherhood and Medicine*, ed. Michelle Stanworth (Cambridge: Polity Press, 1987), pp. 57–80.

9. The fetus was entire (a homunculus), but its cord was severed, and the womb was in half-section with the placenta visibly sectioned as well. The severed cord was painted in such a way as to invite horror at the tearing away of the fetus; but the womb itself was "severed" for no other purpose it would seem than to have it provide a convenient cup for the model of the fetus. A simulated horror.

10. See Michel Panoff, "Marcel Mauss's *The Gift* Revisited," *Man*, n.s. 5 (1970), pp. 60–70; and Jonathan Parry, "*The Gift*, the Indian Gift and the 'Indian Gift,'" *Man*, n.s., 21 (1986), pp. 453–73.

11. The shell is both procreative and procreated. The point is stimulated by two unpublished papers in which Jeffrey Clark has analyzed the remarkable iconography of Wiru pearlshells.

12. David Cheal, *The Gift Economy* (London: Routledge, 1988), p. 19; hereafter cited in text as *GE*.

13. See Rena Lederman, *What Gifts Engender: Social Relations and Politics in Mendi, Highland Papua New Guinea* (Cambridge: Cambridge University Press, 1986).

14. See Jonathan Parry and Maurice Bloch, *Money and the Morality of Exchange* (Cambridge: Cambridge University Press, 1989).

15. See, e.g., Mario Biagioli, "Galileo's System of Patronage," *History of Science*, 28 (1990), pp. 1–62.

16. In the 1990s, life-world-style worlds are already passé, if one is to believe upmarket consumer experts. I refer to the concept of the personalized market here. "If the modern world is based on the notion of an endless repetition of a few products, then its successor is based on the idea of short-runs and the targeting of many, different, products" (Charles Jencks and Maggie Keswick, *What is Post-Modernism?*

2nd ed. [London: Academy Editions, 1987], pp. 48–49) though, as Jencks observes, individual tastes are not as variable as the potential production of variety.

17. See C. A. Gregory, *Gifts and Commodities* (London: Academic Press, 1982).

18. See Lisette Josephides, *The Production of Inequality: Gender and Exchange among the Kewa* (London: Tavistock Publications, 1985).

19. See Faye Ginsburg, "Procreation Stories: Reproduction, Nurturance and Procreation in Life Narratives of Abortion Activists," *American Ethnologist* 14 (1987), pp. 623–636.

20. I read this off from Johnson's presentation of the epigenetic factors. These were indicated in highly generalized terms by contrast with the specific representation of the fetus/person. No doubt his professional view is more sophisticated than the image I have derived from his talk (an organism as a free-standing entity within an environment to which it "adapts"), but for a critique of similar perceptions as they have informed the concept of culture in anthropology, see Tim Ingold, "Culture and the Perception of the Environment" (n.d.); for EIDOS workshop on *Cultural Understandings of the Environment* (London, 1989).

21. Johnson, "Did I Begin?" p. 39.

22. See, e.g., Maurice Leenhardt, *Do Kamo. Person and Myth in the Melanesian World*, trans. Basia Miller Gulati (1947; rpt. Chicago: University of Chicago Press, 1979). For non-Melanesian depictions of the world imagined as a plurality of bodies and of the body containing a plurality of worlds, see the chapter by Malamoud and Levi in Michel Feher, et al., *Fragments for a History of the Human Body*, 3 vols. (New York: Zone Books, 1989).

23. See, e.g., Roy Wagner, *Asiwinarong: Ethos, Image, and Social Power among the Usen Barok of New Ireland* (Princeton: Princeton University Press, 1986).

24. See Daniel Miller, *Material Culture and Mass Consumption* (Oxford: Blackwell, 1987), p. 14.

25. See James F. Weiner, *The Heart of the Pearlshell: The Mythological Dimension of Foi Sociality* (Los Angeles: University of California Press, 1988).

26. See Roy Wagner, "The Fractal Person," in *Big Men and Great Men: Personifications of Power in Melanesia*, eds. Maurice Godelier and Marilyn Strathern (Cambridge: Cambridge University Press, 1991).

27. See James F. Weiner, "Diseases of the Soul: Sickness, Agency and the Men's Cult among the Foi of New Guinea," in *Dealing with Inequality, Analysing Gender Relations in Melanesia and Beyond*, ed. Marilyn Strathern (Cambridge: Cambridge University Press, 1987), pp. 255–277.

28. See Gillian Gillison, "The Flute Myth and the Law of Equivalence: Origins of a Principle of Exchange," in *Big Men and Great Men*; and Jadran Mimica, *Intimations of Infinity: The Cultural Meanings of Iqwaye Counting System and Number* (Oxford: Berg, 1988).

29. See Lynn M. Morgan, "When Does Life Begin? A Cross-Cultural Perspective on the Personhood of Fetuses and Young Children," in *Abortion Rights and Fetal 'Personhood'*, eds. Edd Doerr and James W. Prescott (Long Beach: Centerline Press, 1989). Morgan observes that in the United States it is generally thought that the neonate becomes a person with the cutting of the umbilical cord.

30. See Daniel de Coppet, ". . . Land Owns People," in *Contexts and Levels: Anthropological Essays on Hierarchy*, eds. R. H. Barnes, Daniel de Coppet, and R. J. Parkin (Oxford: JASO, 1985), pp. 78–90.

31. My interpretation of the sequence of statements made to de Coppet by the paramount chief Eerehau.

32. De Coppet, "Land Owns People," p. 87.

33. Giulia Sissa, "Subtle Bodies," in *Fragments for a History of the Human Body*, Part 3, p. 133. See Verena Stolcke, "New Reproductive Technologies—Same Old Fatherhood," *Critique of Anthropology* 6 (1986), pp. 5–31. The term *semen* may be used either as the vehicle that carries sperm or as an alternative for sperm itself. It is sperm donation that is strictly at issue here.

34. Rather in the way that gifts of money in 'Are'Are (see below) encompass, transcend, and differentiate the three components of the person (body, breath, and image) (Daniel de Coppet, "The Life-Giving Death," in *Mortality and Immortality: The Anthropology and Archaeology of Death*, eds. S. C. Humphreys and Helen King [London: Academic Press, 1981], and "Land Owns People"), so Aristotelian semen is the vehicle for the three "principles," soul, form, and movement (Sissa, "Subtle Bodies," p. 136).

35. However, its alienability is a contested point. A recent study by Jeanette Edwards (personal communication) points to diverse views on men's part about the extent to which semen is or is not felt to be disposable in the way body organs potentially are.

36. The relative complexities of the techniques render the physical operations quite different. See Frances Price, "Establishing Guidelines: Regulation and the Clinical Management of Infertility," in *Birthrights: Laws and Ethics at the Beginnings of Life*, eds. Robert Lee and Derek Morgan (London: Routledge, 1989), pp. 46–47. While artificial semen donation is a two-hundred-year-old practice, scientific papers about pregnancies from donated oocytes did not appear in professional journals until 1983–84 (Frances Price, personal communication).

37. A phrase applied to interventionist medicine in general. In a world of punning acronyms, it is no accident that GIFT should occur, though for a process (gamete intra-fallopian transfer) that need involve no "donation" from outside sources.

38. However, see Ray Abrahams, "Plus ça change, plus c'est la même chose?" For Festschrift for J. A. Barnes (n.d.). Ties are occasionally established between the relatives of organ donors and the recipients. Abrahams, drawing on analogies with gift-giving, explores what is both new and old in the identities set up by organ transplant; "racial" origin remains an uninvited guest at the debate. I am grateful for permission to cite the paper.

39. See Miller, *Material Culture and Mass Consumption*; and Daniel Miller, "Appropriating the State on the Council Estate," *Man*, n.s., 23 (1988), pp. 353–372.

40. For nonconsumerist appropriations, I cite two examples. One is Pnina Werbner's remarkable account of "capital, gifts and offerings among British Pakistanis" (*The Migration Process: Capital, Gifts and Offerings among British Pakistanis* [Oxford: Berg, 1990]); the other Mayfair Mei-Hui Yang's critique of "second-economy" arguments in relation to gifts and the state redistributive economy in contemporary China ("The Gift Economy and State Power in China," *Comparative Studies in Society and History* 31 [1989], pp. 25–54).

41. See Gregory, *Gifts and Commodities*.

42. See Debbora Battaglia, *On the Bones of the Serpent: Person, Memory and Mortality in Sabarl Island Society* (Chicago: University of Chicago Press, 1990).

43. Battaglia, p. 191, emphasis omitted.

44. See Debbora Battaglia, "'We Feed our Father': Paternal Nurture among the Sabarl of Papua New Guinea," *American Ethnologist* 12 (1985), pp. 427–441.

45. Parry arguing on this point also reinstates Mauss's purpose in *The Gift* as demonstrating just how we ever came to contrast interested and disinterested gifts. "So while Mauss is generally represented as telling us how in fact the gift is never free, what I think he is really telling us is how we have acquired a theory that it should be" (Parry, "*The Gift*," p. 458, emphasis omitted). I merely point here to the further coercions of choice in the consumer world of compulsory subjectivity.

46. Quoted in Stanworth, *Reproductive Technologies*, p. 15.

47. De Coppet, "The Life-Giving Death," p. 201.

48. See *Death Rituals and Life in the Societies of the Kula Ring*, ed. Frederick Damon and Roy Wagner (DeKalb, IL: Northern Illinois University Press, 1989).

49. See de Coppet, "The Life-Giving Death," p. 188.

50. See de Coppet, "The Life-Giving Death," p. 202, n. 17.

51. Battaglia, *On the Bones of the Serpent*, p. 190.

52. I am compressing several arguments and contested positions here, and do not specify where the view is held. It alludes but does not do justice to Miller's reading of consumption as symbolic labor (the consumer recontextualizes the commodity and objectifies it afresh as a source of inalienable value). See Miller, *Material Culture and Mass Consumption*.

53. See Natalie Zemon Davis, "Gifts, Markets and Communities in Sixteenth-Century France," a paper presented to the conference *The Gift and its Transformations*, National Humanities Center (1990). For a Melanesian Christian counterpart, see C. A. Gregory, "Gifts to Men and Gifts to God: Gift Exchange and Capital Accumulation in Contemporary Papua," *Man* n.s. 15, pp. 626–52.

Notes on Contributors

ÉMILE BENVENISTE (1902–1976) was Professor of Comparative Grammar at the Collège de France from 1937–1976. He wrote several important works on the theory of Indo-European language as well as general and comparative linguistics, including *Problems in General Linguistics* (1966) and *Indo-European Language and Society* (1969).

ROBERT BERNASCONI (1950–) is Moss Professor of Philosophy at the University of Memphis. He is the author of *The Question of Language in Heidegger's History of Being* (1985) and *Heidegger in Question* (1993) and has written numerous articles on various aspects of continental philosophy and the history of social practices.

PIERRE BOURDIEU (1930–) has been Professor of Sociology at the Collège de France since 1981. He has been the director of the École des Hautes Études en Sciences Sociales since 1985 and Director of Studies at the École Pratique des Hautes Études since 1964. He is the author of many books, including *Outline of a Theory of Practice* (1972), *Distinctions: A Social Critique of the Judgement of Taste* (1979), and *The Logic of Practice* (1980).

HÉLÈNE CIXOUS (1937–) is Professor of English Literature at the University of Paris VIII, and director of the university's Center for Research in Feminine Studies. A cofounder of the literary review *Poétique*, her publications include novels, dramas, poetry, literary criticism, and, with Catherine Clément, *The Newly Born Woman* (1975).

JACQUES DERRIDA (1930–) is Directeur d'Études at the École des Hautes Études en Sciences Sociales in Paris and Professor of French at the University of California, Irvine. One of the most influential philosophers of the last fifty years, his important works include *Of Grammatology* (1967), *Writing and Difference* (1967), and *Margins of Philosophy* (1972).

RALPH WALDO EMERSON (1803–1882), American lecturer, essayist, and poet, was a leading exponent of New England Transcendentalism.

RODOLPHE GASCHÉ (1938–) is Eugenio Donato Professor at the State University of New York at Buffalo. His books include *System und Metaphorik in der Philosophie von Georges Bataille* (1978), *The Tain of the Mirror: Derrida and the Philosophy of Reflection* (1986), and *Inventions of Difference: On Jacques Derrida* (1994). His forthcoming book is entitled *The Wild Card of Reading: On Paul de Man*. Currently, he is working on another book-length study on the philosophical concept of "Europe."

LUCE IRIGARAY (1930–) is Director of Research in Philosophy at the Centre National de la Recherche Scientifique, Paris, where she has held a research post since 1964. She is the author of many books, including *Speculum of the Other Woman* (1974) and *This Sex Which Is Not One* (1977).

CLAUDE LÉVI-STRAUSS (1908–) was Professor of Social Anthropology at the Collège de France from 1959–1982 and Director of Studies at the École Pratique des Hautes Études from 1950–1974. The major theorist of structuralism in anthropology, he is one of the best-known intellectuals of the twentieth century. Among his important works are *The Elementary Structures of Kinship* (1949), *Savage Thought* (1962), and *The Raw and the Cooked* (1964). He received the Prix Paul Pelliot (1949), the Huxley Memorial Medal (1965), and the Erasmus Prize (1973), and has been a member of the Académie Française since 1973.

MARCEL MAUSS (1872–1950) began his career as a professor of primitive religion at the École Pratique des Hautes Études in 1902. He was a founder of the Institut d'Ethnologie of the University of Paris in 1925 and Professor of Sociology at the Collège de France from 1931–1942. Mauss worked closely with his uncle Émile Durkheim and helped found *L'Année sociologique*, which he edited following Durkheim's death. One of the first anthropologists to advocate a close relationship with psychology, Mauss's *Essay on the Gift* (1923–24) is one of the best-known works of anthropology.

MARSHALL SAHLINS (1930–) is Professor of Anthropology at the University of Chicago. He is the author of many works including *Social Stratification in Polynesia* (1958), *Stone Age Economics* (1972), and, most recently, *How "Natives" Think: about Captain Cook, for example* (1995).

ALAN D. SCHRIFT (1955–) is Associate Professor of Philosophy at Grinnell College. He is the author of *Nietzsche and the Question of Interpretation* (1990) and *Nietzsche's French Legacy: A Genealogy of Poststructuralism* (1995), and coeditor of *The Hermeneutic Tradition: From Ast to Ricoeur* and *Transforming the Hermeneutic Context: From Nietzsche to Nancy* (1990).

GARY SHAPIRO (1941–) is Tucker-Boatwright Professor in the Humanities and Professor of Philosophy at the University of Richmond. He is the author of *Nietzschean Narratives* (1989), *Alcyone: Nietzsche on Gifts, Noise, and Women* (1991), and *Earthwards: Robert Smithson and Art After Babel* (1995).

ALLAN STOEKL (1951–) is Professor of French and Comparative Literature at Pennsylvania State University. He is the author of *Politics, Writing, Mutilation: The Cases of Bataille, Blanchot, Roussel, Leiris and Ponge* (1985) and the editor and translator of Georges Bataille, *Visions of Excess: Selected Writings 1927–1939* (1985). His most recent book is *Agonies of the Intellectual* (1992), and he recently published a translation with critical preface, of Maurice Blanchot's novel *The Most High* (1996).

MARILYN STRATHERN (1941–) is William Wyse Professor of Social Anthropology at the University of Cambridge. Her interests are divided between Melanesian (*Women in Between*, 1972) and British (*Kinship at the Core*, 1981) ethnography. *The Gender of the Gift* (1988) is a critique of anthropological theories of society and gender relations as they have been applied to Melanesia, while *After Nature: English Kinship in the Late Twentieth Century* (1992) comments on the cultural revolution in England. Her most recent publication is the coauthored *Technologies of Procreation* (1993).

Works Cited

Abrahams, Ray. "Plus ça change, plus c'est la même chose?" For Festschrift for J. A. Barnes. n.d.

Althusser, Louis. "Sur le 'Contrat Social.'" *Cahiers pour l'Analyse* 8 (1966): 5–42.

Appadurai, Arjun. "Introduction: Commodities and the Politics of Value." In *The Social Life of Things*. Ed. Arjun Appadurai. Cambridge: Cambridge University Press, 1986.

Arendt, Hannah. *The Human Condition*. Chicago: University of Chicago Press, 1958.

Aristotle. *Nicomachean Ethics*. Trans. Terence Irwin. Indianapolis: Hackett, 1985.

———. *Physics*. In *A New Aristotle Reader*. Ed. J. L. Ackrill. Princeton: Princeton University Press, 1987.

Bachofen, Johann-Jakob. *Das Mutterrecht*. Stuttgart: Krais and Hoffman, 1861.

Bacon, Francis. *Novum Organum*. 1620.

Barthes, Roland. *L'Empire du signes*. Geneva: Editions d'Art Albert Skira, S.A., 1970. English translation: *The Empire of Signs*. Trans. Richard Howard. New York: Hill and Wang, 1982.

Bataille, Georges. *La Part Maudite*. Paris: Éditions de Minuit, 1967. English translation: *The Accursed Share: An Essay on General Economy, Vol. 1: Consumption*. Trans. Robert Hurley. New York: Zone Books, 1988.

———. "Letter to Blank, Instructor of a Course on Hegel." In *Guilty*. Trans. Bruce Boone. Venice, CA: Lapis Press, 1988.

———. "La notion de dépense." *Oeuvres Complètes*, vol. 1. Paris: Gallimard, 1970. English translation by Allan Stoekl. "The Notion of Expenditure." In *Visions of Excess: Selected Writings, 1927–1939*. Ed. Allan Stoekl. Trans. Allan Stoekl with Carl R. Lovitt and Donald M. Leslie Jr. Minneapolis: University of Minnesota Press, 1985.

———. *Oeuvres Complètes*. 12 vols. Paris: Gallimard, 1970–76.

———. "The Psychological Structure of Fascism." In *Visions of Excess: Selected Writings, 1927–1939*. Ed. Allan Stoekl. Trans. Allan Stoekl with Carl R. Lovitt and Donald M. Leslie Jr. Minneapolis: University of Minnesota Press, 1985.

Batifoulier, P., L. Cordonnier, and Y. Zenou. "L'emprunt de la théorie économique à la tradition sociologique, le cas du don contre-don." *Revue économique* 5 (septembre 1992): 917–46.

Battaglia, Debbora. *On the Bones of the Serpent: Person, Memory and Mortality in Sabarl Island Society*. Chicago: University of Chicago Press, 1990.

———. "'We Feed our Father': Paternal Nurture among the Sabarl of Papua New Guinea." *American Ethnologist* 12 (1985): 427–41.

Baudelaire, Charles. *Paris Spleen*. Trans. Louise Varèse. New York: New Directions, 1970.

Baumgarten, Eduard. *Das Vorbild Emersons im Werk und Leben Nietzsches*. Heidelberg: C. Winter, 1957.

Becker, Gary S. "A Theory of the Allocation of Time." *Economic Journal* 75 (1965): 493–517.

Beckwith, Martha Warren. "Mythology of the Oglala Dakota." *Journal of American Folklore* 43 (1930): 339–442.

Bell, Daniel. *The End of Ideology: On the Exhaustion of Political Ideas in the Fifties.* Glencoe, IL: Free Press, 1960.

Benveniste, Émile. *Indo-European Language and Society.* London: Faber, 1973.

———. *Noms d'agent et noms d'action en indo-europeén.* Paris: Adrien-Maisonneuve, 1948.

———. *Problems in General Linguistics.* Trans. Mary Elizabeth Meek. Coral Gables, FL: University of Miami Press, 1971.

Bernasconi, Robert. "The Ethics of Suspicion." *Research in Phenomenology* 20 (1990): 3–18.

———. "The Fate of the Distinction Between *Praxis* and *Poiesis.*" In *Heidegger in Question.* Atlantic Highlands: Humanities Press, 1993.

———. "The Poor Box and the Changing Face of Charity in Early Modern Europe." *Acta Institutionis Philosophiae et Aestheticae* 10 (1992): 33–54.

———. "Skepticism in the Face of Philosophy." In *Re-Reading Levinas.* Eds. Robert Bernasconi and Simon Critchley. Bloomington: Indiana University Press, 1991.

Best, Elsdon. *Forest Lore of the Maori.* Dominion Museum Bulletin No. 14, 1942.

———. *The Maori.* 2 vols. Memoirs of the Polynesian Society No. 5, 1924.

———. *Maori Agriculture.* Dominion Museum Bulletin No. 9, 1925.

———. "Maori Forest Lore. Part III." *Transactions of the New Zealand Institute* 42 (1909): 433–81.

———. *Spiritual and Mental Concepts of the Maori.* Dominion Museum Monographs No. 2, 1922.

———. "Spiritual Concepts of the Maori." *Journal of the Polynesian Society* 9 (1900): 173–99; 10 (1901): 1–20.

Biagioli, Mario. "Galileo's System of Patronage." *History of Science* 28 (1990): 1–62.

Blake-Palmer, G. "Mana, some Christian and Moslem parallels." *Journal of the Polynesian Society* 55 (1946): 263–75.

Blanchot, Maurice. *Le Très-Haut.* Paris: Gallimard, 1948. English translation: *The Most High.* Trans. Allan Stoekl. Lincoln: University of Nebraska Press, 1996.

Boulifa, S. *Méthode de langue kabyle. Étude linguistique et sociologique sur la Kabylie du Djurdjura.* Algiers: Jourdan, 1913.

Bourdieu, Pierre. *L'Amour de l'art.* Paris: Éditions de Minuit, 1966.

———. "Genèse et structure du champ religieux." *Revue française de sociologie* 12 (1971): 295–334.

———. *The Logic of Practice.* Trans. Richard Nice. Cambridge: Polity Press, 1990.

———. "The Sense of Honour." In *Algeria 1960.* Cambridge: Cambridge University Press and Paris: Éditions de la Maison des Sciences de l'Homme, 1979.

Butler, Judith. *Subjects of Desire: Hegelian Reflections in Postwar France.* New York: Columbia University Press, 1987.

Cahen, Maurice. *Études sur le vocabulaire religieux du vieux-scandinave: la libation.* Paris: Alcan, 1922.

Capell, Arthur. "The word 'mana': a linguistic study." *Oceania* 9 (1938): 89–96.

Cazaneuve, Jean. *Sociologie de Marcel Mauss.* Paris: Presses Universitaires de France, 1968.

Cheal, David. *The Gift Economy.* London: Routledge, 1988.

Cixous, Hélène. "An exchange with Hélène Cixous." Trans. Verena Andermatt Conley. In *Hélène Cixous: Writing the Feminine.* Lincoln: University of Nebraska Press, 1984.

———. "Castration or Decapitation?" Trans. Annette Kuhn. *Signs: Journal of Women in Culture and Society* 7, 1 (1981): 41–55.

———. "Les Comtes de Hoffmann" ["Tales of Hoffmann"]. In *Prénoms de Personne.* Paris: Editions du Seuil, 1974.

Cixous, Hélène, and Catherine Clément. *The Newly Born Woman.* Trans. Betsy Wing. Minneapolis: University of Minnesota Press, 1986.

Coppet, Daniel de. ". . . Land Owns People." In *Contexts and Levels: Anthropological Essays on Hierarchy.* Ed. R. H. Barnes, Daniel de Coppet, and R. J. Parkin. Oxford: JASO, 1985.

———. "The Life-Giving Death." In *Mortality and Immortality: The Anthropology and Archaeology of Death.* Ed. S. C. Humphreys and Helen King. London: Academic Press, 1981.

Dagron, Gilbert. "L'Homme sans honneur ou le saint scandaleux." *Annales ESC* (juillet–août 1990): 929–39.

Damon, Frederick, and Roy Wagner, eds. *Death Rituals and Life in the Societies of the Kula Ring.* DeKalb: Northern Illinois University Press, 1989.

Davis, Natalie Zemon. "Gifts, Markets and Communities in Sixteenth-Century France." Paper presented at "The Gift and its Transformations," National Humanities Center, Research Triangle Park, NC, 1990.

Davy, Georges. *La foi jurée: Étude sociologique du problème du contrat et de la formation du lien contractuel.* Bibliothèque de philosophie contemporaine. Travaux de l'Année sociologique. Paris: Alcan, 1922.

———. *Sociologie politique. Eléments de sociologie* 1. 2d. ed. Paris: Vrin, 1950.

Derrida, Jacques. "Apories: Mourir—s'attendre aux limites de la vérité." In *Le Passage des frontières.* Paris: Galilée, 1994. English translation: *Aporias.* Trans. Thomas Dutoit. Stanford: Stanford University Press, 1993.

———. *L'Autre Cap.* Paris: Minuit, 1991.

———. "Comment ne pas parler. Dénégations." In *Psyché.* Paris: Galilée, 1987. English translation by Ken Frieden. "How to Avoid Speaking: Denials." In *Derrida and Negative Theology.* Ed. Harold Coward and Toby Foshay. Albany: State University of New York Press, 1992.

———. *De la grammatologie.* Paris: Minuit, 1967. English translation: *Of Grammatology.* Trans. Gayatri Chakravorty Spivak. Baltimore: Johns Hopkins University Press, 1976.

———. *Dissemination.* Trans. Barbara Johnson. Chicago: University of Chicago Press, 1981.

———. "Donner la mort." In *L'éthique du don. Jacques Derrida et la pensée du don.* Ed. Jean-Michel Rabaté and Michael Wetzel. Paris: Métailié-Transition, 1992. English translation: *The Gift of Death.* Trans. David Wills. Chicago: University of Chicago Press, 1995.

———. *Donner le temps. 1. La fausse monnaie.* Paris: Galilée, 1991. English translation: *Given Time. 1. Counterfeit Money.* Trans. Peggy Kamuf. Chicago: University of Chicago Press, 1992.

———. *L'écriture et la différence.* Paris: Seuil, 1967. English translation: *Writing and Difference.* Trans. Alan Bass. Chicago: University of Chicago Press, 1978.

———. "En ce moment même dans cet ouvrage me voici." In *Textes pour*

Emmanuel Levinas. Ed. François Laruelle. Paris: Jean-Michel Place, 1980. English translation by Ruben Berezdivin. "At this very moment in this work here I am." In *Re-Reading Levinas.* Ed. Robert Bernasconi and Simon Critchley. Bloomington: Indiana University Press, 1991.

———. "Le Facteur de la vérité." In *The Post Card: From Socrates to Freud and Beyond.* Trans. Alan Bass. Chicago: University of Chicago Press, 1987.

———. *Feu la cendre.* Paris: des Femmes, 1987. English translation: *Cinders.* Trans. Ned Lukacher. Lincoln: University of Nebraska Press, 1991.

———. "Force of Law: The 'Mystical Foundation of Authority.'" Trans. Mary Quaintance. *Cardozo Law Review* 11, 5–6 (July–Aug. 1990): 920–1045.

———. "From Restricted to General Economy: A Hegelianism without Reserve." In *Writing and Difference.* Trans. Alan Bass. Chicago: University of Chicago Press, 1978.

———. *Mémoires: for Paul de Man.* Trans. Cecile Lindsay, Jonathan Culler, and Eduardo Cadava. New York: Columbia University Press, 1986.

———. "Nous autres Grecs." In *Nos Grecs et leurs modernes.* Paris: Seuil, 1992.

———. "*Ousia* and *Grammē*: Note on a Note from *Being and Time.*" In *Margins of Philosophy.* Trans. Alan Bass. Chicago: University of Chicago Press, 1982.

———. *Parages.* Paris: Galilée, 1986.

———. *Passions.* "*L'offrande oblique.*" Paris: Galilée, 1993. English translation by David Wood. "Passions: 'An Oblique Offering.'" In *Derrida: A Critical Reader.* Ed. David Wood. Oxford: Blackwell, 1992.

———. "The Politics of Friendship." *Journal of Philosophy* 85, 11 (1988): 632–44.

———. *The Post Card: From Socrates to Freud and Beyond.* Trans. Alan Bass. Chicago: University of Chicago Press, 1987.

———. *Psyché: Inventions de l'autre.* Paris: Galilée, 1987.

———. "Psyche: Inventions of the Other." In *Reading de Man Reading.* Trans. Catherine Porter. Ed. Wlad Godzich and Lindsay Waters. Minneapolis: University of Minnesota Press, 1989.

———. *Spurs: Nietzsche's Styles.* Trans. Barbara Harlow. Chicago: University of Chicago Press, 1979.

———. "Structure, Sign and Play in the Discourse of the Human Sciences." In *Writing and Difference.* Trans. Alan Bass. Chicago: University of Chicago Press, 1978.

Derrida, Jacques, and Pierre-Jean Labarière. *Altérités.* Paris: Osiris, 1986.

Dostoyevsky, Fyodor. "The Gambler." In *The Gambler, Bobok, A Nasty Story.* Harmondsworth: Penguin, 1966.

Dover, Kenneth J. *Greek Popular Morality in the Time of Plato and Aristotle.* Oxford: Basil Blackwell, 1974.

Dunstan, Gordon. "The Moral Status of the Human Embryo." In *Philosophical Ethics in Reproductive Medicine.* Ed. David R. Bromham, Maureen E. Dalton, and Jennifer C. Jackson. Manchester: Manchester University Press, 1990.

Durkheim, Émile. *Les Formes élémentaires de la vie religieuse. Le système totémique en Australie.* Paris: Alcan, 1912. English translation: *The Elementary Forms of the Religious Life.* Trans. J. W. Swain. London: George Allen & Unwin, 1915.

———. *Montesquieu and Rousseau: Forerunners of Sociology.* Trans. Ralph Manheim. Ann Arbor: University of Michigan Press, 1960.

———. *Le Suicide. Étude de sociologie.* Paris: Alcan, 1897. English translation: *Suicide. A Study in Sociology.* Trans. J. A. Spaulding and G. Simpson. Edited with an introduction by G. Simpson. London: Routledge & Kegan Paul, 1952.

Durkheim, Émile, and Marcel Mauss. "De Quelques formes primitives de classification. Contribution à l'étude des représentations collectives." *Année sociologique* 6 (1901–2):1–72. Republished in Marcel Mauss, *Oeuvres*, vol. 2. English translation and introduction by Rodney Needham, *Primitive Classification*. London: Cohen & West, 1963. Reprint,Chicago: University of Chicago Press, 1970.

Emerson, Ralph Waldo. *Essays and Lectures*. 1844. Reprint, New York: Literary Classics, 1983.

Etymologie der neuhochdeutschen Sprache: Darstellung des deutschen Wortschatzes in seiner geschichtlichen Entwicklung. Handbuch des deutschen Unterrichts an höheren Schulen 4, 2. München: Beck, 1909.

Etymologisches Wörterbuch der deutschen Sprache. Strassburg: Trubner, 8. verbesserte und verm. Aufl. 1915.

Feher, Michel, Ramona Nadaff, and Nadia Tazi, eds. *Fragments for a History of the Human Body*. 3 vols. New York: Zone Books, 1989.

Feist, Sigmund. *Etymologisches Wörterbuch der Gotischen Sprache*. 3rd ed. Leyden: E. J. Brill, 1939.

Finas, Lucette. *Donne*. Paris: Seuil, 1976.

Finley, Moses. "La servitude pour dettes." *Revue d'histoire du droit française et étranger*. 4th series, 43 (1965): 159–84.

Firth, Raymond. "An analysis of mana." *Polynesian Anthropological Studies* (1941): 198–218.

———. "The analysis of mana: an empirical approach." *Journal of the Polynesian Society* 49 (1940): 483–510. Republished in *Tikopia Ritual and Belief*. London: Allen & Unwin, 1967.

———. *Economics of the New Zealand Maori*. 2d ed. Wellington: R. E. Owen, Government Printer, 1959.

———. *Primitive Polynesian Economy*. London: G. Routledge & Sons, 1939.

———. "Themes in Economic Anthropology: A General Comment." *Themes in Economic Anthropology*. Ed. Raymond Firth. London: Tavistock, ASA Monograph 6, 1967.

———. *We, the Tikopia. A Sociological Study of Kinship in Primitive Polynesia*. London: George Allen & Unwin, 1936.

Franklin, Sarah. "Making Sense of Missed Conceptions: Anthropological Perspectives on Unexplained Fertility." Paper presented at the 152d Annual Meeting of the British Association for the Advancement of Science, Swansea, 1990.

Gable, R. W. "Influential Lobby or Kiss of Death?" *Journal of Politics* 15, 2 (1953).

Gasché, Rodolphe. "L'Échange héliocentrique." *L'Arc* 48:70–84 (1972).

Gilligan, Carol. *In a Different Voice*. Cambridge: Harvard University Press, 1982.

Gillison, Gillian. "The Flute Myth and the Law of Equivalence: Origins of a Principle of Exchange." In *Big Men and Great Men: Personifications of Power in Melanesia*. Ed. Maurice Godelier and Marilyn Strathern. Cambridge: Cambridge University Press, 1991.

Ginsburg, Faye. "Procreation Stories: Reproduction, Nurturance and Procreation in Life Narratives of Abortion Activists." *American Ethnologist* 14 (1987): 623–36.

Godelier, Maurice. *Rationalité et irrationalité en économie*. Paris: Maspero, 1966.

Goux, Jean-Joseph. "Numismatiques I." *Tel Quel* 35 (1968).

———. *Symbolic Economies: After Marx and Freud*. Trans. Jennifer Curtiss Gage. Ithaca: Cornell University Press, 1990.

Gregory, C. A. *Gifts and Commodities*. London: Academic Press, 1982.

―――. "Gifts to Men and Gifts to God: Gift Exchange and Capital Accumulation in Contemporary Papua." *Man* n.s. 15 (1980): 626–52.

Grimm, Jacob and Wilhelm. *Deutsches Wörterbuch.* Leipzig: Hirzel, 1854–1922.

Grusin, Richard A. "'Put God in Your Debt': Emerson's Economy of Expenditure." *PMLA* (Jan. 1988): 35–44.

Hanoteau, Adolphe, and Aristide Letourneux. *La Kabylie et les coutumes kabyles.* Paris: Imprimerie nationale, 1873.

Hartmann, Nicolai. *Ethics, Volume II: Moral Values.* Trans. Stanton Coit. New York: Macmillan, 1932.

Hegel, G. W. F. "Der Geist des Christentums und sein Schicksal." In *Frühe Schriften, Werke 1.* Frankfurt: Suhrkamp, 1974. English translation by T. M. Knox. "The Spirit of Christianity." In *Early Theological Writings.* Philadelphia: University of Pennsylvania Press, 1971.

Heidegger, Martin. "The Anaximander Fragment." In *Early Greek Thinking.* Trans. David Farrel Krell and Frank A. Capuzzi. New York: Harper and Row, 1975.

―――. *Basic Writings.* Trans. David Farrel Krell. New York: Harper and Row, 1977.

―――. *Beiträge zur Philosophie. Vom Ereignis,* vol. 65 of *Gesamtausgabe.* Ed. Friedrich-Wilhelm von Herrmann. Frankfurt am Main: V. Klostermann, 1989. French translation of §267 by Jean Greisch. In *Rue Descartes* no. 1, "Des Grecs," (April 1991).

―――. *An Introduction to Metaphysics.* Trans. Ralph Manhein. New York: Anchor, 1961.

―――. *Nietzsche. Volume IV: Nihilism.* Trans. Frank A. Capuzzi. Ed. David Farrell Krell. New York: Harper and Row, 1982.

―――. *On Time and Being.* Trans. Joan Stambaugh. New York: Harper and Row, 1972.

―――. *Sein und Zeit.* Tübingen: Niemeyer, 1984. English translation: *Being and Time.* Trans. John Macquarrie and Edward Robinson. New York: Harper and Row, 1962.

Hirschman, Albert. *The Passions and the Interests.* Princeton: Princeton University Press, 1977.

Hobbes, Thomas. *English Works.* Ed. Sir William Molesworth. London: J. Bohn, 1839.

―――. *Leviathan.* New York: Dutton, 1950.

Hocart, Arthur M. "Mana." *Man* no. 46 (1914): 97–101.

―――. "Mana again." *Man* no. 79 (Sept. 1922): 139–41.

―――. "Natural and supernatural." *Man* no. 78 (March 1932): 59–61.

Hogbin, Herbert Ian. "Mana." *Oceania* 6 (1935–6): 241–74.

Holmes, John H. *In Primitive New Guinea.* London: Seeley, Service & Co., 1924.

Hubbard, Stanley. *Nietzsche und Emerson.* Basel: Verlag für Recht und Gesellschaft, 1958.

Hyde, Lewis. *The Gift: Imagination and the Erotic Life of Property.* New York: Vintage Books, 1983.

Ingold, Tim. "Culture and the Perception of the Environment." Paper presented at EIDOS workshop, "Cultural Understandings of the Environment," London, 1989.

Jakobson, Roman. *Fundamentals of Language.* The Hague: Mouton, 1956.

―――. "Les Lois phoniques du langage enfantin." Communication préparée pour le Cinquième Congrès international de linguistes convoqué à Bruxelles, septembre 1939. Published in Appendix of N. S. Trubeckoj, *Principes de phonologie*; republished in R. Jakobson, *Selected Writings*, 1, *Phonological Studies*. The Hague: Mouton, 1962.

———. "Principes de phonologie historique." Présenté à la Réunion phonologique internationale à Prague, 20 décembre 1930. Published in German in the *Travaux du cercle linguistique de Prague*, 4, 1931; revised for French edition in Appendix of N. S. Trubeckoj. *Principes de phonologie*; republished in R. Jakobson, *Selected Writings*, 1, *Phonological Studies*. The Hague: Mouton, 1962.

———. "Sur la théorie des affinités phonologiques entre les langues." Rapport au Quatrième Congrès international de linguistes, Copenhague, août 1936, publié dans les Actes du Congrès, 1938. Revised for publication in Appendix of N. S. Trubeckoj, *Principes de phonologie*; republished in R. Jakobson, *Selected Writings*, 1, *Phonological Studies*. The Hague: Mouton, 1962.

Jakobson, Roman, and J. Lotz. "Notes on the French phonemic pattern." *Word* 5, 2 (Aug. 1949). Republished in R. Jakobson, *Selected Writings*, 1, *Phonological Studies*. The Hague: Mouton, 1962.

Jencks, Charles, and Maggie Keswick. *What is Post-Modernism?* 2d ed. London: Academy Editions, 1987.

Johansen, J. Prytz. *The Maori and His Religion*. Copenhagen: Musksgaard, 1954.

Johnson, Martin. "Did I Begin?" *New Scientist* 9 (Dec. 1989): 39–42.

Josephides, Lisette. *The Production of Inequality: Gender and Exchange among the Kewa*. London: Tavistock Publications, 1985.

Kaufmann, Walter. "Translator's introduction." In *The Gay Science* by Friedrich Nietzsche. New York: Random House, 1974.

Kierkegaard, Søren. *Fear and Trembling*. Trans. H. V. Kong and E. H. Kong. Princeton: Princeton University Press, 1983.

Kojève, Alexandre. *Introduction à la lecture de Hegel*. Paris: Gallimard, 1947; collection "Tel," 1980. English translation: *Introduction to the Reading of Hegel*. Trans. J. H. Nichols Jr. Ed. Allan Bloom. New York: Basic Books, 1969.

Lacan, Jacques. *Écrits*. Paris: Seuil, 1966.

———. *Encore*. Vol. 20 of *Le Séminaire de Jacques Lacan*. Ed. Jacques-Alain Miller. Paris: Seuil, 1975.

———. "The Meaning of the Phallus." In *Feminine Sexuality: Jacques Lacan and the "école freudienne."* Trans. Jacqueline Rose. Ed. Rose and Juliet Mitchell. New York: Norton, 1985.

———. "Seminar on 'The Purloined Letter.'" Trans. Jeffrey Mehlman in *French Freud: Yale French Studies* 48 (1972).

Lederman, Rena. *What Gifts Engender: Social Relations and Politics in Mendi, Highland Papua New Guinea*. Cambridge: Cambridge University Press, 1986.

Leenhardt, Maurice. *Do Kamo. Person and Myth in the Melanesian World*. Trans. Basia Miller Gulati. 1947. Reprint, Chicago: University of Chicago Press, 1979.

Leibniz, G. W. "De Ipsa Natura." In *Opuscula Philosophica Selecta*. Paris: Boivin, 1939.

Lévi-Strauss, Claude. "Guerre et commerce chez les Indiens de l'Amerique du Sud." *Renaissance* 1 (1943): 122–39.

———. *Introduction à l'oeuvre de Marcel Mauss*. In Marcel Mauss, *Sociologie et anthropologie*. Paris: Presses Universitaires de France, 1950. English translation: *Introduction to the Work of Marcel Mauss*. Trans. Felicity Baker. London: Routledge and Kegan Paul, 1987.

———. *Les Structures élémentaires de la Parenté*. 1949, revised 1967. English translation: *The Elementary Structures of Kinship.* Trans. James Harle Bell, John Richard von Sturmer, and Rodney Needham. Boston: Beacon Press, 1969.

———. "The Tupi-Kawahib." *Handbook of South American Indians* 3 (1948): 299–305.

———. "La Vie familiale et sociale des Indiens Nambikwara." *Journal de la Société des Américanistes* n.s. 37 (1948): 1–131.

Levinas, Emmanuel. *Autrement qu'être ou au-delà de l'essence.* The Hague: Martinus Nijhoff, 1974. English translation: *Otherwise than being or beyond essence.* Trans. Alphonso Lingis. The Hague: Martinus Nijhoff, 1981.

———. *Du sacré au saint.* Paris: Minuit, 1977. English translation: *Nine Talmudic Readings.* Trans. Annette Aronowicz. Bloomington: Indiana University Press, 1990.

———. *Hors sujet.* Montpellier: Fata Morgana, 1987. English translation: *Outside the Subject.* Trans. Michael B. Smith. Stanford: Stanford University Press, 1993.

———. "La signification et le sens." *Humanisme de l'autre homme.* Montpellier: Fata Morgana, 1977. English translation by Alphonso Lingis. "Meaning and Sense." *Collected Philosophical Papers.* Dordrecht: Martinus Nijhoff, 1987.

———. "La trace de l'autre." In *En découvrant l'existence avec Husserl et Heidegger.* Paris: Vrin, 1967. English translation by Alphonso Lingis. "The Trace of the Other." In *Deconstruction in Context.* Ed. Mark Taylor. Chicago: University of Chicago Press, 1986.

———. "Transcendance et Hauteur." *Bulletin de la Société française de Philosophie* 54 (1962).

Linton, Martin, and Nikki Knewstub. "MPs Give Overwhelming Backing to Medical Research on Embryos." *Guardian,* 24 April 1990: 6.

Lysias, "Speech XXI: Defence Against a Charge of Taking Bribes." In *Lysias.* Trans. W. R. M. Lamb. Cambridge, MA: Harvard University Press, 1976.

MacKean, Dayton. *Party and Pressure Politics.* New York: Houghton Mifflin, 1944.

Macpherson, C. B. "Hobbes's Bourgeois Man." In *Hobbes Studies.* Ed. K. C. Brown. Oxford: Blackwell, 1965.

Malinowski, Bronislaw. *Argonauts of the Western Pacific. An Account of Native Enterprise and Adventure in the Archipelagos of Melanesian New Guinea.* London: Routledge, 1922. Reprint, London: Routledge & Kegan Paul, 1978.

———. *Crime and Custom in Savage Society.* London: Kegan Paul, 1926.

———. *Magic, Science and Religion, and Other Essays.* New York: Free Press, 1948. Reprint New York: Doubleday Anchor Books, 1954; London: Souvenir Press, 1974.

Mammeri, Mouloud., and P. Bourdieu. "Dialogue sur la poésie oral en Kabylie." *Actes de la recherche en sciences sociales* 23 (1978): 51–66.

Marcy, Georges. "Les vestiges de la parente maternelle en droit coutumier berbère et le régime des successions touarègues." *Revue Africaine* 85 (1941): 187–211.

Marshall, Lorna. "Sharing, Talking, and Giving: Relief of Social Tensions Among !Kung Bushmen." *Africa* 31 (1961): 231–49.

Marx, Karl. *Capital.* Trans. Samuel Moore and Edward Aveling. Ed. Frederick Engels. Rev. Ernest Untermann. New York: Modern Library, 1906.

———. *Grundrisse.* Harmondsworth: Penguin, 1973.

Mauss, Marcel. "L'âme, le nom et la personne." Intervention à la suite d'une communication de L. Lévy-Bruhl, "L'âme primitive." *Bulletin de la Société française de philosophie* 29 (1929): 124–7. Republished in Mauss, *Oeuvres,* vol. 2.

———. "Anna-Virâj." In *Mélanges d'indianisme offerts par ses élèves à M. Sylvain Lévy*. Paris: Ernest Leroux, 1911. Republished in Mauss, *Oeuvres*, vol. 2.

———. "L'Art et le mythe d'après M. Wundt." *Revue philosophique de la France et de l'étranger* 66 (July–Dec. 1908): 48–78.

———. "Biens masculins et féminins en droit celtique." *Procès-verbaux des Journées d'Histoire du droit* (1929).

———. "Une Catégorie de l'esprit humain: la notion de personne, celle de 'moi'." Huxley Memorial Lecture. *Journal of the Royal Anthropological Institute*: (1938): 263–362. English translation by Ben Brewster. "A category of the human mind: the notion of person, the notion of 'self'." In Mauss, *Sociology and Psychology*.

———. "Commentaires sur un texte de Posidonius. Le suicide, contre-prestation suprême." *Revue celtique* 42 (1925): 324–9. Republished in Mauss, *Oeuvres*, vol. 3.

———. "Dieux Ewhe de la monnaie et du change." Communication faite à l'Institut Français d'Anthropologie; publié dans les comptes rendus de séances, 2, tome 1, supplément à *L'Anthropologie*, Paris, 25 (1914). Republished in Mauss, *Oeuvres*, vol. 2.

———. "Esquisse d'une théorie générale de la magie." En collaboration avec H. Hubert. *Année sociologique*. Paris: Presses Universitaires de France, 1902–3. Republished in Mauss, *Sociologie et anthropologie*. English translation: *A General Theory of Magic*. Trans. R. Brain. London: Routledge & Kegan Paul, 1972.

———. "Essai sur le don. Forme et raison de l'échange dans les sociétés archaïques." *Année sociologique*, Paris, 2e série, 1 (1923–4): 30–186. Republished in Mauss, *Sociologie et anthropologie*. Pp. 143–279. English translation: *The Gift. Forms and Functions of Exchange in Archaic Societies*. Trans. Ian Cunnison. Introduction by E. E. Evans-Pritchard. London: Cohen & West, 1954; reprint New York: Norton, 1967. *The Gift. The Form and Reason for Exchange in Archaic Societies*. Trans. W. D. Halls. Foreword by Mary Douglas. London: Routledge, 1990.

———. "Essai sur les variations saisonnières des sociétés Eskimo. Etude de morphologie sociale," avec la collaboration partielle de H. Beuchat. *Année sociologique* 9 (1904–5): 39–132. Republished in second and third editions of Mauss, *Sociologie et anthropologie*, 1966 and 1973. English translation: *Seasonal Variations of the Eskimo. A Study in Social Morphology*. Trans. J. J. Fox. London: Routledge & Kegan Paul, 1979.

———. "Une Forme archaïque de contrat chez les Thraces." *Revue des études grecques* 34 (1921): 388–97. Republished in Mauss, *Oeuvres*, vol. 3.

———. "Fragment d'un plan de sociologie générale descriptive. Classification et méthode d'observation des phénomènes généraux de la vie sociale dans les sociétés de type archaïque (phénomènes spécifiques de la vie intérieure de la société)." *Annales sociologiques* série A, fascicule 1 (1934): 1–56. Republished in Mauss, *Oeuvres*, vol. 3.

———. *A General Theory of Magic*. Trans. R. Brain. Foreword by D. F. Pocock. London: Routledge & Kegan Paul, 1972.

———. "Gift, Gift." In *Mélanges offerts à Charles Andler par ses amis et ses élèves*. Strasbourg: Istra, 1924. Republished in Mauss, *Oeuvres*, vol. 3.

———. *Manuel d'ethnographie*. Paris: Payot, 1947; 2d ed. 1967.

———. *Oeuvres*. 3 vols. Ed. Victor Karady. Paris: Editions de Minuit, 1969–75.

———. "Les Origines de la notion de monnaie." Communication faite à l'Institut Français d'Anthropologie; publiée dans les comptes rendus des séances, 2, tome 1, Supplément à l'*Anthropologie*, Paris, 25 (1914). Republished in Mauss, *Oeuvres*, vol. 2.

———. "Parentés à plaisanteries." Communication présentée à l'Institut Français d'Anthropologie, 1926; *Annuaire de l'Ecole pratique des hautes études*, section des sciences religieuses, Paris, 1928. Republished in Mauss, *Oeuvres*, vol. 3.

———. "Rapports réels et pratiques de la psychologie et de la sociologie." Communication présentée le 10 janvier 1924 à la Société de Psychologie. *Journal de psychologie normale et pathologique* 21 (1924): 892–922. Republished in Mauss, *Sociologie et anthropologie*. English translation by Ben Brewster. "Real and practical relations between psychology and sociology." In Mauss, *Sociology and Psychology*.

———. *Sociologie et anthropologie*. Précédé d'une *Introduction à l'oeuvre de Marcel Mauss* par Claude Lévi-Strauss. Paris: Presses Universitaires de France, 1950.

———. *Sociology and Psychology*. Trans. Ben Brewster. London: Routledge & Kegan Paul, 1979.

———. "Wette, wedding." *Procès-verbaux de la Société d'Histoire du droit* (1928).

McNeilly, F. S. *The Anatomy of Leviathan*. London: Macmillan, 1968.

Métraux, Alfred. "La causa y el tratamiento mágico de las enfermedades entre los indios de la Región Tropical Sud-Americana." *America Indigena* 4, 2 (April 1944): 157–64.

———. "Le Shamanisme chez les Indiens de l'Amérique du Sud tropicale." Two parts. *Acta Americana* 2, 3 (July–Sept. 1944): 197–219; 2, 4 (Oct.–Dec. 1944): 320–41.

Miller, Daniel. "Appropriating the State on the Council Estate." *Man* n.s. 23 (1988): 353–72.

———. *Material Culture and Mass Consumption*. Oxford: Blackwell, 1987.

Mimica, Jadran. *Intimations of Infinity: The Cultural Meanings of Iqwaye Counting System and Number*. Oxford: Berg, 1988.

Morgan, Lynn M. "When Does Life Begin? A Cross-Cultural Perspective on the Personhood of Fetuses and Young Children." In *Abortion Rights and Fetal "Personhood."* Ed. Edd Doerr and James W. Prescott. Long Beach: Centerline Press, 1989.

Nicolet, Claude. *L'Ordre équestre à l'époque républicaine*. Vol. 1. Paris: Édition de Boccard, 1966.

Nietzsche, Friedrich. *Ecce Homo*. Trans. Walter Kaufmann. New York: Random House, 1968.

———. *The Gay Science*. Trans. Walter Kaufmann. New York: Random House, 1974.

———. *Kritische Studienausgabe*. Ed. Giorgio Colli and Mazzino Montinari. Berlin: de Gruyter, 1980.

———. *Thus Spoke Zarathustra*. Trans. R. J. Hollingdale. New York: Penguin, 1961.

———. *Thus Spoke Zarathustra*. In *The Viking Portable Nietzsche*. Trans. and ed. Walter Kaufmann. New York: The Viking Press, 1967.

Panoff, Michel. "Marcel Mauss's *The Gift* Revisited." *Man* n.s. 5 (1970): 60–70.

Parry, Jonathan. "*The Gift*, the Indian Gift and the 'Indian Gift.'" *Man* n.s. 21 (1986): 453–73.

Parry, Jonathan, and Maurice Bloch. *Money and the Morality of Exchange.* Cambridge: Cambridge University Press, 1989.

Patočka, Jan. "La civilisation technique est-elle une civilisation de déclin, et pourquoi?" In *Essais hérétiques.* Trans. Erika Abrams. Paris: Verdier, 1981.

Petchesky, Rosaline Pollack. "Foetal Images: The Power of Visual Culture in the Politics of Reproduction." In *Reproductive Technologies: Gender, Motherhood and Medicine.* Ed. Michelle Stanworth. Cambridge: Polity Press, 1987.

Price, Frances. "Establishing Guidelines: Regulation and the Clinical Management of Infertility." In *Birthrights: Laws and Ethics at the Beginnings of Life.* Ed. Robert Lee and Derek Morgan. London: Routledge, 1989.

Richman, Michèle H. *Reading Georges Bataille: Beyond the Gift.* Baltimore: Johns Hopkins University Press, 1982.

Rubin, Gayle. "The Traffic in Women." In *Toward an Anthropology of Women.* Ed. Rayna Reiter. New York and London: Monthly Review Press, 1975. Pp. 157–210.

Russell, Bertrand. *Power: A New Social Analysis.* London: Allen & Unwin, 1938.

Sahlins, Marshall. *Stone Age Economics.* Chicago: Aldine de Gruyter, 1972.

Samuelson, Paul A. *Foundations of Economic Analysis.* Cambridge, MA: Harvard University Press, 1947.

Schneep, G. J "El concepto de mana." *Acta Anthropologica* 11, 3 (1947).

Schrift, Alan D. *Nietzsche's French Legacy: A Genealogy of Poststructuralism.* New York: Routledge, 1995.

———. "On the Gynecology of Morals: Nietzsche and Cixous on the Logic of the Gift." In *Nietzsche and the Feminine.* Ed. Peter J. Burgard. Charlottesville: University Press of Virginia, 1994.

Serres, Michel. *The Parasite.* Trans. Lawrence R. Schehr. Baltimore: Johns Hopkins University Press, 1982.

Shannon, Claude E. and Warren Weaver. *The Mathematical Theory of Communication.* Urbana: University of Illinois Press, 1949.

Shapiro, Gary. *Alcyone: Nietzsche on Gifts, Noise, and Women.* Albany: State University of New York Press, 1991.

———. "Debts Due and Overdue: Beginnings of Philosophy in Nietzsche, Heidegger, and Anaximander." In *Nietzsche, Genealogy, Morality.* Ed. Richard Schacht. Berkeley: University of California Press, 1994.

———. "Nietzsche on Envy." *International Studies in Philosophy* (1983): 269–76.

———. *Nietzschean Narratives.* Bloomington: Indiana University Press, 1989.

Simon, H. "A Behavioral Theory of Rational Choice." *Quarterly Journal of Economics* 69 (1954): 99–118.

Sinclair, R. K. *Democracy and Participation in Athens.* Cambridge: Cambridge University Press, 1988.

Sissa, Giulia. "Subtle Bodies." In *Fragments for a History of the Human Body,* vol. 3. Ed. Michel Feher, Ramona Nadoff, and Nadia Tazi. New York: Zone Books, 1989.

Smart, Alan. "Gifts, Bribes, and *Guanxi*: A Reconsideration of Bourdieu's Social Capital." *Cultural Anthropology* 8, 3 (1993): 388–408.

Stanworth, Michelle, ed. *Reproductive Technologies: Gender, Motherhood and Medicine.* Cambridge: Polity Press, 1987.

Stolcke, Verena. "New Reproductive Technologies—Same Old Fatherhood." *Critique of Anthropology* 6 (1986): 5–31.

Strathern, Marilyn. *The Gender of the Gift: Problems with Women and Problems with Society in Melanesia*. Berkeley: University of California Press, 1988.

Teza, Emilio. *Intorno agli studi del Thavenet sulla lingua algonchina: osservazioni*. Pisa: Nistri, 1880.

Trubeckoj, N. S. *Grundzüge der Phonologie*. Prague, 1939. French translation: *Principes de phonologie*. Trans. J. Cantineau. Paris: Klincksieck, 1949. English translation: *Principles of Phonology*. Trans. C. A. M. Baltaxe. Berkeley and Los Angeles: University of California Press, 1969.

Turner, H. A. "How Pressure Groups Operate." *Annals of the American Academy of Political and Social Science* 319 (1958): 63–72.

Von Amira, Karl. *Nordgermanisches Obligationenrecht. 2: Westnordgermanisches Obligationenrecht*. Leipzig: Veit, 1895.

Wagner, Roy. *Asiwinarong: Ethos, Image, and Social Power among the Usen Barok of New Ireland*. Princeton: Princeton University Press, 1986.

———. "The Fractal Person." In *Big Men and Great Men: Personifications of Power in Melanesia*. Ed. Maurice Godelier and Marilyn Strathern. Cambridge: Cambridge University Press, 1991.

Walde, Alois. *Lateinisches Etymologisches Wörterbuch*. Indogermanische Bibliothek. 2. umgearb. Aufl. Heidelberg: Winter, 1910.

Weiner, Annette B. *Inalienable Possessions: The Paradox of Keeping-While-Giving*. Berkeley: University of California Press, 1992.

———. *Women of Value, Men of Renown: New Perspectives on Trobriand Exchange*. Austin: University of Texas Press, 1976.

Weiner, James F. "Diseases of the Soul: Sickness, Agency and the Men's Cult among the Foi of New Guinea." In *Dealing with Inequality, Analysing Gender Relations in Melanesia and Beyond*. Ed. Marilyn Strathern. Cambridge: Cambridge University Press, 1987.

———. *The Heart of the Pearlshell: The Mythological Dimension of Foi Sociality*. Los Angeles: University of California Press, 1988.

Werbner, Pnina. *The Migration Process: Capital, Gifts and Offerings among British Pakistanis*. Oxford: Berg, 1990.

Wiener, Norbert. *Cybernetics or Control and Communication in the Animal and the Machine*. New York: John Wiley & Sons, 1948.

Williams, Herbert. *A Dictionary of the Maori Language*. Auckland, N.Z.: Williams and Northgate, 1921.

Williams, William. *A Dictionary of the New Zealand Language*. Auckland, N.Z.: Williams and Northgate, 1892.

Wolf, Eric. *Sons of the Shaking Earth*. Chicago: University of Chicago Press, 1959.

Yang, Mayfair Mei-Hui. "The Gift Economy and State Power in China." *Comparative Studies in Society and History* 31 (1989): 25–54.

Selected Bibliography

What follows is a list of some recent works addressing questions of gift and exchange. I have tried to cite works that address issues raised in this collection which are not listed among the works cited and I have tried also to include a range of sources that give some indication of the diversity of work that has recently addressed the "logic of the gift."

Ansell-Pearson, Keith. "The An-Economy of Time's Giving: Contributions to the Event of Heidegger." *Journal of the British Society for Phenomenology* 26, 3 (Oct. 1995): 268–78.

Anton, Anatole. "Commodities and Exchange: Notes for and Interpretation of Marx." *Philosophy and Phenomenological Research* 34, 3 (March 1974): 355–85.

Arrow, Kenneth J. "Gifts and Exchanges." *Philosophy and Public Affairs* (Summer 1972): 343–62.

Barnes, R. H. "Marriage, Exchange, and the Meaning of Corporations in Eastern Indonesia." In *The Meaning of Marriage Payments.* Ed. John L. Camaroff. London: Academic Press, 1980.

Baudrillard, Jean. "When Bataille Attacked the Metaphysical Principle of Economy." Trans. David James Miller. *Canadian Journal of Political and Social Theory* 11, 3 (1987): 59–62.

Bataille, Georges. *Visions of Excess: Selected Writings, 1927–1939.* Ed. Alan Stoekl. Trans. Alan Stoekl, Carl R. Lovitt, and Donald M. Leslie Jr. Minneapolis: University of Minnesota Press, 1985.

Beidelman, T. O. "Agnostic Exchange: Homeric Reciprocity and the Heritage of Simmel and Mauss." *Cultural Anthropology* 4, 3 (1989): 227–59.

Bergoffen, Debra B. *The Philosophy of Simone de Beauvoir: Gendered Phenomenologies, Erotic Generosities.* Albany: State University of New York Press, 1996.

Betteridge, Anne H. "Gift Exchange in Iran: The Locus of Self-Identity in Social Interaction." *Anthropological Quarterly* 58, 4 (1985): 190–202.

Biggs, Mary. *A Gift That Cannot Be Refused: The Writing and Publishing of Contemporary American Poetry.* New York: Greenwood, 1990.

Bird-David, N. "The Giving Environment: Another Perspective on the Economic System of Gatherer-Hunters." *Current Anthropology* 31 (April 1990): 189–96.

Carrier, James G. "Gifts, Commodities, and Social Relations: A Maussian View of Exchange." *Sociological Forum* 6, 1 (March 1991): 119–36.

———. "Gifts in a World of Commodities: The Ideology of the Perfect Gift in American Society." *Social Analysis* 29 (Dec. 1990): 19–37.

———. "The Gift in Theory and Practice in Melanesia: A Note on the Centrality of Gift Exchange." *Ethnology* 31, 2 (April 1992): 185–93.

Chiozzi, Paolò, and Rene Konig. "Marcel Mauss: Eine anthropologische Interpretation des Sozialismus." *Kölner Zeitschrift für Soziologie und Sozialpsychologie* 35, 4 (Dec. 1983): 655–79.

Comay, Rebecca. "Gifts Without Presents: Economies of 'Experience' in Bataille and Heidegger." *Yale French Studies* 78 (1990): 66–89.

Conrath, Rob. "Intersubjectivity and Non-Representational Exchange in the Limit Situation: Towards a Shared Body in the Texts of Georges Bataille." *Discours Social: Analyse du Discours et Sociocritique des Textes* 1, 2 (Spring 1988): 201–27.

Damon, F. H. "Kula and Generalized Exchange: Considering some Unconsidered Aspects of *The Elementary Structures of Kinship*." *Man* 15 (June 1980): 267–92.

Davis, J. "Gifts and the U.K. Economy." *Man* 7, 3 (Sept. 1972): 408–29.

De Beistegui, Miguel. "Of the Gift That Comes To Thinking." *Research in Phenomenology* 24 (1994): 98–112.

Dean, Carolyn J. *The Self and Its Pleasures: Bataille, Lacan, and the History of the Decentered Subject*. Ithaca: Cornell University Press, 1992.

Dubar, Claude. "The Methodology of Marcel Mauss." *Graduate Faculty Journal of Sociology* 1, 1 (Winter 1975): 1–12.

Egloff, B. J. "Kula Before Malinowski: A Changing Configuration." *Mankind* 11, 3 (1978): 429–35.

Feil, Daryl K. *Ways of Exchange: The Enga 'tee' of Papua New Guinea*. St. Lucia: University of Queensland Press, 1984.

Fournier, Marcel. "Marcel Mauss ou le don de soi." *Archives Européennes de Sociologie* 34, 2 (1993): 325–38.

Gerrand, Nicole. "The Notion of Gift-Giving and Organ Donation." *Bioethics* 8, 2 (April 1994): 127–50.

Gilmore, David D. "Commodity, Comity, Community: Male Exchange in Rural Andalusia." *Ethnology* 30, 1 (Jan. 1991): 17–30.

Godelier, Maurice. *L'Énigma du don*. Paris: Fayard, 1996.

Goodell, Grace E. "Paternalism, Patronage, and Potlatch: The Dynamics of Giving and Being Given To." *Current Anthropology* 26, 2 (April 1985): 247–57.

Gould, Stephen J., and Claudia E. Weil. "Gift Giving Roles and Gender Self-Concepts." *Sex Roles* 24, 9–10 (May 1991): 617–37.

Goux, Jean-Joseph. "General Economics and Postmodern Capitalism." Trans. Kathryn Aschheim and Rhonda Garelick. *Yale French Studies* 78 (1990): 206–24.

Habermas, Jürgen. "The French Path to Postmodernity: Bataille between Eroticism and General Economics." Trans. Frederick G. Lawrence. *New German Critique* 33 (Fall 1984): 79–102. Reprinted in *The Philosophical Discourse of Modernity*. Cambridge: MIT Press, 1987.

Herring, Phillip F. "James Joyce and Gift Exchange." *Literature, Interpretation, Culture* 1, 1–2 (Dec. 1989): 85–97.

Hirschon, Renée, ed. *Women and Property, Women as Property*. London: Croom Helm, 1984.

Kemp, Peter. "Death and Gift." *Journal of the American Academy of Religion* 50, 3 (Sept. 1982): 459–71.

Koehn, Daryl. "Toward an Ethic of Exchange." *Business Ethics Quarterly* 2, 3 (July 1992): 341–55.

Komter, Aafke E., ed. *The Gift: An Interdisciplinary Perspective*. Amsterdam: Amsterdam University Press, 1996.

Laughlin, Charles D. Jr. "On the Spirit of the Gift." *Journal of the Indian Anthropological Society* 21, 2 (July 1986): 156–76.

Lojkine, Jean. "Mauss et l'*Essai sur le don*.' Portée contemporaine d'une étude anthropologique sur une économie non marchande." *Cahiers Internationaux de Sociologie* 36, 86 (Jan.–June 1989): 141–58.

Macherel, Claude. "Don et réciprocité en Europe." *Archives Européennes de Sociologie* 24, 1 (1983): 151–66.

Marshall, R.C. "Giving the Gift to the Hamlet: Rank, Solidarity, and Productive Exchange in Rural Japan." *Ethnology* 24 (July 1985): 167–82.

McCall, G. "Association and Power in Reciprocity and Requital: More on Mauss and the Maori." *Oceania* 52 (June 1982): 303–19.

McLean, Iain, and Jo Poulton. "Good Blood, Bad Blood, and the Market: The Gift Relationship Revisited." *Journal of Public Policy* 6, 4 (Oct.–Dec. 1986): 431–45.

Milbank, John. "Can a Gift Be Given? Prolegomena to a Future Trinitarian Metaphysic." In *Rethinking Metaphysics*. Ed. L. Gregory Jones. Cambridge: Blackwell, 1995.

Moore, Stanley. "Democracy and Commodity Exchange: Protagoras Versus Plato." *History of Philosophy Quarterly* 5, 4 (Oct. 1988): 357–68.

Nancy, Jean-Luc. "Exscription." Trans. Katherine Lydon. *Yale French Studies* 78 (1990): 47–65.

———."The Unsacrificeable." Trans. Richard Livingston. *Yale French Studies* 79 (1991): 20–38.

Orenstein, H. "Asymmetrical Reciprocity: A Contribution to the Theory of Political Legitimacy." *Current Anthropology* 21 (February 1980): 69–91.

Osborn, Richard Warren, and J. Ivan Williams. "Determining Patterns of Exchanges and Expanded Family Relationships." *International Journal of Sociology and the Family* 6, 2 (1976): 197–209.

Perroux, Francois. "The Gift: Its Economic Meaning In Contemporary Capitalism." *Diogenes* 5 (Spring 1954): 1–21.

Persson, J. "Cyclical Change and Circular Exchange: A Re-examination of the KULA Ring." *Oceania* 52 (Sept. 1983): 32–47.

Poe, Donald B. Jr. "The Giving of Gifts: Anthropological Data and Social Psychological Theory." *Cornell Journal of Social Relations* 12, 1 (Fall 1977): 47–63.

Racine, Luc. "Les Trois Obligations de Mauss aujourd'hui: donner, recevoir et rendre chez les Enga et les Mendi de Nouvelle-Guinée." *Homme* 34, 130 (April–June 1994): 7–29.

Richman, Joel, and W. O. Goldthorp. "Becoming Special: Gynaecological Ideology, Gift Exchange and Hospital Structure." *Social Science and Medicine* 11, 41 (March 1977): 265–76.

Rubin, Z. "Disclosing Oneself to a Stranger: Reciprocity and Its Limits." *Journal of Experimental Social Psychology* 11 (May 1975): 233–60.

Sharp, Ronald A. "Gift Exchange and the Economies of Spirit in 'The Merchant of Venice.'" *Modern Philology* 83, 3 (Feb. 1986): 250–65.

Shaviro, Steven. *Passion & Excess: Blanchot, Bataille, and Literary Theory*. Tallahassee: Florida State University Press, 1990.

Sherry, John F. Jr. "Gift Giving in Anthropological Perspective." *Journal of Consumer Research* 10, 2 (Sept. 1983): 157–68.

Stange, Margit. "Personal Property: Exchange Value and the Female Self in *The Awakening*." In *Contexts for Criticism*. Ed. Donald Keesey. Mountainview, CA: Mayfield, 1994.

Thomas, Nicholas. *Entangled Objects: Exchange, Material Culture, and Colonialism in the Pacific*. Cambridge, MA: Harvard University Press, 1991.

Thompson, David. "The 'Hau' of the Gift in Its Cultural Context." *Pacific Studies* 11, 1 (Nov. 1987): 63–79.

Van Baal, J. *Reciprocity and the Position of Women*. Amsterdam: Van Gorcum, 1975.

Index